Shattered Sense of

I N N O C E N C E

The Elmer H. Johnson and Carol Holmes Johnson Series in Criminology

Shattered Sense of
INNOCENCE

The 1955 Murders of Three Chicago Children

Richard C. Lindberg and Gloria Jean Sykes

Foreword by Larry G. Axelrood

Southern Illinois University Press
Carbondale

09 08 07 06   4 3 2 1

Publication of this book has been underwritten by The Elmer H. Johnson
and Carol Holmes Johnson Series in Criminology fund.

Library of Congress Cataloging-in-Publication Data
Sykes, Gloria Jean
    Shattered sense of innocence : the 1955 murders of three Chicago
children / Richard C. Lindberg and Gloria Jean Sykes; foreword by Larry G.
Axelrood.
        p. cm. — (The Elmer H. Johnson and Carol Holmes Johnson series in
criminology)
    Includes bibliographical references and index.
    1. Peterson, Bobby, d. 1955. 2. Murder victims—Illinois—Chicago—Case
studies. 3. Cold cases (Criminal investigation)—Illinois—Chicago—Case
studies. 4. Hansen, Kenneth. 5. Murderers—Illinois—Chicago—Case
studies. I. Lindberg, Richard C. II. Title.
    HV6534.C4L56 2006
    364.152'3092—dc22   2006018575
    ISBN-13: 978-0-8093-2736-2 (cloth : alk. paper)
    ISBN-10: 0-8093-2736-8 (cloth : alk. paper)

DEDICATION

TO CHARLES SYKES, in loving memory; to all the men and women in the Chicago Police Department, the sheriffs' departments of Cook, Kane, Du Page, and Lake counties, and the federal Bureau of Alcohol, Tobacco, and Firearms who tried to bring closure to the Schuessler-Peterson murders; and especially to James Delorto, whose perseverance and compassion know no bounds.

On September 30, 1995, James "Jimmy" Delorto retired from the federal Bureau of Alcohol, Tobacco, and Firearms. In front of a few hundred friends, family members, and colleagues, Scott Cassidy, an assistant state's attorney, gave Delorto a plaque with the following inscription:

September 13, 1995

Dear Jimmy,

You were a few years older than us back then. We're sure you would have protected us, had you known. But God has something else in mind for you, we now know.

Others have followed similar in age. They, too, did not want to leave, but had no choice. We have told them to be patient. Their time will come. That justice will be served and that in just [sic] world, they have left.

Well, Jim, because of you, our day of justice has arrived. The oldest kids on the block are partying right now. Others here have their hopes high and their spirits are up. Their day will come, too, as long as there are men like you, Jim, and we know there are.

Thanks Jim. Thanks for caring.

Your buddies. Tony, Bobby, and John

Before the state's attorney finished reading the hand-written message, every person in the room was grabbing a handkerchief, napkin, or Kleenex.

CONTENTS

ILLUSTRATIONS

IN THE FALL OF 1955, Chicago was more a collection of distinct neighborhoods than a big city. People felt safe, especially in their own sequestered little areas. The gruesome discovery of Bobby Peterson and brothers John and Anton Schuessler, three murdered boys found lying in a ditch in the Cook County Forest Preserves, forever destroyed that perception of safety.

Besides the unimaginable loss to the families of these boys, the tragedy extended throughout the Chicago area and indeed across the nation. Analyzed with the benefit of hindsight, the massive manhunt that was launched was hampered by infighting, incompetence, and ego-driven lapses of communication. Surely, some of the blame has been tempered by the times. Advances in investigative techniques and scientific applications to law enforcement, the birth of the use of DNA, and the related forensic sciences were far in the future. Yet, most frustrating was that within their investigation, the police had many of the clues that would lead to the apparent solving of the case forty years later.

It wasn't DNA, fingerprints, or some trace evidence examined by a forensic expert that would lead to an arrest in this baffling crime. A casual comment tossed out by a snitch in a seemingly unrelated investigation opened a direct path to a suspect in this long-dormant investigation. Ultimately, prosecutors would weave a case from fragments of information culled from an underworld of murderers, arsonists, swindlers, con men, pedophiles, and what has become known as the Horse Mafia.

After forty years, Kenneth Hansen, a former stable owner who elevated himself to affluence and wealth from humble beginnings, was arrested and brought before the bar of justice. Instead of that ending the story, the saga begins as this extraordinary case starts its crawl through the criminal courts. Is this the man who caused a generation of children to suffer from nightmares of a monstrous killer on the loose? Or is he an old man charged because of his deviant and criminal history?

Two of Cook County's best prosecutors squared off against experienced defense lawyers before a respected veteran judge. Hansen was convicted of murder and received a sentence that would have him spending his last years in prison. In a split decision, an appellate court overturned the conviction and returned the case for another trial. This time, it was assigned to a younger judge considered to be a rising star in the judiciary. It would fall to her to rule on myriad complex legal issues and push the case through to a jury verdict. Forty-seven years after the three murders, Hansen was again convicted and returned to the Illinois Department of Corrections.

A number of disturbing questions remain. Hansen's defense lawyers steadfastly believe him to be innocent despite the two distinct jury verdicts, but others also have lent support to this unsympathetic, aging criminal. Can defense attorneys mount a reasonable defense for a crime that occurred fifty years ago? For those who accept the jury verdicts, the belief is that the punishment has come too late to meet the ends of justice.

As a lawyer with over twenty years of trial experience in the Cook County Criminal Courts, I have seen a lot of such heater cases, those that grab the attention of the media, courthouse regulars, and the public at large. But I've never seen a case like this, one that destroyed two families, more than a few careers, and the trust of a generation. As time passed, the case grew cold, and ultimately, it was believed that it would never be solved.

When an odd sequence of events catapulted this decades-old murder mystery again to front-page coverage, the inner workings of a large and surprisingly interconnected criminal underground in Cook County reminded the good citizens of the Windy City that as much as things have changed since the openly lawless days of Al Capone, the spectral presence of organized criminality continues into the modern day.

In *Shattered Sense of Innocence: The 1955 Murders of Three Chicago Children*, authors Richard C. Lindberg and Gloria Jean Sykes relate a compelling tale of horrific crimes framed within the larger context of a shadowy Equestrian Mafia, but at deeper and more subtle levels, the book shines a spotlight on the underpinnings of the criminal mind and introduces us to a world few people outside of law enforcement and criminal law can possibly imagine.

The crimes were, indeed, horrific. And the media did nothing to spare the public. It was the first, and the last, time that the dead bodies of children were shown on television and in the printed press. Today, the press cannot even report the name of a murdered child until the family has been advised of the tragedy. But 1955 was a different time. Also, in 1955, being gay or bisexual was something to be hidden under a veil of secrecy. Hence, many of Kenneth Hansen's victims remained silent.

Meticulous research and careful reconstruction of historical events in 1955 and beyond, coupled with the authors' intimate knowledge of the political machinations and repercussions surrounding the case, provide the reader with more than a snapshot glimpse of a place and time that has not quite receded in the public memory. With thorough investigative interviewing and the uncanny ability to locate people who may or may not wanted to be found, Sykes and Lindberg also reveal both the human and contemporary sides of the tragedy through the personal observations and the spoken word of James Delorto, a now retired Bureau of Alcohol, Tobacco, and Firearms agent, whose life was forever changed as were the lives of all children by the crime. Other key figures closely connected to the case and possessing vivid recollections and inside information that raise interesting new questions were also interviewed.

Sykes and Lindberg both grew up less than a mile from where the Schuessler-Peterson boys hitched their last ride. The authors' intimate understanding of Chicago's insulated Northwest Side culture, the quiet, tree-lined side streets making up the city's "bungalow belt," and the hopes and dreams of second- and third-generation immigrant families who settled out that way in order to escape crime-ridden inner-city neighborhoods evokes a sense of time and place. So many rank-and-file Chicago police officers, required to reside within the city limits, desired safe streets, good schools, and large backyards. These police officers moved into the bungalow belt for much the same reasons. The authors have managed to convey the bewildering sense of horror and the pervasive attitude among residents who naïvely assumed, *"It can't happen here."*

Except that it did, and after more than a half-century has elapsed, the searing crime still reverberates. It is much discussed and analyzed, even now. There are many complex and underlying threads to this story. You will meet men who are inherently evil and devoid of conscience. The story is supported by the spoken word, excerpts drawn from an interview with Hansen and a collection of Dickensian characters from the underbelly of society who would rather steal a dime than earn an honest dollar. A singularly strange ensemble cast, traversing the divergent worlds of show horses and petty crime, drifting in and out of each other's life, pursuing their criminal enterprises and deviant desires, leaving a trail of victims in their wake. Then a remarkable twist: a key figure in the prosecution's case admitted to his daughter that he had killed the boys.

Since the untimely deaths of Bobby Peterson and the Schuessler brothers, much has happened to alter our perceptions of good and evil. The world as a whole has become a lot more cynical, and the fear of street crime is much more pervasive than it was back in 1955. In the new millennium, we hear a lot about children being kidnapped, molested, and murdered. As a result of the Internet, pedophilia is back in the news in a big way. It has become a worldwide problem—one that law-enforcement agencies seem to be no better equipped to handle than they were in 1955. Therefore, parents throughout America keep closer tabs on their children today, as they know they must.

Kenneth Hansen has grown old. The lawyers in this case remain convinced of their positions. The prosecutors know they convicted the right man. The defense attorneys and the Center for Wrongful Convictions at Northwestern University believe that Kenneth Hansen is innocent.

This is a compelling story based on facts, first-hand interviews, archival newspaper coverage and television footage, and the personal memories of aging baby boomers whose childhoods were torn asunder because of the horrific deaths of these three boys. Many new facts in the book have never been published or were never introduced into trial, and they will allow you, the reader, to draw your own conclusions.

Larry G. Axelrood

Chicago, 2006

Larry G. Axelrood, a former prosecutor and former criminal defense attorney, is author of three novels, *The Advocate*, *Plea Bargain*, and *Death Eligible*.

THIS IS A WORK OF NONFICTION. Except where indicated, all names are real. Some of the descriptive details used to illustrate the lives of witnesses and courtroom scenes and of the Schuessler and Peterson boys and their families were invented to enhance the narrative flow. All courtroom testimony was taken directly from the trial transcripts and/or authors' notes. Most interviews were done in person; some were performed over the telephone. Five hours of interviews with Kenneth Hansen were held at Pontiac Correctional Center in Pontiac, Illinois, and were recorded on audiotape. The authors also consulted federal Alcohol Tobacco and Firearms (ATF) investigation files and archival news reports and conducted interviews with retired Chicago police officials and one investigator still working for the Cook County Sheriff's Department. In addition, the authors drew on extensive interviews with ATF agent James Delorto, who proofread the manuscript and signed off on his investigation and personal story. Delorto said he believes the information gathered by ATF's investigation and the facts and evidence later presented at both trials are completely accurate and is sure that Kenneth Hansen committed the murders in 1955.

ACKNOWLEDGMENTS

WE BOTH FEEL RICHLY blessed and are grateful to many people. We are grateful to Jimmy Delorto for allowing us to tell his personal story, and none of this book could have been possible without his assistance and that of Dave Hamm, two top-notch investigators who shared considerable time and resources with us although our requests to interview other members of the federal Bureau of Alcohol, Tobacco and Firearms (ATF) and the Cook County State's Attorney's office were declined.

From the law enforcement side both past and present, we are indebted to the late Mike Spiotto, a former Chicago Police deputy superintendent, Tony Wilson of the Special Investigations Unit, and James McGuire, former Chicago Police detective and retired superintendent of the Illinois State Police. A very special thanks to retired Chicago detectives James Lanners and Mike Fleming and to Jack Reed, who was a rich source of information about south suburban crime. We'd like to express appreciation to attorneys from the criminal-defense bar: Jed Stone, Leonard Goodman, and Robert McDonnell.

Special thanks goes to executive producer Holly Harter and television agent Marc Wax and to literary agent Michael Hamilburg, who shepherded *Shattered Sense of Innocence* through. If not for Mike's willingness to take a chance on Gloria, who had never authored a book, she would not have had the opportunity to work with Richard, a good friend and neighbor who also grew up in the shadow of the tragedies of the slain boys.

No Chicago crime story is complete without the personal observations of the veteran reporters, TV executives, and cameramen who were privy to breaking developments and insider information, specifically Dick Frisbie, Shirley Haas, Roger Hammill, Steve Laske, Jack Lavin, Sterling "Red" Quinlin, and Dr. Richard Ritt.

Additional thanks to Larry G. Axelrood, retired horse-trainer Robert Breen, Maxie Cassidy, Mark and Debbie Hansen, Cheryl Hollatz, Margie Mack, Al Plotkin, Ralph Schultz, Judge Michael P. Toomin, Al Webber and family, and William "Red" Wemette. We extend appreciation to Sophie and the late Kurt Voderberg, the former owners of Hollywood Kiddieland.

We are also most grateful to Karl Kageff, Barb Martin, and other members of the staff at Southern Illinois University Press and copyeditor Mary Lou Kowaleski for believing in us. The project could not have been successfully concluded without the generous support and cooperation of the aforementioned individuals.

We add special thanks to all of the people who trusted and allowed us to capture their stories. We hope that after all this time we have succeeded in illuminating one of the darkest corners of Chicago history and American life in the second half of the twentieth century while acknowledging that many puzzling questions surrounding the fifty-year-old case are likely to go unanswered.

Gloria Jean Sykes

How well I remember that afternoon in September 1995. My father, retired Chicago Police Sergeant Charles Sykes and a juvenile officer assigned to the Schuessler-Peterson investigation in 1955, greeted me as I walked through the door of my parents' home. He handed me a slip of paper, a Chicago Police bulletin. Once a month, he received a newsletter from Lodge 7 of the Fraternal Order of Police. On the reverse side of this particular issue, my dad had circled an item about ATF agent James Delorto's investigative masterstrokes leading to the resolution of the 1955 Schuessler-Peterson child murders. He suggested that I look into the story but cautioned me, "Keep your eyes wide open."

In 1955, my sister and I rode ponies at Hollywood Kiddieland, and three years after the triple murders, we rode horses at the Idle Hour Stables in Park Ridge, the focal point of this bizarre and wide-ranging story. A year later, my special favorite—a mighty, black quarter horse with a white diamond on his forehead—perished in a barn fire of suspicious origin. My personal connection to the horse world from that point forward was the compelling reason I contacted Agent James J. Grady at the Chicago ATF office about doing a book. He put me in touch with James Delorto, and soon I was talking to the famous investigator who established important linkage between Schuessler-Peterson and the missing candy-heiress Helen Brach.

There are many more people that I would like to thank for their unyielding support, friendship, and love. I wholeheartedly thank my mom, Mary Sykes, who kept me on track during the times when I was ready to give up. Kudos to John Mazzola, Delorto's partner at Delorto and Mazzola detective agency. I want to give a special thanks to Sterling "Red" Quinlan for the many glasses of red wine and the personal insight into the 1955 television coverage of the story. I am so grateful to my dear, dear friends: Paulette Hayden, Lisa Richards, Randy Birch, Dawn Calmentie, Doris Evens, Scott Evens, Lee and Bob Jaffee, Laura Kapp, Gloria Ralph, Pam and John Vennochi, Sergeant Ed Veth, Larry Yellen, and Lisa and Scott Zeien. I thank all of my students and the faculty at Wright College—especially Nancy Schemluck. I am so grateful to my new friends who helped me campaign for alderman of the Forty-First Ward—Randy Lowe, Frank Rosetti, and John and Sylvia Sogal. And I thank my tennis partners Al, Art, Beverly, Gloria, Helen, Ingrid, Jimmy, Matt, Norman, Phil, and Roman for allowing me to play with them, even though my focus was on other things and not on the court. And finally, as a breast cancer survivor, I want to thank the most incredible team of physicians—Drs. John Saletta, Patrick Sweeney, and Pam Keiser at Lutheran General Hospital in Park Ridge and Drs. Donald Novey and Ellen Diamond at the Center for Complimentary Care—and pharmacist Steve Karagiannis. Thank you for my life.

And thank you, Liza Belden. You were one of the strongest and most courageous young women I have known.

Richard C. Lindberg

I would like to recognize and thank Gloria Sykes for bringing me into this project and Carol Jean Carlson for the time-sensitive editorial oversight she lent in the final stages of editing and for the fine organization of chapter content and manuscript assembly. I am most appreciative to the many people who came forward to volunteer their stories, insights, reminiscences, and details of their personal involvement. Particular thanks to Pattie Banas of the Illinois Academy of Criminology; Dennis Bingham, now retired from the Chicago Police Department News Affairs Division, for photo research; Arthur Bilek, criminologist, author, and former investigator with the Cook County Sheriff's Police; and Mary

Claire Hersh for so capably maintaining my Web site. I worked closely with latter-day journalists, true-crime buffs, and research specialists including Lawrence Raeder, Tamara Shaffer, and Susan Zyrkowski.

Thanks also to Judy Varley and Paul Garland, special individuals who shared personal memories about growing up in the Far Northwest Side neighborhood, the grammar school the murdered boys had attended, and the impact of this tragedy on the families of the victims.

Shattered Sense of

I N N O C E N C E

1

The Telephone Call

OCTOBER 1991. The leaden Chicago sky grew even darker as the last of the office staff left for the day. James "Jimmy" Delorto nodded to his secretary, Nadia Martinez, and flashed a broad smile as she rushed for the exit. Every afternoon at 4:30, except for a few field agents and the occasional supervisor, employees of the Chicago branch of the federal Bureau of Alcohol, Tobacco, and Firearms (ATF) eagerly left work, rushing for the corridor and cramming—shoulder to shoulder—into elevators that conveyed them down three floors to Riverside Plaza and the mass of commuters heading home to condominiums on the Lake Michigan lakefront, bungalow-belt neighborhoods, and the bedroom suburbs surrounding Chicago—the city that *almost* works.

This was the city Delorto knew all too well—the city of two Mayor Richard Daleys, two broken-down baseball teams, one football squad, Vienna hot dogs, clout, corruption, and uneasy memories of Al Capone. Chicago has a lot to live for and a lot to live down. After twenty-seven years in law enforcement and a lifetime of working the streets, Delorto's feelings for Chicago were diametrical. He both loved and reviled the town.

Delorto took a long, deep drag on a Marlboro before turning his attention to the two stacks of work piled high on his desk. He deliberately pulled out and opened one of several large files marked "Brach" and leaned back in his chair. Only the sporadic murmuring of the few remaining ATF agents, also staying late at their desks, broke the deep silence in the large room. Delorto reached out and clicked on the floor lamp that stood against his desk. As the sky grew blacker and the room darker, other agents turned on lamps, too. The enormous space looked like the movie set for a science-fiction film, orbs of light denoting the living in an otherwise black universe.

The Chicago branch of the arson division of the ATF had only recently completed its move into more spacious headquarters in the skyscraper at 300 S. Riverside Plaza. The suites were still under construction; many of them were without overhead lights, and some lacked walls and ceilings. It was a hell of a way to run a federal agency charged with the onerous task of collecting revenue, reducing violent crimes, and providing national enforcement authority in all matters pertaining to guns, bombs, booze, and tobacco. Delorto looked at his smoldering cigarette and crushed it out in dismay.

Delorto's desk and those of the arson group he supervised overlooked a large, jammed parking lot. His boss, Joe Vince, however, had a great view of pleasure craft traversing the Chicago River in the foreground. But Delorto didn't mind looking at the parking lot and the old buildings that surrounded it. After all, it was a more authentic panorama of the *real* Chicago, the old Chicago he knew and loved and hated.

Delorto was every inch a Chicagoan—the city was in his bones. He grew up in the Italian section of the Near West Side, near Taylor and Racine, across the street from the Shrine of Our Lady of Pompeii. He was intimately familiar with the denizens of the neighborhood parishes, saloons, bowling alleys, and social clubs, especially the Democratic precinct captains, who came banging on the back door on election mornings and reminded his mother to come out and vote. That was the down payment for delivery of "our Daley bread"—clean streets, efficient garbage pick-up, and city jobs for loyal Democratic-lever–pulling workers.

When Delorto was eight, his family moved to Elmwood Park—one of the western suburbs abutting the city. He was thinking of it just now as he sighed and ripped open another pack of Marlboros. It was his second pack of the day. Delorto leaned back in his chair and collected his thoughts. It had been another one of those anxiety-driven days that inspired his chain-smoking, a habit he vowed to kick but somehow never got around to it. "I'm entitled," he groused as he took in another lungful of smoke.

As the last shred of daylight dipped below the horizon, and the room grew even darker, Delorto glanced, once again, out the window on the other side of his desk. It was difficult for him to concentrate in such a numbing atmosphere. Not that the engineers had planned it that way. No, not at all. The bureaucrats and bean counters had said that all of the construction was to have been completed before the unit moved out of their modest digs in Northbrook, a wealthy bedroom suburb about twenty-five miles north of Chicago and a world apart from the inner city.

The move had set the entire department back more than a few days, and Delorto was determined to sift through all fifteen reports that he needed to review before he could possibly think of heading home for the night. Delorto sighed again and tapped his index finger repeatedly on the top file of those marked "Brach."

"See you, Jimmy," a husky, grating voice echoed inside the room.

Delorto squinted as he stared into the darkness. Unable to identify the voice or the shadow exiting the office, he automatically responded, "Have a good night." Then he lit up another cigarette, forgetting that one was still burning in the ashtray, and took a long, deep drag and exhaled slowly. In a manner that was disturbing, the taste of tar and nicotine relaxed Delorto.

Six months earlier, Delorto had been promoted to supervise the Chicago district-office arson unit. The job upgrade came at a time when he was the lead field agent trying to untangle the threads of one of Chicago's most baffling mysteries—the 1977 disappearance of the wealthy "candy lady," Helen Marie Vorhees Brach. Delorto had begun investigating the case in 1989, when the case was so cold that icicles were beginning to form.

He opened the case file and saw a photo paper-clipped to a report. The picture had been taken of Helen shortly before her disappearance. In 1951, the former Miami hatcheck girl, forty years old, married Frank Brach, the sixty-year-old heir to the Chicago confectionary fortune. She lived contentedly with her wealthy husband until his ticker gave out in 1970. Thereafter, Helen, an eccentric, aging beauty, insulated herself from the candy business, the gossipy North Shore society mavens, and the prying eyes of neighbors. She continued to live in the sprawling Glenview estate that had become a shrine to Frank's memory and the various animal rights and humane causes she had embraced. She avoided romantic entanglements, eschewing the fortune-hunting suitors. Sugar and Candy, her pet poodles and devoted companions, were all the company she required during her prolonged mourning period.

From time to time, it was whispered that the lonely widow had consulted fortune-tellers and soothsayers to help her gain new meaning in what was surely a reclusive existence. But not even the crystal-ball gazers had been able to warn her of the danger that lay ahead.

It was Mrs. Brach's custom to visit the Mayo Clinic in Rochester, Minnesota, for a yearly physical. Those visits were strictly routine; that is, until the afternoon of February 17, 1977. After being given a clean bill of health by the doctors at the clinic, Helen Brach went missing. She was last seen buying a few items in an airport gift shop in Minneapolis. Two days later, her houseman and gardener, Jack Matlick, notified police that she had vanished without notice or reason given. She had disappeared into the mists as effortlessly as New York Supreme Court Judge Joseph Force Crater[1] in 1930 and the redoubtable Jimmy Hoffa in 1975. Neither Judge Crater, Hoffa, nor Mrs. Brach was ever seen again.

How does someone just vanish like that? Delorto asked himself. *And why hasn't the body turned up?*

Brach left behind her lavender Rolls Royce, an eighteen-room mansion, Cadillacs in coral, red, and maroon, $20 million in cash, her two beloved dogs, and a raft of unanswered questions. Every armchair sleuth around town had his or her own pet theory about the fate that had befallen poor Helen. There was a plethora of dead-end leads, a skeleton of a Jane Doe had turned up, and an obvious suspect was Matlick, but there was nothing of substance that Delorto could build a case on.

An uninvited grin appeared on Delorto's face as he thumbed through the case reports. He had thought that the raise in job stature and pay would allow him to spend more time on the golf course and with his family. *Just as soon as I find Helen . . .* Although unraveling the secrets of the pyramids would probably be a hell of a lot easier.

On his desk rested two framed photos. One was of three of his children—Tony, five, Michael, seven, and Amanda, fifteen. The other photo was of his oldest child, Melissa, seventeen, who lived with her mother, Delorto's first wife, in Carterville, Illinois. Missing from his desk was a photo of Debbie, his second wife. Debbie despised having her picture taken, and Delorto was still not certain why he hadn't brought in one of the hundreds of wedding photos of her. The most important part of Delorto's life was family, and for a brief moment, he mused about his father James Sr. ("Giacomo"), who died in 1982. The senior Delorto was a first-generation Italian immigrant from Bari on the Aegean coast.

Delorto made a mental note to call his mom, Maria, and his brothers—Tony, Vito, and Frank—before he left work that night. He beamed with pride as he flipped through the calendar on his desk, searching for a couple of free hours when he could escape and spend some quality time with them. To his complete dismay, he found that he was booked solid for the next two months. Sighing once again, Delorto examined the mountain of work lying before him. The two stacks of files stared back at him. He returned to the Brach file.

The ATF was the lead agency overseeing the federal task force on the Brach case. Assigned to his team was Dave Hamm, a gruff Illinois State Police lieutenant and Delorto's longtime friend, who had been looking into Brach's disappearance as far back as 1978. For a full year, the task force had traveled from the North Shore of Chicago to distant horse farms in Connecticut and the polo fields of Palm Beach following up on rumors and false leads. What they had managed to uncover during this time was a sleazy nether world, a "Horse Mafia" of sorts, populated by swindlers, rogues, and soulless con men who peddled worthless, broken-down steeds to gullible and unsuspecting people eager to gain entrée into the tony world of show horses, steeplechases, champagne-sipping soirees, and late-night socializing.

Exposing a series of murders and insurance scams, the state and federal investigation shook America's riding set right down to its breeches. It took nearly eleven years to identify the owners and operators of this multimillion-dollar racket, but Delorto and Hamm had finally convinced the U.S. attorney's office for the Northern District of Illinois that they had a case ready for prosecution.

After reading a few pages of the court transcripts, Delorto yawned and thought about calling it a night. He felt a pang of guilt. His job had never been nine to five, but he just wasn't up to pulling an all-nighter. "Oh hell," he muttered, certain no one heard him, "traffic will still be a bitch. I'll wait a little longer." Delorto didn't mind bypassing Chicago's brutal rush hours. What should be a simple forty-minute ride to Batavia in the western suburbs of Cook County could turn into an ugly two-hour commute.

Delorto was fifty years old and nearing the end of his career with the ATF. Co-workers would likely describe him as a no-nonsense, Columbo-like sleuth. Delorto was doing exactly what he had always wanted to do. Cold cases like the Brach case were his specialty. The case was seductive, with all of the elements of a classic late-night film noir. The characters were straight out of central casting, white-haired Helen and her pampered pet poodles included. *It will make a hell of a TV movie,* Delorto thought, *if only we can get a conviction.* Delorto signed off on another report and closed his eyes tightly, lost in his thoughts.

In the months leading up to her disappearance, Helen Brach had dated a forty-five-year-old charmer and career con man named Richard Bailey. A former Arthur Murray dance instructor, Bailey had once operated a driving school in St. Louis. He specialized in providing private driving lessons for elderly widows flush with cash and stock portfolios, but seduction was his real game. A late night tête-à-tête in an expensive little bistro, with just enough shadows to comfort a female companion sensitive about her age and appearance, was his special skill. The French wines and champagnes flowed generously as he whispered platitudes of affection. Bailey, by nearly all accounts, was a sensitive and caring man who made women of sixty feel young again. But in reality, Bailey was the master of the long con, the sophisticated swindle that bleeds the victim dry slowly over a period of months, even years. The key to his success was to steal the money a little at a time, never all at once, preying on the victim's foibles and fragile vanity as well as her desperate desire to savor the thrill of new romance one last time before the onset of old age and its attendant miseries.

In time, the authorities in Missouri learned of Bailey's lonely-hearts treachery. One of his victims had finally had enough and reported him to the police. It seems that one of his driving school pupils had failed to become proficient behind the wheel, even after months of instruction and thousands of dollars. The Missouri regulatory board intervened and revoked his license. Even the most accomplished con man knows that the game can only go so far. That is why you have to keep them guessing. Stay on the move, keep your wits about you, and adapt to changing conditions.

In 1970, the faker and his wife relocated to Chicago, a city of boundless possibilities with old money scattered up and down the North Shore, which stretched from the pricey condominiums and boutiques lining Michigan Avenue north to the Wisconsin border. At first, Bailey intended to open a dance studio catering to an affluent clientele of bored, rich ladies with Astor Street addresses and Saks charge cards. But the plan changed overnight when a rich and diabolical horseman named Silas "Si" Jayne sold him a broken-down horse.

Bailey, one of twelve children born to a farmer from the Kentucky bluegrass region, thought he knew horses pretty well, but he was just another easy mark ripe for the taking. Rather than kick about his ownership of a worthless horse, he was genuinely impressed by Si Jayne's business acumen or gall—depending on how one looked at it, of course. Bailey thought smugly that Si Jayne was a man he could do business with, and thus an unexpected opportunity arose.

For Bailey, some might say, his introduction to Si Jayne, the treacherous godfather of suburban Chicago's Horse Mafia, was serendipitous. The master conniver and the crass horseman with a penchant for murder, fraud, and arson hit it off immediately. Suddenly, everything began to fall into place. The high-stakes con game espoused by Jayne involved the sale of horses to those who loved them best—cash-rich society women who never outgrew their girlish love of horses. Helen Brach easily fit into that category, and Bailey's brother Paul sold her three horses for $98,000—but they were worth less than $20,000.

Many stories floated around as to how Bailey met Brach, but the most reliable and most memorable came in 1998 from the candy heiress's best friend, Molly Goldberg. The gracious, elderly woman had greeted Hamm, Delorto, and Delorto's partner, John Mazzola—a short, stout, cigar-smoking Italian—with a large pot of fresh homemade matzo-ball soup. The hungry field agents eagerly accepted the meal, and while they ate, Goldberg rambled on. According to her account, Bailey learned that Brach's Florida condo was up for sale. In 1973, a real estate broker introduced the lonely and vulnerable Brach to Bailey over the telephone. Within a few minutes, Brach was totally smitten by the sweet-talking devil, who professed a love of ballroom dancing, quiet evenings on the veranda, and after-dinner strolls along a moonlit beach. Bailey did not purchase the condo, but he agreed to a date to meet Helen in person when she returned to Chicago a few weeks later. They had dinner in Greek Town and enjoyed many more fabulous nights on the town in the weeks and months that followed. That fateful meeting, as far as Delorto could surmise, was the beginning of the end for Helen Brach. Bailey had been a viable suspect in her disappearance ever since an anonymous tipster alerted the feds to a message scrawled on the sidewalk outside the Brach residence in 1981. The message to the best of Delorto's recollection read: "Richard Bailey knows who killed Helen Brach."

But without a body . . . Delorto mused as he signed off on another report. Delorto then paused in his reverie to stand up and stretch his arms, arching his back like a cat after a nap. He needed to get out some of the stiffness before re-seating his five-foot-eight-inch frame. Worn down by endless hours of work, Delorto smoked more and exercised less. Debbie had quit smoking over the summer, but he wasn't quite ready to stop. He held the flame to the tip of yet another cigarette, and the weary ATF agent inhaled long and deeply.

Engrossed by thoughts of the Brach case and his reports, Delorto didn't realize how much time had passed. He had not noticed that everyone else in the office had left for the night. It was times like these, in the stillness of an empty office, that the veteran agent longed for the earlier days of his career when he was assigned to the Organized Crime Division (OCD), tracking the movement of the juice-loan[2] collectors, professional killers, thieves, labor-union slugs, and their associates in the Chicago Outfit from the penitentiary to their home turf and back again. Delorto missed working the streets, especially with Mazzola, his long-time partner, and the camaraderie that came with being one of the boys and not the boss.

Ever since he was a boy, Delorto had dreamed of becoming a cop. As a teenager in the fifties, Delorto was a devoted fan of TV's *M-Squad* and *Dragnet*. The ambition to join law enforcement burned in him through high school. He chose a course of college study that he hoped would catapult him into the FBI and filled out enough applications to wallpaper his bedroom, but the outcome was always the same: rejected. Delorto suspected that his Italian heritage blackballed him from the Bureau. The same ethnic prejudices held true for Arabs, African-Americans, and Hispanics as well as other olive-skinned Europeans whose ancestors hailed from the areas in and around the Mediterranean. Back then, hiring practices reflected J. Edgar Hoover's fierce biases. The director only wanted angular, fair-complexioned men with Anglo- or Nordic-sounding surnames attached to the Bureau. The unspoken word was that the FBI considered all Italians a security risk.

In 1966, Delorto enlisted in the U.S. Army. For six months, he trained to be a "tunnel rat," part of an elite detail of soldiers with slighter builds who would be sent into the dismal Viet Cong tunnels to "ferret" out the enemy. Luckily for Delorto, an ankle injury sustained in advanced infantry training kept him out of the war. The army believed that an operation on his ankle would not be successful because Delorto had flat feet. Much to Delorto's private horror, more than half of the soldiers in his unit who had trained as tunnel rats were killed in Vietnam.

It wasn't until he was twenty-eight, after he had spent a few years teaching history and art at Chicago's Steinmetz High School, that Delorto applied to the ATF and was accepted as an agent. This was in the fall of 1969, when the nation was engulfed in civil unrest stemming from militant opposition to the Vietnam War by the nation's alienated youth. The irony of the situation was that Delorto believed the FBI bypassed him because he was Italian, but for precisely the same reason, the ATF quickly assigned him to the Organized Crime Division, where he developed cases against the Chicago Outfit, then at the apex of its power and influence. It was during this time that Delorto uncovered the delicate threads linking Si Jayne and his Equestrian Mafia to the Chicago Outfit and its seven insular street crews.

As Delorto drained the last of his now-cold cup of coffee, his phone rang. Dropping the report he was perusing, he reached for the receiver and glanced at his watch. He stopped cold. It was only about 5:30 PM, but somehow it seemed much later. Delorto thought it was a routine call from Debbie, checking in and questioning his ETA for dinner. He picked up the phone and in a cheerful tone said, "Hey!"

To his surprise, the caller was a long-time informant, William "Red" Wemette, former proprietor of the Peeping Tom adult bookstore at 1345 N. Wells St. in the then-trendy Old Town neighborhood and a much sought-after hanger-on in Mob circles.

Delorto was familiar with Red's background. They first met in 1987, four years ago. The ATF had requested a meeting in order to learn more about the Chicago Mob. Red had become an FBI informant in 1971 after he was caught red-handed selling a machine gun to undercover agents. For that offense, he was kicked out of the Marine Corp with a dishonorable discharge, but because of his youth—he was eighteen at the time—Wemette was given only a slap on the wrist. To atone for his earlier indiscretions, Wemette invested his time and energies helping the Bureau penetrate and bring down members of the Outfit. It was his personal calling in life, and he was very good at it. As a confidential informant (CI) for over twenty years, Wemette supplied his handlers with valuable information about his association with members of the Rush Street and Grand Avenue crews. Testifying before a subcommittee investigating Mob infiltration of the Laborer's International Union of North America (LIUNA), retired Bureau Agent Jack O'Rourke said that Wemette's "information was independently verified and found to be reliable by the FBI." Red did not trust most federal agents, but he had a warm regard for Delorto. It took only a handshake and few words for him to feel safe with the dogged investigator. They formed an instant bond, one that was based on mutual respect.

Red had helped the government put away the notorious loan shark and feared syndicate assassin and enforcer Frankie "the German" Schweihs, believed responsible for two sensational gangland hits linked to porn and vice operations in the Windy City.[3] Beyond what Red already knew about Schweihs's terrible reputation for violence and his alleged involvement in the two unsolved Mob murders, Red had had a vested interest in sending the psychopath off to jail for a long period of time. Schweihs, his garrulous henchman, and street collector Anthony "Jeeps" Daddino extorted $21,450 from Red and his one-time bookstore partner Leonard "Lenny" Cross. Red and Cross had been required to pay a syndicate street tax ranging from $250 to $1,000 a month for the privilege of keeping their vice emporium open.

In 1987, Red was at the end of his tether. He told the FBI about thirteen years of difficulties with the Outfit, not exclusively limited to Schweihs. Louis "the Mooch" Eboli, Marshall Caifano, and Albert "Obbie" Frabotta were other syndicate heavyweights also interfering with his operations. Wemette had been prepared to make a deal and allowed the federal agents to come to the apartment he rented above his seedy Wells Street porno shop to secretly videotape and audio-record the German's attempted shakedowns. Fifteen months went by before the feds were finished compiling their evidence against the extortionist. As a result of Wemette's cooperation with the feds, Schweihs was arrested on September 16, 1988, moments after picking up a cash shakedown from the owner of Old Town Video on Wells Street.

"There are strong indications this man [Schweihs] is one of the most violent people to have come before this court," said prosecutor Thomas Knight. Sentenced on February 16, 1990, Schweihs was ordered to pay restitution to Wemette before being shipped off to federal prison for thirteen years. Angered by these developments, the Outfit put out a contract on Wemette, but it was too late for bloodshed. Wemette chose not to enter the Federal Witness Protection Program but did accept the assistance of the government with regard to his personal security. His personal possessions, photographs, and childhood mementos were taken by the government, however, and to date have not been returned.

"Remember me?" The voice was cautious but eager.

Delorto hadn't heard from Red since 1987. "Hey, Red, long time no hear."

Delorto impatiently tapped his knuckles on one of the Brach files and lit up another cigarette. Over the years, Delorto had cultivated many informants like Red, from bank presidents and corporate CEOs to bust-out, low-life criminals, all willing to talk to cops in exchange for a "consideration" or some personal benefit.

Red was a talkative and colorful guy, and he liked the action. He had that reputation. More importantly, he knew everyone that mattered in Chicago and, *oh, the stories he could tell*. Despite his borderline lifestyle and reputation, Red had always been truthful with Delorto, and the agent respected that. Oddly enough, Wemette demanded nothing from Delorto; no money, no favors, nothing this time except for somebody to listen patiently. He said he had another story to tell. Delorto knew that Red was "on the run" and that it wasn't a very good idea to communicate directly with an informant under government scrutiny, but he also knew that if Red was risking the call, he had something important to share.

"I understand you've arrested some horse killer in Florida?" Red said.

Delorto was surprised and impressed by Red's up-to-date knowledge. Details about the Brach investigation and its connection to the Horse Mafia had yet to hit the news, but one item had appeared in a local newspaper about a horse being killed as part of an insurance swindle.

"How's this for an irony?" Red said with a snicker. "I once met that broad—Brach!"

In all the years that Delorto and his team had been investigating the Chicago Horse Mafia and its connection to the Brach murder, Red's name had never come up, not even in the rumor mill. For a second, Delorto tried to make a mental connection between Wemette and the candy heiress. Clearly, she hadn't been into the kind of sleazy pornography Red peddled. "Helen Brach! How the hell did you ever meet her?"

"I used to live with Kenny . . . Kenny Hansen. You know," Red said, his voice faltering for just a second. "I lived in a trailer at his stable. I was kind . . . of a . . . kind of a ranch hand."

Delorto was surprised. No, shocked was a better word for it. "You lived with Hansen? How is that possible?"

"I loved riding and caring for horses," Red whispered in response.

"A real cowboy, eh, Red?" Delorto replied with a snort.

At the time Red said he lived on Hansen's property—in the early seventies—Red was only eighteen years of age and fresh out of the Marines. Having known him for all these many years, Delorto couldn't imagine Red on horseback. The sordidness of the equestrian industry, however, was personally troubling to Delorto. In his line of work, he had encountered many rough and dangerous characters who were horsemen or were somehow related to the frauds perpetrated by members of the horsey set.

"I lived at Hansen's ranch for three, almost four years, off and on. I don't remember. It's no big deal," Red said in a nervous, retreating tone. "You know Kenny, don't you?"

"Yeah, I know Kenny," Delorto responded. "He was arrested in '71 in connection with the murder of Si Jayne's half-brother, George. I never met the guy, but I heard about him. How'd you meet Kenny?" Delorto was trying to piece together what all of this could possibly mean.

Red told Delorto about Kenny's crazy, mean-spirited brother, Curtis Hansen, who was connected to the syndicate and reputed to be a stone-cold killer. According to Red, soon after being discharged from the Marines, he initiated a relationship with Curtis, and Red uttered his usual words of regret about his teenage follies to Curtis.

It seemed clear to Delorto that Red's heart was at least in the right place with his dream of bringing an end to the Outfit's reign of terror.

At first, Curt trusted Red and offered him room and board at a teenage social club he owned out on the Lincoln Highway called the Valley View YAC (Young Adult Club, pronounced *yak*), often visited by such 1960's celebrities as Buddy Rich and the rock group Procol Harum.

"One night around eleven o'clock, Curtis barged into my room and urged me to leave immediately. No one messed with Curtis, you see." Local Mob watchers believed Curtis was an enforcer aligned to Jimmy "the Bomber" Catuara and the Chicago Heights crew in the vice-ridden southern suburb taken over by Al Capone in the 1920s. Curtis was also good friends with and a disciple of the late Sam "Mad Sam" DeStefano, a ruthless mobster who was known to torture his victims for days if need be, usually with an ice pick, blowtorch, or broken pool cue. Delorto had had a few dealings with Mad Sam and understood the basis for Red's fears.

"Curtis introduced me to Kenny, and after I left Curtis's place, I went over to Kenny's." Red was silent for a moment. "Curtis was a mean son of a bitch with no respect for life. Kenny is a piece of shit, too." Then Red let it slip. In a casual tone, he added, "Oh, by the way, Kenny told me he killed two kids back in '55."

"What the fuck are you talking about?" Delorto shot back. "What kids, Red?"

"Kenny told me he killed these kids a long time ago. Peterson, or something like that." Red drew a deep breath, as if he had just remembered an important fact that might jump up and bite him if he wasn't careful. "It was like in '55, maybe '56." He hesitated. He seemed to be hedging.

Delorto knew exactly what Red was alluding to. Delorto had lived through that terrible time when confidence in law enforcement was shaken, and the insulated world he knew was forever changed. He remembered the incident vividly, and it was all coming back to him now, like an old black-and-white newsreel. Delorto's face grew visibly pale, and a knot formed in his stomach as Red repeated his confession. "There were two boys. Kenny said he killed them!"

Actually, three boys had been murdered. Their names were etched in Delorto's memory. Bobby Peterson was the oldest at thirteen. The other two boys were school friends from the neighborhood—Anton and John Schuessler. Delorto had lived less than ten miles from the Schuessler and Peterson boys. Although he didn't know them personally, they all played baseball in the same neighborhoods, rode the same CTA bus line, and ran in familiar circles. Delorto had been the same age as Bobby Peterson, but they hung out with different crowds.

The horrifying crime scene had played out in the grainy film footage on WGN TV. Delorto's dad had discouraged his sons from watching the unfolding account. But as Delorto listened to Red's rambling, he vividly recalled the *Chicago Sun-Times* news photo of the unclothed bodies lying in a ditch in the Robinson Forest Preserve—close to a bridle path where he and his buddies had often ridden their bikes. The photo was circulated in his classroom, and the deaths of Tony, Bobby, and John affected all the kids. It was personal, *very personal*.

A new, all-pervasive fear had gripped all of Chicagoland that autumn. Anxious mothers warned their offspring that the same fate could befall them if they accepted a ride with strangers or talked to unfamiliar men. Delorto picked up the photo of his own sons. He thought back to the young lives that were snuffed out. The slayings of Tony, Bobby, and John changed the way people thought and lived. Life was never quite the same after that.

The vivid memory of the newspaper photo of the crime scene again flashed through Delorto's mind. The boys had been out on a Sunday lark, only to end up murdered and tossed naked into a ditch. The image brought back the fear, the revulsion, and the panic that gripped the entire city. The murders had turned people's lives upside down. "Who killed those boys?" Delorto's voice was soft, almost imperceptible.

Now, after thirty-six years of wondering, thirty-six years of waiting for the solution to the horrific crime, Delorto received a phone call that moved the murder mystery closer to resolution. After thirty-six years, the identity of the killer was still a mystery. And now Red Wemette comes forward with information on the triple homicide. Delorto sat in stunned silence, as if he were unable to wake up from a four-decade-old nightmare. Red's revelation was the first tiny crack in the rock-hard mystery of the horrific crime that had altered Delorto's childish notions of right and wrong, good and evil—a crime that had long since receded into the cold-case files of the Chicago Police Department.

"Kenny said he killed the kids, but he didn't want to, but he had to," Red casually related, as if the lives of three innocents were negotiable, some kind of bargaining chip. Silence. Neither man said anything. Numbed by Red's admissions, Delorto knew better than to interrupt. Rule Number One of successful investigations: Listen before talking. Rule Number Two: Don't venture an opinion or talk, if you don't have to. Still, Delorto gingerly pushed for more details after sensing that he might be losing Red at this critical juncture. Red simply had no idea how critical this information could be. "This is important, Red. What the hell else do you remember?" The silence continued, unusual for Red who talked nonstop most of the time.

"We were in Kenny's trailer, drinking and stuff, that night. Curtis had kicked me off his place. And Kenny got weird and emotional when he drank."

This time, his voice filled with rising excitement, Delorto asked, "Why didn't you tell me about this before? Did you tell anybody about this?" There was a high probability that Red had already mentioned it to other cops, FBI agents, and U.S. marshals, who were usually on first-name basis with their guarded informants. But if he had told somebody who wasn't familiar with the magnitude of the Schuessler-Peterson case, he or she would not have known what he was talking about and may have just dismissed it as the ramblings of an overly talkative snitch. Federal law-enforcement agents were transferred in and out of cities like pawns on a chessboard. The federal agents Red might have confided his suspicions to would have most likely been out-of-towners, and it was almost certain that the murders would have occurred well before their time.

One thing Delorto was fairly sure of, however, was that Red had had no intention of bringing up Kenny Hansen during this phone call—at least not in respect to the slayings. Red had merely called Delorto to relate a chance meeting with Brach and to notify him that two other people were present at the stable gathering—Si's cousin, Frank Jayne, and the slippery toad Richard Bailey. Together they had pulled up in a big black Cadillac, and, by chance, Red had been walking by when Bailey whistled him over. Red recalled his first meeting with the candy heiress. He suspected at the time that the fawning, insincere con man Bailey and the Jayne gang were out to scam her. The slayings of the Schuessler and Peterson boys and how they happened to fit into this widening circle of intrigue were just other tidbits of information that Red threw out for dramatic effect.

Kenny said he killed the kids, but he didn't want to, but he had to. Red's voice echoed in Delorto's ears. His heart was pounding, and he could barely contain his excitement. *Could Brach's disappearance provide a motive for the murder of the Schuessler-Peterson boys?* Delorto wondered. It all seemed too farfetched, almost unbelievable. *Were the Jayne brothers involved, too? Did Kenny confess to the slayings to anybody else? Or maybe, Kenny was simply in a drunken stupor and grandstanding to anybody within earshot.* Delorto muttered these questions to himself as he swept his fingers through his hair.

"What?" Red asked. "What did you say?"

"Nothing. Nothing," Delorto replied in a breathless manner. His tone then turned gentle and persuasive. "So Kenny confessed to the killings while drunk?"

"That's what Kenny told me, Jimmy. Take it or leave it," Red said.

As one question after another popped into Delorto's head, he became more and more doubtful about the truthfulness of Red's allegations. And yet, if it was true, this was the only lead that had surfaced in almost forty years. Red continued talking, but Delorto was only half-listening as he began calculating how far he could delve into proving Red's claim—one way or another.

Red suddenly jolted Delorto back into the conversation. "This shit is just hearsay. Isn't it?"

"It's not hearsay, Red. It's direct testimony. *Important* shit!" Delorto's eyes rolled upward, and a slight smile spread across his face. "Kenny told you he killed the boys, right? It's not hearsay. It's evidence. I'll need more, but it's a damn good start."

"Yeah, but he just blurted it out," Red argued, as if he was trying to protect Kenny Hansen or hide some darker truth. Red had spent many years running and hiding from the Outfit. Clearly, he had also been avoiding Kenny. "Uh, it wasn't the only time he mentioned it either."

"Think really hard about everything that was said and done, Red, then call me in a couple of days, and we'll talk more about this," Delorto said as if he desperately wanted to end the conversation. "This is really important. Can I count on you?" Delorto tapped his pen on the desk impatiently, waiting for a reply.

An awkward moment of silence followed before Red responded, "Yeah, sure, Jim. I'll call you." And then he hung up.

Delorto held the receiver in his hand for a few minutes before he disconnected the telephone. Call it instinct. Call it gut-check time or maybe just plain old intuition, but the inflection in Red's voice was a concern to Delorto, who sensed that his informant was holding back something important. There was another part to this story and a reason why Red wasn't coming clean.

A tidbit of information, anything, would be crucial for successful prosecution. Delorto had been a cop too long, and he knew that promising leads were often discarded. But now he was getting way ahead of himself. Delorto had plenty of questions to ask Red, but he had to cut him off. He needed time to sit back and draw a breath before moving on to the next step. He scanned his desk. As the supervisor of the arson division, he had to oversee all of these other cases. He reminded himself that he was still the lead investigator on the Brach case. There was too much work to be done, and yet his mind kept pounding with questions about the '55 slayings. *What were Red and Kenny doing before the confession? Who else was in the room? What were they talking about before Kenny said he killed the boys? Did Kenny ever say "we" rather than just "I killed those boys"? What about Si Jayne, Bailey, or Curtis?* The answers were important because one corroborated response just might connect to a piece of evidence. Substantiation by others would be a daunting task, however. *What others?* It was, after all, thirty-six years after the fact. *How many of them would still be alive?*

Delorto did the math. Red Wemette could not have been a witness to the crime. He was still wearing his Dr. Denton's[4] and mastering the ABCs in 1955. Maybe Red's calling had to do with something that happened to him in the intervening years, something he wasn't proud of or might even be afraid to tell. Or, maybe Red was just being a good guy and simply trying to make up for the foolish things he had done in the past. With Curtis Hansen and Si Jayne, thankfully, dead, perhaps Red no longer feared retribution from the Horse Mafia. Only time would tell as to whether Kenny Hansen had killed the boys or had simply been acting out as a bragging drunk. None of that mattered right now. What did matter was that *he, James Delorto,* got the information. What was the chance of a lead like this dropping into his lap so late in his career? The clue to cracking one of the oldest and most famous murder mysteries in Chicago history could fire the imagination of even the youngest recruit in the Bureau. They were, after all, murders that had shattered all sense of innocence.

Delorto glanced at his watch. He had been on the telephone with Red for about an hour. He scanned his desk and realized that he had hardly made a dent in the pile of paperwork, which had been his only reason for staying late. Still, he felt energized, seized by a renewed sense of purpose.

"I've got to call Hamm," he said out loud. Dave Hamm possessed a wealth of knowledge about the Equestrian Mafia. If anyone knew anything about what Kenny might be up to these days, it was Dave. Delorto dialed his friend's number from memory.

"Hello," a gruff voice answered the telephone.

"Dave, you're not going to believe what I just heard." Delorto paused for a moment, drawing a deep breath and collecting his thoughts. "I just got done talking to one of my CIs. Are you sitting down?"

"Okay."

"He said that Kenny Hansen told him he killed two boys named Peterson a long time ago."

Without hesitation, Hamm said, "You're shittin' me. I always figured that son of a bitch was good for those murders."

For another hour or so, Delorto moved about the darkened office, walking in and out of the shadows, smoking and thinking. There was a lot for him to do before he told his boss about the confession. From time to time, images from his favorite childhood Western, *The Lone Ranger*, flickered through his thoughts. An hour or so later, he returned to his desk, pushed aside the paperwork, and wrote in bold letters on a Post-It note: RED. He took a second Post-It and scribbled down his last known confidential telephone number for Red, folded the note, and placed it in the back of his wallet. Delorto stuck the first note on the lampshade and chuckled to himself—as if he would ever forget the conversation that night. Then he gathered up the few reports he had signed off on and placed them on Martinez's desk. And finally he wrote, "Make copies and distribute. Thanks. J."

Delorto was anything but certain that night. His thoughts turned to the uncomfortable childhood memories he had tried to erase and to a time in the distant past when family and friends called him Jimmy-boy. The name stuck with him through the years even when no one else from his adult life called him that. "Jimmy-boy, you might have stumbled onto the mother lode!" The world-weary agent switched off the lamp next to his desk and began to make his way to the door.

2

No Indian Summer This Year

A COLD WIND SWEPT down from the Northern Plains late that Saturday night in October 1955, bringing the region's first snow flurries. The older residents of the Jefferson Park neighborhood in the extreme northwest corner of the city dreaded the sudden cold snap and its attendant winds, knowing that winter wasn't far behind. Dilatory motorists hustled to fill their radiators with the proper mixture of antifreeze and water, gardeners covered the houseplants on the back porch, and everyone prayed that there would be Indian Summer, at least for a few weeks. As any weary resident knows, there are really only three seasons in Chicago: the scorching months of summer, followed by a season of football, and then the seemingly interminable winter.

Malcolm Peterson, a workaday carpenter, had moved his family into Jefferson Park in 1944 for much the same reasons as the rest of his neighbors in the 5500 block of Farragut Avenue—good schools and high moral values.

Jeff Park, as it was called by the locals, was perceived to be a safe, God-fearing community, a place where kids could be kids without experiencing the pull of street gangs and juvenile delinquency, which were fast becoming important social issues in 1955. *Life* magazine and scores of sociologists were analyzing and debating the phenomena of rebellious youth and the rising criminality among the nation's younger set.[1] What was wrong with these kids, anyway? Parents were demanding answers.

The many citizens who prospered in postwar America often lived lives much like that of Sloan Wilson's Tom Rath, the corporate striver in *The Man in the Gray Flannel Suit*. They either indulged their young ones with money, cars, and too much freedom or flat out ignored them. They were the cocktail generation, and without knowing it as they drank their martinis and made merry with the neighbors in their backyards, the good-looking husbands in the starched white collars and the attractive wives in high heels and billowing sundresses were making a fashion statement of their own about child-rearing. Many disillusioned teenagers, left to their own devices and with time on their hands, drifted into gangs, experimented at an early age with booze and sex, or danced to "Rock Around the Clock."[2]

Built up along an old Indian trail that later became Milwaukee Avenue, Jefferson Park, with its bungalows, two-flats, Dutch Colonials, sleepy taverns, and corner candy stores, was an almost perfect example of the orderly lifestyle Americans in the 1950s found so desirable. Known as "The Gateway to Chicago" and "The Cradle of the City's Northwest Side," Jefferson Park had residences that were well-maintained and residents who were conformists in thought and deed.

Bulwarked by its many Protestant churches and Catholic parishes with their devout families, Jefferson Park and the surrounding communities of Irving Park, Norwood Park, Gladstone, Forest Glen, and Mayfair were insulated from the horrors of big-city living. Beginning in the 1920s, the families who settled in these neighborhoods were unassuming folk—working-class Europeans mostly, who never looked back but did not want to look too far into the future either, always wary of the calamities that might lie up the road. Getting along day by day, month by month, with a roof over their heads and the mortgage paid on time, was often the primary goal. By the thousands, they had managed to escape Chicago's crowded ethnic ghettos, but they still desired to maintain some of the flavor of city living while in a quasi-suburban setting, free of the blacks and the more recently arrived immigrants, whom they regarded as lower on the socioeconomic ladder and, therefore, objectionable. The Northwest Side satisfied all of their requirements. Prejudice was implied but never spoken about out loud. Most of the residents had been brought up to believe that racist thinking was vulgar and crude, an undignified practice of the hillbillies and rednecks terrorizing blacks in the Jim Crow South. And yet, intolerance always lurked just below the surface. It was whispered over the backyard fences in easily understood code words like "maintaining property values" and "preserving the quality of education in the neighborhood schools." Before restrictive covenants[3] were struck down in the 1940s, homeowners relied on an exclusion clause to protect the homogeneity of their neighborhoods. More registered Republicans lived in Jefferson Park and Norwood Park than in any other neighborhoods in the whole of the Democratic-machine town of Chicago.

It was a different world (a man's world, most were willing to concede[4]), existing in a very different time. Northwest Side husbands went off to factories and put food on the table by working as punch-press operators, sanders, or tool-and-die men. Others labored as carpenters, garbage collectors, city cops, motormen, firefighters, and shopkeepers. The Far Northwest Side of Chicago was strikingly blue-collar, but as the years wore on, more and more men in gray flannel suits turned up. The college-educated GI-bill boys, the schoolteachers, and political insiders began buying up pricey cottages with attached garages in Forest Glen, Edgebrook, and Sauganash, the tonier eastern exposure of Jeff Park where the residents fiercely resisted the installation of sidewalk curbing because they wanted to preserve the quaint "rustic" charms of the area. The real reason, envious Jeff Park homeowners bristled, was the "highfalutin notions of the politicians who live out that way and just want to put on airs." There was an element of truth in that statement.

Malcolm Peterson was neither a harried downtown executive racing to catch the 7:10 to the Northwestern Station nor a boozy egotist seductively eyeing the lady next door. He was a modest, forty-year-old, blue-collar worker raising children and caring for an elderly mother-in-law who lived in the house with Dorothy, his wife of seventeen years, and their four children—Tommy, Barbara Ann, Susan, and Bobby—ranging in age from three to thirteen. A tall, striking man of Swedish descent, Malcolm married Dorothy Anderson just two years after she graduated from Lakeview High School, just a little south and west of Andersonville and Clark Street, Chicago's famous Scandinavian main street. The couple didn't care much for gossip, and they resented neighbors who were suspicious and prying. Malcolm just wanted to collect his weekly paycheck from the Strom Construction Company, go home, coach a neighborhood Little League team on weekends, and get along as best he could.

The Petersons, a close-knit family, lived in a large Dutch Colonial house with a simulated brick front that might have easily been mistaken for a country hay barn by outsiders unfamiliar with the architectural landscape of the area. ("Hey, yer barn door is open!" bungalow owners would tease.) The high gambrel roofs and spacious rooms were ideally suited to accommodating larger families or monthly boarders. Many immigrant Poles, fleeing the Iron Curtain country for the safety and comfort of the largest Polish settlement outside of Warsaw, rented attic apartments in the Dutch Colonials until they could get better situated. The corner newsstand at Milwaukee and Lawrence avenues on any given day sold more Polish-language newspapers than were peddled on the streets of Warsaw.

Robert, or Bobby as his friends at the James B. Farnsworth Elementary School called him, was born on February 11, 1942, the eldest of the

Peterson offspring. He was a bright and assertive eighth-grader, whose most serious known or talked about offense against parental authority was playing hooky for a few days the previous school year.

The local churches were an important source of weekend and after-school recreation for young people and a hedge against street-gang activity, particularly that in the adjoining Albany Park neighborhood, where young hoodlums inspired by Marlon Brando's motorcycle bravado in *The Wild One* were becoming something of a nuisance. AKA greasers or hot-rodders, the black-leather-jacketed toughs in chinos and T-shirts hung out in local bowling alleys and other, seedier gathering places, copping an attitude with the adult males and mingling with down-and-out idlers. It was the corrupting influence of this latter group of restless transients that parents feared the most.

An epidemic of teenage gang crime overtook Chicago and, for that matter, the rest of the nation's larger cities beginning in 1955. The four Chicago newspapers published disturbing accounts of street-gang fights occurring in nearly every neighborhood in the city. The word *rumble* drifted into the argot of the day. Writing for *Parade Magazine* over the Fourth of July holiday weekend that year, William Blankenship issued an urgent wake-up call to parents who were unaware of what their children might be up to when they were away from home. "You pick up the paper and read another terrible story of teen-age crime, of bloody 'rumbles,' of young boys and girls killing each other. And you think: This happens only in slum neighborhoods; it can never hurt me, or my kids. But it can. Teen-age crime is more your problem—as good parents—than anyone else's. For without you it can't be licked. And if it isn't licked soon it may someday strike *your* home."[5]

Malcolm and Dorothy Peterson spent endless hours with their children. The Petersons were a family that prayed together and played together. Malcolm loved sports just as much as his son Bobby. The games they watched on the field, the teams they rooted for, and Bobby's growing proficiency in baseball, bowling, and football made Malcolm very proud and brought the father and son close together, more like older and younger brothers rather than father and son. Sunday afternoons in the fall meant Chicago Cardinal football in the Peterson household. The beloved "Big Red" was the city's South Side team, which had played second fiddle to George Halas's North Side Bears through many long and bitter seasons but somehow always managed to show them up in head-to-head matches. This did not exactly sit well with the majority of

Northwest Siders, who pulled for the Bears who played their games in Wrigley Field. But Bobby was always a contrarian. He chose the Cards over the Bears and preferred the White Sox to the Cubs, the latter because Malcolm was a dyed-in-the-wool Sox fanatic. That fateful Sunday afternoon when he went out, Bobby would proudly wear his black satin jacket with the official Sox logo emblazoned over his heart.

Bobby occasionally went with his dad to the Monte Cristo bowling alley just to study his dad's moves and ball release. Malcolm belonged to two company leagues. Sports of all sorts were the great unifiers in many Northwest Side families.

Bowling was a sport that united fathers and sons, but police and some educators viewed many of the ten-pin emporiums as seedbeds for crime, places to go for older boys who were up to no good and populated by homosexual hustlers and other predators who plied adolescents with booze and change for pinball-machine play.

In 1955 in the Irving Park Police District (which included Jefferson Park), however, the police flatly denied that young hooligans were stirring up trouble, not in the district's many bowling alleys or in any other gathering places. Most people agreed with Captain Russell F. Corcoran's calming assessment of local conditions. In the usual parlance of the Far Northwest Side, gangs were "a city problem." In other words, it was someone else's problem. And as long as peeling tires and late-night drag races did not occur on Milwaukee Avenue and disturb the slumber of the homeowners, the community was at peace with itself, and the hooligans were confined to elsewhere. Ignored were the occasional whisperings of "unnatural acts" and sex orgies that supposedly took place deep inside the nearby forest preserves.[6]

The Reverend William F. Eifrig, who confirmed Bobby Peterson in the spring of 1955, had observed him closely in the youth programs sponsored by the Jefferson Park Lutheran Church. Bobby sang in the children's choir and was sports minded. In those days, the latter was always a good thing to be. Bobby played baseball in a Norwood Park Pony League sponsored by the local Kiwanis Club. He belonged to the YMCA and bowled with his father twice a week. "His home had a lot of burdens, but he never gave his parents any worry," recalled the reverend, who said he had taught a lot of youngsters over the years. He noted in Bobby a "good Christian lad" who was never "spontaneous or sensational" and had never "tried to rip the place apart" or "get away with anything." Bobby's favorite church hymn was "Jesus Savior, Pilot Me." The theme of Reverend Eifrig's confirmation class that year was "Deliver Us from Evil."

John Schuessler and Anton Schuessler Jr. were friends of Bobby Peterson, and John and Bobby were also classmates. The Schuesslers' home was a small, yellow-brick ranch house at 5711 N. Mango Ave., approximately six blocks northwest of the Peterson residence, in a part of the neighborhood known as South Edgebrook. Anton Jr., called Tony by his classmates, was "fun-loving and full of life"—code words that teachers sometimes used to appease anxious parents at PTA conferences when minor disciplinary issues needed to be addressed. Grammar-school classmate Paul Garland, who grew up in nearby Forest Glen, recalled that the Schuessler parents "were kind of old country" in their attitudes toward childrearing, and, undoubtedly, that sparked defiance in their youngest son when he was outside of the home. "I remember Anton as a nice kid but kind of tough at times, with a pretty raspy vocabulary on the playground," said Garland. "He was well liked by the students. He was certainly not withdrawn. He liked to play sports during recess, and I seem to remember that he was athletic."

Tony told his parents that he wanted to go to Quigley Seminary in Chicago and study for the priesthood. The boy was described as deeply religious, and in time, he might have realized his ambition.

Everyone on the Schuesslers' block, especially the parents who carefully noted the appearance and manners of the school friends their children dragged home, remembered that John and Tony were active in the Boy Scouts at St. Tarcissus and that the boys were respectful to their parents. When her husband was away, Eleanor Schuessler refereed the usual childhood squabbles. The Schuessler boys had received a stricter upbringing than Bobby Peterson. Their parents kept a close watch over them and disciplined them when they were rambunctious and acting up. But these were minor issues, easily resolved over the dinner table and forgotten by breakfast. Theirs, like the Petersons', was a close family. The Schuessler brothers were inseparable. The brothers, neighbors recalled, rode bicycles and took care of Penny, a seven-year-old cocker spaniel. John was passionate about animals and talked about becoming a veterinarian. Soft-spoken and reserved, the older Schuessler brother once nursed an injured crow back to health, and from that day forth, his tenderness and compassion for animals were duly noted and talked about by the neighbors on the block. In the room they shared, the two boys' model airplanes, battleships, and cars, glued together with plastic cement and a boy's precision, decorated the shelf directly over a chest-of-drawers.

Anton Schuessler Sr., an emotional, often-high-strung man owned the Alpine Cleaners and Tailor Shop at 5200 Sheridan Rd. in Uptown, a neighborhood along the Chicago lakefront due east of Jefferson Park. The stocky, forty-two-year-old tailor often worked twelve to sixteen hours a day in his little shop, mending holes in children's britches and letting out the seams of their fathers' dress slacks. "Tony really struggled to get that business going and make something of it," remembers Ralph Schultz, the son of Emma Schultz Alexander, Eleanor Schuessler's aunt. (Ralph's mother treated Eleanor like a daughter. Eleanor and Ralph grew up together and remained very close for most of their lives. At the time of this writing, Ralph was in his seventies.) "Tony did everything except the cleaning, which he farmed out to someone else. He did all of the repair work. He did the pressing and the spotting. He could even sew you a suit if you wanted one, and, in fact, he made my first tuxedo."

By 1955, Anton Sr. suffered from arthritis and asthma. Years of struggle and financial worry had taken a toll on his health. He was also hard of hearing but stubbornly refused to wear a hearing aid. In recent months, heart complications were detected. He would have liked to have taken a more active role in his sons' lives, but there were times when he could barely rise from his chair. Looking back on it, Ralph was struck by the elder Tony's good cheer and keen sense of humor despite his problems. Tony was quick with a joke and always eager to share some odd but amusing little story with his customers.

Anton Sr. was born in Chicago to immigrant parents. His mother was from Yugoslavia but of German descent. When Anton was only nine months old, she abandoned her husband and took Anton back to Yugoslavia, where, as a young lad, he was forced to steal apples and scraps of bread in order to stay alive. The mother had changed his last name to Petri. The boy did not fit in with the other children and was teased and hounded relentlessly. Not until 1930, when Anton was eighteen years old and apprenticed to a tailor, was he able to return to the United States and resume a more normal life.

In Chicago, Anton attended language classes at Carl Schurz High School at Milwaukee Avenue and Addison Street on the Northwest Side, becoming proficient in six languages. In 1934, he met his future wife, Eleanor Lillian Holz, at a Saturday night *Schühplatteler* dance[7] on Halsted

Street, which was sponsored by a German American fraternal organization. Eleanor had gone to the dance with her cousin Ralph, who was often her escort. When Eleanor glimpsed Anton for the first time, he was wearing Bavarian *lederhosen* and looking perfectly ridiculous. But it was still love at first sight. A few days later, Anton called her up for a date. He showed up in more acceptable American attire, and soon they became a couple. Anton and Eleanor went steady for two years, until they could no longer wait to be together. With $6.00 he borrowed from a friend, the recently repatriated young man, whose whole life revolved around mastering his trade, eloped with Eleanor to Waukegan, Illinois, on May 9, 1936. The marriage bureau was closed, however, and the young couple had to turn around and drive south and east. They finally tied the knot later that day in Crown Point, a tiny town in northwest Indiana.[8] Crown Point marriages were fast and convenient for lovers in a hurry.

The Schuesslers began their child-rearing years in a small flat near Broadway and Bryn Mawr in what is now the Edgewater neighborhood of Chicago. For the next decade, theirs was a nomadic existence, moving from place to place, wherever Anton's work took him. After World War II, they relocated to a tiny apartment above a grocery store at 3835 W. North Ave. in a tough industrial and commercial corridor in Humboldt Park, a drab working-class area northwest of downtown. North Avenue was an arterial street and noisy, crowded, and increasingly crime ridden. The Germans, Poles, and Scandinavians who settled the area decades earlier were fleeing the neighborhood en masse, being replaced by an emerging mixed-Hispanic community, including Puerto Ricans.

Looking back on the years of struggle, Eleanor remarked, "Everything I had was his, everything he had was mine. I had more happiness than some women married fifty years. I have nothing to regret about my life with Anton."

Anton and Eleanor's first son, John, was born November 30, 1941. Anton Jr. came along November 12, 1943. In 1947, John and his father were struck by an automobile and badly injured. The tragic accident placed a terrible burden on the family. John, in particular, was psychologically scarred by the ordeal and appeared to Eleanor to turn inward. He began to allow himself to be dominated by the rougher boys in the neighborhood.

Anton Sr. continued to seek a good-paying position in the needle trade and, for his boys, quieter, safer surroundings. The Schuesslers were cautious, frugal people who saved and invested their money wisely. In 1950, with their economic circumstances improving, the family settled comfortably into a slightly more-upscale brownstone apartment building at 2705 Mozart Ave., located in the once-fashionable Logan Square neighborhood, north of Humboldt Park. Parlaying a $5,000 windfall from a real-estate investment with a $4,000 cash settlement received from the accident, the Schuesslers were finally able to move up in the world. They fled Logan Square in the early 1950s, abandoning apartment living for 5711 N. Mango St. with few regrets.

At that time, work was about to commence on the new Northwest Expressway. For thousands of less-fortunate apartment tenants denied cash relocation settlements by the city and too poor to find a place of their own, the decision to demolish hundreds of buildings blocking the "pathway to tomorrow" was a calamity. Though the Schuesslers' building on Mozart Avenue was spared the wrecking ball, the new superhighway, once complete, would slice through the neighborhood less than three city blocks away. Always mindful of the boys' safety, Anton and Eleanor were thankful to plant roots on Mango Street, where they knew they would not hear the constant din of automobile traffic or, worse, face the threat of another accident. In Jeff Park, there would only be the contented chirping of the cicadas on warm summer evenings. The little place became a sanctuary for the boys and a shelter where Anton Sr. could retreat from the world. "We bought this house for them (the boys)," Eleanor later recounted.

The Schuesslers did not own a car, and neither of them knew how to drive. Each morning at 7, Anton Sr. boarded an eastbound Foster Avenue bus to convey him to his shop near the lakefront. Long days left precious little time for him to enjoy life's simpler pleasures. In the months after the move, the Schuesslers talked about buying a new Ford station wagon; that is, if they could figure out a way to pay for it.

The Schuesslers suffered repeated financial hardship. In order to keep up with the steep rent payments on the tailor shop and the $72-a-month mortgage payment for the six-room house, which, in truth, they could not afford to own, Eleanor worked on the assembly line at Crescent Industries Inc., a maker of radio speakers located on Touhy Avenue. Eleanor belonged to Local 1031 of the International Brotherhood of Electrical Workers, AFL. Hers was a solid-paying, union position in an era when good manufacturing jobs were still plentiful.[9]

German Americans were one of the dominant ethnic groups living on Chicago's Northwest Side. Nightmares of the recent war and the humiliation of the Nazi scourge plagued first-generation immigrants. The plight of the refugees and the sorrow for the missing were indelibly inked into the collective memory of a community only one generation removed from Europe. While anxious parents and grandparents dispatched letters (many finding their way back to the Jeff Park post office on Lawrence Avenue and stamped undeliverable), food packages, and money to ease the sufferings of relatives left behind in the bombed-out regions of the old country, the grammar-school boys at Farnsworth and St. Tarcissus played war games in the streets, inside basement "bunkers," in alleys, on playgrounds, and from behind garbage cans. Iwo Jima, Berlin, and the beachhead at Anzio were recaptured many times by post-war kids armed with imaginary machine guns and plastic rifles. The neighborhood "wars" were inspired by the countless television documentaries watched in the company of their dads and by the oft-told tales overheard during moments of unguarded conversation at the dinner table. Blood and sudden death were imaginary events on the Northwest Side but a staple of the popular culture in John Wayne's America where the good guys always triumphed over cattle rustlers, Nazis, communist spies, and bank robbers.

Riding bicycles to school afforded youngsters an excellent opportunity to mimic television's best-known and widely loved Western stars like Richard Boone, the haughty bounty hunter in *Have Gun Will Travel*. With imagination, daring, and imitation-leather holsters strapped around their waists, grade-school boys hummed the *Have Gun Will Travel* theme as they rode their imaginary steeds to and from the assigned street corners where they served their school, gym teacher, and younger classmates as patrol boys. *Paladin, Paladin, where do you roam? Paladin, Paladin, far, far from home.*

Saturday, October 15, 1955, dawned bright and clear. For some, Saturday was marketing day on the Northwest Side, the customary time to shop for groceries at the IGA, Kroger, or National Tea and for kid's clothing at Shopper's World, a noisy wholesale outlet on Milwaukee Avenue just around the corner from the Petersons. For others, Saturdays on the Northwest Side meant clean-up day—a time to mow the lawn, sweep the twigs and leaves from the sidewalk and lawn, trim the hedges, or clean out the garage before the onset of winter. The neighborhood residents attended to these things with a devotion bordering on fanaticism. It was not uncommon for homeowners to water their park-like lawns well past 10:30 at night. No one dared allow the front-yard grass to grow tall, the leaves to go uncollected, or the paint on the eaves to crack and peel.

These same neighbors also kept a careful watch on who came into the neighborhood. To not do so would be an open invitation for dope fiends, hot-rod lunatics, or other "unwanteds" to move in—especially if the property values managed to dip just low enough, as they surely would because of the careless neglect of the few.

On Saturday, everyone pitched in and did his or her part. That meant boys and girls, too. No one wanted to be viewed as lazy or a slacker. In the springtime, the Chicago public-school system sponsored an annual clean-up week in accordance with the time-honored Yankee values of thrift, self-reliance, and pride in maintaining a proper appearance. "Keep Chicago Clean!" was the slogan of the day, and everyone subscribed. Twice, the Citizens for a Cleaner Chicago committee bestowed upon Jefferson Park the highly regarded honor of being named the "most beautifully landscaped community" in Chicago. "We can rightfully take pride in title and credit to our well-kept homes and grounds in the Jefferson Park area," beamed one local historian.

John and young Anton Schuessler raked and bagged the falling leaves, dashing indoors every few minutes or so for an update on the University of Illinois versus University of Minnesota football game on WGN radio. Sagging in his easy chair, too tired to work in the yard this autumn afternoon, Anton Sr. decided to let go of the chores just this once. With his *Chicago Tribune* spread out across his lap, he nodded off, the latest news of President Dwight D. Eisenhower's recent heart attack, his convalescence, and anticipated return to the golf links lulling him to sleep. It had been a long and tiring week.

"Dad! Dad!" Anton Jr. interrupted in an excited voice. The elder Schuessler opened his eyes, cleared the cobwebs from his mind, and peered at his son.

"Are you done out there?" he whispered, still half asleep.

"Uh, yeah, just about, I suppose." Tony's gaze wavered. "Some of the fellas are going bowling. Can we go, too?"

"Jeez, how many times a week do you think you have to go bowling?" Anton Sr. replied in an irritated tone. The night before, John had accompanied Malcolm Peterson and Bobby to the Faetz and Neeson alleys at 5961 N. Ridge Ave. in Chicago. Anton Sr. thought about the yard chores and wondered just how much his sons had managed to accomplish in so short a time.

"We want to go up to Natoma Lanes," the boy said somewhat hesitantly. The second-floor Natoma bowling alley straddled the city's northern limits separating Chicago from suburban Niles. Natoma Lanes was part of an adult "entertainment complex" of backroom gambling, sleaze, and B-girl hustlers crammed into one square block of what was then a shady Northwest Side no-man's-land that existed between the ragged periphery of the bungalows and a Cook County forest preserve.[10] In hindsight, it is remarkable that community residents were so unconcerned about this dangerous area that they would allow their children to stray into it without adult supervision. "It seemed that as kids we had a lot of freedom to move around—going downtown on the bus at ten and eleven years old, hanging out in the forest preserves, and staying out at night with very little to worry about," Garland recollected from his home in California.

The Schuessler brothers, like many boys of that era, loved bowling to the point of obsession. They listened religiously with their dad to sports announcer "Whispering" Joe Wilson as he described all the action of *Championship Bowling* over the air waves of WBKB-TV, channel 7, in Chicago. The boys frequented ten-pin lanes all over the Northwest Side, regardless of the unsavory reputation of a handful of these establishments. Bowling was big-time fun in the 1950s, and all over the city, wheezing, overweight, and overwrought middle-aged men belonged to company leagues that met regularly on weeknights. Champion PBA bowler Dick Weber was everyone's special favorite—the Babe Ruth of the Ten Pins.

Still half asleep, Anton Sr. nodded his consent and told his sons to be home before dinner. He picked up his paper from his lap and tried to focus on the important news of the day.

The two brothers rode their Schwinn bikes one mile to the Natoma Lanes where they met up with Bobby Peterson, ten-year-old Richard Padal, and several other Farnsworth schoolyard chums in the upstairs room—a narrow, smoke-filled hall featuring ten or twelve lanes and a liquor bar from which they rented shoes and bought their Cokes.

The boys bowled the customary three games, paid the attendant their bill of two bits a game, and exited Natoma Lanes, racing past the darkened vestibules of the Riviera Lounge and Guys and Dolls and home for supper.

"Well, maybe we'll see you at Mass tomorrow. Are you going?" Anton Jr. asked Richard.

Richard, who lived down the street from the Schuesslers, shrugged his shoulders, "I guess so, but I'm not sure what time."

On Sunday, October 16, 1955, the hand of fate would reach out to protect Richard and another neighbor boy, ten-year-old James Schemitsch, both of whom frequently went with the Schuessler boys to the movies. Through the luckiest of circumstances, both boys left home early on Sunday for pleasure drives with their parents. Otherwise, the boys might have been with Bobby, Anton, and John on Sunday afternoon.

Eleanor and Anton Schuessler Sr. entertained company late into the night on Saturday. On Sunday morning, worried about her husband's fatigue, Eleanor insisted he stay home and rest up. That meant skipping Mass at St. Tarcissus for Anton Sr., but the boys changed into their Sunday best—sports jackets, ties, and polished black Oxfords. Eleanor gave them each quarter for the collection plate and a rosary and told them not to dawdle or they would be late for the ten o'clock Mass, which would be presided over by Father Raymond G. Carey. Eleanor remained behind to finish up the last of the breakfast dishes and change into a fashionable dress for eleven o'clock Mass.

Around the same time that Sunday morning on Farragut Avenue, Dorothy Peterson was also busy getting her children ready for church, except for Bobby, who decided not to go this one time because he and his dad were working on a big fixer-upper project of extending the garage by four feet.

Shortly after 1:00 PM, when the girls came back from Sunday School at Jefferson Park Lutheran Church, Dorothy served up a meal of fried chicken and mashed potatoes. After dinner, Malcolm and Bobby returned to the garage addition. The telephone rang, and Bobby answered. He spoke to the caller briefly before phoning John Schuessler to invite him to the movies. Mrs. Peterson never found out who spoke with her son that Sunday afternoon.

Dorothy sat down with Bobby to review the movie listings, but as far as appropriate subject matter for children, the choices that week were very slim. Bobby had already seen *The McConnell Story* at the nearby Balaban and Katz Gateway Theater on Lawrence Avenue. *Kiss of Fire* and *Five Guns West,* a Technicolor double feature at the Portage Park, also nearby, wasn't appealing to him (of course, the real adventure was not the movie but the chance to "mess around" downtown). At the Oriental on Randolph Street in the heart of the Loop theater district was the musical comedy *It's Always Fair Weather* starring Gene Kelly, which sounded boring to Bobby (teenage boys found musicals boring). *The Tall Men*, a

Clark Gable Western at the State and Lake streets, and Audie Murphy's war epic *To Hell and Back* at United Artists were rejected by Dorothy, who thought there was enough war in this world. The crime thriller at the Roosevelt and *Lucy Gallant*, a Charlton Heston–Jane Wyman love story at the McVickers, did not seem right to her either, the subject matter and all. After some mild debate, mother and son agreed on *African Lion*, playing at the Loop Theater on State Street near Randolph. The award-winning Walt Disney nature documentary was about a family of lions surviving the changing seasons in their natural habitat, with *Peter and the Wolf* as the side feature. Bobby knew this choice was wholesome and acceptable entertainment and would not jeopardize the expedition into the city.

But Malcolm and Dorothy conceded that Bobby was a teenager now and in another year would be starting high school. Malcolm respected his son's physical capabilities and increasing maturity. As the boy got older and progressed through the juvenile sports programs, the father treated him more and more like a best buddy rather than a son. An unspoken bond existed between them, one based on mutual trust and admiration. After talking it over with Dorothy, Malcolm, with an understandable reticence, decided to allow Bobby to go downtown to see a movie with his friend. What could be the harm in that? Bobby was familiar with the bus routes and for the past year had taken his younger sister, Barbara Ann, to her downtown optometrist for eye exercises, sometimes in the company of Terry Reilly, one of Bobby's school friends.

Going downtown was an important rite of passage for boys living in the outlying areas of the city, forcing parents to give the matter careful consideration because of the distances involved and the modes of transportation. From the Far Northwest Side, the boys would catch the Milwaukee Avenue CTA (Chicago Transit Authority) bus and take it to the Logan Square terminal, at which point they would transfer to the subway in order to complete the final leg of the journey. The bus passed through several rough neighborhoods en route to Logan Square, and the CTA subway and elevated line also had to be viewed with supreme caution.

A few minutes past noon, Eleanor Schuessler returned from church to prepare the afternoon meal for her family. She was experimenting with a new soup recipe with shell macaroni and wasn't sure how it would turn out. She called her boys down to the kitchen and, with a sigh of disappointment, she filled their plates with the soup that more closely resembled a macaroni mush. She had used way too much macaroni. "I'm sorry, Tony," she said to her husband. "I thought it would turn out a lot better than this." "That's okay, Honey," Anton Sr. said with a pleasant smile. "It tastes just fine to me." He cleaned his plate without complaint. That's the kind of tender, loving man he was. Sunday dinner was nearly over when the phone rang. It was Bobby Peterson calling for John.

"He said he wants to go to a movie and wants me to come with. Is that okay, Dad?" Nothing was mentioned about a downtown movie. To ask permission to do so would have invited a firm "No!" and the customary parental retort to foolish notions that sometimes got into a kid's head. "Just because somebody else on the block thinks it's okay for a boy who is still wet behind the ears to go downtown alone doesn't mean that you can!" John could count on those words pouring out of his father's mouth like hot lava, and no logic would have gotten him to change his mind. So, why waste the time trying? The trip downtown with Bobby Peterson would remain a private matter between friends.

Anton Sr. lit up a cigarette and thought for a moment. "What about your brother? I bet he'd like to go along with you boys."

"Dad!" young Anton protested. "They don't want me around!" He was close to his brother, but he recognized that in certain social situations, sometimes younger brothers were considered a distinct liability.

Ignoring Tony's plea, the senior Schuessler instructed John to call Bobby Peterson back to tell him that Anton Jr. would be tagging along.

"Do you really think that's a good idea?" Eleanor asked. She mentally questioned the wisdom of allowing the younger boy to go out on a Sunday afternoon with the older boys, then she chided herself for being an overly protective parent. Besides, Anton Sr. needed some more quiet time to rest up for the week ahead. In recent days, Eleanor had noted with growing concern that her overworked husband's complexion was sallow. He complained that he wasn't feeling well and had been listless all weekend long. She didn't want young Anton irritating his father. "Don't be silly, Dear. I want Tony to have a good time, too. Go on, John. Call Bobby back now."

John informed his father that he had accidentally left his bicycle at the Peterson home the day before, and that with Tony along with his bicycle, they could ride both bikes back to Mango Street later that day. John made the call.

"Do you have homework to do?" Anton Sr. asked.

"Nope," beamed Tony. "I finished it on Friday night!"

"What about you?" the father asked, casting a glance toward John.

John nodded sullenly. He was feeling sly about concealing the fact that they were going downtown and not to the Gateway, Portage, or Harding theaters, and that brought on a rush of guilt feelings. Hiding something like this from the old man was never a good idea. It brought to mind that old familiar parental admonition, *When you don't mind, something always happens!*

"I want you boys home before dark," Eleanor said, meaning they were to be home before 7 PM. "Monday is a school day. And I don't want you bothering that boy's parents. Do you understand?" Eleanor had no idea where the Petersons lived, nor did she bother to ask John for their telephone number. It did not seem important at the time.

Tony and John had already changed into their casual clothes at their dad's insistence. John put on a brown shirt. Young Anton selected his black-and-white flannel shirt with the buttoned-down collar. Eleanor handed them their blue satin Chicago Cub jackets; the *U* was missing from Anton's emblem.

"The streets are wet. I want you to be careful and watch for traffic," Anton Sr. warned. "Be home by sundown."

The brothers went out through the back door, mounted Tony's bike, and headed toward Mango Street. Tony turned and waved. "Mommy, if they don't want me with, I'll be back by 3:30." Eleanor smiled ruefully and shook her head. The little dog by her side barked happily.

According to the 1955 newspaper reports, the Schuessler brothers turned up at the Peterson front door at three o'clock, having parked Anton's bike in the gangway next to the house. When Bobby noticed John's blue zippered jacket with the Cub emblem stitched on the front, he grimaced, "What are you wearin' that for?"

"There's only one team in this town worth anything."

"Yeah, the Sox!" Bobby shot back.

Anton Jr. chuckled. The baseball banter went on for only a few minutes more before Dorothy reminded them that they had better get going if they wanted to be on time for the previews. She zipped up her son's jacket, knowing full that it would be unzipped the second they turned the corner onto Milwaukee Avenue. "Oh, well, boys are boys," she consoled herself as she watched them from the enclosed porch.

"Bob, please be careful now, seriously. I want you home before seven, sooner if possible. Tomorrow is a school day," she said, frowning. The boys bounded down the front steps and turned left toward the bus stop. She felt a momentary shiver as she caught sight of her boy glancing over his shoulder at her that one last time.

Bobby waved casually to his dad, who was up on a ladder, now working on a storm-window project. Bobby and his friends disappeared down the street, unshackled by any of worries adults have to deal with.

"I wish I was that age again, Dotty," Malcolm softly whispered to his wife after he had climbed down from the ladder and come back into the house.

"I wish you would finish taking down the screens and stop being an old fuddy-duddy!" Dorothy slapped her man playfully on his rear as she retreated into the spacious living room of the Dutch Colonial.

"No Indian summer this year, I expect," said Malcolm, looking out once more at the quiet side street and his next-door neighbor raking up leaves. But Dorothy did not hear. She was already in the kitchen and lost in her own private thoughts.

According to neighborhood friend Glenn Carter, he and his brother Bruce met up with Bobby and the Schuessler boys in an alley not far from the Peterson home at approximately two o'clock on Sunday. The Carters attended the same church as the Petersons. Glenn and Bobby were also both active in Boy Scout troops that occasionally had joint functions at Jefferson Park Lutheran Church. During the past year, Glenn had ridden horses at a stable out on Higgins Road known as the Idle Hour Stables. On several occasions, he had seen Bobby at the same stable.

The boys chatted for awhile, and Glenn asked, "So, where are you going?"

"To the ice cream parlor on Lawrence Avenue and then we're going to get a ride to the horse stables," Bobby answered.

At that moment, a slow-moving car passed the mouth of the alley. The driver honked his horn.

"Is that Hansen?" Tony asked.

"Shut up!" John barked. "You've said enough already."

Bobby added guardedly, "We're going to get a ride to the stables from Hansen."

The Carter brothers said their good-byes and walked off. They glanced back, but the other boys had turned the corner and were already gone.

"So, who's Hansen?" asked Glenn.

3

The Last Bus Ride

THE CITY BECKONED. With four dollars in change among them, Anton, John, and Bobby figured they could live it up in style and be back home by nightfall. Of course, if it turned out to be 9:00 or even 9:30, they might be inviting a heap of trouble, but on the surface of things, it seemed to the boys a risk worth taking. Whether or not they made a spur-of-the-moment decision, shortly after Bobby waved good-bye to his dad, to go bowling or if they headed straight downtown to see *African Lion*, the reported movements of the three boys raise many questions and form the nexus of the impenetrable mysteries surrounding this case and a controversial theory that refuses to die.

Armed with student bus passes, three boys boarded the southbound #56 Milwaukee Avenue bus at Central Avenue. Chicago Transit Authority driver Thomas J. Meagher was convinced these were the boys in question—the same three boys who had paid their discounted student fare of twelve cents and quizzed him with boyish excitement about the downtown movies playing that day. He was certain that he picked them up at "around 2:30," but, if true, the time contradicts Malcolm Peterson's assertion that they did not leave the Peterson home until 3:00.

"On Sunday, most boys are dressed up for church. These boys were not. That's why I remember them," Meagher said emphatically.

The boys rode as far as Logan Square in a busy commercial strip five miles south of Jefferson Park. In the 1950s, the Logan Square area was a community of non-English-speaking Poles, with a smattering of other Eastern European and Norwegian residents, living in row after row of Victorian graystones. In those days, the northwest extension of the CTA rapid transit line (the El) traveled only as far north as Logan Square. People from the Far Northwest Side neighborhoods who relied on public transportation to get downtown made their connection at this busy hub. Meagher said he remembered watching the boys dart towards the elevated terminal and thought nothing more about them until he read the newspaper accounts the following week.

Allowing for the possibility that they changed their minds, as boys so often do, they would have transferred at Logan Square to the Kedzie

Avenue bus line and conceivably reached the Monte Cristo Bowl by 3:45 but certainly no earlier (witnesses said the boys were spotted there at 3:15). The Monte Cristo was a short bus ride away but a world apart from the security of the boys' homes. The rough character of the Albany Park neighborhood, due east of Jefferson Park and centered on Kedzie Avenue between Lawrence and Montrose avenues, made it an improbable destination for the three young boys from Jeff Park who told their parents they were on their way to see a Walt Disney nature film in downtown Chicago.

In this sagging, working-man's Albany Park neighborhood defined by rows of shabby storefronts with second-floor apartments, package liquor stores, currency exchanges, and small industrial factories, the Monte Cristo lanes (at Montrose and Christiana) were a magnet for small-time drinkers, company-league bowlers, and the usual collection of after-hours city folk hanging out and marking time. The place reeked of stale beer, hangovers, and bad memories. Dust gathered on the championship trophies from years past. The Seven-Seven was the mixed drink of choice among the middle-aged bowlers in flowered shirts smoking LaPalina cigars. It was a gritty, Pabst Blue Ribbon setting.

Edward Davis, manager of the Monte Cristo, swore he had seen the boys wander into his place but only for a few moments. In the noisy clamor, could he *really* be sure? Was he *really* paying attention? Disappointed because the lanes were all in use, the boys exited the bowling alley and possibly headed downtown, though there were no actual eyewitnesses who spotted them on a bus or the elevated line or inside what was supposed to be their final destination—the Loop Theater on State Street near Randolph.

The Disney documentary ended shortly before six. The boys presumably exited the theater and walked one block east to the Garland Building, 111 S. Wabash Ave., a 1915 brick skyscraper brushing up against the Loop elevated line. Bobby Peterson told the lobby attendant that he needed to use the washroom up on the ninth floor. This is the building to which several times during the past year Bobby had accompanied his younger sister, Barbara Ann, to her eye doctor appointments and, therefore, knew the location of the men's restroom. He told the Schuessler brothers to wait for him on the ground floor. "Be back in a few minutes," he might have said. In hindsight, it seems very odd that Bobby and his friends would walk over to the Garland Building just to use a restroom when there were more convenient locations in the Loop Theater and in nearby restaurants. Why would he go over there unless, maybe, he had made an arrangement to meet someone? Perhaps it had something to do with the phone call Bobby had taken moments before calling John Schuessler. The question remains unanswered.

Less than five minutes later, Bobby rejoined his companions in the lobby, and they left the building without incident.

The Garland Building, with its many medical offices, towers over a stretch of Wabash Avenue known as Jewelers' Row—Chicago's encapsulated version of Manhattan's famed diamond district on West 44th Street. In the 1950s, the lobby of the old skyscraper was infamous. The cops knew it as a hangout for hustlers, creeps, junkies, prostitutes and their pimps, homosexuals, the homeless, and the class of men who preyed on little boys. The Chicago Police Department, Eleventh and State streets, drew no distinction among these idlers and tarred them all with the same broad brush—morons and perverts. This was the terminology universally accepted by the police reporters working the pressroom at Eleventh and State during those politically incorrect times.

The skies grew dark, and a steady, mean-spirited drizzle blanketed the city during the early evening hours of October 16, 1955. John, Tony, and Bobby made their way back to the Northwest Side intent upon bowling a few games in the neighborhood before calling it quits for the night. For the second time that day, they tried to rent a lane at the Monte Cristo, but, once again, the place was filled. The boys parked themselves on a bench between the seventh and eighth lanes and with only passing interest watched the older men bowl. It was 7:00 PM. The sun had already set an hour earlier. The boys were spotted by a neighbor of the Schuesslers, seventeen-year-old Ernest Niewadomski, a student at Gordon Technical High School, who was accompanied by his two sisters, Leona, twenty, and Delphine, age ten.

Niewadomski later said he did not personally know Robert Peterson, but from time to time, he had allowed John and Tony and some of the other younger boys on the block to play baseball with the older high school guys. "Every so often we would need extra players, and the younger kids got to fill in, to play right field or what have you, positions that we didn't think very important, but everybody got to play."

Niewadomski, the last person to positively identify the boys that night, recalled that the boys had left the bowling alley "in good spirits" a little after 8:00 PM. The older boy chatted pleasantly with them about their downtown adventure and the Disney movie. Bobby and his friends told how they had taken the El back to the Northwest Side, likely the same

Logan Square elevated line where they would have transferred to a north-bound Kedzie Avenue bus.

Niewadomski asked if they wanted to bowl a few games.

"Not unless you pay for it!" they replied.

Niewadomski remembered, "I said, 'Well, my sister is paying for me so I don't have any money.' So, we just had some small talk, and that was basically it." Bobby disappeared into the washroom of the Monte Cristo, rejoining them five minutes later. "C'mon, let's go!" Bobby said in a purposeful tone that suggested to Niewadomski's sister Leona that they had a definite plan in mind for the remainder of the evening.

Sunday night was a quiet time in the neighborhoods fanning out from the inner city. Sunday nights in the mid-1950s meant a late supper and then an evening of television with Ed Sullivan[1] and his *Talk of the Town*, followed by the *Alcoa Hour* and at nine the *Loretta Young Show*, and capped off by the 10:00 news with Walter Cronkite, before the porch lights flickered on and people settled in for the night.

At home, Eleanor Schuessler looked at her watch and her husband with mounting apprehension. It was past seven; Ed Sullivan was warming up his studio audience in New York. "And tonight we have with us . . . Rosemary Clooney, Dave Brubeck, Liberace, Andre Kostelanatz, and Edward R. Murrow—"

A crack of thunder and a fierce sheet of rain startled Eleanor. "Tony, you don't think anything is wrong, do you? I mean, where are they?"

When rain pelts the city streets, only the bus drivers, cops, cabbies, short-order cooks, newspaper deliverymen, and creatures of the night can be found out and about. On this particular night, the October rain was a stroke of bad luck for the police because it reduced the number of potential eyewitnesses who otherwise might have been outdoors that night. "Traffic is not so heavy on a rainy Sunday night that three boys could be forgotten by a [bus] driver or fellow passengers," a *Chicago American* reporter noted, as he sifted through a maze of conflicting, unconfirmed police reports placing the boys here, there, and everywhere except where they were supposed to be. The city never seemed so big, yet as small as that night.

After leaving the Monte Cristo bowling alley, the boys proceeded west on Montrose Avenue in the general direction of the Drake Bowl, four blocks away. The trio darted in and out of the rain, headstrong about getting to bowl—one way or another. Ernest Tucker, a popular and well-versed *Chicago American* columnist, had to wonder: "Why the urge to go bowling? Why the visits to several alleys and projected visits to at least one other? Through the whole thing runs the theme of bowling. They were good boys. Why were they so far out of routine? Why were they nearly three miles from home at 7:45, long after dark, long after their parents had begun to worry? Was it just the heedlessness of the boys?" Or did they just want to go bowling?

At the Drake Bowl, 3550 W. Montrose, manager Waldorf Lundgren spotted them inside the doorway. It was 8:00 PM, and all sixteen lanes were in use. It was busy but not so busy that Lundgren would have missed spotting the three kids in his establishment. "Sorry, boys, nothing going on tonight!" They looked dejected.

Inside the taproom adjacent to the cashier station, men huddled around the bar swapping stories about "the one that got away" as they gazed up at the black-and-white TV and quaffed their lager. The Drake is a relic from another time—mostly unchanged from its heyday in the 1950s. It is a cozy neighborhood setting with sixteen lanes, wood paneling, glass-block doorways, and vintage décor. The sense is that the modern-day kings of the hardwood are on a first-name basis with the counterman. The atmosphere at the Drake spirits one back to a time in American culture when bowling and not the current leisure-time pursuits of jogging, golf, or tennis was the number-one participation sport. Maybe when all is said and done, the Schuessler-Peterson boys wanted nothing more than to end this evening of unexpected freedom bowling to their hearts' content.

At 8:05, twenty-year-old truck driver Harold Blumenfield eased his rig to the curb to pick up three boys standing forlornly at the edge of the sidewalk at Montrose and Kimball with their thumbs out. "Hop in. Where you headed?"

The talkative one, who identified himself as "Peterson," stood five feet three inches and had blue eyes and brown hair. He seemed to be the natural leader, the one in charge.

Bobby jumped into the front seat alongside Blumenfield, telling him about their present difficulties finding an open bowling alley.

"Gosh, that is tough," the driver said in mock sympathy. "Are you any good at it?"

"Yeah, not bad," replied Bobby, casting a glance toward the back seat. "Of course, these guys are still learning!"

Blumenfield drove on for a half-mile. He remembered one of them saying they wanted to go only as far as Elston Avenue, a diagonal street intersecting Montrose, but instead they continued to Kenneth, a block west.

"Do any of you boys happen to know what time it is?" asked Blumenfield.

Bobby told him that it was 8:21. A few minutes later, they pointed to the northwest corner of Kenneth and Montrose and said, "Okay, here." They thanked the driver for the ride and climbed out of the truck. By now, the rain was coming down in sheets, and upon further reflection, Blumenfield though it odd that they would want to get off at this quiet, out-of-the-way side street. Where were they going in such foul weather and at this time of night? "Hmmm," Blumenfield said, shook his head, and drove off.

At Milwaukee and Belle Plaine in Portage Park just south of Jeff Park, CTA bus driver Bruno Mancarini told police that he picked up three adolescent boys around 8:40. He remembered that the two older boys had their school bus-fare cards and paid their dime, but Anton Jr. did not. The boys were still searching for an open bowling alley, and Mancarini said he joshed with them, "Well, you can try your luck at the Jefferson Park Recreation Alleys. Of course, it's rather late now, don't you think?" In order to connect with Mancarini for this conversation to occur, the three would have had to walk nearly a half-mile in the pouring rain. "They were wet as though they had walked a couple of blocks," Mancarini said.

Why did they venture so far out of their way, ending up at Belle Plaine Avenue? The boys could have just as easily caught the #56 bus at Montrose rather than walk three extra blocks south on Milwaukee. There was one possible explanation. According to witness Jack Johnson, whose testimony was publicly disclosed long after the main investigation had ended, the boys wandered into the Garden Bowling Alley at 4074 Milwaukee Ave. around 8:40 PM. The smallest of the three approached Johnson and asked, "What time is it, Mister?" Johnson identified the lad as Anton Schuessler Jr.

A few minutes later, they boarded Mancarini's bus. The driver was positive that it was them, and the police accepted his story conditionally because they still had some doubts.

"They were quiet, and that's unusual for kids. They looked just like any other kids going to a show. They sat on the long seat near me," Mancarini remembered.

Bobby Peterson and his dad frequented the Jefferson Park lanes and were well-known customers of co-owners John Mendes and Jack Sampayo. On the night in question, neither Mendes nor Sampayo reported seeing the boys in their modest second-floor establishment. They agreed to take a lie-detector test to back up their statements.

Others in the Jefferson Park community told of observing three boys— but much earlier in the day. Joseph Stanton, the owner of a Milwaukee Avenue hobby shop, informed police that three boys matching the descriptions were in his place around 4:30 PM asking questions about converting a model-airplane engine for use in a boat. Stanton's Hobby Shop was only two doors away from Henri's, a saloon where homosexuals congregated. The owner of a tile-and-linoleum store at 4746 Milwaukee Ave. said the Schuessler brothers walked through his front door at 5:30 PM, inquiring about a birthday present for their mother. Waitress Elsie Weisgerber at the C & L Restaurant at Montrose and Milwaukee said there was no doubt in her mind that she had served the three boys an early dinner around 5:00. She remembered them because "they were so polite." It would have been impossible for them to have gone to a downtown movie and made it back to Jefferson Park by public transportation in time to visit Stanton's, shop for tile, and eat at the C & L. These discrepancies in time as well as the shaky eyewitness accounts of Stanton, Weisgerber, and others conflicted with the known facts of the case and only served to create confusion in the minds of investigators.

At 9:05 PM, an hour when most grammar-school children were at home completing their schoolwork assignments or preparing for bed, Bobby, Anton, and John were spotted in front of the S. Rosenau Jewelry Store at 4787 N. Milwaukee Ave. on the southeast corner of Milwaukee and Lawrence avenues, directly across the street from the Hoyne Bank. As they waited for the traffic light to change, a man and woman traveling west on Lawrence Avenue on their way to a late-night movie at the Portage Park Theater studied the three lads with growing interest. One of them was standing with one foot in the street and the other resting on the curb. His thumb was out, and he was hitching a ride. The other two boys, appearing miserably chilled to the bone, huddled underneath the store awning with their hands jammed inside their pockets. "Now why would those boys be out on a night like this without warmer clothes on?" the woman wondered. She noticed that the two positioned nearest the wall of the jewelry store were wearing Cub jackets, and the hitchhiking boy, a Sox jacket. "When I was a girl, a Sox fan and a Cub fan never would pal around together," she remarked nonchalantly. "They would be sure to argue. I think it's nice that children nowadays feel differently."

The light changed, and Bobby Peterson, noting the directional on the couple's car indicated that they were turning south onto Milwaukee, stepped back up on the curb. The motorists, who told their story under the condition of anonymity, turned left from Lawrence Avenue.

Additional details provided to the state's attorney's investigators by this young couple might have proven critical if only the investigators had been willing to share with other agencies, but Chicago Police Lieutenant Mike Spiotto[2] did not get ahold of the information until months later, long after Cook County State's Attorney John Gutknecht and his staff abandoned the lead.

"I first heard about it around the time I was pulled off the Schuessler case," said Spiotto. "If I had gotten it in time, well, maybe I could have done something with it."

Near the intersection, the couple reported seeing a beat-up, white "farm truck," the kind of shabby, low-sided, flatbed vehicle with attached wooden slats that a junkman might use to haul away old appliances or a rancher to hold bales of hay in place.

"They said that the kids waved to the truck and one of them called out a name—'Hey, Ed!'—but that was only part of it," Spiotto remembered. "They couldn't make out the rest of the name or distinguish the license plate. But it seemed like important information all the same."

Who was Ed, and what was his connection to the boys?

There were still others who claimed to have spotted the Schuessler-Peterson boys hitchhiking in the Jefferson Park business district that night. Ralph Helm, a fifteen-year-old Lane Technical High School student walking his girlfriend home from the movies, independently confirmed the couple's story. Ralph told police that he, too, had observed three boys thumbing a ride east on Lawrence Avenue—away from the general direction of their homes. Ralph vividly described what he had seen that windswept evening: "South of Lawrence Avenue on the curb, it would be the east curb of Milwaukee Avenue, I observed a young boy standing, facing more south than any other direction, with his right hand extended with the thumb extended from his right hand as if to be hitchhiking. I thought this was a dangerous situation . . . to have a young boy that late at night to be hitchhiking."[3] After dropping off his girlfriend, Ralph returned to the intersection ten to fifteen minutes later to catch the southbound Milwaukee Avenue bus, but the boys had already gone.

Where were they going? What could they possibly be up to? They must have known their parents would be frantic with worry at this late hour.

Anton Schuessler Sr. had issued strict orders for his boys to be home by sundown, and sundown on this drizzly October night arrived at 6:00 PM. The mystery deepened.

Reports from two other witnesses placed the boys at Lawrence and Elston avenues, a mile east of the Hoyne Bank, at 10:35 PM. Police paid close attention to the testimony of forty-eight-year-old motorist Margaret Crimmins, a divorced Glenview waitress, who said that around that time of night, she watched three young boys enter a light-colored DeSoto sedan driven by a "well-dressed" man "in his fifties, wearing a fedora hat." Because of the falling rain, Mrs. Crimmins said she could not identify the license plate numbers on the car she described as light green with yellow or chartreuse paneling. "I noticed two fives in the number though." A second witness agreed that the car was a DeSoto.

By a quarter to nine, a nervous, gnawing dread overtook Eleanor Schuessler. It was just not like her two boys to flagrantly disregard their parents' instructions like this. She tried, however, to be sensible and not a nervous Nellie. "They must have stayed over for the second half of the double feature," she said weakly. What movie they'd gone to see, she did not know, but the neighborhood theaters like the Portage Park and the Gateway showed two movies continuously throughout the day, sometimes interspersed with a short subject or newsreel.

"Maybe they're over at the Petersons," Anton Sr. suggested, "and just lost track of time. You know how boys are." He tried to mask his own apprehension. Something was not quite right. He felt it in his bones. "Maybe we should give them a call. Do you have the Petersons' phone number?"

Eleanor pensively ran her hands through her hair. "The boy's name is Robert. That's all I know!" she said in an agitated tone. "Damn!"

"Get me the phone book." To his dismay, Anton Sr. discovered twenty columns of Petersons listed in the Chicago directory. Eleanor and Anton did not have a clue as to the name of Bobby's father. All they could do was dial the phone and hope to catch a break. What was the neighborhood exchange? It was PE for Pensacola, of course. The anxious mother tore out a page from the phone book and called dozens of Northwest Side Petersons in the PE area, repeating the same tired lines over and over, "I'm sorry to bother you at this hour, but I'm wondering if you have a son named Robert? You see I have two boys who have been out with him all afternoon and haven't come home . . ." The minutes ticked away. Eleanor nervously twisted the phone cord, her voice beginning to crack under the terrible mounting strain.

Finally, she reached the residence of Malcolm Peterson at PE-6–2591.

Dorothy, whose frantic tone mirrored her own growing desperation, said, "No, they haven't returned, Mrs. Schuessler. I don't know . . ." Eyes wide, Dorothy looked at her husband.

There was silence on Eleanor's end when she discovered that her sons had gone with Bobby to a downtown movie and not the closer Portage Park or Gateway. The awful truth sunk in. She and her husband had just assumed all along that it would be the Gateway. By accident or design, John and Tony had withheld the truth from their parents about their plans for that day. *When you don't mind, something always happens!* Anton lowered his gaze and said somberly, "I think we should first make some calls in the neighborhood and then to the police."

And so began an agonizing thirty-six-hour vigil for these two ordinary, hard-working Northwest Side families forced to confront the terrible possibilities and the unexpected hand that fate had dealt them. With the passing minutes, their feelings of bewilderment and helplessness were given up to a more visceral sense that something was horribly wrong. Malcolm Peterson contacted the neighbors up and down the street.

Around 9:15 PM, Mrs. Charles E. Ebert of Farragut Street contacted the police. The well-meaning neighbor telephoned the desk sergeant at the Irving Park (thirty-third district) police station on Gale Street, which lay exactly halfway between the safety of Farragut Avenue and Milwaukee and Lawrence where the boys were last seen hitchhiking, to report them missing.

The Petersons were told to keep checking in the neighborhood. Maybe Bobby and his friends just lost track of the time. Boys are like that sometimes. "If they haven't returned by midnight, well, then maybe you should come in and file a report," the sergeant advised.

Phone calls went back and forth between the anxious parents each hoping to hear an encouraging word from the other that one of the boys might have had the good sense to check in. But there was only silence.

Malcolm Peterson tried to be rational. "You know, maybe they spent all of their money and are stuck somewhere. That would be just like them! Maybe they are walking home from downtown . . ." His voice trailed off. That was too farfetched to believe, but nothing could be left to chance. "Mr. Schuessler," he said. "Do you drive?"

"No, I don't," Anton replied, in a voice barely above a whisper.

"Well, let me come over there, and we'll go out and look for them. We'll drive all the way downtown if we have to." Malcolm put on his coat and drove over to Mango Avenue, where the two men exchanged uncomfortable formal greetings and briefly shook hands before setting out.

During the next hour and a half, they drove slowly south on Milwaukee Avenue, past the darkened storefronts of the neighborhood shopping centers in Portage Park, Avondale, and Logan Square and into the heart of West Town, bordering the outer edge of downtown Chicago. Malcolm scanned the sidewalk to his left, and Anton focused on street activity to the right, looking for the three lost boys, but the rain kept falling, and the city was already asleep. Every ten minutes or whenever they could spot a pay phone, Malcolm stopped the car and telephoned Dorothy and Eleanor for some further word. "Have they come home? Did they call?" But there was no word from the missing boys.

The two men peered intensely into the windows of the all-night snack shops. The warm, inviting glow of the diners and burger joints illuminated the faces of grizzled men, the third-shifters conversing over coffee with their bored and indifferent servers. And still no sign. As the two fathers inched ever closer to downtown, they noticed the profound shift between the well-maintained communities of the Far Northwest Side and the poorer and rougher inner-city neighborhoods. Metal pull-down grates protected the plate-glass windows and doors of the ma-and-pa stores from vandals and burglars. South of Logan Square, broken sidewalks were littered with paper refuse, and the weather-beaten facades of nineteenth-century buildings stood in stark contrast when compared to the quiet, well-manicured homes of Jefferson Park. This stretch of Milwaukee Avenue had been called "Dinner-Pail Row" by the tenement-dwelling immigrants of former years. "You don't think they would be all the way down here, do you, Anton?" Malcolm asked, worried that the boys might have been struck by a car and were lying in a hospital somewhere, and shook his head.

"No, but let's just drive on."

Few words passed between the two men, each lost in their own private thoughts and worries.

The downtown movie houses were closing. Many of them were already dark, and the final showing of *African Lion* at the Loop Theater had commenced at 10:40. Malcolm and Anton made an inquiry, but neither the ushers nor the managers on duty that night remembered seeing the boys. With the exception of a few stragglers, the rows of seats inside the movie theater were nearly empty. The fathers peeked into the lobbies of the other theaters and were told essentially the same thing.

Their spirits deflated, Malcolm and Anton turned and headed home, retracing their earlier path on Milwaukee Avenue. With a heavy sigh, Malcolm turned left onto Gale Street, driving slowly past the Jefferson Park Masonic Temple and into a parking spot adjacent to the small Art Deco police station that served the greater Northwest Side. The two men filed missing-persons reports with Sergeant George Murphy, who on this dreary Sunday evening was marking time until his shift was over. It was past midnight, and Murphy was cooperative. He telephoned the downtown theaters and the ten-pin alleys where Malcolm and Bobby often went to bowl, but there was nothing to report. Both fathers attested to the good character of the boys. Not one of them had ever been in trouble or involved with gangs. The sergeant nodded grimly and provided assurances that the other city police districts would be notified. ("Bobby Peterson never hung around with gangs. He spent most of his time playing baseball or football," recalled Carol Walsh, a classmate who had lived at 5857 Mango, a block from the Schuessler family. Carol admitted she had had a crush on the athletic John Schuessler as did a number of little girls at Farnsworth during that last summer.)

Shortly after midnight, every North and Northwest Side district station was placed on high alert and told to be on the lookout for three lost boys. At 12:30 AM, a Teletype message was delivered to all city police districts informing them of the disappearance.

Full of fear and dread, the two men walked slowly out of the station, their shoulders sagging and their hearts heavy. "Please let us know as soon as you hear something," murmured Anton. Sergeant Murphy nodded. Without telling either father, he placed a private call to the Sex Bureau and alerted them to the disappearance of the three boys. With so many curfew violators and missing children reported to police every night of the week, it was a highly unusual step for Murphy to take at this early juncture, but his instincts told him that the disappearance of these boys was about to become a very serious matter.

For a few hours more, Malcolm and Anton drove aimlessly through the neighborhoods, rechecking the bowling alleys, driving past bus stops and hamburger stands, unwilling to contemplate the darker possibilities. At 3:30 in the morning, Malcolm Peterson dropped Anton Schuessler Sr. off at his doorstep and went home to comfort his wife and speak to their other children.

Sleep was not possible for any of them that night. Anton found Eleanor seated on the green couch in the living room with pillows propped up behind her back, waiting for some hopeful sign or a bit of encouraging news. But he could only shake his head in dismay. Eleanor stared vacantly at the wall and in a barely audible voice said, "None of them ever stayed away from home before." She was unable to fight back the tears welling up in her eyes.

With bitter irony, Eleanor thought back to the recent visit of the boys' great aunt, Mrs. Emma Schultz Alexander, who had enjoyed several care-free weeks in Chicago vacationing with the family. Only a week earlier, Mrs. Alexander and her second husband, Otto, had driven back to their home outside of Miami, Florida. Eleanor remembered loading up the car and how John and Tony had expressed a strong desire to accompany the two on their return trip, yearning to enjoy a few days in the sun and surf. "If there's no room in the car, we'll ride in the trunk!" volunteered John. Anton Jr. piped in, "Sure! Can we do that, Mom?" But Eleanor smiled and said that that wasn't a very good idea, was it? Now it seemed like it had been the very best idea in the world.

4

A Time to Grieve

AUTUMN IS THE LOVELIEST time of year for nature lovers to commune in the swathes of green spaces that make up the Cook County forest preserves. The trees and bushes are at their peaks of their beauty and with the arrival of the first cold snap, the bothersome mosquitoes and gnats are nearly all gone. In October in years past, it was the custom for Northwest-Siders to drive out to Robinson Woods to buy Halloween pumpkins from roadside stands. In 1955, the area was not yet incorporated into the city.[1] Twenty-two riding stables provided recreation to horse lovers of all ages in rustic settings that had not yet succumbed to the urban sprawl and increased population density that would result from the rapid expansion of O'Hare International Airport and its adjacent bedroom suburbs in the 1960s.[2]

The Des Plaines River bisects Robinson Woods and runs parallel more or less to River Road near Lawrence Avenue. Robinson Woods contains the only marked Indian burial ground within the Chicago city limits.

In the opinion of folklorists and students of the paranormal, Robinson Woods is awash in psychic unrest. Haunted, they say, by the restless spirits of the Native Americans who inhabited the area until the early 1830s, when the government relocated the indigenous tribes to the Western Reserve.

In 1829, Alexander Robinson, one of the defenders of old Fort Dearborn when the military garrison was attacked and besieged by Indians, ceded the tract of the land to the U.S. government. Robinson's mother was a full-blooded Chippewa Indian, and his descendents continued to live in the vicinity until the City of Chicago, with its inimitable sense of fair play, decided that the family should be evicted.

The remote location of the woods and the sense of isolation from the outside world appealed to nature lovers, picnickers, hikers, and couples in love. However, the forest preserves of Cook County, protected by a thinly deployed contingent of rangers unable to effectively patrol such a vast expanse, were, at their worst, an irresistible lure for criminals, substance abusers, vagrants, and sexual predators. The density of the underbrush made the forest preserves a natural place for criminals and deviates to hide themselves and their nefarious deeds. In 1955, Herbert Holm, owner of the Rocking Horse II Stables, told police that twice a month, on average, riders were accosted by someone in the woods. Only the rangers on horseback were able to get far enough back into the woods to investigate the complaints.

Tuesday, October 18, 1955, started out sunny, but there was a chill in the air. Victor Livingston was a beer and liquor salesman by trade, but he did not drink. In the 1930s, he worked as an extra in Hollywood, appearing in a string of B-movies. By 1955, however, Livingston's acting days were well behind him, and he was back in Chicago living on Rascher Avenue with his second wife, Sadie. Victor, according to his nephew Al Plotkin, was in the habit of packing a lunch bag before he set out to make his daily rounds of the local taverns and roadhouses in Chicago and its close-in suburbs. When the mood suited him, the fifty-five-year-old salesman would eat his lunch in his car, parked in some remote spot where he could listen to the birds, close his eyes for a moment, and unwind. That morning, Plotkin continued, Livingston called on the proprietor of Heuer's, a tavern at 5600 River Rd., one of several drinking places close to Robinson Woods. Around noontime, after concluding his dealings at Heuer's, Livingston steered his car toward a driveway running south from Lawrence Avenue into Robinson Forest Preserve. About two hundred feet in, the driveway widened into a parking area. Livingston stopped his automobile, shifted into park, turned off the engine, and leaned back. He was facing a low, weedy culvert. It was 12:15 PM.

Just as Livingston was about to reach for his lunch in the back seat, he glanced over his dashboard, and three strange objects lying in the ditch caught his attention. "What the devil—?" Livingston peered for a moment at what he had seen. At first, he believed he was gazing at three department store mannequins, stripped of clothing and carelessly thrown into the ditch by a litterer. But, he got out of his car, and as he got closer, he noticed a spot of blood on one of the pale, white forms and realized that he had stumbled into a crime scene. These were not discarded display dummies but the lifeless bodies of three boys. Livingston gasped, "Oh, Jesus God!"

He was not thinking clearly, and his heart was pounding. *What to do? What to do?* The salesman jumped into his car and broke out into a cold sweat. Breathing heavily, he turned on the engine, jerked the gearshift into reverse, straightened the vehicle, and raced back to Heuer's, the only place he could think of at the moment. Only a handful of people were in the bar when Livingston burst through the door. In a strangled voice, he blurted out the details of the gruesome scene he had just witnessed. Don Gudeman, owner of the Mel-O-Rust riding stables on River Road, picked up the phone and calmly called Forest Preserve Ranger Headquarters at Harlem Avenue and Lake Street in west-suburban Oak Park. Because the crime appeared to have occurred on forest preserve property, Gudeman's first reaction was to contact the rangers, though they had only limited jurisdiction in the matter and lacked the necessary resources to conduct a major criminal investigation.[3]

When he received the phone call, Ranger Roy Haslam told Gudeman to take Livingston back to the crime location and wait there for someone from his department to show up.

The first responder at the crime scene was not a sworn city police officer as would have been expected, but a part-time news reporter for WGN-TV, channel 9, who showed up prepared to shoot the grisly crime-scene footage with a heavy and cumbersome Bell and Howell model #70DL 16 mm camera. Richard Ritt had been finishing lunch at his North Side home when the assignment editor from WGN called. In an excited tone, the editor ordered Ritt out to Robinson Woods with his camera. The newsroom had intercepted a police radio call, and though details were very sketchy at that point, three dead boys lying in a ditch somewhere out in the woods was much more than an average run-of-the-mill story for the evening telecast.

"I was going to school on the GI Bill at the time," vividly recalled Ritt, a retired optometrist in his seventies at the time of the interview. "I was actually in optometry school and working as a night man for WGN. I made about three hundred films for them, all told, but this one . . ." Ritt collected his thoughts. "I made it to the crime scene in less than fifteen minutes in my Dodge. As I approached, I saw what appeared to be a forest-preserve employee hovering over something. Then I saw the kids lying there. This was not a pretty sight you know." Ritt began filming anyway. He was on location a good ten minutes before any sworn law-enforcement personnel arrived.

Ranger John E. Byrne was dispatched from the Belmont and East River Roads station to rendezvous with Gudeman and Livingston at the crime site. Byrne was told that he would be joined by reinforcements.

Meanwhile, Livingston and Gudeman went to the crime scene. Pale, trembling, and unable to drive, Livingston asked Gudeman to take the wheel. When they arrived, the liquor salesman pointed out the location of the tangled mass of arms and legs that was the three slain boys, then looked away. Gudeman in shock and disbelief exclaimed, "My God, would you look at that!" The horrific image was too much for him to comprehend. The three boys had been tossed into a runoff ditch as if they were sacks of garbage. Chicago had long been viewed as a dangerous, crime-ridden town, but the slaughter of three school-age youths was extremely disconcerting even by Chicago standards.[4]

Detective James Lanners responded quickly after hearing of the discovery of the boys' bodies and arrived shortly after the coroner. He told his new captain, Russell Corcoran, "I'm going to go locate a friend of the Schuessler boys." He recalled that no one was home at the Peterson residence. "I found out about a man by the name of McMahon, a fireman, who lived next door" to the Schuesslers. Lanners drove the concerned neighbor to the crime scene "and we went up by the bodies, and he identified the Schuessler boys." The detective was insistent that he was not one of the men "who rolled the bodies over or contaminated the crime scene."

Lanners was a "licensed embalmer funeral director," the job he had before becoming a Chicago Police detective. "I was looking to see if they were buggered. And there was nothing that would indicate that."

Chief Ranger Daniel Conway, beleaguered and in over his head, was the next to arrive. He was followed by Captains James McCann and Walter Fleming from the Cook County Sheriff's Police; Cook County Coroner Walter E. McCarron, a self-important political hack who owned a trucking company, and his deputy Harry Glos; Lieutenant James McMahon, head of the Chicago Police Department's vaunted homicide squad; Detective James Lanners from the Gale Street station; and Sergeant Ray Young of the mobile crime laboratory.

"Within fifteen minutes, the crime scene was swarming with people," cameraman Ritt recalled.

Detective Lanners alone was warned "to mind his own business." "I was told that it wasn't Chicago's jurisdiction," Lanners said. "I was told to put my pen and paper away and not take any notes. So I put my hands behind my back. In other words, I'm interfering with their job. They didn't want the city coppers messing with their murder."

McCarron, the first Republican to occupy the coroner's office since 1928, was long on ambition but short on practical experience. "He was telling everybody what to do and warned me that I had better stop taking pictures or he would confiscate the film," Ritt recounted. "Hell, I kept filming." McCarron and Glos trampled the crime scene and may have inadvertently destroyed evidence with their posturing. In a shocking display of official incompetence captured on film moments before Ritt was ordered to turn off his camera, Glos is seen "inspecting" deep parallel wounds on Robert Peterson's scalp, moving the boy's head from right to left.[5] The field footage was given to Cinema Processors,[6] located at 161 E. Grand in Chicago, for processing. Within hours, the film was developed and edited. In the sequence aired by the three local network affiliates as well as WGN, no compassion or decency was shown the dead or the living. Not only were the faces of the murdered boys visible, but they were naked, their genitals exposed.

"In 1955, it wasn't unusual for police officers to move bodies, adjust bodies, or change their positions even before the coroner's officers got there," recalled police photographer Roger Hammill, who was among the early responders at the scene. The crime scene was not secured. Within minutes, the course of the investigation was compromised. In those days, police did not use the now-familiar yellow tape to cordon off the crime scene from the politicians, press, and curiosity seekers. The professional politicians worsened a bad situation.

"What he [McCarron] was trying to do was get as much publicity and exposure for himself as he could," adds Ritt. "An election was coming up,[7] and he was trying to 'play it.' He figured that if his photo was going in some newspaper, it was all right, just so long as I wasn't filming the kids." Dr. Ritt also remembered the anger and frustration of the city police after they found out that Glos had decided to play Dick Tracy and move the bodies around for ease of examination. "He just walked in there and rearranged them. One was on top of the other two, but he changed their positions. Incredible."

The coroner's actions that afternoon were even more despicable. "It was a hot day, and McCarron left those kids lying in the sun for nearly three hours," Ritt said angrily, still upset by the lack of human decency. "He was playing a game because he was running for political office."

Police conjectured that the boys had been dumped at the site at around 11 that morning. No one ever bothered to cover the boys' remains with a blanket. In death, Tony, Bobby, and John were not only stripped of their clothing but also any semblance of dignity.

"I raced like hell to get to the woods," recalled Steve Laske, a still photographer for WBKB-TV (the former ABC affiliate in Chicago). "There were no expressways back then, so the sirens on my car really helped. In those days, reporters could literally put a camera in the mouths of the victims and shoot photos. That's how close we were allowed. Then I remember Walter McCarron blurting out, 'It's a sex crime!' and the members of the press just laughed at him. Here was a guy in the trucking business who knew nothing about child molestation or murder."

The death scene was more than a half mile from the nearest regular telephone service, but Illinois Bell Telephone dispatched two emergency mobile units to within a few feet of where the bodies were found, making it possible for the gaggle of newsmen and TV reporters to file minute-by-minute reports with the newspapers and television and radio stations. News of the crime spread quickly across the city.

Journalists intermingled with case-hardened detectives, youth officers, rangers, the coroner's men, and throngs of curiosity seekers who had come out to gape at the human remains baking in the sun. It was a shameful scene of rampant egotism and disorganization bordering on chaos—cold and ghastly.

"Some of the finest and most capable Chicago detectives were eventually assigned to the special task-force investigating the murders," explained Art Bilek, criminologist, author, and former chief of the Cook County Sheriff's Police. "Unfortunately for the families of the young victims, the first responders were not the seasoned homicide dicks from the city districts. The whole damned thing was badly bungled from the very beginning by some thoroughly corrupt and ignorant pinky-ring politicians who drove up in their big Buicks puffing on fat Cuban cigars."

The cops and politicos intuitively understood that the triple homicide was destined to become one of Chicago's biggest crime stories, perhaps the biggest in the nation to involve children. There would be substantial rewards in the form of promotions and media publicity awaiting the resourceful and enterprising investigator or prosecutor who could bring the killer or killers to justice.

"Sergeant's stripes and captain's bars were up for grabs, not to mention political advancement for the men wearing the fedoras," Bilek added. "Reputations were at stake. There was a lot riding on the outcome of this case."

One by one, the investigators (none of them trained pathologists or physicians) took turns examining the wounds. All three boys had been strangled but in different ways. It was surmised that Bobby had been garroted with a long, flexible object, while Tony had been hit with a judo chop. It appeared that John had been strangled. Investigators also noticed that a section of tissue had been removed from one of John's thighs—a careful and deliberate act. Eleven jagged and irregular wounds were inflicted on Bobby's skull. There was no evidence of gunshot wounds, however. Whoever was responsible for this carnage had used raw, brute force to overpower and murder the three boys. The savagery perpetrated against the boys was the thing that stood out in the memory of all who were present that day.

At 2:30 PM, a hearse finally arrived to transport the remains to the county morgue where a postmortem was to be conducted. Detective Lanners recalled that the hearse was supplied by Oehler Funeral Home on Minor Street in Des Plaines. "Now the first thing we [the Chicago Police Department] would have done is put the bodies in the police wagon. It's evidence. You don't let anything contaminate it. So right from the beginning, they did!"

Jack Lavin, a Pulitzer-Prize–winning *Chicago Daily News* reporter who helped expose a major political scandal that rocked the office of the Illinois state auditor one year later, described the coroner's inquest as "absolutely atrocious."

Looking back on the way things were routinely handled in the 1950s, the city reporters sent out by their assignment editors to cover the proceedings were not so much startled by the thorough and on-going lack of professionalism in the coroner's office as they cynically noted the shocking levels of incompetence. The people in charge of the inquest from the lowliest stenographer to the deputy coroner were political hacks and pay-rollers—untrained and ill-prepared to perform precise scientific and medical procedures.

"It was a mob scene, it was terrible," Lavin remembered. "The press was in a feeding frenzy and every kind of jurisdiction you can think of was involved. But the coroner, of course, has the highest jurisdiction when it comes to violent death."

Coroner McCarron almost single-handedly botched the critical first stage of the investigation and postmortem, but with the television cameras rolling, looking nervous and tired, he gave an off-handed assessment of the situation and even offered a plausible reconstruction of the crime: "The killers used one-inch adhesive tape to blindfold the boys and put two-inch tapes over their mouths. Then the killers removed the tape after the boys were killed, to make sure they left no fingerprints." Subordinates carefully scripted McCarron's press-conference remarks.

"Who could have done this?" someone asked.

"I have no clear-cut idea as to who the murderers might have been," McCarron drawled. "They could have been a gang of young toughs."

"McCarron was very political but he didn't know his ass from fat meat," Lavin chuckled. "We'd be at an inquest and I'd always say [to McCarron], 'Now, Walter, you're going to conduct this one. Make sure you ask these questions of the witnesses.' And he'd say, 'Okay.' We would not suggest. We would tell him what questions to ask. And then he would ask the questions of the various witnesses."

Meanwhile, the Schuesslers, who had survived the Great Depression, a world war, and the tragic automobile accident that nearly claimed John's life, had been experiencing an aching void every moment since the disappearance. Comforted by five neighbor women, Eleanor maintained an around-the-clock vigil from her living room couch waiting for her boys to come home. The mother of the teenage boy who was the last known person to speak with the Schuesslers on Sunday sent her son over to the Schuessler home.

"We told Mrs. Schuessler that we had seen the boys [at the Monte Cristo bowling alley] and that there was another boy with them and not to worry because there was safety in numbers," recalled Ernest Niewadomski. "There was three of them, and they just probably went someplace."

As the minutes and hours dragged by, anxiety gradually gave way to a profound sense of despair. Neither the comforting words of her sister,

Mrs. Beatrice Blane, and her neighbors nor the quiet strength of her husband calmed the stricken mother. Eleanor took her desperate feelings as a sign that her boys had been killed, but she dared not verbalize her darkest fears. In what was like an unfolding Greek tragedy, all who were present in that room sensed the eventual outcome.

Retired *Tribune* reporter Shirley Haas, then a feature writer for the "World's Greatest Newspaper," remembered being sent out on assignment by her editor George Schreiber to capture the "personal angle" of the breaking story. She was told to go and interview the Schuesslers while they waited for an encouraging word or some bit of good news about their missing boys. She vividly recalls the large number of family members and friends milling around inside the small ranch house.

"I rang the doorbell, and when I told Mrs. Schuessler I was with the *Tribune,* she fainted right in front of me," Haas recollected. "The poor woman thought that I had come to the door to bring her the news that her sons were dead."

In Robinson Woods, about seven miles away, the task of identification fell on the shoulders of Lieutenant John M. O'Donohue of the Chicago Fire Department. Acting on behalf of his Mango Street neighbors, he positively identified the battered remains of the Schuessler brothers. Mrs. Marian Kolk, a family friend of the Petersons, performed the same sad duty for her friends.

Captain Russell F. Corcoran, who had arrived at approximately 1:00 PM that very same day to begin his new assignment at the Jefferson Park police station, barely had time to introduce himself before being asked to accompany Mrs. Kolk, Detective Lanners, and Lieutenant O'Donohue to the crime scene. Corcoran was one of eleven new police captains promoted to command by Police Commissioner Timothy O'Connor only two days earlier. A waiting reporter shook his head and expressed sympathy, "You, my friend, have one of the roughest crimes in the history of Chicago on your hands." Corcoran nodded grimly. The Schuessler-Peterson murder investigation with all of its political ramifications, professional jealousies, and second-guessing was to be his baptism by fire.

Other family members first heard the news over the radio and television. Bobby's grandparents in McHenry County about sixty miles away did not know of the matter until a special report flashed across their television screen around 5 PM on the eighteenth of October. They immediately drove into Chicago. Imagine the pain and anger upon seeing a beloved grandson in death stripped naked and lying in a ditch.

By the time the inevitable phone call from law enforcement finally came, Eleanor was on the verge of collapse. "My life . . . my arms . . . my life . . . now gone." Inconsolable, she repeated those words over and over in a scene of terrible sorrow. When she attempted to arise from the sofa, crying, "I want my boys! I want my boys!" the other women in the room had all they could do to restrain her. A parish priest from St. Tarcissus arrived at the home and read a soothing prayer. Anton J. Schuessler Sr. smoked a cigarette in the kitchen. He approached his wife lying in grim repose, fell to his knees, and broke down. "Mother, what kind of land do we live in?" His heart ached, and he cried out for justice, but there was no answer.

"The words were sobbed in shock and anguish," the *Chicago Sun-Times* noted in a solemn editorial the following morning.

> How do you answer that question from the father of two boys brutally murdered and tossed naked into a ditch? How do you answer the question of Malcolm Peterson, father of the third murdered boy, "Why does it take a crisis to alarm a community?" How do you answer these same questions from the parents of three other children who have also been murdered in Chicago this year? It is not enough to answer with words of horror and sympathy and with angry demands that the killers be caught.

A great fear-laden pall shrouded the Northwest Side that night. Doors were locked tight. Children, who would have otherwise been playing on the front lawns of their homes, were kept indoors once the sun had set. The belief held by residents was that a depraved gang of killers was in their midst. Teenage "hot-rod hoodlums" were singled out for blame. Chicago Police detectives in unmarked squad cars cruised up and down the deserted streets of Jefferson Park, South Edgebrook, Norwood Park, Gladstone, and Mayfair, but there was nothing suspicious to report. Parents gathered around their television sets and radios to hear the latest developments unfold. Inside the Gale Street police station, Sheriff Joseph D. Lohman, Ranger Chief Conway, and John T. O'Malley, Chicago PD chief of detectives, huddled around Captain Corcoran plotting investigative strategy and trying to figure out ways to calm the nerves of the jittery community. But as the *Sun-Times* ruefully noted, "A community that can spawn killers of children must do some soul searching before it tries to answer the question sobbed out by the father of two boys who lie dead."

The following morning, the *St. Louis Post Dispatch* and many other newspapers across the country and around the world published on the front page the frightening details of the Chicago child murders. The shock and horror of the thing aroused the nation. Quickly a local story had national implications. In a photo essay on October 31, *Life* magazine called it "the most heinous and senseless crime in the annals of a city which has long been blasé about its shocking record of professional violence." *Newsweek* said, "Chicagoans, not easily aroused by murder in their midst, were shaken."

The privately owned hearse delivered the remains of Bobby, John, and Anton Jr. to the Cook County Morgue, a gray, dismal building at 1828 W. Polk St., shortly before 4:00 PM, Tuesday, October 18. The bodies were placed on stainless-steel carts and removed to one of three autopsy rooms. What the reporters remembered most about the place was the smell of fifty years of mysterious and violent deaths that had soaked into the plaster walls. It was not a place for the faint of heart or people with weak stomachs or delicate constitutions.

It was left to the fathers to view the battered remains of their sons. While Dorothy Peterson waited outside the inquest room of the morgue tucked in back of Cook County Hospital on the Near West Side, Malcolm Peterson went in alone. "I want to see him! Please, Honey, take me to see my boy!" pleaded the emotionally drained mother, but her husband shook his head sadly. "Honey, I don't want you to see him. You won't be able to recognize him."

Detective Lanners accompanied Malcolm into the room where the body was on view. "So I first talked to the coroner," Lanners recounted. "'Goddamn you, you'd better have the boys covered.' Well, what do you think they did? The morgue people took him up, and would you believe it? There was his son, damn it . . . his chest wide open. I had to grab him [Mr. Peterson] because he passed out."

The Petersons had already left by the time Anton Schuessler Sr. and his two brothers-in-law, Ernest Doll and John Holz, arrived. Eleanor remained at home. She was too weak and in too terrible a state of shock to attempt the horrendous task of identification. Seeing his youngest boy in death proved too much for the disconsolate father. He collapsed on top of the prostrate remains of little Anton and had to be dragged into the waiting room by a morgue attendant and a deputy Cook County sheriff.

"Why? Why? Why?" Anton Sr. pleaded. "All I had were the two boys. And now they are gone.

"If you have any kids, you know how I feel," he sobbed. "Get down to the bottom of this. There have been some [other slain children] before. Maybe there will be some again."

Propped up by a deputy sheriff and a morgue attendant, Anton staggered outside into the cool night air, but once he was seated in Holz's automobile, he fainted. A *Chicago Sun-Times* still photographer standing two feet away from this tormented man was on hand to record the image of grief for the back page of the morning edition and for posterity.

One by one, in a cold, dispassionate tone, Coroner McCarron grilled the parents, the neighbors, and a handful of witnesses at the inquest on the following day.

Unable to conceal the roiling emotion he was feeling in the pit of his stomach at that moment, Anton Schuessler told how he never knew his sons were going downtown. "This was the first time they did that. And the next time I saw them, they were dead."

McCarron asked Malcolm Peterson if there had ever been any trouble at school. "Do you recall if the boy was threatened by teenaged gang members?"

"No," Peterson replied. "There was one incident about a year ago or so, when a boy brought a gun or a knife to class at Robert's school, but he did not threaten anyone with the weapon as far as I know." Malcolm related an incident from the seventh grade that had not seemed terribly important at the time, but now he began to wonder. The Petersons were called in for a parent-teacher conference after Bobby admitted that he had ditched school for several days. The boy explained rather mysteriously that he "hid out" in the garage and basement on the days in question. Puzzled by his response, the parents asked if he was with anyone during his time away from school, but Bobby was silent, withdrawn, and appeared somewhat fearful. It struck Malcolm as unusual behavior because his son "always took things with a laugh."

At least, that is how Allen Haber, a Farnsworth classmate, remembered Bobby: "He never took things too seriously."

The police asked Malcolm if his son had received a phone call before he left the house.

"You'll have to ask my wife," he said. "I could have been outside working around the garage."

"Yes, he did receive a phone call," Dorothy interjected.

"Who was the call from?" the detective asked.

"We don't know," she replied.

Only seven days before the remains of the boys were discovered in Robinson Woods, the Farnsworth eighth graders were given a personality and aptitude test. One of the questions on the printed form asked, "Do you know anybody who is trying to do you harm or hurt you?" Robert Peterson and John Schuessler were the only students out of a class of thirty who answered, "Yes."

Detective James Kelly recalled a chilling interview with a schoolboy who reported talking to Robert at a store near Farnsworth on Saturday, October 15. "Young Peterson rode up on his bike." The boy said Bobby was very white—like he had powder on his face. "He had trouble talking. He stayed a little while there . . . and then he rode off."

All through Monday and up until the early afternoon hours of Tuesday, the children in Mrs. Bernice Jonas's sixth-grade classroom at Farnsworth waited pensively for some news about the mysterious disappearance of their schoolmate Anton. "Late in the day [on October 18], perhaps 2:30 or so, an adult came to the class doorway," said Paul Garland, drawing a word picture of a moment in his life he will never forget.

I don't remember if it was the principal or another teacher. This person motioned Mrs. Jonas into the hall. A few seconds later, Mrs. Jonas returned to the class, a stricken look on her face. I can almost remember it exactly. She said, "They have found the three boys; they are not alive." It was of course very, very quiet. Like we were all in shock. Class was dismissed, as it was the end of the day. The following days I don't remember much being said by the teachers. Everybody was very somber. There was not any special assembly. Recess and school rules I don't think changed. One thing that did change was that there was a shortcut through an alley the Forest Glen[8] kids used to take [that] suddenly became off-limits to us. It was about a block from the school.

Shock and disbelief gave way to feelings of bitterness and anger among the Jefferson Park–Gladstone–Forest Glen neighbors. "Most of all, we want the killers to be caught and get the punishment they deserve," said one resident. "We're afraid that they're liable to get off easy, and then we'll have the same thing all over again."

Fretting parents reported that their youngest children were having difficulty sleeping through the night. "My parents were horror-struck by the incident as I'm sure all parents were," recalls Garland. "My mother in particular seemed to be almost in shock although she did not know the boys personally. She had a sister living outside London at the time, and her sister called within a day or two to tell her about what a big story this was even halfway around the world."

During a PTA meeting held at the Farnsworth, there was talk of extending curfew hours for younger teenagers. This did not happen. One mother candidly admitted that for the time being, she was escorting her kids to class. In the 1950s, very few school children rode school busses or were afforded the luxury of being driven to class every day by overly protective and indulgent parents. Responsible patrol boys from the sixth, seventh, and eighth grades were assigned to look after and safeguard the younger kids crossing the busy intersections. No one seriously believed that there was any necessity to take more drastic security precautions.[9]

"We want to come and get them but if we do the kids will be terrified," said one mother. "We're worried, yet we want them to lead normal lives. But I know I feel better when they ring the bell to let me know they're home safe."

Farnsworth Principal Wesley B. Thorsen arrived at school the Wednesday morning following the discovery of the bodies to face down a battery of reporters and anxious newsmen clamoring for interviews and photos of the boys' classmates. The reporters demanded unimpeded access to the classrooms, but Thorsen was adamant in his refusal: "No useful purpose would be served. The children are disturbed enough as it is."

In those years, the media presence during major crime investigations was pervasive. Far greater collegiality existed among reporters, homicide detectives, veteran street cops, and evidence technicians than today. The old-time police reporters often became active participants in the story and sometimes impersonated sworn personnel in order to make news. They drove to crime scenes in private vehicles equipped with sirens and flashing lights and very often got to know family members of the victims intimately and were thus able to play up the "human-interest angle" demanded by their editors. Print reporter Jack Lavin remembers calling on the Schuessler home many mornings during the height of the investigation and, over coffee and rolls, sorting through a raft of "wacko" notes arriving in the mail from total strangers. Eleanor "was as pleasant as a person could be under those circumstances," Lavin said. "And cooperative with the press! I was fortunate to get her respect. I must admit that there were times when I thought Eleanor would have a heart attack. There was so much stress and sadness." Imagine such a thing today, even in this overheated age of information, tabloid reporting, twenty-four-hour news coverage, and the crass commercial exploitation of human tragedy that have become so commonplace. There is a profound difference in reporting methods from then to now. For example, today, a journalist would never dare publish in a by-lined story the home address of a criminal or a victim. But it was common practice in the 1950s and for years thereafter.

The older children at Farnsworth understood the gravity of the crime, but it is less likely that the little ones were able to comprehend very much of it beyond what their parents had been whispering to one another. "The youngsters have shown wonderful self-control despite the emotional upset of this tragedy," commented Principal Thorsen. "It's a reflection of their home training and the type of thing we're trying to teach here in school."

In Mrs. Jonas's room, the third desk in the sixth row where Anton Jr. had sat was empty. The teacher bit her lip and lowered her gaze, reminding herself that it was her duty to be strong . . . for the sake of the children. Cecilia A. Schwachtgen wore black on Wednesday the 19th. She had been teaching at Farnsworth since the school opened in 1925, when the bungalows were just beginning to fill with city people moving up from poverty. Mrs. Schwachtgen had taught several generations of Farnsworth kids, including many of the parents of the children enrolled at the time of the tragedy. Bobby Peterson and John Schuessler were two of her eighth-grade pupils. She came to know all of her children as if they were family. Mrs. Schwachtgen told a reporter from the *Chicago American* that in all those years, not one Farnsworth boy had ever been sent to the reformatory or the Audy Home (a temporary juvenile detention center). The children at Farnsworth were well behaved and respectful. "The less said now, the better. The thing to do is go on with our work." She turned away from the reporter, lest he catch a glimpse of the tears in her eyes.

At the point of physical collapse and against the concerned advice of neighbors and relatives who wanted him to slow down, Malcolm Peterson obtained a leave of absence from his job in order to press on with the inquiry. Aided by CTA supervisors, Peterson maintained a vigil at the busy Milwaukee and Lawrence intersection, flagging down bus drivers for small scraps of information. "Did you happen to see these boys at anytime last Sunday?" he asked. With deep sympathy to the plight of the father, they sadly shook their heads. Failing to turn up any substantive clues, Malcolm next ventured into Robinson Woods to conduct an investigation of his own with a pair of German pointers named Baron and Duchess. Malcolm's friend Jack Sampayo, owner of the Jefferson Park Bowling Lanes, owned the dogs. Taken to a location within a hundred feet from where the boys were found, the hunting dogs were given a shoe belonging to Bobby to sniff, in the vain hope that the animals could pick up the scent of a trail or, perhaps, discarded clothing items. But like the police evidence technicians before them, who scooped up blades of grass and clumps of earth for clues, Sampayo's prized tracking dogs turned up nothing.

The City of Chicago, a local Kiwanis Club, two labor union locals, Joseph Lohman of the sheriff's police, and Dan Ryan, a powerful Democratic politician and president of the Cook County Board, all posted substantial cash rewards for the arrest and prosecution of those responsible. Within the first seven days of a drive to add to the reward, more than $30,000 was raised. The money poured in. School children sent in their nickels and dimes. Mayor Richard J. Daley put up $10,000 from the contingency fund, because as he explained it, "I would have felt I was not doing right as an elected official if I hadn't made the offer to increase the rewards. We must do everything and anything to bring to justice those responsible for such a dastardly act."

Malcolm Peterson was overwhelmed by the public response. Each night after dinner for over a week, the neighbors augmented a police house-to-house search by scouring the side streets of Jefferson Park and South Edgebrook for clues. In the days following, well-intentioned people telephoned the parents night and day offering ideas, theories, and suggestions. Nothing came of it, but Malcolm mulled over the bitter irony of his situation. On the night of October 16, "we went to the police to get help to find our boys," he said. "But only a few people seemed interested. But now look! Everybody's interested! I just came back from the television studio. They were going to broadcast the description of the boys, but now it is too late."

The intrusive media, the badgering questions, the telephone calls, and the stream of crank notes arriving at their homes day in and day out did not allow the parents a moment's peace.

At the Robert Peterson memorial service on Thursday, October 20, 1955, before the boy's earthly remains were committed to eternal rest at Rosehill Cemetery, Malcolm made his intentions known. He asked that the generous gifts of money be turned over to the Norwegian Lutheran Children's Society because he remembered Bobby praising the sportsmanship of the boys who belonged to its baseball team.

The children's choir of the Jefferson Park Lutheran Church sang Bobby's favorite hymn, and Reverend Eifrig, who had been called to Jefferson Park in 1944 and would attend to the devotions of his parishioners for yet another fourteen years, recalled the courage and self-sacrificing spirit the boy had shown in life. "Robert attended our Sunday School from primary to senior classes. Through all these years, his record was above average in both interest and conduct. At one point when his mother suffered from a prolonged illness, Robert, even as a ten-year-old, assumed duties and responsibilities unknown to most boys that age."

Tears welled up in Malcolm's eyes, tears borne of tenacious resolve. "I'll never rest in peace until they find those who killed my son. I'm going to see that no stone is left unturned to bring to justice those responsible for his death."

A spray of red roses adorned Bobby's casket. The inscription was simple and plaintive. "Our loving son—Mother and Father."

On Saturday, October 22, 1955, a thousand people filed slowly past the caskets of the Schuessler brothers, waked at the Koop Funeral Home, a stolid two-story brick mortuary on Milwaukee Avenue, only a mile north of where the boys exited Bruno Mancarini's bus just a few nights earlier. Those nights had seemed like an eternity.

A telegram of sympathy from Samuel Cardinal Stritch, the archbishop of Chicago from 1946 to 1958, comforted the parents. "I beg almighty God and pray that out of this tragedy there will come a better public conscience for the protection of our youth," he wrote.

That evening, many pitiful, broken sobs punctuated the quiet of the chapel. The great crowd who had come to pay their respects was mostly silent, however. The grieving mother, laid low by the tragedy, looked around, but it was hard for the mourners to summon the proper words of comfort. My God, what can one say under such circumstances? "Two . . . they took two, not one . . . but two. All I had!" Beyond tears, Eleanor collapsed onto a sofa in the funeral parlor.

An honor guard of Boy Scouts from Troop 962, who had known the brothers in better days, flanked the open caskets in a touching tribute to their slain comrades. From the closing of school until 10:00 that night when the chapel closed, pairs of scouts stood at solemn attention in one-hour shifts.

The brothers were dressed in blue suits, each boy clutching a rosary and a Bible. Eleanor complained to her husband, "They don't look like themselves. That isn't how my boys looked!"

Rev. Raymond Carey spoke a few words to the then-assembled, but still the mourners poured in, an endless procession of friends, neighbors, and total strangers. "Even truck drivers passing by stopped, parked their trucks, and came in," funeral director Charles Koop reported. Catholic mourners knelt and prayed. Others stood by helplessly. They shuffled uncomfortably from foot to foot, unsure of the changing world in which they lived.

On the day of the funeral, a private limousine donated by Mrs. Marion Thorne, the wealthy Chicago socialite whose son Montgomery Ward Thorne had died mysteriously on June 19, 1954, was parked at the curb for the personal use of the Schuessler family. Mrs. Thorne's heart went out to the stricken parents because she, too, had endured a similar horror.

Through the night, undercover police officers kept a watchful eye on the gathering. Sometimes killers, with perverse delight, attend the wakes of their victims. At the closing hour, four teenage boys in grubby clothing tried to elbow their way into the chapel to catch a glimpse of the boys, but they were turned away at the request of the family. The four unkempt boys were seized by the arm and removed to Gale Street for questioning. They provided contradictory stories about why they were there, and the cops were suspicious.

Early the next day, an enormous crowd gathered under a bright autumn sky outside the doors of St. Tarcissus Roman Catholic Church on Ardmore Avenue. Prayers of sympathy were murmured aloud as Eleanor ascended the steps of the church for Rev. Carey's requiem Mass. The stricken woman was in a state of shock. As she crumpled into the arms of her brother-in-law and had to be carried into the church, a faint gasp issued from the throng of mourners. Every pew in the church was filled—twelve hundred in all. Outside, a great human tide, which had swelled to thirty-five hundred, silently observed the grim spectacle of death from the sidewalk. They prayed for resurrection and peace. Rev. Carey related the Biblical tale of Lazarus to his listeners. "They, too, have the happiness of Lazarus, not for life but forever. They died with sanctifying grace on their souls." Undoubtedly, more than a few people that day were filled with the desire for vengeance. Silently they demanded swift and harsh retribution from the Maker for those responsible.

An honor guard of Boy Scouts acted as pallbearers and carried the caskets through the front doors and into the hearse that would transport the slain boys to St. Joseph Cemetery in suburban River Grove, their final resting place.

Soon after the funeral, Anton Schuessler was seen knocking on the doors of neighbors with photos of his two sons in hand, asking, "Have you seen either of my boys?"

Two days after Eleanor and her family said their final good-byes to John and Anton Jr., the family was stunned by the news of a near-tragedy befalling one of their sons' Boy Scout pallbearers. A neighbor boy named Thomas Fijak had miraculously survived a kidnap attempt. Fresh hopes were raised that the fourteen-year-old Taft High School freshman would be able to supply an accurate description of the assailant, who was likely to be the murderer of the Schuessler-Peterson boys. Fijak, his face bloodied and clothes disheveled, stumbled into the Cook County Sheriff's Police Station in Niles, the same station from which Lohman had deployed his investigators during the opening phase of the murder investigation. The boy said he found the intruder prowling in the basement of his parents' home on Miltimore Avenue, only a few blocks away from the Schuessler residence. Confronted by Fijak, the tall stranger overpowered the boy, dragged him to a car, and proceeded to beat him about the face. The boy said he was a friend of the Schuesslers and had served as a pallbearer at the boys' funerals. At that point, the sheriff's men became suspicious. They grilled Fijak for seven hours straight before calling his father. Finally, the boy admitted that he had staged a cruel and deliberate hoax.

"Why did you do it, Son?" Not even the case-hardened detectives could figure this one out. *Just when they thought they had seen it all . . .*

Tom Fijak explained that he concocted this strange deception in order to "give Eleanor Schuessler fresh hope" that the killer might yet be found. He said he "felt sorry for her."

"Okay, well that makes perfect sense to me," sneered the detective. "So how did you get that bruise on your head, Son?"

Fijak said he struck himself on the forehead with a brick. Then he said he walked from his home in Gladstone Park all the way to Milwaukee Avenue and Golf Road in Niles—a distance of six miles. At that point, he said he was physically drained and collapsed from exhaustion, falling asleep in a roadside ditch. For his youthful indiscretion, Fijak was remanded to the custody of his father and required to undergo further questioning by juvenile detectives at the Gale Street station.

5

The Mysterious Marks

EVEN AFTER BOBBY, JOHN, AND ANTON JR. were laid to rest, the case would not fade away for the grieving families and friends or the city of Chicago. As the details of the postmortems were revealed, there were more rather than less questions and few answers. Pathologist Dr. Jerry Kearns conducted complete postmortems during the four hours following the identification of the bodies by the parents. Kearns was not a criminologist, and mistakes were made. He was not interested in a killer's motive or malice aforethought. He was concerned with only two things—determining the hour and cause of death. With cold, clinical detachment, Dr. Kearns had examined thousands of human remains. He went about his work as a trained professional. It was a job, and the doctor had the good sense not to take it home with him.

The deaths of these young boys, Dr. Kearns concluded, had occurred between 9:00 PM and midnight on Sunday, October 16. The variables of their age, physical condition, and outside temperatures made it impossible to affix a precise time of night. But there seemed to be little room for doubt as to *how* they had met their demise. Anton Jr. was struck in the neck. A karate chop, perhaps? Dr. Kearns wondered about that. Evidence that both Anton and John were strangled was easily verified by the presence of fingernail marks on their necks. The brothers had been attacked from the left rear. Though it had all the earmarks of a sex crime, there was no evidence to suggest that the boys had been molested prior to death. "This was not done by a boy or boys their own age." Dr. Kearns was certain of that much. "Nor was it done by a single man of eighteen or twenty. One man might kill one boy but not three boys."

Bobby was savagely beaten about the head and was garrotted. Deep, parallel wounds in the back and left side of the boy's scalp suggested to Dr. Kearns that the killer wielded a pronged implement, perhaps a rake of some kind or a garden tool commonly used to pull weeds. "The only real obvious fact is that the Peterson boy fought for his life," McCarron said. "His head injuries show that."

That the murders were not premeditated seemed beyond dispute. One was thought to have died by accident, and the other two were killed to prevent identification. The chances were good that they had "stumbled into something" they were not supposed to have seen and were grabbed. The belief held that more than one person was responsible for the outrage.

All of the Chicago newspapers were provided with photographs of the bodies taken at the morgue. It was routine practice in those days for reporters to share with each other information about sensitive case files in matters of great public interest. Sometimes, a reporter got lucky and spotted something the pathologists overlooked. The Schuessler-Peterson photographs were carefully studied and analyzed, and nothing unusual was detected until the *Chicago Daily News* published a set of startling drawings and photos on December 7, 1955, illustrating a set of curious markings found on John's left thigh, midway between his knee and hip. An oval wound measuring four inches by two inches had within it a pattern of stars and letters that were imprinted on the fatty layer of tissue below the skin. Prominent was the word *BEAR*. What could the markings mean, and why hadn't Dr. Kearns noted them in his preliminary findings?

Frank San Hamel was a highly regarded *Daily News* artist, who by 1955 had logged thirteen event-filled years with the afternoon paper. During that hectic time, he had covered other high-profile murder cases including the arrest and prosecution of William Heirens, a seventeen-year-old University of Chicago student, for the 1946 abduction of seven-year-old Suzanne Degnan from an upstairs bedroom in her Edgewater home. The little girl was eventually murdered and dismembered. San Hamel was destined to play a key role in fingering Heirens for the crime. Chief of Detectives Walter G. Storms, in charge of forty-eight teams of detectives combing the buildings and alleys of the North Side for the missing girl, had asked the *Daily News* man to render an opinion on the ransom note allegedly penned by Heirens. Storms had a hunch that it was a fake—that it was written by the killer *after* the child was slain—and quickly acted upon it. In the media feeding frenzy that followed, San Hamel reported that his careful examination and analysis of the note revealed the presence of "hidden indentation writing"—faint impressions of doodles that the cops traced back to Heirens. In the opinion of the police, this piece of evidence conclusively linked Heirens to the Degnan murder, although later doubts were raised.

Now, nine years after the Degnan tragedy, San Hamel and *Daily News* reporter Jack Lavin set out to trace the origins of the mysterious marks on John Schuessler's thigh. "We were certain they were Ursa Major. When I asked my editor to run the story," Lavin recalled, "he said, 'You're fucking nuts! Smoking something?' This wasn't a random removal of flesh. Shit, the markings could have led us to the bastard who killed those boys."

A month after the murders, San Hamel prepared drawings of the unusual skin patterns on the Schuessler boy and advanced an intriguing hypothesis with police. San Hamel suggested the marks were a representation of the star pattern associated with the constellation Ursa Major, but there was sharp disagreement among rival experts hired by the other afternoon journal, the *Chicago American*.[1]

The *American's* team of pathologists included Dr. C. W. Muehlberger, director of the State of Michigan's crime laboratory, who was provided with a duplicate set of photographs of the skin tissue purportedly showing the strange markings. He said there was a simple explanation for the presence of the stellate (star-like) marks. They always appear when incisions are made at right angles to each other. The skin at the incision point simply spreads out, and it was inconceivable, the *American* reported, to think that vague impressions would remain on subcutaneous tissue after death. The *American* bluntly stated that there were no stars or constellations or the word *BEAR* discernible in any of the autopsy photos. "Blow-ups were made of the portions of the pictures under discussion, and these were inspected," the paper reported on January 12, 1956. "Stereoptican or three-dimensional slides were constructed and viewed. Nothing was found which could not be seen in the original photos."

San Hamel and Lavin had come across the single most important clue to unlocking the riddle, but the combined resources of the pathologists, police, and crime-lab technicians never completely accepted their evidence. The *Daily News* was, in so many words, accused of using the unfortunate occasion to jack circulation by attempting to outdo the hired experts of competitor papers. "It is reasonable further to conclude that the clues of stars and letters are not clues at all, but merely an over-imaginative flight of fancy," sulked the *American*, but San Hamel and Lavin pushed and prodded the cops to give the Ursa Major clue highest priority. Apparently, the police chose not to. The other newspapers around town, according to Lavin, "pooh-poohed it because they didn't get it first."

At first, Dr. Kearns said the wound was caused by a rodent bite, but additional slash marks found on the leg convinced him and the other pathologists that the killer might have noticed incriminating patterns in the skin (be they stars, constellations, the word *BEAR*, or whatever) and made attempts to cut them away with a dull-edged knife. Later, three East Coast pathologists who were provided with photographs of the obliteration marks by the *Daily News* changed Kearns's mind. He retracted his initial findings after he removed a portion of the skin and subcutaneous tissue. "The person had to be handy with a knife," he conceded. "The shallow depth of the cut indicates he had complete control of the knife. It was not a gouge." Kearns also failed to detect bone fractures in the Schuessler brothers. A funeral home attendant made the shocking discovery as he prepared them for the wake.

There was also one other important forensic evidence to consider. Coroner McCarron and his staff determined that adhesive tape measuring one-half-inch to two-inches wide had covered the boys' faces, but the tape was removed prior to the time the bodies were left in the ditch. "The roll probably is of the twelve-inch-long types used in hospitals, gymnasiums, locker rooms and carried by some doctors in their professional kits," the *Daily News* theorized. Dr. Kearns concluded that the tape was applied to their mouth and eyes after they had been beaten.

"The ones who did the crime knew what they were doing," Coroner McCarron said. "They were careful to remove the tape used to blindfold and gag the victims since it might have shown fingerprints."

Critical to the investigation was a greasy black substance found on the feet of all three boys. Were they murdered inside a machine shop or near some heavy equipment? The mastic stains on the boys' feet contained casein and emery dust and were consistent with lubricants used to oil machinery. The evidence pointed to the probability that the assailants had driven the Schuessler-Peterson boys to a sequestered location either in the city or the suburbs where some form of manual labor was performed. A factory? A garage? Detective Lanners is convinced the deed was done in a steel factory/warehouse across the street from the Monte Cristo bowling alley because an informant named Bobby Harter, now deceased, tipped him off to allegations that J. W., the factory owner,[2] was reputed to be a pedophile who had been "caught in a lot of sexual episodes with teenagers.

"You see, the [Chicago] Outfit had an area on Milwaukee Avenue from Cicero [Avenue] all the way to Lawrence [Avenue] that was controlled by [Sam] Puleo," Lanners related. "Puleo was a Mr. Fix-It, and every time J. W. would get into a jam, he'd call Puleo. He [J. W.] was a millionaire, this guy. His criminal lawyer told me, 'If you ever go near my client, I'm going to have you knocked off.' A handful of lawyers used to run the Goddamned lawyer business in Chicago and worked for all the hoodlums. So the cops didn't do a damned thing about this guy. If you got the right lawyer, you could do anything."

Chicago Police Commissioner Timothy O'Connor had good reason to be proud of his department. In the five years since he had taken over the reins of a police bureaucracy mired in decades-old politics, patronage, and graft with unremitting cycles of corruption and reform, serious crime—the indicator of how well a big-city law-enforcement agency performed its duties—had actually decreased in Chicago.[3] Nationwide, however, crime was on the rise, despite prosperous times and low unemployment. "I am proud of the record of Chicago's *most* maligned police department," O'Connor said with more than a hint of bitterness to his voice over past criticisms. "It shows that the morale and efficiency of the force are high and greatly improved."

O'Connor, a ruddy-faced, balding Irishman, quit high school in his third year to fulfill his lifelong ambition of becoming a policeman. In November 1950, he took over the reins of a scandal-ridden department that had recently been investigated by Senator Carey Estes Kefauver, a Democrat from Tennessee, for its deep and pervasive ties to syndicate gamblers. O'Connor was an honest cop, and his appointment was seen as a sincere attempt on the part of the mayor to clean things up. Those who worked alongside O'Connor during the difficult years described the commissioner as the best-grounded and most thorough and industrious police officer the City of Chicago had ever seen. The *Sun-Times*, however, took a skeptical, wait-and-see attitude: "It takes more than intelligence and honesty to run an organization of more than seven thousand men. It takes more than good intentions and a hatred of criminals and corruption. It takes real executive ability. The department must be run by the Commissioner, not by individual captains in 39 districts, each a little czar. Time will tell whether O'Connor has it."

Then came the shock of the decade. The Schuessler-Peterson case represented the first serious test of the crime-fighting abilities of the commissioner who, until now, had mostly concerned himself with the campaign to drive out the corrupt political cops and restore honesty and integrity into the law-enforcement apparatus. It was now up to O'Connor to move the investigation of the murders along cleanly and efficiently. How well "Honest Tim's" heavily politicized department would perform in the critical weeks ahead would reflect not only the overall morale, efficiency, and public confidence vested in the police but also the commissioner's administrative abilities and the leadership of Chicago's freshman mayor, Richard J. Daley. Because of the decentralized nature of big-city police work in those days, the commissioner's duties at Eleventh and State streets were largely ceremonial. Well-intentioned, with his sterling reputation for honesty still intact, Tim O'Connor was a marginalized cabinet figure serving at the privilege of the mayor. Real policing power, as the *Sun-Times* gently reminded its readers, rested in the detective bureau and the districts with the captains, who oversaw every aspect of deployment, discipline, community relations, and major crime investigation. How well a commissioner was viewed depended on the abilities of the men below him in the chain of command.

The appointment of Russell Corcoran and ten other new police captains just three days before the triple homicide on the Northwest Side was bitterly assailed in the Republican press, notably the *Chicago Tribune*. "Commissioner O'Connor had to reach pretty close to the bottom of the barrel of eligibles," sneered a *Tribune* editorialist. "In the Chicago Police setup, a district captain is a key man. He is the person with whom politicians deal on all matters of privilege. No Police Commissioner is going to make eleven new captains without talking to the mayor. All of the new captains we have been assured are 'good' Democrats."

Corcoran was one of the youngest captains in the department at the time of his appointment. His background was in police administration, not major homicide investigation. In the eight years leading up to his promotion, Corcoran helped reorganize the traffic division and received praise for streamlining a bloated bureaucracy. Nevertheless, this rising young performer was a crime-fighting tenderfoot, ill prepared to assume the awesome responsibilities involved in overseeing an investigation of any magnitude. Maintaining his composure, Captain Corcoran called on all good citizens of the Northwest Side to step forward and work with the police, but when the information he desperately solicited from the public was not immediately forthcoming, he complained bitterly to the press. "Our investigation is hampered because we have not yet been able to piece together their [the Schuessler-Peterson boys] complete itinerary [on the day of their disappearance]. The only way it will be solved will be through a break that will come from a citizen. The public just isn't cooperating."

It was a case of bad luck and poor timing for an inexperienced man to begin a demanding new assignment in the Jefferson Park district[4] at so critical a moment. Malcolm Peterson's complaint (echoed by Anton Schuessler Sr.) that they "could not get any action" after filing their first report by phone and then later talking to the desk sergeant at 5430 W. Gale St. weighed heavily on the tenor and conduct of the investigation to follow. With politics, professional jealousies, and rival policing agencies from other jurisdictions figuring so prominently in this heater case,[5] seamless, competent investigative work was compromised from the very moment the two worried and frazzled fathers voiced concerns for their missing sons a few minutes past midnight on October 17, 1955.

The murder of the Schuessler-Peterson boys had to be solved . . . at all costs. What kind of message would it send to parents (i.e., to the voters!) if the killers of children were allowed to roam free on the streets of Chicago? An election was coming up in five months, and too much was riding on the outcome of the case to leave anything to chance. But in the rush to press into duty competent professionals from six separate branches of Cook County law enforcement, scant attention was paid to the efficacy of such a massive effort. In the first leg of this investigation, every local agency jumped haphazardly into the fray—the homicide bureau and crime-detection laboratory of the Chicago PD; 135 highway patrolmen from Sheriff Joseph D. Lohman's staff; 57 city policemen assigned to Cook County State's Attorney John Gutknecht's detail; Coroner McCarron's deputies (responsible for presiding over inquests); the Illinois State Police personally led by Governor William G. Stratton's man Lieutenant Edward Stanwyck; and the forest preserve rangers. The archaic system of multiple policing agencies claiming primacy in major homicide investigations contributed to unnecessary duplication of effort, the jealous guarding of information, the refusal to share leads, petty bickering, and jurisdictional rivalries. Long-standing political antagonisms and infighting were dramatically underscored throughout the Schuessler-Peterson investigation by some particularly vicious political feuding between the Republican McCarron and the spry but belligerent sixty-six-year-old state's attorney Gutknecht, a Democratic party stalwart facing a tough reelection challenge in 1956.

Gutknecht was the brother-in-law and political protégé of "Colonel" Henry Crown, the rich and highly connected founder of the powerful Material Services Corporation (MSC), supplying ready-mixed cement to the city and campaign contributions to Democratic politicians. A former company lawyer for MSC and its vast holdings, John Gutknecht parlayed his cozy thirty-three-year ties with the influential company patriarch right into the state's attorney's office, where his prosecutorial record was regarded by many as lax, but his loyalty to the Democratic Machine was unquestioned. McCarron bitterly denounced Gutknecht for refusing to cooperate with him in the sharing of information and deliberately leaving his name off of the invite list to case debriefings held inside the County Building.

If ever there was a case to be made for the immediate implementation of a unified system of metropolitan policing (one police department for the city and all of the surrounding suburbs), it was with the balkanized nature of Cook County law enforcement that plagued the Schuessler-Peterson case from the very start. Sheriff Lohman, a forceful and catalytic teacher to a generation of criminology students at the University of Chicago long before entering public life in 1949, was the most persuasive proponent of the metropolitan-policing concept. "There are eleven thousand policemen in the county," Lohman explained at a city press conference convened nine days after the slayings. "But they operate under more than two hundred separate and uncoordinated agencies. It's not so much too few policemen which bedevils us but the inflexibility and inefficiency created by legal limits." The Lohman protocols were heartily endorsed by Mayor Daley and Commissioner O'Connor, but the protocols were doomed from the start by the outlying suburbs' sound rejection, fearing the inevitable loss of political control to Chicago. The pressures brought to bear by Lohman, O'Connor, and Mayor Daley for a metropolitan force were guided by common sense and practical political considerations not altogether altruistic. The suburban mayors correctly sensed a potential power grab by the Democratic machine of Chicago, slowly approaching the apex of its power, clout, and influence. Even the Chicago Crime Commission, a nonpartisan civic watchdog agency above the fray, expressed reservations. "Any proposal which ignores local authority as a basic principle in any proposed police organization will probably not receive the proper acceptance necessary for its adoption in the foreseeable time," wrote Virgil Peterson, executive director.

Sheriff Lohman was an anomaly in the maelstrom that is Chicago politics—a tweedy Hyde Park academician with a University of Chicago pedigree, high ideals, and impeccable paper credentials. He was a nationally recognized expert in corrections and penal reform and had served as chairman of the Division of Corrections for the State of Illinois from 1949 to 1952. Pleased with the tenor of his work, Governor Adlai Stevenson elevated Lohman to the chairmanship of the Board of Parole and Pardon for the State of Illinois in 1952. Two years later, the Cook County Democratic screening committee considered Lohman for the sheriff candidacy. The office had been a cesspool of corruption longer than anyone could remember because it was one of the richest political plums in Cook County government. In the mid-1950s, the sheriff had on his payroll 1,016 employees. None of them were subject to Civil Service, meaning that they could be hired or fired on a whim at any time. The Democratic organization looked to a cosmetic "reform" candidate to balance the ticket, appease the voters, and instill a degree of professionalism in the ranks. Lohman, the vigorous academic, was an impressive talker, but opinions were divided, and the vote was deadlocked at 12 to 12, when in a curious twist of fate, a notorious West Side political hack named Arthur X. Elrod stepped into the caucus room at the old Morrison Hotel to cast the deciding vote in Lohman's favor.

In the fall election of 1954, Lohman, who was never free of controversy, won a bitterly contested race against William "Bud" Runzel. It was a vicious, mud-slinging, name-calling campaign tarnished by accusations that Republican Governor Stratton took statements out of context from a tape-recorded speech of Lohman's and accused the candidate of saying police officers had a disproportionate number of wives who were former prostitutes. Stratton said that Lohman had made the slanderous comment two years earlier while addressing a gathering of parole agents. Lohman called the accusation a "monstrous fraud" and responded by accusing his opponent of Mob ties.

With an election win now sewn up, Lohman leapfrogged into office with the zest and determination of Don Quixote, the wisdom of Solomon, and the naïveté of Pollyanna. He viewed the sheriff's office as a great "laboratory" for social science experimentation—an extension of the ivy-covered walls where theories could be tested, measured, and evaluated. (Those who had gone before him had only considered it a license to steal.) In December 1955, as a consequence of the Schuessler-Peterson investigations, Lohman launched *Searchlights on Delinquency*, a thirteen-week, public-service series airing on WTTW-TV (today, Chicago's public broadcasting station) that focused on the root causes of juvenile crime and how this growing menace could be eradicated. With his unintentionally amusing deadpan delivery, Lohman came across sounding more like Jack Webb of *Dragnet* fame than the serious-minded criminologist he intended. He became Cook County's first television sheriff and was derided as a consummate publicity hound intoxicated by media attention. For fifty-three weeks, his *Your Sheriff Reports* program was aired over station WBKB-TV. Another long-running series, *Community of the Condemned*, studied the national penal system. Meanwhile, Lohman's own Cook County Jail remained a disgraceful and festering sinkhole run by barn bosses, the toughest, meanest, and most aggressive of the inmates languishing in the cells at Twenty-Sixth Street and California Avenue.

The sheriff was stubborn and obdurate and made political enemies all over town. "He can't admit he is ever wrong," a former aide confided. "He can't face reality. He'll never apologize" for anything. Within six weeks of his election victory, Lohman fired twenty employees and replaced them with his own political loyalists. He even fired the hapless shoeshine boy who was working for tips in the Criminal Courts Building at Twenty-Sixth and California. Long accustomed to the cerebral pace of academia, Lohman was suddenly thrust into the world of backroom wheeler-dealers, men he would have earlier tarred and feathered from the lecture-hall rostrum. Once Sheriff Joe was firmly entrenched within the cabal, he set out to please his political masters in Cook County so they would award him a spot at the top of the ticket in 1956. Despite early missteps, Lohman seemed to the voters to be the right man for a tough job—fair, levelheaded, and pragmatic. That is, until he was caught up and seduced by the electoral process and the trappings of office. Before he was sheriff, he said it was a disgrace for public officeholders to be chauffeured around in Cadillacs and surrounded by bodyguards. Critics could only smirk when Lohman showed up for press conferences in his new Coupe de Ville with guards positioned at his side.

All of Lohman's good intentions burned up on the pyre of his driving ambition that had him daydreaming about the governorship of the State of Illinois before Daley or the Democratic slate-makers had given the matter a second thought. More than anything, however, the "man who talked like a textbook" was motivated by the desire for political revenge against Governor Stratton, the politician who had publicly humiliated him. Cracking the notorious Schuessler-Peterson murder case would be a good place to begin his campaign for the governorship.

Doing what he believed to be a necessary first step, Captain Corcoran ordered 150 uniformed officers into the boys' neighborhood to canvass residents, in what amounted to a house-to-house search. He either underestimated the enormity of the task or failed to take into account that the Jefferson Park (Thirty-Third) Police District covered twenty-three square miles and a population of 159,000—in 1955, the second largest police district in the City of Chicago. It would have been an impossible assignment for 1,000 men, let alone 150. Fanning out from Milwaukee and Lawrence, the police searched for discarded items of clothing and clues pointing to the three boys' whereabouts on Sunday night. Long-time residents who lived through those wrenching days shuddered nervously as they recalled so many uniformed police officers converging on the side streets of their usually placid neighborhood.

In the early spring of 1955, Alfred and Catherine Webber and their four children had moved into a two-story frame house in the 5300 block of Lynch Avenue, very near the Peterson house. The Webbers worshipped at the same church as Malcolm and Dorothy, but they didn't know the Peterson family all that well at the time of the tragedy. "When we saw the [crime scene] photos, we were shocked because we lived so close to them," Catherine said. "Back then we didn't have that kind of crime going on. That's why it was all so gruesome." Alfred will never forget the climate of fear permeating the neighborhood in the days that followed the murders. "The police were all around here. They knocked on our door," he recalled. "We couldn't even throw our garbage out. The garbage men were looking in everyone's trashcans and reporting back anything suspicious they found." The Webbers were very protective of their own offspring. Like so many other Northwest Side parents of baby boomers, they based their home-buying decision on the persisting perception of the community as a desirable place to raise children. "It was such a *good* neighborhood," said Al, registering a sense of disbelief that still resonates all these years later. "That's why we were so shocked by the whole thing. We were scared to death! There were a lot of kids around here back then, and they [the murdered boys] were the same age as my children. But after this horrible crime, we wouldn't let our youngsters out the front door or leave them home alone when we went shopping! We made them stay in the backyard."

The presence of so many uniformed police officers and plainclothes detectives canvassing the neighborhood was also upsetting to the business owners. But the investigation pressed on. Captain Louis Capparelli of the traffic division pulled an additional two hundred officers from his detail. All two hundred voluntarily surrendered their weekend in order to assist in the manhunts in Jeff Park and Robinson Woods. It was a first for the Chicago PD "I never saw anything like it," beamed Capparelli. "To a man, every officer who possibly could make it offered to be there." Members of the Forty-Ninth Anti-Aircraft Battalion of the National Guard assisted the police volunteers combing Robinson Woods for clues. The soldiers were deployed at three-foot intervals to fine-screen every inch of ground near where the bodies were found. The praiseworthy but unsuccessful efforts reflected the sincere commitment of these men to get to the bottom of the mystery. So many of them were young fathers in their late twenties and early thirties. They commiserated with Malcolm and Anton in their losses and were anxious to help out. "There but for the grace of God go I" was their unspoken bond.

Barely a week had passed before the investigation foundered. The massive deployment of uniformed officers yielded tantalizing possibilities but nothing of substance to present to a grand jury, not even scraps of the boys' missing clothing. The press was increasingly impatient, prompting one paper to take a proactive stance in the investigation and thus *become* the news story. Accusing the police of overlooking the obvious, the *Daily News,* a spunky and opinionated Chicago afternoon newspaper, hired a team of four diving experts to scour the muddy bottom of the Des Plaines River in Robinson Woods because it seemed "a likely place to dispose of clothing or weapons [used] in the killings." But after several hours of fruitless searching that yielded a collection of discarded tin cans, a bedspring, and useless concrete fragments, the search was called off, and the chilled divers were sent home.

Sheriff Lohman set up his temporary command post at the Niles police station out on Milwaukee Avenue, well north of the city limits and out of the way of Captain Corcoran, who ran his house-to-house search detail from Gale Street. Both men tried hard not to step on the other's toes, but patience was strained, and egos were badly bruised. "A metropolitan force would help immeasurably toward solving murders of this kind," urged Commissioner O'Connor. "And it would also permit us to go after hoodlums who operate in Chicago and live in the suburbs. We could go after them right in their backyards." But no one person was granted the authority needed to marshal the troops and coordinate activity in all six jurisdictions. Arresting the killer in his "own backyard" was not so simple a task if the local chief or mayor voiced objections. The enactment of an effective system of metropolitan policing might have ended the despicable practice of pulling in everyone who happened to look suspicious or fit a certain ethnic or racial profile.

In an interview published in 1956 in the *Chicago American,* legendary Chicago crime reporter Leroy F. "Buddy" McHugh described the chaotic and often disorganized police tactics of the era, when suspects were routinely grabbed off the street and brought in to the station for the "show-up" without rhyme, reason, or specific purpose other than to demonstrate to superiors that the officers in the field were managing to keep profitably busy.[6]

> As a police reporter of many years standing, I can recall the old-time "tough stuff." The endless parade of suspects who weren't really suspects but just somebody to point out to as "having been questioned." In those days one police group was working against another, each seeking the credit for solving the crime and going blindly ahead without first making elementary and intelligent observations.

McCarron, the grandstanding coroner, crossed partisan lines to endorse the Lohman proposals in order to curry political favor in the next election, find a way to undermine his political foe Gutknecht, and incidentally solve the crime. His next move came as no surprise to veteran city-hall watchers. McCarron, convinced that the killers were "a gang of young toughs, probably in the nineteen-to-twenty age group," offered to deputize city police in order to allow them to extend the manhunt throughout suburban Cook County. Working hand-in-hand with O'Connor, who approved the formation of a handpicked, fifty-two-member Special Investigations Unit (SIU), McCarron deputized the squad leaders in the private office of the Cook County State's Attorney on day five of the investigation. The brightest minds in the Chicago PD—including fifteen of the best men from the detective bureau, four policewomen, and four juvenile officers—were entrusted with the solemn task of identifying the killer or killers and bringing that person or persons to justice. It had worked before, so why not now?

The precedent was set in June 1946, when a coordinated task force tracked down and arrested William Heirens. As a consequence of his splendid work on the case, Commissioner O'Connor—working six straight days without sleep and refusing to take a day off in three months—was made chief of detectives, driving home the point that prominent murder cases capturing the public imagination were career makers . . . or breakers if the outcome was unsatisfactory.

This time the anointed powers settled on Chicago Police Lieutenant Patrick J. Deeley to head the Special Investigations Unit (SIU). A policeman since July 2, 1929, Deeley had graduated from the FBI National Police Academy in Washington in 1953.[7] The balding, 220-pound veteran was the acting captain of the Racine Avenue station when he was tapped to spearhead the Schuessler-Peterson task force at 5:00 PM on October

20.[8] Commissioner O'Connor announced the appointment a scant two hours ahead of Deeley's scheduled departure on a seventeen-day vacation junket with his wife and two young boys. "This has happened before and will happen again," O'Connor said with weary resignation. Pat Deeley was considered one of law enforcement's "rising young men" and his willingness to forsake a vacation when duty called was a departmental imperative. Between 5:00 PM that Friday afternoon, October 21, and 3:00 AM on Sunday, the husky crime fighter managed only three hours of sleep.

Barking orders to subordinates like an old-fashioned Marine drill instructor, Deeley was a hard-nosed, old-time political cop, who grew up in St. Mel's Parish on Chicago's West Side. He had struggled to complete the demanding eight-week FBI course, but with perseverance and a strong work ethic, he saw it through. "I thought all it took to make a policeman was a star and a gun," he laughed. "But now I realize what really goes into the making of a good policeman." A decorated war hero who pinned four battle stars on his chest during a hectic tour of duty in the South Pacific, Deeley made sergeant in 1947 and lieutenant six years later.[9]

"Deeley was a big strapping Irishman who smoked Luckys and died of cancer," Jack Lavin remembered. "He was around fifty at the time of the murders and was a heavy drinker and a protégé of the big-shot West Side politicians. He might have let a saloon or two stay open," Lavin admits, but otherwise he was regarded as a pretty good cop from the rough-and-tumble era of Chicago policing.

"He was a West Side guy," recalls James McGuire, a retired detective who was assigned to the Schuessler-Peterson investigation and worked under Deeley's direction. In those days, the men from the detective bureau were generally free to roam the city but tended to remain close to the geographic areas they grew up in or where they happened to be residing at the moment. "Of course, I was a very young cop then, and Deeley was one of the old-timers, but he just seemed like a big blowhard," McGuire chuckles as he recalls one of his supervisor's nifty job perks. "He got all of his groceries for nothing."[10]

Joining the Schuessler-Peterson task force from the sex bureau were Harry Town and John Griffith, in their early thirties, who had sent a dozen men found guilty of sex crimes to the penitentiary. Also assigned were burglary detectives Michael Glynn, Byron Conley, and George O'Brien, considered top men in their field. Ed Cagney, an ace detective who would later put in many long hours during the 1957 Judith Mae Andersen murder investigation,[11] was one of the department's best interrogators. His powers of persuasion were about to be put to the test. "He had the ability to gain a suspect's confidence," recalled Ed Flood, his partner of many years. "He used sugar rather than vinegar." Lieutenant Frank Pape, a tough old bird who held the unofficial departmental marksmanship record by sending nine felons to an early grave "in the line of duty" (or so it was said), volunteered McGuire, Charlie Fitzgerald, Pat Driscoll, and Herbert Wilk from his vaunted robbery unit. Fitzgerald typically worked fifteen-hour days and, in that respect, was a mirror image of his case-hardened boss. Respectful colleagues in the department called Fitzgerald "the relentless pursuer of evildoers." "What a lot of people don't know is that he was also part Indian," recalled McGuire, one of only a handful of Chicago Police officers who rose to command in *three* separate Illinois law enforcement agencies.[12] "Some of us called him the 'Crafty Navajo.' He wasn't a very friendly guy, and he had his ways, but he was a good policeman who put a lot of effort into it. He eventually retired a lieutenant in the Town Hall District."

Two of Chicago's most famous and highly regarded policewomen, Antoinette Quinn and Frances Herb, were added to the detail because of their impressive skills in crime detection. Obsessing over the smallest details, Quinn had chipped in three months of overtime without pay during the tense days leading up to the arrest and capture of the accused child-murderer William Heirens.

Added to the mix was veteran Detective Sergeant Otto Kreuzer, described by subordinate Wes Hunter as a street dick "with great eyes," in other words, keen powers of observation. Kreuzer was a tough street cop from the old school who went on to become chief of detectives. Four other Chicago Police sergeants—Thomas Mulvey, John Cartan, John Konen, and John Hartigan—coordinated much of the day-to-day field work with Kreuzer and Mike Spiotto. The *Tribune* praised all four for their "dogged checking" and probing of "one of history's roughest crimes."

Despite long-standing patterns of unchecked corruption and bribe-taking and a reputation for brutality, the Chicago Police Department could take comfort and pride in the abilities of its homicide detectives, the antiquated tactics of the "showup" notwithstanding. They are to this day without peer in the Midwest. There was, however, one problem during this investigation. Central coordination of the Special Investigations Unit (SIU) was transferred out of Gale Street and moved downtown to Room 111 of the Central Police Headquarters, 1121 S. State St. Spiotto remembers Deeley telling him, "Mike, we're taking this case downtown," which indicated just how serious a matter it was. The unit was now required to file headquarters reports, and this resulted in a logistical boondoggle and heated complaints from the street detectives. It was a serious tactical blunder, indicative of the divisive politics of the day made worse by political drag and the raging turf battles of Sheriff Lohman, Chief O'Connor, Coroner McCarron, and State's Attorney Gutknecht. Each had his own agenda as he vied for the honor of being the first to "make the case." Gutknecht despised Lohman and dismissed him as an arrogant "egghead." McCarron hated Gutknecht on general principles. Tim O'Connor tried to maintain civility and keep his chivalrous reputation for professionalism and honesty intact. When that failed, the best he could do was to keep the combatants at arm's length from one another.

The hunt for an unknown killer was conducted on two fronts—out in the streets and in Chicago's well-equipped scientific crime laboratory on the twelfth floor at Eleventh and State. John Ascher (now promoted to a captain) and Lieutenant Francis N. LaVelle, an expert lie-detector operator trained in lab work, supervised forty-six technicians and ballistics experts analyzing microscopic evidence from the thousands of pieces of discarded clothing, shoes, and assorted junk picked from the trash bins, streets, and weed lots and delivered to the task force. "If we had kept everything we examined, we could open a junkyard," LaVelle said later. About 99.99% of the material was worthless. "We've used all our resources except ballistics experts, tool-mark experts, and handwriting experts."

Only one clue was given serious attention by Sergeant Claude B. Hazen, a veteran Chicago cop in charge of microscopic analysis. A set of parallel striation marks found on the chest of Anton Schuessler Jr. indicated that the corpse had been pressed up against a corrugated object, perhaps a rubber floor mat or some metallic object found in the trunk of an automobile. These impressions did not disappear from the skin after death. "Lividity is the process of blood settling to the lowest portion of the body," explained James Delorto. "Without blood flow, these strange marks will not go away. They were spotted during the autopsy, then later in the crime lab." Frederick Bird of the *Chicago American* prophetically noted, "A picture of the marks may be the key to unlocking the cells of death row, or it may become only a souvenir from Chicago's greatest manhunt."

After wrapping up one of the lengthiest Cook County autopsies on record, Dr. Kearns convened a press conference at the morgue to explain to reporters the cause of death of each of the boys and how death came about. Exhausted and drained by the ordeal, the pathologist patiently answered the reporters' questions for nearly an hour. "If you had to speculate—"

Kearns cut off the reporter in mid-sentence. "I do not speculate."

There was no evidence the boys had been drugged, this according to Dr. Walter J. R. Camp, the state toxicologist from the University of Illinois.

"Any idea what they had eaten?"

The physician answered the question by saying that Mr. Schuessler had told him that his sons had eaten lunch at 1:00 or 1:30 PM. The physician said Eleanor Schuessler had prepared a noodle soup, and the family enjoyed their customary Sunday afternoon lunch. Furthermore, the results of the postmortem seemed to tally with the statements of Elsie Weisgerber, the C & L waitress.

"But she said the bill was $5.57, and the boys left home with only $4.00 in their pockets? What do you make of that?" one of the reporters inquired.

The pathologist shook his head and shrugged his shoulders. "That is a question best left to the police I'm afraid."

"Is it a sex crime then?" asked another reporter.

Dr. Kearns said it was not a sex crime. From the autopsy report, there was nothing to suggest that sexual penetration had occurred. Nor did the Schuessler-Peterson murders conform to the established criteria of sex-related homicides with the four predictable categories: (1) interpersonal violence-oriented disputes (husbands and wives, a jilted boyfriend, a lovers' quarrel turning violent, etc.; (2) rape- and/or sodomy-oriented dispute (resulting from unintentional or intentional sadistic violence during a heterosexual or homosexual encounter); (3) deviant-oriented assault (a premeditated lust murder); or (4) a serial murder (a pattern of multiple homicides committed against strangers over a period of time).

"That is all for today, ladies and gentlemen." Kearns exited the room.

With that, the vexed reporters arose from their chairs each looking to the other for interpretation. At Riccardo's, the Billy Goat Tavern, and other watering holes along the avenue where the fourth estate of Chicago gathered to guzzle highballs and swap war stories, much of the table gossip that night concerned the Schuessler-Peterson case. The press veterans of 1946 spoke of the Degnan case, but they could draw no parallels. A man who had kept watchful eye on the girl before making his move grabbed little Suzanne while she slept. As shocking as it was, the Degnan abduction was premeditated and seemed to fit the definition of a deviant-oriented assault. This time, though, it was something all together different. The cold-blooded randomness of these current murders and the apparent lack of motive sent a chill throughout the city. The postmortem had stirred considerable controversy and raised many more questions than were answered. The reporters and the cops correctly sensed that the investigation was back to square one. If it wasn't a sex crime, then what was it? Chicago's greatest crime fighters were, for the moment, dumbfounded.

A rumor that gained currency among the cops and reporters was that the slain boys and their schoolyard chums were in the habit of extorting money from known homosexuals—demanding cash in return for silence. The adolescent boys who engaged in these kinds of petty shakedowns were described by the police as "fruit hustlers."[13] For this reason, investigators took a hard look at the gay community, but no evidence pointed to blackmail revenge as a motive or the likelihood that the murdered boys were fruit hustlers. Given their tender ages, their conservative families, and the strong influence of the church in this tightly woven community, the accusation was impossible to believe, but it wasn't completely discounted.

With so little to go on, plenty of room existed for conjecture. "There was diabolical cleverness on the part of the murderer or murderers," conceded Sheriff Lohman.

"When these killers are found, we will find there were at least three of them under twenty years of age with disturbed minds of course," predicted Harry Glos, the coroner's investigative pit bull who had cast suspicion on Anton Sr. early on in the investigation. The ailing, grief-stricken father enduring his own private agony volunteered to take a lie-detector test with his wife "so there would be no doubt." The Schuesslers were tested at a private laboratory by Lohman's staff and ruled out as suspects after they passed the test.

On November 3, Malcolm Peterson drove to the private residence of State's Attorney Gutknecht to express outrage over the vicious insinuations he had heard to the effect that the fathers of the boys were involved in the murders. Gutknecht said that he had "reviewed every detail of the case" and "could find no hint of the fathers' implication." Nevertheless, Bobby's father volunteered to undergo a polygraph test in order to explode rumors but asked that the results be kept secret. A few days after being cleared, Peterson reconsidered. He returned to Gutknecht's residence to authorize release of the findings to the media with the hope it would dispel any lingering doubt. "There were no clues or facts that in the slightest way pointed any finger of suspicion at any of the parents," said State's Attorney Gutknecht.

Assessing results of the investigation after the first two weeks, general agreement among the rival law-enforcement agencies was that for all of the intelligence they had gathered, it added up to a big zero. "I have no theory," admitted John T. O'Malley, the soon-to-be defrocked chief of detectives. "This thing is wide open for speculation until we can develop some further clues."

"I have no clear-cut idea as to who the murderers might have been," Walter McCarron chimed in. "They could have been a gang of young toughs. If the killers have any shred of conscience, they will surrender. They cannot live with this."

For the moment, the SIU and the other police agencies blamed it on the gangs—the most convenient target. Beyond that, anything else was just too sinister for them to contemplate.

6

Deadly Screams

LETTERS AND TELEGRAMS OF sympathy and small donations poured in from across the country. Every morning for the next month and often accompanied by cops and reporters who brought boxes of jelly dough-nuts, Anton and Eleanor Schuessler sorted through the mail, dismissing the obvious cranks but taking great comfort in the solicitude of strangers. Most of the letters radiated warmth and tenderness. "People can be wonderful," Eleanor said. "They've written to us from everywhere—New York, Virginia, California—all kinds of people rich and poor. A lot of them have lost children of their own and just want to offer their sympathy." The story of the three boys tugged at the heartstrings of the nation. How senseless. How very tragic.

"In that era of general good will and expanding influence," wrote author David Halberstam, "few Americans doubted the essential goodness of their society. After all, it was reflected back at them not only by contemporary books and magazines, but even more powerfully and with even greater influence in the new family sitcoms on television." A paroxysm of horrifying crimes against children jarred Americans out of their complacency and was all the more unsettling when juxtaposed with television's wholesome portrayals of family life. This crime wave against juveniles suggested that in large measure, Americans were no longer living in the safe and secure world they thought was theirs after the turmoil of the first half of the twentieth century.

On August 27, 1955, outside Money, Mississippi, the battered, bullet-ridden remains of Emmett Louis Till, a fourteen-year-old African American vacationing from the South Side of Chicago, had been pulled out of the Tallahatchie River. Till was the victim of white segregationists, and an ugly rumor quickly spread up north that the Schuessler-Peterson boys were abducted and murdered by a vengeful black man. The vicious rumor had no merit, of course, but the slaying of Till became a watershed event in America's evolving civil-rights movement.[1]

Peter Gorham, a twelve-year-old from Evanston, Illinois, disappeared from a Boy Scout camp near Muskegon, Michigan, over the Fourth of July holiday. His skeletal remains were found in a wooded area on August 14, 1955. The investigation into this murder dovetailed with the Schuessler-Peterson case.[2] On September 12, the decomposed body of fourteen-year-old Peter Certik of Bannockburn, Illinois, was pulled from a thicket near Libertyville, north of Chicago. Like the bodies of the Schuessler-Peterson boys, the Certik boy was slain elsewhere, and the body was dumped in a location where it would be easily found. Although these and other juvenile murders attracted national headlines, the Schuessler-Peterson murders remained singular because never before had three children been killed at the same time in so violent a manner.

In a public statement made days after the murders, the Schuesslers cried out for justice, not vengeance. "We can't allow such vicious criminals on the streets," Malcolm Peterson warned the public. "They killed once. They can kill again."

The two sets of parents put up their homes as a reward for the capture of the responsible party or parties. "We've lost everything," Eleanor sighed, as she emptied the closet of winter coats and other items of clothing that had belonged to her sons. The boys' personal effects were painful reminders of young lives never to be lived and were given over to charity.

"Neither we nor the Petersons can rest until the killers are captured," the Schuesslers said. "What's the difference whether we give up our house?" With the Schuesslers backed into the corner financially, the people of Chicago opened their checkbooks for the family. Celebrity-gossip columnist Irv Kupcinet of the *Sun-Times* appealed to his readership for generosity, and $6,500 was sent in. The message was loud and clear—the parents of the boys were not alone in this terrible ordeal.

Hundreds of Jefferson Park neighbors canvassed the streets each night after work for clues. Many more telephoned the families with helpful suggestions and ideas. Meanwhile, police agencies continued to mobilize. A call center was set up at Chicago Police Headquarters to ensure the prompt checking of all leads phoned in to the switchboard. Detectives searching the neighborhoods were ordered to channel all tips—oral or written—to the message center. Sheriff Lohman ordered a surprise roadblock on Lawrence Avenue near the entrance to Robinson Woods. Motorists were asked if they had witnessed suspicious persons coming or going from the woods on October 18. Six people indicated that they "might have seen something," but they weren't sure exactly what it might have been. Captain Norman Hawthorne of the Cook County Sheriff's Police timed the roadblock to catch drivers who regularly traveled this way on Tuesday mornings—the day of the week when the boys were found in the ditch. Lieutenant Deeley pressed Commonwealth Edison workers and highway-maintenance men into service to assist in the hunt for clues.

Deeley also called on twenty-five thousand Northwest Side schoolchildren to share what little information they might have with their parents, teachers, or other trusted adults. Chicago School Superintendent Benjamin C. Willis said, "Juvenile officers are welcome to discuss possible clues with principals, adjustment teachers, counselors, and other school employees."

"Perhaps some student will tell of being approached by suspicious characters lately," Deeley said, begging for cooperation. "And maybe somebody can throw new light on the movement of Robert, John, and Anton just before they disappeared that Sunday night." Deeley guaranteed the young tipsters anonymity, but a number of parents were understandably fearful that the killer might return and seek reprisals against the children if accusations were made public or hearsay repeated. School officials provided the police with truancy and absentee lists from October 17 through 19. Circulars with sketches of the slain boys were posted in seventy-eight Chicago elementary schools. Five juvenile officers assigned to eight Northwest and West Side high schools—Austin, Foreman, Kelvyn Park, Roosevelt, Schurz, Steinmetz, Taft, and Von Steuben—quizzed older students.

On the fifth day of the investigation, Coroner McCarron deputized twenty-five members of "Scotland Yard," the Chicago PD's ultra-secret, undercover investigative unit headquartered on Canalport Avenue on the South Side.[3]

The massive investigation involving so many disparate agencies and special units of law enforcement was unprecedented in Chicago Police history. But then, the city had never fully experienced a murder case of this type. It was a strange and frightening time, not only for the children and parents traumatized by the event but also for postadolescent males from the immediate area who were branded "hoodlums" and "hot-rod lunatics" by well-meaning but anxiety-ridden neighbors who reported these young men to the police just because they were of a mind to. Single men living unconventional lifestyles and other persons unable to make a good accounting of their whereabouts on the nights in question fell under suspicion. All were detained and questioned, many of them relentlessly. An ex-Marine residing in the 4900 block of Lawrence Avenue told of being "brainwashed" and "threatened" during an interrogation. Two former service buddies echoed his complaint.

Sheriff Lohman conferred with four northwest-suburban police chiefs and urged them to keep the murder investigation "uppermost in their mind." This meant bringing drivers in for interrogation on the slightest pretext. "When stopping motorists for traffic violations," Lohman advised, "look in their cars for suspicious things. Look for nervous drivers, and if reasonable, haul them into the station for questioning." The Miranda warnings, a four-part warning that includes police inform a detained individual of his or her right to legal counsel, would not be decided until 1966. At the time of the Schuessler-Peterson investigations, it was still acceptable to arrest a person "on suspicion," a practice that often left police vulnerable to charges of coercion and brutality.

Others caught in the dragnet and then cleared by the police and sent home often endured the terrible humiliation of seeing their pictures and home addresses published in the newspapers, subjecting them to public ostracism. Even in better times, choosing to live under the Dutch elms of the Far Northwest Side was often a difficult social adjustment for singles, married people without children, divorced mothers, ethnic and racial minorities, and nonconformists.

In late October 1955, in a small Catholic church in the town of Brookville, Indiana, forty miles northwest of Cincinnati, Ohio, one of society's throw-away people told the good Reverend Kenny Sweeney a curious tale. Gloria Vazquez was only nineteen, but she was hard-edged, streetwise, and cynical beyond her years. She said she was reared in San Jose, California, but had been a creature of the open road for many months now. There had been numerous arrests for burglary, arson, and narcotics possession. She also dabbled in prostitution. But that wasn't why she had come to St. Michael's Parish.

"The car outside?" she said, flashing a grin. "I took it."

The priest suggested that it was in her best interests to surrender, and the raven-haired girl of Portuguese-Mexican ancestry did just that. She put up no fuss when Franklin County Sheriff James Hixon arrived and took her into custody.

"So what are you doing down here, anyway?" the lawman demanded.

Gloria told how she had come down from Chicago. Only a week earlier, she had been lolling about her room inside the Roosevelt Hotel, a dingy flophouse at Twelfth Street and Wabash Avenue, drinking and getting high with a man named "Paul."

Sheriff Hixon wanted to know if the woman had any direct knowledge of the hideous murders of the three Chicago boys that everyone was talking about.

"Sure I do!" There was an unnerving eagerness in her voice as she told how she "was with them" the night they dumped the bodies from the automobile.

"Now hold on there, Miss, you say you were *with* them?"

Vazquez said she fled Chicago in the company of "Paul," the man with no last name. "If I would have stayed, I would have got into terrible trouble!" she said.

In a truck stop outside Cincinnati, she split up with Paul to accept a ride from two other men who drove into the African American neighborhood of the Queen City, up the hill and north of downtown, to score $30 of cocaine and Benzedrine from street traffickers. When one of her companions drifted away and the other passed out, Vazquez stole the automobile and drove straight to St. Michael's.

"So why were those young boys killed?" asked Hixon.

"If they hadn't gotten nosey, nothing would have happened to them." That was all she would say about that.

Hixon pressed her for more information, but Vazquez was high as a kite and in no mood to talk just now. The sheriff incarcerated her in the juvenile detention center, but she kicked out a window and was transferred to a solitary-confinement cell. A call was placed to the Cook County Sheriff's office. "I think you boys better get down here PDQ," Hixon advised.

In a remote part of northern Wisconsin, north of Ladysmith, Ed Kline, a thirty-year-old army veteran, and his youthful companion Charles Driscoll were dragged from a rusty bed in an abandoned farmhouse. The isolated farming community forty miles north of Eau Claire and 380 miles northwest of Chicago is a good place to hide out for people running from the law. In this case, the scraggily looking pair had fled the Northwest Side of Chicago under circumstances that the cops found to be very suspicious.

Driscoll and Kline, unkempt and bearded, surrendered to Rusk County Sheriff Peter J. Sybers, who turned them over to the custody of the local police chief, Orville Woods. Woods found it very unusual that neither Kline nor Driscoll asked why they had been arrested, so he called Lieutenant Deeley in Chicago to advise him of the arrest. The suspects were placed in separate cells. The pair had become suspects after a sixteen-year-old in Jeff Park tipped police to an earlier conversation he had with Driscoll, who told him, "We're going to blow town and maybe go to Florida." The conversation took place the day the bodies were found in the woods.

Patrick Deeley acted quickly and dispatched detectives Arthur Kelly and Donald Verkle along with crime-lab technicians and Assistant State's Attorney Frank Ferlic to Wisconsin to put the two suspects under a hot light. "Do not touch anything in their car until my men get there," Deeley asked of Woods. Kline owned a 1947 maroon Oldsmobile that had seen better days. But it was the items in the trunk that drew the sharpest attention. Bloodstains were found inside and on sections of rope and a discarded handkerchief. Scrapings were removed and sent to the crime lab for analysis. Of particular interest to police was a homemade floor mat with lined squares not unlike the impressions found on the boys during the postmortem. On January 12, 1956, Ernest E. Tucker of the *Chicago American* reported, "In photographs of the forehead of one of the slain boys were similarly 'brought out' impressions of shields, designs, and portions of letters. These were all presented as indicative the boys' bodies had laid on metal stampings or dies."

Thrown off balance by the staccato questioning of the cops, Driscoll and Kline gave confusing and contradictory statements concerning their movements in Chicago on the night in question and the presence of incriminating bloodstains in their vehicle.

"Oh that," Kline shrugged uncomfortably. "I bumped my head, and it started bleeding, that's all." He told Ferlic that he was divorced and missed his two children very much.

"Would you have taken three schoolboys out and beaten them up because you were angry at your wife for taking your own children?" badgered Ferlic.

"No, I don't believe I would have done that," Kline replied.

Kline and Driscoll agreed to submit to polygraph tests and were whisked back to Chicago. Driscoll, however, was overwrought, way too upset for the test results to be conclusive. Nevertheless, the investigators kept at him. He told police that his grandmother, Mrs. Chester Winters, owned the farmhouse, and he had come up north to look after her.

"But where were you on Sunday night?" Ferlic wanted to know, directing his question back to Kline.

"Just riding around," the man fired back. Lowering his voice, Kline suddenly looked Ferlic straight in the eye and told how he had seen the three boys walking northward on Milwaukee Avenue. Afterward, he said, he had gone to the Hub Roller Rink, a popular Northwest Side hangout for teenagers on Harlem Avenue, where he met up with Driscoll around 11:15 PM.

Pressed for more details by a *Chicago Tribune* reporter who had journeyed up to Ladysmith for an exclusive interview shortly before the two men were extradited back to Illinois, Kline changed his story and said he was "watching television" and hadn't been out at all. "I said it because I was nervous," Kline added. "I have my own theories about it [the murders]."

Kline recited Biblical scriptures and spoke of his past troubles in the army. While stationed in Germany in 1953, he had suffered a nervous breakdown and was hospitalized for nine months. He said his father was a nondenominational minister. The weepy-eyed service veteran said many things, much of it vague and inconsistent.

Before the cops administered the polygraph test, they spent a few minutes conferring with Anton Schuessler Sr., who recalled seeing a beat-up maroon jalopy that looked an awful lot like Kline's oil-burner cruising slowly up and down Mango Street the night of the disappearance. He said the car nearly struck a parked automobile, and the driver appeared drunk or distracted, almost as if he was peering inside the houses and wasn't keeping his eyes focused squarely on the street in front of him.

Charles Driscoll explained that he had worked at his job all day Monday, October 17, and all day Tuesday, the eighteenth. His alibi was ironclad, but there was good reason for the Chicago PD to be so interested in these two characters and why detectives solicited assistance from the Rusk County officials. Kline and Driscoll, Chicago Police were told, frequented a horse stable at 8600 Higgins Rd., 2.7 miles northeast of the desolate spot in Robinson Woods where the boys were found. And that happened to be near where Park Ridge neighbors claimed to have heard the deadly screams.

James Chase, a teenage stable hand, added another strange twist when he told the cops that Kline and Driscoll were inseparable, and they had confided that they were planning to run away together. The stable in the woods was known as the Idle Hour and the property owner by the name of Silas Jayne, a gruff horse breeder with a police record.

In the forest preserves, the hunt for clues moved forward at a plodding pace. Tough, new measures to beef up security were already in place as Cook County officials tried to implement workable procedures in the forty-two thousand acres of unpatrolled woods. While teams of workmen were busy installing chains and steel posts to seal off the parking lots from nocturnal trespassers, Rangers Merliss Booth and Richard Gudeman were on their hands and knees scratching around in the soft, wet loam for fresh evidence. Seventy-five feet from where the bodies were found, Booth extracted a dirt-encrusted matchbook cover, advertising the "air-conditioned comfort" of three bowling alleys—the Monte Cristo, the Austin Bowl, and the Drake. The clue took on added significance because of the known movements of the boys on Sunday night, but hopes were quickly dashed when the parents told police that neither Bobby nor John smoked cigarettes, and Anton was too young to be tempted; nor did the boys collect matchbooks, and there was no other reason for them to have them in their pockets. It was just a coincidence, or was it?

In the days and weeks following October 16, the bowling alleys loomed large in the investigation. On the Saturday after the boys were found, Malcolm Peterson and two close friends dropped by the Monte Cristo to question owner Lou Gelfand. He was not in the building when they arrived, but the attendant on duty said Gelfand was anxious to help out or, at the very least, extend his sympathies to the father. Malcolm was asked to wait a few minutes while an employee summoned Gelfand by phone from another bowling emporium he owned. While this was going on, a stocky, bushy-haired man between the ages of forty-five and fifty loitering in the aisle caught Malcolm's attention. He subsequently learned that this individual had made "improper advances" to a seventeen-year-old earlier in the evening, but Gelfand said he could not shed any light on the matter. The bushy-haired man in the blue suit panicked and fled, just as Malcolm gestured in the stranger's direction and started walking toward him. He turned quickly and raced down the stairs from the second-floor alleys and cut around the corner. Malcolm gave chase and after a fast run caught up with him, but the man dashed off after exchanging only a few words. For the next hour, radio squad cars from the Albany Park station canvassed the side streets, but the bushy-haired man had disappeared, never to be found.

Using the laws of eminent domain, the city had purchased the properties that stood in the path of the oncoming Northwest Expressway for fair-market value. Heart-broken residents, many of them reluctant to leave and filled with bitterness, were forced out. In October 1955, nearly two thousand vacated apartment buildings and abandoned single-family homes stood forlornly awaiting demolition in the residential neighborhoods of the Northwest Side. For persons with sinister intent or something to hide, it was the perfect place in which to disappear for a couple of hours. The empty buildings scheduled for the wrecking ball became an easy target for vandals, dopers, scavengers prying loose resalable fixtures and woodwork, and other undesirables. Police patrols were minimal, and parents constantly fretted that mischievous children would get hurt exploring these unstable, vandalized hulks or would be overtaken by a far greater human evil lurking inside these abandoned buildings. "We would require a special round-the-clock police guard, and that's impossible," countered Roger Nussbaum, state expressway engineer. William J. Mortimer, county highway superintendent, passed the buck to recalcitrant and uncooperative property owners. "It's first a human problem. We can't get tenants to vacate all buildings in a given area on any set day. It's also a matter of cost. Unless we contract for wrecking a large number of buildings, the cost gets out of hand." Complaints mounted, but nothing was done.

Lieutenant John Lynch of the Thirty-Third District ordered twenty of his best men into these places to hunt for clues. Dorothy Peterson believed that the tottering, ransacked shells along Avondale Avenue (less than a half mile from the family home) might contain some small piece of physical evidence that might unlock the mystery of her son's death. But there was no proof that the boys were taken to an empty house where they were stripped naked and murdered. Not one person living along Avondale heard screams that Sunday night.

Police spent hours grilling Edward Rohlfes, a forty-seven-year-old retired railroad worker on disability, who had spent all of Monday night (the seventeenth) in the forest preserves because he "often slept out." Rohlfes had parked his truck twenty-five feet from the shallow ditch where the boys were later found. He said that things were not good at home. He was living with his wife, Muriel, in a motel near Arlington Heights but spending much of his time in the company of his deaf-mute brother, Herman, a factory worker who could neither read nor write. The men dozed inside their red, 1951 half-ton rig from 6:45 PM Monday until 6:00 AM the following day when it was time for Herman to go to work.

Ed Rohlfes passed much of Tuesday with his married daughter, Joanne Malecke, and two-year-old grandson, Leonard. They visited the family plot in a local cemetery and then stopped off at Ed's sister's home in Elmwood Park. On the return trip, Ed and Joanne passed by the location in Robinson Woods where he had crashed for the night. "You want to have a look at my outdoor hotel room?" Ed, wanting to kill time, winked at his daughter and turned into the woods. It was past 10:00 AM. Both Rohlfes and his daughter said they spotted a beat-up blue Ford turning into the parking lot. Three men were in the car—all of them bareheaded, and that was an unusual fall fashion statement in the 1950s. Ed Rohlfes, speaking for his brother, swore to police that they had driven past the ditch several times earlier in the morning but had not noticed anything in particular. Ed Rohlfes underwent two lie-detector tests and passed them both.

Sheriff Lohman accepted the story, which narrowed the time frame the killers could have disposed of the three boys, from 10:30 AM to noon on Tuesday. It had rained into the morning, but the bodies were dry, though the grass beneath them was still wet. There could be no doubt. Police had to wonder what purpose was served by keeping the bodies all night. And why would the killer hurriedly drop them in a roadside ditch in broad daylight and risk detection?

The tenuous connection between the Rohlfes brothers and the discovery of the bodies in the ditch added a new spark to this combustible murder mystery five months later in March 1956, when Herman Rohlfes, the fifty-two-year-old deaf-mute, communicated a weird story that baffled investigators and sent evidence technicians scurrying back to Robinson Woods to tear up ground near the crime scene for further analysis. Representatives of the Illinois State Department of Rehabilitation and the National Fraternal Society for the Deaf examined Herman at intervals of twelve hours to determine whether or not he was delusional, demented, or actually on to something.

Herman Rohlfes, with only a fragmentary knowledge of sign language, indicated that he had seen the bodies eleven hours before they were actually discovered. He went on to say that around 1:00 AM, he had observed a man and a boy fighting in the darkness; the young one was stripped naked and beaten senseless. The attacker was short. He had a round face and a stubby beard. After the boy was rendered unconscious, the man set fire to the boy's clothes. Moments later, the man walked right up to the cab of their truck and shined a flashlight inside but ran off when Herman indicated that he could not speak or hear what was being said. Herman said he thought the assailant might be Native American, but brother Ed dismissed the story as the ramblings of a "child-like" man who still believed in the Easter Bunny and Santa Claus.

"Herman is always watching television shows in which Indians are killing cowboys," Ed told police. "He might have imagined all the things he has been telling about." Or he might have been drinking. When asked about that, Herman indicated to his niece Joanne that he had consumed two beers that night. Joanne defended her uncle, "Herman does not make up stories. Whenever he has any information, he passes it on immediately."

Then why hadn't he mentioned this sooner?

The woman said he was probably afraid of the police and did not want to be questioned.

"This is all nonsense!" countered his brother, who said that Herman would have awakened him in the truck and alerted him to the presence of danger if indeed he had actually witnessed a crime in progress.

Investigator Deeley listened to the story thoughtfully and asked Herman if he could lead police to the exact spot where the boy was allegedly assaulted and the clothes burned. "This is a very peculiar situation," Deeley admitted. "I can't recall anything like it. All we can do is go ahead. We can't afford to overlook anything. But I have never seen a tougher thing to cope with."

Investigators and a police sketch artist watched closely as Herman Rohlfes led them to a spot in Robinson Woods exactly 250 feet east of where Edward had parked the truck on the night in question. Herman pointed to a grassy area and said that was where the clothes were burned. Three hundred feet away from where the car was parked, Herman identified the approximate location where the fight and the stripping occurred.

"I'm telling you that if Herman saw a fight between a man and a boy, he would have hit, pinched, or kicked me at the time he saw it to let me know," Edward kept insisting.

There was silence as veteran investigators contemplated possible explanations. How could Herman have witnessed a fight 250 feet away in the dead of night? Or did he see these events unfold in a vision or a supernatural dream sequence? There was no moon that evening, and it was raining. None of it made much sense.

One fact was confirmed—during the night, Ranger Peter Carlino had rapped on the side of the truck, warning Edward to turn on his parking lights or risk a ticket. Lieutenant Mike Spiotto, by this time in charge of the task force, called that minor little detail "the most important result" of the interview. With Carlino making the rounds, it was a fair assumption that if anything untoward had gone on in the woods that night, the ranger would have spotted it. "We've checked on much weird information in this investigation," Spiotto said impatiently. "Some of it was on the basis of people's dreams. But we'll continue until we break this case."

There was no accounting, however, for the presence of ashes found in the exact spot where Herman indicated the clothes were torched or for a location three-quarters of a mile away where a Cook County deputy sheriff and a National Guardsman found the ashes of a bonfire. A pair of badly burned blue jeans was found in the pile. All three of the boys had worn jeans the day they disappeared. The police speculated that someone unconnected to the case had set fire to his discarded rubbish . . . by the sheerest coincidence.

Harry Glos, the unflinching, battle-scarred chief investigator in Coroner McCarron's office, said he had personally known Herman Rohlfes for ten years and recalled Herman's uncanny "sixth sense" about fires. While stopping short of vouching for Herman's credibility (or his sanity), Glos drew upon memories of a fire that had occurred in suburban Schiller Park only eighteen months earlier. "Though Herman had been many miles away, he described the fire dramatically and in detail," Glos remembered. "I think Herman believes he is telling the truth. But only a psychiatrist could evaluate his real mentality."

Neither the police nor Herman's immediate family put much stock in his version of events—likely the result of an addled child-man's overheated imagination. After all, Herman did still believe in Santa Claus. Any other explanation defied logic and crossed over into the realm of the paranormal. And that was unacceptable to the tough Chicago homicide dicks that neither had the time nor the inclination to listen to fortunetellers, psychic dreamers, kooks, cranks, or crazies.

On November 2, 1955, the season's first snowstorm blanketed the Chicagoland area. Twenty-mile-an-hour winds buffeted the city, and deep drifts formed. The heavy coating of early snow hampered efforts at the crime scene. For the first time, police publicly admitted they were up against a blank wall in the hunt for a killer. Both Lieutenant Deeley and Captain Corcoran were laid up with flu-like symptoms and hundred-degree fevers while Coroner McCarron accepted help from an unlikely source. William "Bud" Runzel, political foe of Sheriff Joe Lohman and the unhappy loser of the 1954 race for Cook County sheriff, volunteered the services of his two prized German shepherds. With Harry Glos and the coroner's deputies leading the charge, the dogs were given a scent of the boys' apparel and began the hunt despite the snow. However, the second attempt to track down overlooked clues with hunting dogs was no more successful than the first.

With hopes for swift resolution beginning to fade, the *Chicago American* called upon the state's attorney to use his powers of immunity to encourage informants to speak up.

> Under the law State's Attorney Gutknecht is authorized to grant immunity from prosecution to minor participants in crimes so that they can be used as witnesses against the actual criminals. There is a chance that Mr. Gutknecht could hasten the solution of the murder of the three schoolboys by announcing that anyone whose part in the crime was that of an accessory and not a killer, can clear his conscience by exposing the murderers without running a risk of being sent to prison himself. We think it should be tried.

Gutknecht, an important cog in the city Democratic Machine and accused by the Republicans of refusing to seek indictments against politically connected building inspectors lax in condemning fire-trap slum buildings, ignored the cogent editorial advice of the *Chicago American* in the belief that something would soon turn up. When it did not, Gut-knecht's political agenda, his refusal to work with the coroner, and personal motives were called into question. "It's a sin to play politics in a tragedy of this type," sniped Walter McCarron.

Down in Brookville, Indiana, Jacob "Dutch" Bergbreiter, a corrupt vice-lieutenant (who later admitted to being on the crime syndicate's payroll), and Policewoman Sylvia Cammy from Joe Lohman's staff pounded away at Gloria Vazquez, the glib junkie/prostitute whose cryptic remarks about "nosey boys" getting their comeuppance raised eyebrows. But after many hours of interrogation, Bergbreiter and Cammy gave up. "She's all yours, Sheriff," the lieutenant said in a disgusted voice. Vazquez, they finally decided, had invented a time-consuming and costly hoax. She had read the newspaper accounts of the murders and cooked up a fairy tale, nothing more. The nineteen-year-old woman was held over by Sheriff Hixon on the unrelated auto-theft charge while the Cook County Sheriff's team returned to Chicago to assist one hundred deputy sheriffs and bailiffs who had agreed to work as search volunteers on their off days.

The hunt for clues had widened to include a thirty-six-square-mile area in the eastern part of Du Page County, a suburban area west of Cook County. Here, Lohman replicated Captain Corcoran's earlier house-to-house efforts in Jefferson Park but with the same dismal results. One by one, the most promising leads were either discounted or abandoned altogether. After two weeks, there was no more to go on than there had been hours after the disappearances were first reported to the police. Police could not even establish a proper motive for the crime—all they could do was conjecture. "We went more than six months in the Degnan case before we got a break," Police Commissioner O'Connor reminded the press. "I am confident we'll get such a break this time, and I am hopeful that it won't take that long."

Eleven days after the boys' remains were removed from the woods, Lieutenant Deeley summoned his elite fifty-two-member SIU squad to central headquarters for a debriefing—and what amounted to an admission of failure. Responding to repeated criticisms that the brass had failed to keep the men in the field properly informed of breaking developments uncovered by the sheriffs in other jurisdictions, Deeley announced that the unit headquarters would be transferred back to Gale Street, with only a skeleton staff of record keepers remaining behind. "There is no excuse for lack of coordination and cooperation among various investigating agencies," asserted Virgil Peterson of the Chicago Crime Commission.

More suspects were released as hopes dimmed. The grieving parents pleaded with Lohman, Deeley, and O'Connor not to waver in their efforts. "Please ask everyone that any bit of information . . . no matter how small or insignificant it might be, it might help the police catch the killer," Eleanor Schuessler urged. Malcolm Peterson went on the radio and made a separate appeal for Chicagoans to come forward and help solve the case.

A few weeks after his sons' funerals, Anton reopened his little tailor shop on Sheridan Road, but his shattered nerves would not permit him to go about his daily tasks. His customers were polite and solicitous, but they noticed a marked change. The bereaved father had slipped into an emotional abyss. He could not concentrate, lost in a fog of psychic pain. Unable to go on, he closed the shop and returned home. In the next few days, Anton made frequent visits to the Gale Street Police Station to chart the progress of the investigation, but the sergeant on duty shook his head sadly and told him there was nothing new to report. The dawn of each new day brought only more sorrow. Anton's depression deepened to the point where Eleanor considered institutionalizing her husband. It would be a painful step to take but perhaps a necessary one.

The hunt for a killer also involved a search for the killer's automobile, which was based on the most promising clue so far—parallel striation marks found on the chests of Anton and the stomach of John. It appeared as if the marks found on the boys were caused by the bodies having been pressed against a rubber, ribbed floor mat from an automobile, possibly a Packard. Before the investigation had run its course, detectives questioned the owners of 970 Packard automobiles from the model years 1942 through 1950, as well as the owners of certain 1947 Cadillacs and 1953 Fords because the impressions on the boys closely resembled the manufacturers' designs for the floor mats in these models as well. As it turned out, all of the interrogated Packard owners were interviewed and released.

In early November when the owner reported his car taken, a three-state alarm was sounded for a white-and-green Chevy sedan stolen from Raymond Lierman October 16 near the intersection of Belmont and Central avenues. A second car stolen from this same corner on October 16 was later recovered—but a set of green-plaid seat covers was removed by the police, fueling speculation that an attempt had been made by police to destroy blood stains or other physical evidence. The car was sent to the crime lab for examination, but the results were inconclusive, and the car was returned to its owner.

The *Daily News* invited readers to call them at DEarborn 2–1111 with information to aid the cops in their work. In the days that followed, cryptic messages appeared in the paper, including this one: "A letter writer who signed the name 'Jada' and another who wrote on a torn piece of yellow paper are especially requested to telephone the city editor. Their identities will be protected."

Charles Driscoll took a second polygraph test and passed it. Detective Chief John T. O'Malley said there was "nothing inconclusive" about the results, and the earlier inconsistencies in Driscoll's testimony were chalked up to extreme nervousness. Driscoll and Ed Kline, his confused and shell-shocked friend, were both ruled out as suspects. The police dismissed scores of others who were at one time seriously considered as suspects. Among those were Jack McKinney, who had been extradited back to Chicago from Tazewell, Tennessee, and forty-year-old Arthur Prowski, whose only offense was his possession of pornographic photos, confiscated from his apartment by Chicago Police.

An isolated location two-and-a-half miles northwest of Robinson Woods became of primary importance to members of the SIU when reports began filtering in from area residents who claimed to have heard the muffled cries of a young boy begging for his life at around 11:30 PM, Sunday, October 16. Today, the neighborhood is densely populated and hardly recognizable from what it was in the 1950s when a good deal of the immediate area was undeveloped prairie. At the time of the Schuessler-Peterson murders, much of it was a garbage dump. The area was notorious in the 1950s as a lovers' lane, and the cops were always on the lookout for suspicious behavior. A smattering of homes, horse stables, and roadside stands was in the area, but much of the vicinity (bound by Higgins Road and Harlem, Bryn Mawr, and Odell avenues) remained well off the beaten path from central Chicago until the opening of O'Hare Field jump-started a remarkable period of sustained residential and commercial development.

"No! No! Don't!" The screams of a young boy were unmistakable. The anguished cries for help awakened several people who repeated to police essentially the same story. Based on that information, a team of policemen, aided by a German shepherd, three schoolboys, Malcolm Peterson, and Anton Schuessler Sr. conducted a thorough search of the empty fields. The hunt yielded a couple of promising new leads. In the parkway of a lot at 7200 Bryn Mawr Avenue, eighteen-year-old Ray Quinn found a diamond-patterned, blue-and-red sock with a piece of tape clinging to it. It was established that the tape was very similar to the two-inch variety used by stable hands to bind the ankles of horses. Recognizing Malcolm Peterson from newspaper photos, Quinn walked up to him to share the find with the hope it would spark a glimmer of recognition. Peterson, who had already examined the great mounds of discarded clothing brought in every day to the Gale Street station in the hope that some small item that might have belonged to Bobby, could not say for sure whether or not this particular sock belonged to his boy.

"We had a special laundry-mark unit within the department in those days," former SIU Chief Mike Spiotto relates. "In many instances, we were able to trace scraps of clothing back to the manufacturer and the store where it was sold. Once in a while, we even found the former owner."[4]

More significantly, Quinn found the sock near from where the screams were said to have emanated—a prairie adjoining the residence of Edward and Dolores Wisilinski at 7236 Higgins Rd. in the Oriole Park neighborhood. The Wisilinskis, the couple who first heard the piteous screams and reported them to police, lived approximately two-and-a-half miles from Robinson Woods. "I am certain those screams came from a boy," Dolores told reporter Elgar Brown of the *American*. "At one stage I heard him cry, 'No! No! Don't!' After that, I heard a car door slam and the screech of tires. I tossed on a robe and hurried outside but the car had disappeared."

Anthony F. Walloch, a seventy-five-year-old retired engineer, and his forty-four-year-old son, Sylvester, were roused from a light sleep at 11:30 PM by the sound of screams coming from the darkened prairie near their home at 5520 N. Octavia. The sound came from the general direction of the Wisilinski residence, Anthony told police.

> I lay in my bed at 11:30 PM a week ago Sunday when the first awful screams from that prairie were heard. I thought they came from a phone cable near my window, but soon I realized this wasn't so. The shouting and yelling continued four or five minutes, then suddenly ceased. Only a few minutes later there were other screams continuing briefly, and it seemed to me like the voice was muffled. I heard somebody getting killed.

Walloch, who said he never bothered reading newspapers or listening to television or radio newscasts, provided cops with a chilling account. "There was another ominous pause, and by this time I was tense, listening closely. A little later, perhaps almost at midnight, there was a third outburst. This time the voice was hoarse, and it sounded like somebody might be pleading for mercy. I stared out my window repeatedly, but I couldn't see nothing." Walloch said he saw "hot-rods" parked near his home and heard the unmistakable roar of dual-quad carburetors. This caught the attention of police, who were told of the presence of two other cars described as hot-rods near a grassy strip behind the driveway leading into Robinson Woods. Witnesses placed the cars at 7:30 AM on Tuesday, October 18, in the vicinity of where the bodies were found at 12:15 PM.

Lieutenant Deeley ordered an immediate search of the prairie when it was discovered that a greasy film, not unlike the substance found on the boys' feet during the autopsy, covered sections of the ground. A mother of two adolescent boys said the neighborhood children often liked to play in the prairie. "Many times when they returned, I have noticed oil or grease spotting their clothes," said Mrs. Stephen Tisinai, one of the Octavia Avenue neighbors. "I am sure they can lead police to the spots where they acquired this grease."

Lohman, O'Connor, Gutknecht, and the SIU detectives were beginning to wonder where it would all end. The most extensive manhunt in modern Chicago Police history turned up a myriad of dead-end leads and clues. The task force chased down suspects from Michigan to Tennessee to Indiana and up into Wisconsin, but the expected break never materialized. More than a thousand letters were sent to police, but it all added up to nothing.

After three frustrating weeks, the task force revised its original hypothesis. It was possible, the SIU experts conceded, that the murders could have been the work of one man. Each of the boys was killed in a different fashion, leading Detective Leon Sweitzer to advance the notion that the murderer lured one of them (possibly Robert Peterson) away from the other two. Then, as the killer grappled with the first victim, who put up a terrific fight, the other two burst in upon them from another room or some partitioned area and were quickly subdued.

At the Koop Funeral Home, a closer examination of the Schuessler brothers prior to the wake revealed that Anton had a broken nose, and John a fractured cheekbone—important details somehow missed during the autopsy. Detectives surmised that one person could have easily rendered the brothers unconscious by slamming their heads together in a brutal, violent fashion.

Bobby fought back savagely. He sustained a fractured rib and had been beaten on the left side of his head with a pronged tool resembling a hand garden rake. His right hand was swollen, suggesting that he landed several telling blows on his assailant before he was killed. When asked about his son's ability to defend himself from attackers, Malcolm Peterson recalled how he had "told Robert to use his feet and his hands, to kick if anyone molested him. We said he was not to give up unless somebody pushed a gun at him."

Detective Sweitzer, a veteran of many homicide investigations, speculated that the killer must have felt safe leaving the corpses at the murder scene overnight in order to await the perfect moment to dispose of them: "If there had been more than one person involved, it is reasonable to believe the bodies would have been disposed of that night."

A few miles from the Walloch home, Park Ridge resident Stanley Panek and his neighbors Vince and Hetty Salerno told of hearing screams emanating from an area four blocks southwest of their homes and near the Idle Hour Stables at 8600 Higgins Rd.[5] Panek, a used-car salesman, was out walking his dog when he first detected the sounds of a distant struggle. The Salernos lived across the street from Panek at 1016 W. Peterson in a tri-level home with an open breezeway and attached garage. Mrs. Salerno reported hearing the disturbance at 11:30 PM Sunday. "Somebody must be getting the hell beat out him," murmured Vince to his wife. The couple was standing in front of the door saying good-bye to departing guests when the sharp, piercing screams were first heard. "I heard two screams," Hetty recalled. "The first scream, it was loud . . . piercing. It was a young voice, and it was a frightened scream. Then a little while later, the next scream came, lower than the first scream. They came from the west, from towards the stables. Mr. Panek came across then," said Hetty, who served as an ambulance driver during World War II. "He was talking to my husband. And actually I was scared. I went in the house [and] stayed there."

The search near the horse stables was widened. Thirty police officers scoured every inch of the open fields. "They were at arm's length, side by side in a row," recalled Violet Sable who lived at 1024 W. Peterson, down the street from the Salernos. "They went from Higgins Road to Peterson, which is a long block." Based on the tip supplied by Panek and the Salernos, detectives interviewed between fifteen and twenty Idle Hour stable hands and other employees, along with the employees of Smitty's Timber Ridge Stables at 8700 Higgins (a block north of the Idle Hour) and dozens of other horsemen working at other local stables up and down Cumberland Avenue and Dee, Higgins, and River roads. A *Daily News* reporter sent by his assignment editor to interview the employees of the stables in the area found no one who recalled hearing anything unusual that night. On any given night, a dozen grooms and stable hands bunked down at the Idle Hour. A night watchman and his German shepherd guarded the premises. A four-foot-high rail fence surrounded the clubhouse, barns, outdoor ring, and tack room. It is a reasonable assumption that someone would overhear the commotion. Was that person so afraid of the consequences that he refused to cooperate with the police?

Bob Breen, a veteran horse trainer and championship rider, and his wife, Elsie, and two teenaged daughters were guests of Ralph Fleming, the caretaker, at the Idle Hour for a few weeks in 1955. Breen slept soundly that night. In an April 2003 interview with the authors, Breen was unequivocal: "I know there were four or five of these kids sleeping there as well. They were provided double-decked beds. My wife and daughters were there. So were Ralph Fleming and his wife. There were no screams. We heard nothing of the kind." During a brief telephone conversation with the authors, one of Breen's daughters, an out-of-state college professor, corroborated her father's story: "We didn't hear any screams the night the boys were killed. I heard no screams. [The Idle Hour Stables] was locked down with Dobermans running free" that night. She asked that her name not be disclosed and refused to answer further questions.

On Wednesday morning, just twenty-four hours after the discovery of the bodies in Robinson Woods, stable owner Silas Jayne, Ralph Fleming, and Bob Breen sat around the kitchen table discussing the triple murders over their cigarettes and morning coffee. On the one hand, Si Jayne was a well-known equestrian, skilled businessman, and veteran horse trader. However, the flip side revealed a convicted rapist and cutthroat swindler, who sported a sixteen-carat diamond ring on his finger. Over the years, his name has been associated with a variety of fraudulent schemes, arsons, and other crimes. If one of his employees had lured the boys to the stable for immoral purposes, and Jayne knew about it, the logical question to ask is would he deal with the offender on his own terms, covering up the crime, or go to the police?

Breen's contention is that neither Silas Jayne nor any of his cohorts had anything to do with it. "Si said to us, 'This is a terrible thing! *But at least the homosexuals didn't get to them.*' Si was a rough character. If he caught anyone doing such a thing as that, he would have blown the person's head off." And yet, all of the available evidence, from the first moment the unfortunate boys jumped into the stranger's car on Lawrence Avenue to the reliable reports of deadly screams and screeching tires emanating from the edge of the prairie, pointed in this one direction. In April 2003, Bob Breen was ninety-eight years of age. He was mentally alert, and his recollections of past events were clear. There is no reason to believe he was making up stories for the sake of protecting the memory of Silas Jayne who was by then dead.

Jayne's offhanded remark that he was thankful that "*at least the homosexuals didn't get to them*" is quite an astonishing admission. How would he have known such a thing on the morning of October 19, assuming that Breen is accurate and this conversation occurred when he said it did? It would have been impossible for *anyone* to draw a conclusion that the boys were *not* molested at this early stage of the investigation. Before the autopsy reports (ruling out the possibility of molestation) became a matter of public record a few days later, it was assumed that a sex fiend had abducted the boys because of the absence of clothing at the crime scene. Extensive newspaper coverage reflected this thinking.

Even though law enforcement and the Illinois National Guard scoured a wide swath of prairie, it is conceivable, perhaps even likely, that the boys were *taken* to the Idle Hour but were murdered out on the empty prairie. On Sundays in the 1950s, the Idle Hour closed at 5:00 PM. The public "had to be out" at that time, Breen remembers, and the entire compound was locked down for the night. The grooms and stable hands had the choice of bedding down or running off to the city to unwind. The killer essentially had the entire spread to himself. Not wanting to disturb the Flemings, the Breens, or any of the stable boys, is it possible a horse was removed from the corral for the boys to ride as a pretext to isolate them in a desolate spot on the prairie? That would certainly lend credence to the reports of "deadly screams" coming from a generalized location radiating away from the Idle Hour. The stable had already acquired a somewhat steamy reputation. Several Rosemont police officers had heard scuttlebutt, and, from time to time, they would feed the gossip mill.

Without the children, Eleanor Schuessler felt isolated and alone in the little house on Mango Street. Now, all that remained of her former life were the painful reminders—the little dog, Penny, a collection of toys, winter clothing, and Boy Scout uniforms that would never be worn again. Eleanor's fortitude was remarkable, given the tragedy and all of the hardships she had had to endure. And now her poor, befuddled husband, no longer able to find solace or peace in his home life and unable to sleep through the night, was rolling down a ruinous path towards self-destruction. In diminished health long before the tragedies occurred, Anton Schuessler was losing his grip on reality. Lost in a fog of self-blame and guilt, he came to believe that he was somehow responsible for his sons' deaths and was in fact the real murderer. The doctors described his condition as a paranoid psychotic state. When Anton talked of suicide, his doctors advised an extended period of rest and convalescence. Eleanor turned to the church for comfort and guidance. She was, however, no longer able to transfer a measure of hope or the spiritual strength she tapped from her God to her ailing husband. On November 9, with a heavy heart, Eleanor committed Anton to the care of Dr. Julius J. Steinfeld, director of the Forest Sanitarium and Rest Home in suburban Des Plaines. "He's going to stay in the home at least a week, maybe two, and get a complete rest," Eleanor said, but she wasn't at all confident that the maladies of spirit and mind would be cured so quickly. As it turned out, her husband had lost the will to live.

Anton was permitted to roam freely through the corridors of the sanitarium; none of the staff members believed he was a threat to himself or anyone else, though Dr. Steinfeld reaffirmed the opinion that Anton was in the throes of a "paranoid, psychotic stage, with delusional thinking separate from the fact of the death of his boys." Dr. Steinfeld raised the eyebrows of the press when he declared Anton's ailment a "pre-existing condition," *present long before* the boys were abducted and murdered. Unaware of Schuessler's rapidly deteriorating physical condition, Dr. Steinfeld ordered electroshock therapy to help Anton "get over" his severe mental illness. On the twenty-sixth day of his ordeal, Anton Schuessler Sr. expired, tragically becoming the killer's fourth victim. His weak heart simply couldn't stand the strain and gave out. He died despite three hours of attempted resuscitation.

The death of the senior Schuessler (in the opinion of Dr. Thomas A. Carter, a member of Coroner Walter McCarron's staff) resulted from a coronary attack induced by shock treatment. "I wouldn't have a cardiac patient of mine take any shock treatments," Carter said. "He might have lived for some time, if not for this."

"Well, that is simply not so," Steinfeld countered, defending his controversial decision as best he could.

The inquest verdict carried with it strong language recommending that in the future, all private sanitariums in Illinois be equipped with electrocardiogram equipment to monitor a patient's condition before such a risky procedure was even attempted. Ralph Schultz, Eleanor's cousin, was not aware of Anton's nervous breakdown or the subsequent hospitalization. "As far as I know, he died of a broken heart."

Anti-Semitic zealots pinned Anton's sudden and unexpected death on a Jewish physician acting on behalf of Zionist conspirators to cover up a series of worldwide ritualistic murders blamed on the Jews. World War II was still fresh in the public memory in 1955. However regrettably, the specter of anti-Semitism lived on long after Hitler and his government were vanquished. The Schuessler-Peterson slayings according to the irrationality espoused by these hatemongers seemed to fit the profile of a pattern of unsolved murders of Gentile children described by the notorious British fascist Arnold Spenser Leese[6] in his inflammatory polemic *Jewish Ritual Murder,* originally published in Europe in 1938.

The absurd rumor gained currency not long after a Chicago woman named Mrs. Lyle Clark Van Hyning (publisher of a newsletter *Women's Voice)* allegedly mailed Mr. Schuessler a copy of the Leese pamphlet imploring him to read it immediately and heed the warnings. Alarmed by the "revelations" contained therein, Anton, according to Van Hyning, "made the mistake" of going to Sheriff Lohman to demand that the ritual-murder angle be investigated. Van Hyning was convinced that Anton Schuessler Sr. was put to death on the operating table before he could go public with these damning disclosures. The inference, of course, was that Lohman, being Jewish, was somehow involved in a cover-up with Steinfeld. To support the allegation, Van Hyning offered as proof copies of a *Chicago Daily News* article blaming the murders of the three boys on an unspecified religious sect. She boldly accused the *Daily News* of pulling the edition out of newsstand circulation ten minutes after the paper hit the streets in order not to offend the Jewish community and spark "racial unrest." Copies were forwarded to Leese to use in his propaganda machine against European Jewry.

There is no record of Eleanor being troubled by any of this twaddle, and it is unlikely that her husband had actually received the Leese pamphlet or digested any of its hateful content. Discounting the opinions of crackpots and bigots, McCarron tried to be sympathetic, but Dr. Carter's raw accusation of Steinfeld reduced Eleanor to a state of emotional and physical collapse. "I don't like pursuing this line of questioning, but I have to," prodded McCarron.

"Go ahead! Go ahead! I have taken so much, I can take this!" wailed Eleanor.

"He was on his way to death when they gave him the shock treatments," Dr. Carter added, as if this would somehow ease the grief or improve the situation.

"I'm all alone now," Eleanor said softly. "All I have left is a bird and a dog."

Broken by the loss of her husband and sons, Eleanor scraped together the last of her life's savings, nearly $2,000 in total, to pay for her husband's wake and funeral. "I figured he worked so hard," she said. "That's all I could do for him." More than seven hundred letters of condolence poured in from across the city pledging financial help to the widow. The next-door neighbors expressed their sorrows and vowed to do what they could. "I know what Mrs. Schuessler's circumstances are," said Mrs. Charlotte Spitzer of 5701 Mango. "She's up against it. You know how it is when everything is taken away and nothing is coming in. I don't know which way she can turn now. I don't see how she can work in her present state. She doesn't take any food."

On November 12, the *Chicago American* published an open letter that Eleanor had composed to the killer.

You have ruined my life. I hope you are satisfied. Everything I ever had, you have taken away from me. The nineteen years of happy, family life we had have been burned out in twenty-five days. You may as well come and get me. Finish your job completely. I have nothing to live for. You saw to that. You killed my husband just as surely as you killed Robert Peterson and my two boys. My husband and I would have celebrated our 20th anniversary next May 9, but we weren't even allowed that bit of happiness. You may be sitting smirking and laughing at me as you read this, saying I'm a fool for writing you, but I wanted you to know what a complete job you have done of ruining my life. You've already broken my heart into little pieces. Why not finish the job?

Relatives feared for her sanity. The dark possibility that she was suicidal and determined to follow her husband into the grave was more than just a passing concern.

Chicagoans, rich and poor, mailed in their contributions following a direct appeal from Mayor Richard J. Daley. "Isn't this a tragic thing!" exhorted the mayor. "It's so shocking. How that poor man and his wife have suffered! Our policemen are not letting up on this case. I would rather see this case solved than anything I know. We need everybody's help." With the mayor's blessing, so it would come to pass. Forty-fifth Ward Alderman Charles H. Weber, a wheelhorse in the formidable Democratic Machine, wrote a check to the relief fund launched by the *Chicago*

American: "Her parents live in my ward. She needs help. Here's $500 to start it off."[7]

Daley, his wife, Eleanor, and State's Attorney John Gutknecht were on hand for the wake. The powerful political leaders each promised additional resources to Mrs. Schuessler in a private meeting held inside the Koop Funeral Home.

Before a respectful gathering of three hundred parishioners who had come to mourn the passing of their neighbor Anton Schuessler, the Reverend Theodore Stone of St. Tarcissus Church spoke to the sufferings of the widow. "Long ago there lived a man named Job. He had seven sons and three daughters and lost them all. But he still turned to God. Our Lord asks us to suffer so that we can help other souls get to heaven." Then he added, "Because some men are wicked, the innocent must suffer."

In the days and weeks following the murders of her sons and the death of her husband, Eleanor Schuessler's weight dropped from 142 to 118 pounds. Unable to rebuild her torn and shattered life while trapped inside the house on Mango Street, she decided to leave the city for the holiday season. Without informing the press, she spent the next month recuperating with her aunt, Emma Schultz Alexander, and her aunt's husband, Otto, in South Coral Gables, outside Miami, Florida. "Eleanor was a survivor," recalled her cousin Ralph Schultz. "She was resilient . . . but how the hell do you put something like this behind you?" When Eleanor returned to Chicago in late December, she moved in with her mother and began life anew on the North Side of the city.

The Petersons regrouped and tried to make the best of things for the sake of their other children, attempting to show them a good Christmas despite what had happened. But their sense of well-being was forever shattered for the Petersons and for their neighbors as well.

Finally, on June 8, 1956, the dark clouds parted, and Eleanor was allowed to smile again. On that Friday afternoon, she was joined in marriage to Valentine "Bud" Kujawa, a thirty-seven-year-old widower who had lost his wife two years earlier. Reverend Carey performed a simple Catholic ceremony before a small circle of well-wishers at St. Tarcissus, where, nine months earlier, solemn funeral services for her boys were conducted. Kujawa was a family friend from the neighborhood with a teenaged daughter and a ten-year-old boy to look after. The kids had known the Schuessler brothers and on occasion walked to school with them. "Eleanor is a wonderful person. She loves me and my children," Kujawa said. "They love her, too. We've both been lonely but we're young and we only want to live an ordinary life together. We'll be thankful for all the happiness granted us." Eleanor hoped that her troubles were at last over. "I have been terribly unhappy since my boys and Anton were taken away from me," she said. "In Bud I have found a considerate, home-loving companion. I have found happiness again."

The Kujawas settled into a new life, freed of torment. They were devoted to one another, and their family flourished. But Eleanor kept the bronzed baby shoes of her two boys on the nightstand so the memory would never fade away. Eventually, the family abandoned Northwest Side living all together. They relocated to a small Wisconsin town—away from the meddling neighborhood gossip and away from the smug disapproval of total strangers who questioned her right to marry so quickly and start anew.

On a sunlit July afternoon in 1956, Mr. and Mrs. Malcolm Peterson participated in special ceremonies dedicating an athletic field at the Norwegian Lutheran Children's Home in the memory of their son. It was recalled that Bobby had played at this field on the Little League team sponsored by the Edison-Norwood Kiwanis Club. Superintendent Fred W. Schroeder and the Petersons paused to reflect on the many friendships that Bobby had forged with the youngsters residing in the home and the kindness he had shown the less fortunate boys. They agreed that this was Bobby's very special place, and a portion of the money donated to the Petersons in the aftermath of the tragedy was turned over to the home to construct a new backstop on the baseball diamond. More than three hundred people turned out to cheer the formal opening of the new Robert M. Peterson Athletic Field in Park Ridge and the dedication of a plaque bearing Bobby's name.

The parents of the slain boys marked the one-year anniversary with prayers and tears. Eleanor Kujawa had a Mass said for her boys at St. Tarcissus. Malcolm and Dorothy Peterson attended memorial services in the Jefferson Park Lutheran Church. Not far away, the earthmovers and dump trucks noisily dug the extended ditch that in a few years was destined to become the busy Northwest Expressway.

Malcolm Peterson never abandoned hope that the killer would one day be found. For many years thereafter, he made it his solemn duty to appear before the desk sergeant at Gale Street, knowing in his heart of hearts that the answer to his question would always be the same. "Nope, nothing to report today, Mr. Peterson."

Though he has only a faint recollection of his older brother, in many ways Tom Peterson shares a special kinship with Robert. There is an unbroken spiritual bond between the brothers transcending death, including a lifelong affection for the Chicago White Sox baseball team. Malcolm and Dorothy Peterson could take great solace in the athletic accomplishments of their youngest son, a gifted athlete. Tom fulfilled Robert's early athletic promise by lettering in basketball and baseball for the Eagles of Taft High School. The Petersons waited until Tom graduated in 1970 before abandoning their old life in Jeff Park–Gladstone. They left behind the Dutch Colonial and everything the house represented to them in good times and in bad.

7

A Case Grown Cold

THE REST OF 1955 passed quietly and soberly in Jefferson Park and South Edgebrook. Parents of school-aged children took time to reflect on the events of autumn and give thanks that the angel of death had mercifully passed over their homes. By December, news of the ongoing police investigation gradually vanished from the front pages of the morning and afternoon papers, but the tragedy was never far from the public conscience. At least once a week, some bizarre new development caught the media's attention, underscoring the baffling and paradoxical aspects of the case. No description can do justice to the climate of fear that engulfed the neighborhood in the aftermath of the murders. "Don't get into a car with strangers, or you *might* end up like the Schuessler-Peterson boys!" The dire warning was passed from parent to child for many years to come. To baby boomers struggling to grasp the larger political issues of the day, such as the Cold War, Sputnik, and the omnipresent threat of "the Bomb," the parental scare tactic was confirmation that a more tangible evil lurked closer to home. The manifestation of that singular evil—the Halloween "bogeyman" in human form—kept to the shadows. The police, who were looked up to by many conservative citizens as our "peacetime army," spent vast resources on manpower and scientific analysis to catch this killer. But in the end, they seemed powerless to stop him from striking again, if that was what he wanted to do.

All through that difficult first year, Lieutenant Spiotto kept fifty-four

SIU men and women working 24/7 on the case. Aided by anonymous tipsters sending daily notes and letters to the city desks of the four major metropolitan newspapers, hundreds of fresh leads were passed on to police. "We had so many leads to follow, no one was shirking," recalled Spiotto, a spry eighty-nine-year-old at the time he was interviewed. Spiotto rose to the rank of acting superintendent before calling it a career. "We split them up in teams of two, and they brought back people for crimes I never heard of."

In March 1956, after weeks and weeks of careful analysis, the Chicago Police crime lab came up intriguing new evidence from the original autopsies that sent eighteen of the SIU investigators out on a frantic, cross-town search of machine shops, steel-fabricating plants, and foundries. Filings of a rare metal were extracted from under Robert Peterson's fingernails and analyzed by chemists. The fingernails of the Schuessler boys were too short to have retained any of the material, but additional scrapings from the soles of their feet turned up the same substance. The investigation took on added significance when the microscopic filings were identified as rare forms of nonmagnetic, heat-resistant stainless steel known to metallurgists as SS309 and SS310. Traces of brass, zinc, and other metals were also found, but it was the stainless-steel filings, used in the manufacture of airplane parts and "candle carburetors" (steel coils placed over candles in nightclubs to scatter smoke), that attracted the most attention. Also found were traces of dolomite, common in household cleansers.

Because police often look to the textbooks for answers to vexing crime problems, Commissioner O'Connor decided to seek out the opinions of two private research groups. Experts from Standard Oil's engineering division and the Armour Research Foundation at the Illinois Institute of Technology were called in to examine the material and offer opinions. The general consensus among the lab-coated technicians was that the unusual shavings must have come from a place engaged in grinding, welding, buffing, or metal spinning. Under these circumstances, gypsum, alpha quartz (sand), dolomite, and lead oxide were other likely abrasives that would be used to grind down softer metals.

The citywide search included a twenty-square-mile area bounded by Fullerton Avenue on the south and Ashland Avenue on the east and extending west into Du Page County and north to Lake County. All of law enforcement was focused on the 1,783 metal plants within this perimeter. The task force interviewed scores of junk dealers, factory owners, foremen, and metalworkers to see who had access to the shops the night of October 16. "We wondered who could possibly have access to a manufacturing plant around midnight," Spiotto said. "Well, when we got through, we ended up with 916 people who had that kind of clearance. I'll never forget one officer who came back to us and said that we had arrested his uncle. I told him we would try to keep the uncle's name out of the papers."

The primary focus, however, centered on eighteen Northwest Side manufacturing plants where steel and dolomite compounds were frequently used. In one of the factories, eight policemen in overalls sifted through fifty wheelbarrows full of ashes. They broke up a barrel of concrete found on the property and interrogated the owner of the machine shop after it was learned that he was on probation for a sex offense against two girls, ages seven and thirteen.

Deeley and Spiotto were convinced that they were finally on to something important, something that might unravel the deepening mystery. "We figured the stainless steel would give us an entrée, and we made numerous arrests," Spiotto said. "We'd find these guys molesting children—a boy comes home one day with an expensive new wristwatch, and his mother asks, 'Where did you get it?' The mother would get suspicious and call us, and we would go check it out."

Efforts were redoubled after Dorothy Peterson told police that it was impossible for her son to have picked up the steel filings before leaving home. "Robert was very careful about getting cleaned up that night," she recalled. "He was more than unusually careful about his nails."

Then in early May, O'Connor summoned pathologist Dr. Kearns and Coroner McCarron to his office for a private conference to review their options. It was simply not known at the time of the original autopsy how valuable these metal particles might be to the investigation. But there would be no shadow of doubt, or blame, attached to the good name and reputation of Jerry Kearns—that much was decided. After all, he was generally considered to be one of the nation's preeminent pathologists, despite some obvious bungling during this particular postmortem. Kearns had taken a more or less permanent "leave of absence" from the coroner's office in 1956 in order to accept a full-time position as pathologist at St. Elizabeth's Hospital on the West Side.

The coroner, acting on the advice of Dr. Edwin Hirsch of Presbyterian St. Luke's Hospital, believed that the next logical step should be the exhumation of the boys—a decision likely to be controversial, wrought with emotion, and terribly risky. Dr. Kearns, linked forever to this case and given a renewed vote of confidence by the chief, was appointed to lead the new investigation. "The question now arises as to what kind of instrument caused the wounds found on the head of Robert Peterson," explained Kearns. "These wounds may contain some particles which will provide a clue to the murders." It was agreed. An exhumation would proceed but only with the full consent of the parents of the victims.

The newspapers reported these macabre events as they unfolded. The entire city was on edge, expecting the imminent capture and prosecution of the Northwest Side bogeyman. Only one man grimly understood that the machinery and filings associated with the crime were also commonly used in riding stables to shoe horses. While SIU narrowly focused on the city factories, Jim Delorto surmised that Silas Jayne was shaken by the newspaper accounts and the dreaded prospect of a bunch of nosey cops poking around his property, especially now, only a month after the Chicago City Council annexed much of the surrounding area into the city limits. And so, with the simple flick of a match in the early morning hours of May 15, 1956, the Idle Hour hay barn burst into flames imperiling nearly eighty horses in an adjacent building. The combined fire-fighting resources of Norwood Park, Niles, Franklin Park, Park Ridge, River Grove, and Elmwood Park struggled to contain the blaze that threatened not only animals and property but the nearby woods as well. The fire was eventually brought under control, but in a matter of minutes, Silas Jayne, colorfully described by attorney F. Lee Bailey[1] as a "big strong-looking man who resembled a heavy Joseph Cotten," eliminated a serious problem and pocketed a hefty insurance settlement after reporting $30,000 in losses.

Dr. Kearns was supposed to be in charge of the exhumation, but in truth, Edwin Hirsch and Walter McCarron were calling the shots. Driven by the hope that science would succeed where police work failed, the coroner and his lackeys moved forward with haste. Whether nagging doubts tormented him, second-guessing from political adversaries annoyed him, or just the sheer horror of the thing grated on his conscience is hard to say, but McCarron vowed "that no one would obstruct anything which would help in solving this crime. . . . I saw those little boys and was troubled each night by it. . . . I was the first major law officer at the scene of the discovery."

Mike Spiotto was one of a handful of dissenters who had serious reservations about proceeding with the exhumation. "I mean, what could you gain by it?" the veteran street cop wondered. "It was Hirsch's idea. He said there might be a fingerprint on one of the boy's arms that we could have missed, but those boys were scrubbed clean prior to the wake. Never in the annals of police science has anyone ever lifted a print off of a human body."

Showing contempt for Dr. Kearns and the obvious errors he had made in the first postmortem, McCarron summoned to Chicago to assist in the examination Dr. Richard Ford, assistant professor of pathology at Harvard University Medical School, and Dr. Allan Moritz from Western Reserve University in Cleveland and the president of the American Academy of Forensic Sciences. The critical issue was the passage of time— nearly nine months had elapsed since interment. "It is feasible provided the embalming had been done properly," advised state toxicologist Dr. Walter J. R. Camp. State's Attorney Gutknecht, opposed to McCarron on personal and political grounds, called the exhumation a "shot in the dark" and was extremely reluctant to badger the parents for their approval to open the graves. A conference was held in Gutknecht's office, but initially a consensus could not be reached. Malcolm and Dorothy Peterson were against it. Mrs. Schuessler was distraught and did not have the willpower to decide.

The nightmarish ordeal exacted a terrible emotional toll on everyone. To disturb the graves at this time seemed to be a travesty against the memory of the three boys. The bereaved parents turned to the clergy for advice and mediation. Speaking for the families, Bobby's minister, the Reverend William F. Eifrig, with understandable reticence, nodded his assent: "We made up our minds to permit the exhumation because we didn't want to appear we would impede justice." The caskets came out of the ground in June 1956.

Mike Spiotto shook his head in grim bemusement as he recalled Harry Glos's exuberant, nearly breathless tone as the day of the exhumation drew close. "I got a kick out of him. He said to me, 'Say, do ya want to go watch?' I said, 'No, I don't want to go watch!' In my mind and heart I didn't want to see those boys disturbed. When you see a kid like that . . . well, it just breaks you up." It was all for nought, the results of the exhumation yielded nothing new as regards evidence or leads.

By now, SIU had mostly dispelled lingering notions that hot-rodders or street gangs were responsible for the Schuessler-Peterson murders. More likely it was the work of one person, or perhaps two, who knew enough about police work to destroy the most important physical evidence—the clothing. Most homicides involve people who know each other, and those homicides are often the easiest to solve. Conversely, when there is no link at all or the victim has been chosen at random, the odds of not getting caught are heavily stacked in the killer's favor. This was not a perfect crime, but neither was it sloppy or unprofessional. Most likely, there was no premeditation to murder the boys, but once the deed was done, the killer brilliantly camouflaged his every movement.

With better coordination between law-enforcement agencies willing to share resources and leads, greater separation between politics and policing, and a leadership team unfazed by the allure of promotions and fame, the triple homicide might have been solved quickly. In the first six months of its existence, the SIU interviewed 20,000 persons, interrogated 2,340 individuals considered to be "suspects," and investigated 1,296 leads. Seven thousand homes, vacant structures, and commercial businesses were visited by police and searched between October 18, 1955, and the end of May 1956. In the process, eighty people were arrested for crimes unrelated to the Schuessler-Peterson murders, and, from this pool, twenty-one criminal indictments were filed, resulting in seventeen convictions. Commissioner O'Connor drew attention to the impressive scope of the investigation in his *Report on Chicago Crime for 1955*, but partially out of personal embarrassment, he deliberately omitted any direct reference to the names of the three murdered boys or the failure of his department to attach a name and a face to the killer.

Days and weeks rolled into months. Winter gave way to spring, and, one by one, SIU members assigned to the Schuessler-Peterson case were transferred to other areas in the department to attend to more pressing matters. From time to time, new theories would emerge, and the name of the SIU's latest "hot suspect" would appear on page one of the afternoon "green-streak" edition, kindling false hopes and a sudden spike in newspaper circulation.

In January 1957, William Brooke, a poised and dapper businessman, was seized moments after he stepped off a KLM jetliner at New York's Idlewild Airport on his way back to Chicago. Brooke had been conducting an oil survey in Iran for a Chicago LaSalle Street firm when word reached police that he had allegedly taken part in sex orgies with young boys at a flat in the 5100 block of Ashland Avenue on the North Side. Found among Brooke's possessions were a cache of pornography and a bundle of newspaper clippings pertaining to the Schuessler-Peterson case. Nothing further is reported about this suspect.

In June of 1957, Charles L. Dahlquist, a thirty-three-year-old golf caddy and former railroad switchman, was arrested in Hollywood after making an illegal U-turn in front of a patrol car. A fast check of the plates by the Los Angeles Police Department revealed that the vehicle was stolen. Dahlquist was detained at police headquarters, where he was questioned about the recent strangulation of Marjorie Hipperson, an attractive twenty-four-year-old Los Angeles nurse engaged to a Chicago man.[2] As details of the Dahlquist interrogation and the victim's connections to Chicago filtered back to the homicide bureau in Chicago, Pat Deeley assigned Lieutenant Joseph Morris to coordinate local efforts with the LAPD. Dahlquist, a towering, angular Swede known to the SIU as "the Giant," was a sexual predator. Morris advised LAPD Lieutenant Fred Earl that Dahlquist had jumped a $4,000 bond after failing to appear in Cook County Felony Court, November 23, 1955, on a sex charge involving indecent liberties taken with a fifteen-year-old boy at an Edgebrook golf course on August 22 of that same year. "Would this guy waive extradition?" Morris wanted to know. In 1955, while residing with his father, Leonard, at 5915 Peterson Ave. (four city blocks from the Schuessler home), Charles was picked up in Chicago on the basis of an anonymous phone tip and grilled by the SIU homicide dicks within the first few hours of the Schuessler-Peterson homicide investigation.

Additional information received from Frank and Magdalena Kruell, a Northwest Side couple in their late sixties, brought Dahlquist into much sharper focus on police radar. The Kruells supplied police with startling information, raising many new and puzzling questions. On July 15, 1955, the Kruells said they observed a boy they believed looked a lot like Anton Schuessler Jr. and the pedophile Dahlquist loitering under a bridge spanning the Des Plaines River at Belmont. The couple explained that they were walking toward the bus stop when they noticed a man with a boy. It seemed very odd, and they reported the matter to police after reading about the triple murders in the newspapers.

That stretch of Belmont Avenue, which is about two miles south of Robinson Woods, is a few hundred feet east of Des Plaines River Road and about three and a half miles southwest of the Idle Hour Stables. The stretch is surrounded on both sides by woods and on a part of the south side by a cemetery. In 1955, it was a sparsely traveled country lane—hardly the kind of place where a chance meeting would be likely to occur between a thirty-three-year-old, six-foot-five-inch tall "giant" and an eleven-year-old boy. The cemetery, about five hundred feet east of River Road on Belmont Avenue, was St. Joseph's. Adding a strange ironic twist,

Anton Jr. would be laid to rest under the green lawn of St. Joseph's less than three months after his alleged rendezvous with Dahlquist under the bridge. Even today, with the hubbub of increased automobile traffic, it is hard to imagine a clandestine meeting of this nature occurring on the edge of the forest preserves unless it was for some untoward purpose.

The two-hundred-pound sometime-caddy was unemployed at the time the police seized him on a warrant and rushed him down to the Cook County State's Attorney's sex bureau at Twenty-Sixth and California for grilling. In a candid and revealing admission that failed to register with Gutknecht's gumshoes, Dahlquist informed them he had previously worked in a greenhouse/nursery.[3] Early on, detective Jim McGuire was assigned to canvass Chicago-area floral shops and greenhouses looking for the particular type of pronged garden hand tool that the killer had wielded on Bobby Peterson.

On the night of the murders, however, Dahlquist said he was home alone watching television from 8:00 PM until noon the following day. He vividly recalled the programs he had tuned into that evening and provided an accurate description of their content, satisfying police that he was being upfront with them.

Dahlquist was paraded before the Kruells at the detective bureau. The husband and wife were positive that this was the suspicious man they had observed with a boy only three months prior. "That boy passed within five feet of us on his bicycle!" Frank Kruell said in a heated voice after being shown a photograph of Anton Jr. "They both ran off when they saw us watching them." Dahlquist flatly denied the charge. Frank, a foreman with the Railway Express Company, said he was able to pinpoint the exact date and time because it happened to be an important moment in his life. He had just exchanged marriage vows with Magdalena. The couple were honeymooning at the time.

Detectives questioned Mrs. Schuessler. When asked if she remembered what her son might have been up to the afternoon of July 15, Eleanor recalled that Anton had ridden all the way out to Harlem and North avenues on the West Side of the city—an astonishing distance for an eleven-year-old Jeff Park boy to travel alone, peddling his bicycle. It is possible, one must concede, that Anton Jr. could have ended up near Robinson Woods, where he encountered Dahlquist either by accident or design. "If the Chicago detectives believed for a moment that Dahlquist worked at Idle Hour and knew the boys, they would have been all over him," countered Jim Delorto. "And if, in fact, he worked as a stable hand, as some people believe, it was never fully substantiated, and, if true, it might have been before the boys were even born."

The important questions to ponder: Who *was* the young boy keeping company with Dahlquist? If it was little Anton, what could he possibly have been doing under the bridge with a grown man of suspicious repute so far from home? Or was it a simple case of mistaken identity by the Kruells, both well up in years and suffering impaired vision?

Traumatized by John's car accident, Eleanor and Anton Sr. had became overly protective of their older son. As a result, the boy became far more hesitant in his dealings with others. Anton Jr., on the other hand, was not scrutinized as intensely and was outgoing and more adventurous. Was Anton Jr. engaging in improper behavior with this older man as a fruit hustler extorting money from him, or had he been lured into a sexual liaison that ultimately led to murder?[4]

Whether or not Charles Dahlquist was telling the truth, nobody corroborated his story—every aspect, every tangible clue in this high-velocity murder investigation pointed police in the general direction of Silas Jayne's Idle Hour.

Dahlquist, sporting a fashionable DA[5] haircut, underwent three polygraph tests on Chicago Police equipment. The first test cleared him, but the second and third tests were termed "inconclusive." Arraigned on the unrelated sex charge, Dahlquist jumped bail and headed west and, for the time being, was forgotten by the Chicago P. D.—until his traffic stop in California. Dahlquist was no more forthcoming with the LAPD than he had been in the interrogation room in 1955 located at Eleventh and State. He indignantly informed his captors at the time of his arrest that he had fled Chicago because he had grown weary of answering pointless questions about the murders: "I'm not going to tell you anything more than I told Chicago Police!"

After receiving a communiqué from Los Angeles that the suspect Dahlquist was agreeable to a waiver, Lieutenant Morris prepared the necessary legal papers for Governor Stratton to sign, authorizing the extradition of the fugitive back to Chicago. By the time of his arrest in California, Dahlquist was under renewed suspicion after the Chicago crime lab discovered particles of insecticides and grass fertilizers on the skin of the murder victims during the 1956 exhumation. Suspicion grew that the boys met with foul play inside a greenhouse, based on the trace material found on the bodies. Scalp wounds on Robert Peterson indicated that he had been "struck by a pronged garden tool," giving further credence to the theory.

Once he was returned to the Windy City, Dahlquist was dragged before Chief Justice Wilbert F. Crowley to answer for the 1955 molestation charge. Dahlquist pleaded guilty to a "crime against nature" and was sentenced to one to five years. No further investigation into his possible involvement in the Schuessler-Peterson case was made.

Based on the science of "link analysis" (an investigative technique that establishes probability of action by linking suspects and victims together through their personal associations and patterns of contact), the chance that Dahlquist was a conduit to the sexual predator who carted the boys off to Idle Hour Stable or some place close or that he met up with the Schuessler brothers earlier that summer and introduced them to their pedophilic killer must be weighed carefully against all of the available evidence.

Tony Wilson, a retired Cook County Sheriff's Police Department detective, told the authors that the name Dahlquist certainly "sounded familiar" but wasn't sure that was his suspect's name. Wilson explained that he and two other colleagues were ordered to open the cold-case files of the Schuessler-Peterson murders and those of the two Grimes sisters and Judith Mae Andersen. (The latter two crimes occurred in 1957.) "We had a lot of circumstantial evidence on one suspect in particular," continued Wilson. "The fellow we were following was employed in Brighton Park, Illinois, at a factory where employees worked with gasket-boring tools. We were certain the hole in the thigh of one of the Grimes girls was made with that tool. Flesh was cut off of the thigh of one of the Schuessler-Peterson boys, too, if I remember correctly. Also, the same fellow had access to chemicals, which were used in the Judith Mae case."[6] According to Wilson, their suspect hung around the Habetler bowling alley on the Northwest Side and was a known homosexual and pedophile. "His wife left him for his mother. I thought that was queer," Wilson said and then paused. "His mother had an old cottage in the Fox Lake area, and we learned that our suspect had lived there. We did a search of the cottage, and what was curious was what we found in a dresser drawer. There were articles about the Schuessler-Peterson boys' murders, the Grimes sisters, and Judith Mae Andersen. It was our opinion that this guy had a lot to do with their deaths."

Whatever horrible secrets Dahlquist may or may not have harbored accompanied him to the grave. He died anonymously and long forgotten in San Mateo, California, on February 16, 1991.

Hot leads were discounted and promising suspects faded away. The Schuessler-Peterson case inevitably drifted into cold-case oblivion—three drawers in a metal filing cabinet at Eleventh and State, crammed with dog-eared file folders gathering the dust of the passing years. Coroner McCarron's callous shot-in-the-dark decision to exhume the bodies revealed nothing that was not already known to police and pathologists. It only served to prolong the personal grief of the Schuesslers, the Petersons, and persons of compassion and goodwill whose prayers of sympathy went out to the families throughout the ordeal.

Taking into account the bitter lessons of October 1955, it would be logical to assume that the principal law-enforcement agencies of Cook County would be better prepared to engage in the next high-profile investigation in a spirit of cooperation and equanimity. The Chicago Police Department had, after all, taken drastic steps to improve efficiency, beginning with a substantial increase in the size of the force. Nearly seven-hundred sworn personnel were added to the duty roster in 1956. For the first time, policewomen were required to wear uniforms and with that came a sense of dignity and greater respect among the public for the important role they played in law enforcement. The SIU unit was kept intact, but the rest of the detective bureau was decentralized in June 1956 and splintered into three geographical sectors—D-1 (south), D-2 (west), and D-3 (north)—to better respond to crimes of the magnitude of the Schuessler-Peterson murders. O'Connor and his deputies did not have to wait long to put their new setup to a most stringent test.

On a cold winter's night, January 22, 1957, motorist Leonard Prescott was passing through a heavily wooded subdivision in the remote southwest suburbs of Chicago when he spotted something unnatural in a culvert behind a guardrail running alongside German Church Road, a narrow two-lane highway. The location was two-hundred feet east of the Cook and Du Page county line. Two tiny, unclad figures were lying motionless in the melting snow. At first, Prescott thought they were discarded department store mannequins. (Victor Livingston had had the same startled reaction when he found the Schuessler-Peterson boys in Robinson Woods.) "Passing over Devil's Creek I saw something in the grass off the highway," Prescott recounted. "I couldn't make out what it was at first. When I stopped the car and looked closer, it looked like a couple of store-front dummies—or like bodies." Prescott raced home to tell his wife, Marie, what he had discovered. Together they returned to the gloomy location to confirm that these were actual human beings—not mannequins.

On February 15, 1995, journalist Ray Gibson of the *Chicago Tribune* received a letter from an anonymous person with whom he had attended grammar school in LaGrange.

I do not wish to divulge my name in order to protect certain individuals. This has to do with the Grime sisters' murder that happened in the late 50's. I think it was 1956 or 1957. . . . Anyway, these two young girls went to see an Elvis Presley movie and were never seen alive again. Some time later they were found dead in the ditch in front of Cathy Werner's house. She lived on German Church road near County Line Road. The police in Summit did bring in some guy and strung him up by his thumbs for a while but he was released. My father worked the night shift at the Fisher Body plant on Willow Springs Rd. He was coming home around midnight the night the girls disappeared, and he saw this man that he worked with in his car with these two young girls and they were parked on 79th street near Willow Springs Rd. He witnessed a struggle in the car but went on. This man lived in Balboa Trailer Park and he had an auto body shop across from the Edgewood Country Club next to that swimming pool and other trailer park on Willow Springs Rd. . . . His name was Joe [D———].[7] I'm not sure if I am spelling the name correct. Anyway, Joe had not been to work that night. The next day when he showed up, his face had many deep scratch marks and his arms were all scratched up. When he was asked how he got the marks he said a cat scratched him. This car that Joe drove was very unusual. It was made in the 1940's and it had a split windshield. The police did say they were looking for that type of a car. After the police announced that, no one ever saw Joe drive this car again. Joe has since died. . . . One of Joes' close friends was a man named Bill Benedict. He worked in the hourly payroll dept at [F]isher [B]ody. In the late 50's, he was sent to jail for killing his wife and her boyfriend. He got out of jail in 1986. Maybe he might know something. Good luck.

The information corroborates much of what was provided by Tony Wilson.

In every way imaginable, this shocking crime was an eerie repeat of the tragic events of October 18, 1955. "It was all the same," wrote Ernest Tucker of the *American*. "Chicago has lived through this before, just fifteen months ago, and the horror of that first shock has not yet worn off. And now this. The similarities are awful and obvious."[8]

Despite exposure to the elements, the remains of the two youthful victims were easily identified as Barbara and Patricia Grimes, ages fifteen and thirteen. The sisters had vanished into thin air the night of December 28, 1956, after attending the Elvis Presley movie *Love Me Tender* at the Brighton Park Theater only a few blocks away from the comfort and safety of their mother's home at 3634 S. Damen Ave.[9] Police at the Brighton Park Station were notified of the disappearance at 11:45 that night.

"So there was the question," the *American*'s Tucker posed. "Had the same killer who drove into Robinson Woods in October 1955 driven into the lonely road near Devil's Creek? If this is true, what lives among us? Who did these things?"

Within minutes, the same men as before—the ones in the long camel's hair coats, fedoras, and horn-rimmed glasses—descended on the crime scene like a plague of locusts, trampling the perimeter and obliterating clues that might have revealed some important bit of information. They fussed and they fumed and speculated on motives to Jack Lavin and the throng of other reporters trailing in their wake.

"This follows the same pattern as the Robinson Woods killings," said Sheriff Lohman. "The same person or persons could have been responsible."

"I have never seen another case like the Grimes and Schuessler-Peterson killings where the clothes have disappeared," said Lieutenant John Ascher of the Chicago crime lab, who during the investigation was promoted to captain.

Dr. Edward A. Kelliher, psychiatrist of the Municipal Court, believed the two cases were intrinsically linked. Dr. Samuel Liebman of the University of Illinois medical school faculty concurred, "It makes no difference to the criminal pedophile whether it's that of a boy or a girl. Youth is the great attraction, and these kids were all around the same age."

The Grimes sisters had been carelessly tossed from an automobile in the same cavalier fashion as the boys but with one important difference. Neither Barbara nor Patricia bore any visible marks of violent struggle. Absent from the girl's bodies were the tell-tale strangulation marks around the neck and the vicious body blows administered by the killer or killers of the three boys. How they died, *where they died*, and the time of death were at the heart of the mystery.[10]

Calling the original autopsies of the Schuessler-Peterson boys badly blundered and "carelessly performed," the *Daily News* warned local law enforcement, "This time there must be no mistakes. In our crazy-quilt patchwork of official jurisdictions it is not easy to achieve complete co-ordination of police effort. This time it must be achieved. No overriding authority can compel it. But absolutely complete coordination of effort must be achieved by voluntary agreement."

The incompetence of the coroner's office was dramatically underscored by the raging controversies to follow. Based on the analysis of their stomach contents, toxicologist Dr. Walter J. R. Camp affixed the time of death as occurring five to six hours after the girls disappeared. Never one to mince words, Harry Glos publicly defied his boss, Walter McCarron, by going to the press and boldly accusing Dr. Camp and pathologist Dr. Jerry Kearns of botching the inquest. With clinical and gruesome exactitude, Glos asserted that the girls were held captive for several weeks and were repeatedly beaten, tortured, and sexually molested. He further stunned reporters by accusing the Chicago P. D. of withholding critical evidence of sexual abuse in order to spare the divorced mother the pain of knowing that her girls were hurt in this way. Chief of Detectives Patrick Deeley was forced to admit the accusation was true but said that departmental secrecy was the only way of aiding the investigation.

With no other recourse in the matter, McCarron fired Glos, who fell happily and contentedly into the arms of Sheriff Lohman, who was about to build a case against a twenty-year-old skid-row hick from Paris, Tennessee, named Edward "Bennie" Bedwell. Bedwell was living in a Salvation Army halfway house and working as a dishwasher when Lohman's men picked him up on suspicion and pried loose a confession to the girls' murders through physical and verbal intimidation. After the Bedwell arrest, Lohman appeared on national television waving a signed confession and posing for photographs, beaming over his success. The press conference drew hostile criticism from editorial writers who reminded the sheriff that in the wake of a terrible tragedy such as this one, it was highly inappropriate for anyone to gloat. Lohman was steadfast in his conviction that Bedwell was responsible. He had no doubt whatsoever, and Glos nodded approvingly. It was their personal moment of triumph, and with certitude, Lohman believed he had effectively demonstrated his abilities as a tough lawman.

With reporters in tow, Under-Sheriff Thomas Brennan personally dragged the dull-witted flophouse hillbilly out to German Church Road. Ignoring strong protests from the American Civil Liberties Union,

Bedwell was forced by Lohman's men to "reenact" the crime. Bedwell concocted a story that played to the press and Lohman's overriding desire to vindicate his earlier failures in the Schuessler-Peterson tragedy.

Despite growing evidence to the contrary, Glos and Lohman refused to waver from the belief that Bedwell was the actual murderer. After being dumped by McCarron, Glos volunteered his services as an unpaid deputy sheriff to help expose a "conspiracy to preserve virtue," one that made it a higher priority to protect the good name and reputation of the girls than prosecute the man authorities believed to be the only viable suspect.

Meanwhile, neither Kearns nor McCarron were able to satisfactorily explain how the Grimes sisters met their deaths or how they were rendered so powerless that they fell victim to the sub-zero temperatures and possibly perished from exposure. The pathologist's final report on the matter concluded that the sisters died from secondary shock and exposure; a coroner's jury sent back a verdict of "murder by persons and means unknown."

The official incompetence evident in these two sets of unsolved murders was fast becoming a national news story after Dr. Alan Moritz blistered the coroner and his staff before the national press corps. "I'm curious," he said, "to know how bad things have to get in Chicago until some real steps are taken in the matter of better medical investigations in violent deaths. It's almost incredible to have this going on in Chicago, known as the medical center of the nation, if not the world."

At first, Benjamin Adamowski, the new Cook County State's Attorney, conditionally accepted Lohman's theory and was prepared to indict Bedwell for murder. But as Adamowski probed deeper, he concluded that Lohman did not have one-tenth the evidence he claimed to have. The confession simply did not jibe with the known medical facts of the case. And Lohman and McCarron were bickering over who was really in charge of the case. The state's attorney became fed up and chastised them both in the strongest of terms. Based on the inconsistencies in Bedwell's story, Adamowski dropped the murder charges and sent him on his way with an apology.[11]

Lashed by criticism, Joe Lohman fared no better than the witless down-and-outer he tried to frame for murder. The Grimes case was a humiliating and near-fatal political setback for the embattled sheriff, who was skewered by the media and skating on thin ice with Mayor Daley and the Cook County Democrats. They had had about enough of well-meaning but ineffective university eggheads. "I'll weather the storm," vowed

Lohman ever so meekly, but any remaining hopes he might have had of running for governor went up in smoke. Before he could reevaluate his future, he had to first prepare to defend himself against the threat of a lawsuit filed by Bedwell's attorney charging false arrest.

A final sad note to the Grimes horror occurred only a few days after the girls were buried. A mystery man speaking in a lowered voice telephoned the grieving mother and threatened her surviving children. "I helped undress your girls," he said. "This isn't over. The next one will be found floating in the river." Mrs. Loretta Grimes notified the police, but the call could not be traced. The poor woman's terror must have been unimaginable after the voice on the other end of the line accurately described how Patricia's little toes on both feet crossed over her fourth toes. Patricia crossed her toes out of habit. Her toes were not crossed in death. This information had never been previously divulged to any police officer or reporter attached to the investigation. Mrs. Grimes told reporters that she was convinced the same madman who killed her daughters also murdered Judith Mae Andersen and the Schuessler-Peterson boys. There are many people today who still subscribe to that notion.[12]

A sense of frustration and outrage over the endless contretemps and heavy-handed tactics among the politicians and heads of the major law-enforcement agencies seared the public conscience. In February 1957, Illinois State Senator Robert J. Graham called upon the General Assembly to investigate the larger failure of the city and county authorities to contain lawlessness and solve the murders. The agencies "are now withholding information from each other and are generally hurting the possibility of catching the killers," Graham asserted. "Somebody is fooling somebody when these authorities go off in all directions and make conflicting statements." Graham, a Democrat out of Chicago, called for the formation of a five-member committee with subpoena powers to investigate, but the Republican Senate majority leader Arthur J. Bidwell said it was not the Senate's concern. "It is no responsibility of the Senate how authorities in Cook County investigate murder cases. They were elected to function as they do, and presumably if they don't do a good job voters will take care of the situation. It's their problem and they will work it out."

The voters of Cook County, as Senator Bidwell correctly prophesied, would have the final say in their choice of elected officials involved in law enforcement. And after the Schuessler-Peterson case had run its course, the public had had their fill and soundly rejected John Gutknecht in his bid for another four years as state's attorney. His defeat was as much a public referendum on the Schuessler-Peterson murders as it was a political blow to the party. Gutknecht's opponent was Benjamin Adamowski, a turncoat Democrat pledged to fight the Daley Machine and drop the hammer on rampant waste and corruption in Cook County. One example of questionable practices emanating from the state's attorney's office was the awarding of secret cash bonuses. It was common practice in those days for Gutknecht (and his predecessors) to pay certain preferred assistants a monthly cash stipend, in addition to their paycheck, from a secret contingent account. In 1956, Gutknecht drew heavily from the contingent fund to award staffers kickbacks ranging from $100 to $1,100 a month. In a campaign pockmarked by personal attacks and massive vote fraud, Adamowski, a self-styled reformer, prevailed. His stunning upset marked the first time in twenty-four years that the Democrats had lost control of the state's attorney's office. Two months into his term, the Grimes girls were slain, and Adamowski's overwhelming self-assurance withered in the face of the Bedwell storm.[13]

Walter McCarron, Cook County's brusque and outspoken coroner, built his political strength on the financial and voting support of the members of his Illinois Motor Truck Operators Association, which he headed for twenty-five years. They served him well throughout the 1950s as he bridged the divergent worlds of business and public service. McCarron always maintained that the duties of the coroner were administrative and not medical, but after he had blundered the two most horrendous murder investigations of the decade, the entire office and the qualifications of the man who occupied it for eight years were reevaluated and found wanting.

The ineffectualness of this political animal was dramatically underscored once again during the inquest into the Our Lady of Angels School fire on December 1, 1958. Eighty-seven children and three nuns perished inside this West Side firetrap because the building lacked fire doors and other preventive measures to stop the flames from shooting up the stairwells. It was easily ascertained that the blaze had been deliberately set by an underage pyromaniac, who was later institutionalized. McCarron, however, was evasive in his responses to the hard questions being asked of him by anguished parents. He refused to affix blame, admit the possibility of criminal arson, or hold the archdiocese directly accountable for what was so obviously a case of gross negligence.

The realization took hold that it was time to unshackle Cook County from the politics and patronage of the antiquated coroner system. The legal hearing into the Lady of Angels fire conducted by the deputy coroner and a six-person jury was farcical, and the press made jokes about it. The Grimes case and, to a lesser extent, the Schuessler-Peterson postmortem illustrated that the coroner and his designates were impotent except in the most routine death inquests. In 1959, McCarron followed up on recommendations from a citizens' committee and hired a full-time chief pathologist, but it was not enough to assuage the dissatisfaction of the public. The Our Lady of Angels School fire was the final straw. Immediate adoption of the medical-examiner system was strongly urged.

A tireless campaigner, McCarron ran for reelection in 1960 and was confident of victory, but this time, the Democrats pulled an ace out of their sleeve by slating Dr. Andrew J. Toman, a physician who was also the son of a well-known former sheriff. Toman was a respected surgeon and something of an expert on gunshot wounds. His message to the voters was simple and direct—a doctor for doctor's job. Toman promised to push for the medical-examiner system for public inquests in determining causes of death.

To the charge that his office was a poorly functioning political trough impeding law enforcement every step of the way, McCarron fired back, "The coroner's office performs an important function. It serves as a check and balance to the police department and the State's Attorney's office." One of the strongest arguments for abolishing the coroner's office was given by one of McCarron's presumed allies, Assistant State's Attorney Robert Cooney, during the inquest into the murder of Judith Mae Andersen: "I've never known a coroner's inquest to do one thing toward solving a crime. Instead it usually raises obstacles in the prosecution of suspects."

Weighing the evidence and his rather dismal eight-year record, the voters found the coroner's argument no match for Toman's irrefutable logic concerning the urgency of properly trained MDs running this office. McCarron went down to defeat and was washed up politically, but because the wheels of reform turn slowly in Cook County, the appointment of the medical examiner was put on hold—and would languish on the drawing board for the next sixteen years. Toman served four terms of office as coroner before the office was permanently abolished on December 6, 1976.

McCarron's much-maligned sidekick Harry Glos hoped to succeed Joseph Lohman as Cook County sheriff. He entered the political arena on a wing and a prayer in 1958 but was unable to wrest the nomination away from Peter J. McGuire, veteran chief investigator for the Illinois attorney general, who secured the blessing and endorsement of the GOP party regulars. Nobody in Cook County expected Glos to win, and he didn't. It was McGuire's margin of victory that left political observers gasping in astonishment. Peter McGuire polled 99,000 votes to Glos's paltry 25,188. Statehouse reporters made a fast beeline to the library to see if there had ever been an Illinois candidate who endured a worse royal thumping than poor Harry.

In 1961, after an awkward interval of time had passed, the embittered Glos severed all ties with the Republican party. He switched allegiance to the Democrats and volunteered his services to Governor Otto Kerner and the party stalwarts in Springfield. Except for a stint as police chief of Northlake, Illinois, Glos's ambitions were mostly thwarted and his accomplishments overlooked until the mid-1990s when ATF agents examined his case files, which contained voluminous reports and correspondence pertaining to the original Schuessler-Peterson investigation. In the end, death cheated Harry Glos out of the opportunity to vindicate his controversial handling of Chicago's unsolved child murders. Glos passed away in May 1994 at age eighty, before he had the chance to articulate his controversial theories to a new generation of law-enforcement officials eager to hear what he had to say.

The Schuessler-Peterson boys were in the ground less than a year when Sheriff Joe Lohman submitted his resume to the county slate-makers for promotion. "I would be a good candidate [for governor] out to win as soon as I am picked," he said, firing salvos at his archenemy, Governor Stratton. Mayor Daley and his Democratic strategists took a pass on a man they considered a loose cannon and chose instead Judge Richard B. Austin as their party's standard-bearer for the 1956 election. Lohman took the snub personally and fought back by forming a coalition of independents to buck Daley, whose name was added to the peevish sheriff's expanding roster of enemies.

Because a Cook County sheriff could not stand for reelection once his four-year term expired, in 1958 Lohman found himself adrift and on the verge of exile to the political desert. One faction of Democrats touted him for the post of state school superintendent, citing his academic background and growing popularity on the lecture circuit. Lohman was an articulate and facile speaker (albeit an often tactless one), but the Schuessler-Peterson and Grimes murders had left a bitter taste in the mouths of many party stalwarts. A compromise was struck, and Lohman was slated to run for state treasurer, but it was not the political payoff that he had envisioned.

Helped by a landslide in Cook County, Lohman confounded political analysts and managed to pull off a surprise election-day victory with precious little support coming from his own party. Lohman made political hay out of Daley's mistrust and dislike, convincing skeptical downstaters that he was a party independent with no machine ties. Reforming the treasurer's office, however, was not nearly enough of an ego trip to satisfy Lohman's insatiable ambition. He tried again in 1960 for the gubernatorial nomination but was passed over a second time. But he wasn't through, not quite yet. Lohman expressed interest in becoming the Democratic candidate for the U.S. Senate in 1962, but after disparaging Daley and calling him a "political boss," he was frozen out.

Frustrated, and undoubtedly resentful, by the turn of events, the roly-poly little malcontent who "talked like a textbook" left political life and fled the State of Illinois on May 21, 1961. With two years left to go as state treasurer, he walked off the job to accept the deanship of the School of Criminology at the University of California. Few tears were shed when the news of his departure circulated through City Hall. Joe Lohman resumed his nomadic life in Berkeley where the campus longhairs expressed far greater admiration for his scholarly aptitude than he was ever shown by the Chicago pols.

In 1959, Patrick Deeley was promoted to captain and given command of Jefferson Park—though his departure from the detective bureau can hardly be considered a strong vote of confidence from the departmental brass. Deeley's colorful forty-year career in Chicago law enforcement bridged the eras of gangster Al Capone and protestor Abbie Hoffman. Confident and robust following his official retirement from the Chicago P. D. in January 1970, the tireless gumshoe finagled a plush patronage job as an investigator assigned to Mayor Daley's office. He was hired to ferret out corruption and malfeasance in Chicago. Did he find any? The political wags lunching at the Blackhawk and Drake's Mayor's Row Restaurant in the shadow of City Hall were grimly amused. Whatever else may have been said about the spate of unsolved murders occurring under his watch, there was no denying Pat Deeley had an in with the right people. In Chicago, the word most often used to describe this characteristic is clout.

If there was such a thing as a "Schuessler-Peterson curse" attached to the failed investigation, then Commissioner Tim O'Connor, the buoyant "last honest man" in the Chicago Police cadre, suffered the most from it. After weathering a storm of criticism for his department's handling of the Schuessler-Peterson, Grimes, and Judith Mae Andersen murders, O'Connor was blindsided by the worst police-corruption scandal to occur in fifty years.

In January 1960, eight uniformed officers were arrested and indicted for burglarizing a string of North Side retail stores. Ben Adamowski "made" the case, and the Summerdale Police Scandal, as it is recorded in the history books, was a pox on the department that cost O'Connor his job and his good reputation. Even though Commissioner Tim had nothing to do with the thievery and always boasted that his evenings home with his wife was "time well spent," the indignant Mayor Daley fired back that maybe if he had spent more time on the street looking after his men instead of watching television, the integrity of the department might not have been so shamelessly compromised.

The political Sturm und Drang was of little more than passing interest to the family and friends directly affected by one of Chicago's most horrific child murders. Reforming the mechanisms of law enforcement and the endless finger-pointing and bickering among bureaucrats would never bring their boys back. One year to the day of the murders, Commissioner O'Connor reaffirmed his pledge to keep the Schuessler-Peterson investigation going. Lieutenant Joseph Morris, transferred from the Scotland Yard detail for political reasons and placed in charge of the twenty-seven-member special unit, vowed "that the killers would be caught . . . even if it took five years."

"In the year police have interviewed more than 38,000 persons and questioned 1,700 suspects," the *Tribune* noted. "They have solved more than 100 sex crimes. All Chicago, except the killers, hopes that the next one to be solved will be the 'triple murder.'"

In 1961, following the Summerdale-scandal embarrassment, the new Police Superintendent Orlando W. Wilson eliminated layers of bureaucracy by consolidating the thirty-eight police districts into twenty-one districts during a major departmental reorganization. The Thirty-Third District became the Sixteenth District within Area 5, and Captain Corcoran was succeeded by Jim Rochford, who later went on to become superintendent of police in the 1970s.[14]

Beginning on March 15, 1961, the D-1, D-2, and D-3 geographic setup—a reactive measure put in place in June 1956 to address the failures of the Schuessler-Peterson investigation—was eliminated in favor of a new, unified command structure with detectives deployed to each of the six area headquarters. The new chief of detectives replacing Lieutenant James McMahon was Captain Maurice Begner, who organized a special investigative unit in 1961 to take a second look at the Schuessler-Peterson case and the other unsolved child murders in the Chicagoland area. Though well intentioned and worth the commitment of personnel and resources, this latest effort yielded nothing new.

Maurice Begner assumed command of the Sixteenth District in 1963. After his sudden and tragic death in an airplane crash in the interior of Mexico in September 1969, a succession of new men followed, each younger than the last, until the inevitable day arrived when there was no one left in Sixteen with living memories of the Schuessler-Peterson nightmare.

8

Suspects in the Shadows

IN THE LAST WEEK of June 1957, four months shy of the two-year anniversary of the murders, an intriguing new lead arrived that ultimately pointed in the direction of a man whose nefarious deeds would one day make headlines around the world. John Sarnowski and his partner, Edwin Kocinski, called on Dorothy Peterson one afternoon with the intention of searching Bobby's room. It was an admitted long shot, but Sarnowski was playing a hunch that the police may have missed something in earlier investigations. One thing always had bothered him. Why had his parents let Bobby go downtown like that—given his age and all? Chicago homicide detective John Sarnowski was one of the original fifty-two detectives assigned to the special task force to lead the Schuessler-Peterson probe but one of only a handful who kept at it and pursued leads even after the investigation had been tossed into the cold-case file. Promoted to the detective bureau in 1954 when he was only twenty-four, Sarnowski did not have a whole lot of practical experience behind him, but he had good street sense and was extremely tenacious. Sarnowski believed that he could penetrate the enigma that was the Schuessler-Peterson case.

At the Peterson house, Sarnowski chatted pleasantly with Bobby's seven-year-old sister, Barbara Ann, and noticed that she wore eyeglasses. When he asked her mother who her daughter's eye doctor was (Sarnowski's son suffered from poor vision, and he was curious), Dorothy revealed that Bobby had often escorted his sister to Room 820 of the Garland Building, where Maria Gonzalez, an eye-training technician, kept an office. Barbara Ann first began eye-exercise therapy in July 1954. Her most recent trip downtown with Bobby occurred on October 12, 1955—Columbus Day—a public holiday for all Chicago schoolchildren. His interest piqued, Sarnowski wondered if there was a chance that Bobby might have visited the building the same day that he disappeared.

And so, twenty months after the crimes were committed, Sarnowski and Kocinski interviewed Thomas Meehan, the twenty-seven-year-old elevator operator on duty at the Garland Building the day of the boys' disappearance. By a stroke of luck, the sign-in sheet maintained by Meehan on October 16 was still on file in the security office of the building and available for inspection. Mrs. Darling, the custodian for the records, presented the ledger to the two detectives. To their complete astonishment, the detectives found Robert Peterson's signature. He was one of twenty-three people who signed Meehan's logbook that day. Lieutenant David Purtell of the Chicago Police crime lab compared it to Bobby's handwriting samples from Farnsworth School and verified its authenticity.

The Peterson boy had affixed his name to the sheet at 6:00 PM and signed out at 6:05 PM, proving beyond a doubt that the boys had been downtown and likely sat through at least an hour and a half of the intended double feature or perhaps some other movie in the Loop. Meehan recalled that Peterson took the elevator alone up to the washroom facility on the ninth floor, while his friends waited in the lobby. Meehan told Sarnowski that he had refused to allow all three boys to go upstairs. Puzzled as to why the watchman had not reported this visit during the course of the police investigation, Meehan explained that he only read the Irish newspapers and never watched television. He said that he did not know anything about the disappearance and murders of three boys.

The eye therapist added another curious twist. Gonzalez said that on at least three different occasions between July 1954 and October 12, 1955, an older boy with a DA haircut—the style favored by the 1950s' "greaser" crowd—wandered into her waiting room. She remembered that on one occasion, the youth leaned over and spoke in low tones to Bobby, who seemed agitated and was doing his best to ignore him. "Do you have any business in here?" demanded Gonzalez. The boy shrugged his shoulders impassively and exited the office. Gonzalez remembered that the sinister-looking youth walked with a noticeable limp and, in an odd sort of way, reminded her of Mr. Potato Head, a popular toy in the 1950s. She described the youth as being seventeen to nineteen years old and standing five-foot ten-inches tall with heavy shoulders and a broad chest. He wore a beach shirt with an unusually loud floral pattern and spoke with several of the other children waiting for their appointments. "After I ordered him out of my office, he walked away, appearing to be walking off balance, sort of listing to the right," the dark-haired, middle-aged practitioner told the police. "He had such a strange look in his eyes that I thought he must be a patient of some psychiatrist in the building. He had a high forehead set over a small face, but his cheeks seemed to be fat.

"There is at least the possibility that he and the Peterson boy met by prearrangement," she conceded.

Maria Gonzalez, with a busy downtown office and a full appointment book, failed to connect the slain boy dumped in Robinson Woods with his two friends to her patient, Barbara Ann Peterson, until June 1957. Dorothy Peterson provided a simple explanation. "I have been there a number of times with Barbara Ann since it happened, and I have never spoken of it. Curiously enough, even our own insurance man didn't connect the family association for some time after it occurred."

The Loop eye technician expressed grave fears for her own safety. "I haven't had any police protection, and I don't want to be the next card of the deck," Gonzalez anxiously told reporters who honored her request that her home address not be published in the newspapers. Assured of anonymity, and protection, Gonzalez fully cooperated with the SIU and provided an accurate description of the suspect. The unit sprang into action. Eight officers under the direction of Sergeant John Hartigan set up a temporary command post on the fifteenth floor of the Garland Building in a suite formerly occupied by a beauty shop. Police learned that only three people including Meehan were working in the Garland Building on October 16. All were questioned and cleared.

Meanwhile, police artist Adolph Valanis prepared a drawing of the suspect based on Gonzalez's best recollections. After Valanis finished his sketching, he turned to Maria and with a look of alarm registering on his face, he said, "I have drawn this man's face before." Arising from his chair, Valanis opened a cluttered filing cabinet and rifled through his folders until he pulled out a drawing of a man bearing a remarkable resemblance to the Garland Building youth. "Does this look familiar to you?" he asked, handing the sketch to the shaken Gonzalez. The subject depicted by Valanis in the older drawing was a likeness of one of two men who had abducted a twenty-two-year-old woman from her parked car at 703 N. Central Ave. on October 18, 1956—a year from the very date the Schuessler-Peterson boys were found in the woods.[1]

A few days after Gonzalez provided her description to the police artist, a North Side cabdriver said that he had spotted the Garland Building suspect loitering near his taxi stand at Bryn Mawr and Clark Street. The cabbie based his conclusion on Valanis's drawing of the mystery man who had appeared in the afternoon *American*. His call was one of five thousand tips about the limping man received by the SIU in the next few days. "The guy caught my eye because of his peculiar walk, like he was walking on air with a little bounce," the driver recalled. "And he had very big upper arms . . . all out of proportion to his body, as though he was a weight lifter. Also, he had very blond hair combed straight back and sticking up a bit." Ironically, the taxicab driver insisting that he stood face to face on Clark Street with the man the police were seeking was named John *Gracey*.[2]

The drawing of the blond-haired suspect struck a responsive chord with Terry Reilly, a former schoolmate of Bobby's who had once accompanied Bobby and Barbara Ann to the eye therapist in the Garland Building. Reilly moved to Memphis, Tennessee, with his family not long after the triple murders. Detective Sarnowski traveled to Memphis to interview the fifteen-year-old and to see if the Valanis sketch triggered a spark of recognition. Although Reilly did not remember seeing such a person on his visit to the Garland Building, he said the sketch bore a strong resemblance to an individual he remembered terrorizing the playground at Farnsworth School. He went on to say that that man was much taller, however, and had a name.

"'Frankenstein' was a big guy who used to chase the kids around the block making gestures," Reilly said. The Farnsworth children knew the boy as "Willie" but tagged him with the Frankenstein moniker shortly after the murders. Reilly, however, did not think that this eccentric bully walked with a limp and vividly remembered loitering inside Find's Candy Store, 5301 Berwyn Ave., with friends one afternoon when Willie suddenly appeared. The tiny corner candy store fronting busy Central Avenue was only half a block away from the Peterson residence on Farragut, and Bobby, John, and Anton knew Willie because Find's was where the local kids bought and swapped Topp's baseball cards and chugged Kayo.[3] The Schuessler brothers, Reilly said with conviction, were terrified of the thuggish Willie.

For classmate Paul Garland of Forest Glen, the candy store was well off the beaten path, but even so he had been there: "Kids from different areas played in their own neighborhoods after school. Find's Candy Store was a store Farnsworth kids visited at lunchtime. I don't know if kids hung out there after school, but I bought my first *Mad Magazine* there."

Judy Varley, whose older brother had been a classmate of Anton Jr. at Farnsworth School, has only vague recollections of Frankenstein and those strangely innocent but violent times. "As kids, we were so free and easy until those murders," she said. "I was eight when they were killed, and I remember a small park near Beaubien Elementary School. My mother always told me to stay out of it because there was a strange man rumored to be harassing kids there." Varley, who now resides in Calgary, Alberta, did not think much of it at the time. When a kid is eight and feeling secure in his or her surroundings, stern parental warnings often go in one ear and out the other. "I went to the park all the time and never witnessed anything unusual. Needless to say, I didn't always listen to my mother."

Lieutenant Joseph Morris was convinced that Terry Reilly was telling the truth and ordered an immediate search of the area for the neighborhood tough known only as Frankenstein. But if Frankenstein existed at all, he could not be found in the Farnsworth or Beaubien areas.

Detective Sarnowski and his partner retraced their steps back to the Peterson household for another interview with Barbara Ann. Sarnowski asked her to describe what she might have observed inside the waiting room at the Garland Building.[4]

QUESTION: Did you ever see any strange men in Miss Gonzalez's office who tried to talk to Bobby or to you?

ANSWER: No, I never did. I would always go right into the other room to have my eye exercises with the other children, and I couldn't see Bobby when I was in there.

QUESTION: Did you ever see any men in the outer office with their children?

ANSWER: Hardly ever. Mostly the mothers brought their children or maybe their brothers or sisters did.

QUESTION: Did anyone go with you besides Bobby?

ANSWER: Sometimes my mother took me, and a couple of times
    Johnny Schuessler went with Bobby and me.
QUESTION: Did you ever see any man try to talk to Bobby?
ANSWER: No. Johnny and Bobby just sat together and waited for me.
QUESTION: Were Johnny and Bobby always nice to you?
ANSWER: Oh, yes, they were awfully nice.

A year later, in 1958, a troubled teen matching the original description supplied by Maria Gonzalez was admitted to Northwest Hospital after suffering repeated seizures. Disoriented and confused, the muscular boy was found lying on the floor of his room babbling. "I didn't do it! I didn't do it!" he cried hysterically. The psychotic youth who was checked into the hospital that night in 1958 was John Wayne Gacy—destined to become one of the worst serial killers of the twentieth century.[5] What it was that he didn't do remains a mystery.

In December 1978, just after the news of Gacy's crimes made the national wire, John Sarnowski thumbed through the yellowing pages of his Schuessler-Peterson case file and began to fixate on the 1957 Valanis rendering, comparing it to the mug shots of the adult Gacy. It was a wild leap of imagination, but Sarnowski, who was by then retired, cobbled together a highly speculative theory that the thirteen-year-old but no less lethal John Wayne Gacy was Mr. Potato Head and had murdered the Schuessler-Peterson boys.

Sarnowski based his entire theory on that one police sketch and the hearsay of Terry Reilly and Detective Robert Ekenborg, who back in 1955 had rousted the denizens of Henri's Tavern, a gay bar at 4734 N. Milwaukee Ave. in Jeff Park. The hunt for the "pervert," "fruit," or "sex fiend" they believed abducted and killed the Schuessler-Peterson boys inevitably led police to the underground haunts of the gay community, which hid under a cloak of darkness in the moral climate of the mid-1950s. Granger's out on Mannheim Road in Franklin Park was another such place. There, undercover Chicago cops posing as gay men to gain intelligence angered the owner of the establishment. "I don't mind the guys here getting butt-fucked," he said. "What I do mind is the cops fucking them!" Henri's also was closely watched. The fearful clientele had to keep one eye on the front door for the sudden arrival of the Cook County Sheriff's Police working "pervert patrol" and looking to arrest and incarcerate gay men loitering inside the tavern. Law enforcement and the judicial system in the 1950s considered homosexuality a crime of moral turpitude and not a lifestyle.

Hours after the discovery of the lifeless forms of the Schuessler-Peterson boys, an anonymous tipster phoned the newspapers and the Chicago Police to let them know that the "joint [Henri's] was a favorite gathering place for perverts." Owner Larry Smith conceded that "a certain percentage of the men who frequent the place are of the homosexual type." Detective Ekenborg, following up on the tip, seized a teenage boy inside the tavern but let him go because of his youth. In hindsight, he believed the boy was Mr. Potato Head and, by extension, the deranged serial killer whom the world would eventually come to know as John Wayne Gacy.

In 1955, Gacy was only thirteen but already causing trouble for his teachers at Prussing Elementary School, 4650 N. Menard Ave. A victim of his father's repeated alcohol-induced tirades and beatings, Gacy spent his unhappy teenage years in a common brick bungalow at 4505 Marmora Ave. According to Chicago writer Richard Vachula, who published Sarnowski's intriguing hypothesis in a 1989 *Chicago Magazine* article, "Gacy was introduced to hustling at the Garland Building, that he hung out there, that he may have first met Robert Peterson there, and that when Peterson went to the Garland Building on the evening of the murder, he was looking for Gacy, perhaps by prior arrangement."

By Sarnowski's own admission, the idea of a thirteen-year-old overpowering and murdering three boys close to his own age did not seem believable at first blush. But as he probed deeper, he discovered that a Gacy uncle named Raymond Robertson lived just seven doors away from the Petersons on Farragut. There was a strong probability that Bobby knew and associated with Gacy, who moved into the neighborhood in 1952. The boys attended different schools but occasionally crossed paths at neighborhood hangouts—the candy store, Whealan Pool in the summertime, and nearby Jensen Toboggan Slides after the winter snows accumulated. According to Gacy's former classmates, John was an above-average bowler, and the Monte Cristo was one of his favorite hardwood lanes. Sarnowski hypothesized that it was at the seedy Montrose Avenue bowling alley where Gacy lured the Schuessler-Peterson boys to their deaths.

While their movements earlier in the day remain in dispute, it is accepted as fact that Bobby, Anton, and John returned to the Monte Cristo between 7:15 and 7:45 PM, looking to bowl a game or two before calling a night. However, all the lanes were occupied, even at this late hour. Ernest Niewadomski, the teenaged youth who bumped into the boys at the bowling alley that night, never noticed a "puffy-faced" boy (i.e., Mr. Potato Head) in their company. Gacy was a braggart and an overbearing loudmouth who most likely would not have been able to resist the impulse to intrude into the conversation if, in fact, he was with the boys on that fateful night. If the Schuessler-Peterson boys had no money to bowl, why were they so intent upon finding an alley? And was John Wayne Gacy with them?

Detective Sarnowski conjectured that the sly Gacy stood off to the side, shuffling nervously and biding his time until Niewadomski walked away. Then he made his move. Sarnowski offered the following scenario as a conjecture as to how Gacy drew in the boys: "C'mon, let's go over to my house. What do you say? I got some stuff I want to show you." Bobby and the Schuesslers followed John back to Marmora Avenue. There, he allegedly fed them a bowl of noodle soup from a pot that his mother had left on the stove for him earlier in the day. (Gacy's parents were conveniently away.) When they finished eating, Gacy, according to the theory, convinced the boys to follow him into the dirt-floored garage where he promised to show them a special kind of "rope trick" he had devised or, in the opinion of a preeminent psychiatrist Richard Vachula interviewed in the course of Sarnowski's research, to initiate them into a "secret society" he had invented. Sticking to the theory, the boys were caught off-guard, overpowered, and viciously assaulted by Gacy, who clubbed them with a garden tool before binding them up with a length of rope.

How could it be possible for the plodding Gacy to subdue three boys near his own age inside a tiny garage without one of them escaping into the alley or the neighbors hearing their anguished screams and becoming suspicious? In order for this farfetched scenario to play out, John Wayne Gacy would have had to load the three lifeless bodies into the trunk of the family Packard. When the senior Gacy came home, John would have had to convince his raging, alcoholic father to agree to become an accomplice to a murder cover-up. It is extremely unlikely that either the peevish John Stanley Gacy or his silent and browbeaten wife, Marion, would have become a party to such a scheme. It is possible the boys might have known Gacy or associated with him at the neighborhood playgrounds and bowling alleys, but it is almost certain that this "puffy-faced" boy was *not* the actual murderer. Gacy stood five-foot-eight inches tall and weighed 210 pounds. The man that Maria Gonzalez described to police was at least five-feet-ten-inches tall and had much lighter hair. The cops never learned the identity of the Frankenstein character who struck terror among school-aged children in 1955. Frankenstein and Mr. Potato Head seem to be two different people, but in Sarnowski's overheated imagination, they became the manifestation of one terrifying presence—John Wayne Gacy, the epitome of all earthly evil.

Detective Sarnowski, an otherwise capable and conscientious officer, went to his grave embittered. Sarnowski and his colleagues assigned to the Garland Building detail questioned five hundred tenants and known visitors on the Sunday evening in question. He and his partner, Edwin Kocinski, spent the next five frustrating years working every conceivable angle, even after his boss, Lieutenant Morris, offered him the chance to go back to his unit in the district and be reassigned to another case where there was a possibility of attaining closure. Armed with highly charged but unverifiable circumstantial evidence, Sarnowski tried to convince his superiors in the Chicago Police Department of the legitimacy of his theory, but the brass was uncooperative, and Gacy, languishing on death row, certainly wasn't talking. Failing to interest local law enforcement in pursuing the investigation any further, Sarnowski indignantly accused the department of covering up their blundering incompetence by turning a blind eye to what he perceived to be the raw truth about one of Chicago's most insidious crimes. While it is a compelling yarn that adds a dash of mystery and intrigue to the case, Sarnowski's theory is unsupported and simply not believable. The neighborhood children identified the neighborhood bully, the Frankenstein of the parks and playgrounds, only as "Willie." There is no record of John Wayne Gacy ever answering to that name.

The inquest into the unsolved Schuessler-Peterson murders was officially closed on November 27, 1961, with a verdict of murder by "person or persons unknown." The inquest was closed so that permanent death certificates could be issued for the boys. Police estimated that a "minimum" of a hundred hours a month were given over to the investigation from 1955 to 1961.

9

Wild Horsemen

ILLINOIS HORSE COUNTRY IS the fashionable acreage of Lake, McHenry, and Kane counties where the wealthy social elite gather to appraise prized thoroughbreds and indulge their children with ponies and riding lessons. A figure that loomed large in that particular milieu was millionaire sportsman Silas Jayne, a man with a dark and sordid past, the supreme overlord of a gang of horse-trading swindlers known as the Equestrian Mafia or Horse Mafia.

If a person is known by the company he keeps, then the genteel folk residing in the stately mansions of the nouveaux riche ought to have been more careful. Si Jayne was a brawling roughneck in a sheltered world of style and grace. The rich upper crust, however, did understand the rules of the game as had been set down for generations in the broad green pastures behind the white-railed fences of horse country. And the rules of this particular game decreed that if one wanted to gain entrée into the world of pure-bred show horses, sooner or later it would come down to doing business with Si and his kin, otherwise known as the Jayne Gang. This was not a term of endearment or anything to be taken lightly. Investigators uncovering a litany of crimes ranging from the doping of horses and insurance fraud to car bombs and murder-for-hire schemes tagged the Jayne Gang and their confederates for what they really were, a sinister organization engaged in crime that was allowed to flourish amid affluence and privilege.

From Lake County, well north of Chicago, stretching to the distant southwestern suburbs, the Jayne Gang and their allies established a chain of profitable riding stables catering to the eclectic tastes of wealthy Chicagoans and suburbanites anticipating the day when their privileged offspring would cart home blue ribbons in organized show competition. "Riding in show" is the dream of every little girl who fancies horses. Well-intentioned parents with the means to pay for Saturday morning lessons, riding getup, and tack eagerly obliged, if for no other reason than to bring joy into the eyes of their daughters.

The popular culture of the 1950s promoted Western folk heroes, clean air, and the wide-open spaces. It encouraged baby boomers at an early age to get up off the couch and learn to ride the dusty trails. Wholesome depictions of ranch life touting the adventures of happy-go-lucky stable hands grooming their horses in such popular serializations as *Spin and Marty*,[1] proved an irresistible lure for preadolescents weaned on television. According to published newspaper reports, in 1955 Robert Peterson and some of his pals from church and school lived out their dreams of horses and cowboys and ranch life at Silas Jayne's Idle Hour Stable in Park Ridge. (However, there is no information that the Schuessler brothers rode horses at the Idle Hour.)

"If parents only knew the kind of things that went on in some of those stables, they wouldn't allow their sons and daughters within a thousand feet," opined Jimmy Delorto, speaking to young parents of the Dr. Spock generation who "only wanted to do what was right" by their kids. "Not knowing any better, parents dropped their kids off with perverts and sex idiots, and what went on after that often went unreported."

To minimize overhead, disreputable stable owners tapped into a readily available and abundant labor pool of runaways, grifters, petty crooks, pedophiles, and other aberrant types who were circumspect about revealing too much of their past. But in the twilight world of horse breeding, championship competition, and the buying and selling of million-dollar "hunters and jumpers," the stable owners were nondiscriminatory in their hiring practices for all the wrong reasons.[2] Character references and background checks normally required of job applicants were not a prerequisite to employment. Suspicious characters were routinely recruited to perform menial tasks. In return, they were allotted three square meals a day, a place to bunk for the night, and a few bucks rubber-banded together and distributed at the end of the week—it was a cash business, and the IRS was none the wiser.

There was always the chance that the mentoring relationship between a rakish young trainer and his callow teenaged charge, dropped off for a riding lesson on a Saturday morning by mom and dad, could easily evolve into something far less wholesome than a pleasing canter around the corral perched atop gentle old Buckshot. Delorto, as well as other officers, believes the character of some of these stables was unwholesome: "Let's say the lesson starts at ten and is supposed to be over in an hour or an hour and a half, but then around noon the parents get a call from their daughter telling them not to come around until four in the afternoon because she's been asked to 'help out' around the stable with the grooming of the horses. Well, is she really grooming the horses, or is she sexually involved with her trainer?" Occasionally, the victim would confess to mom and dad, or the parent would stumble across the ugly truth quite by accident, but social pressures and the threat of public humiliation and an ensuing scandal likely to devastate the girl's reputation for years to come reinforced a strict code of silence—one that allowed the illicit seduction of minors by pedophiles engaged in the horse business to go unpunished. Boys were equally at risk from sexual predators.

Kenneth Hansen was a city boy. But he had been around horses for much of his life. The youngest of four children born to Ethan and Lucille Hansen—second-generation Norwegians—Ken was an intelligent boy, handsome and well liked by his classmates.

In the worst years of the Great Depression, the Works Progress Administration (WPA) employed Ethan. Lucille, suffering from poor eyesight, had dreams of a musical career. Despite her handicap, Ken's mother was an accomplished piano player, who, according to her grandson Mark, gave comedienne Joan Rivers her first lessons on the keyboard. During the Depression while her husband worked for the WPA, Lucille performed at local taverns. The Hansen family lived in a tiny flat at 421 N. Claremont Ave. on the Near Northwest Side of the city, not far from where the Schuesslers resided in the early years of their marriage. Ethan and Lucille were industrious people. They went to church and attended to their three children—Curtis, Marion, and Kenneth—as best as their limited finances would allow in those tough times. A fourth child had died years earlier in an accident.

Tragedy nearly claimed the lives of the surviving Hansen kids the night of April 22, 1936. Ethan had left twelve-year-old Curtis in charge of the little ones while he went over to pick up Lucille, who was attending a church social. An hour after Curtis read his brother and sister to sleep, a fire of unexplained origin broke out underneath the porch. Flames shot high into the air, threatening to consume the entire building. With dense smoke rolling in, Curt Hansen staggered from his bed to rouse his siblings. He picked up three-year-old Ken and ordered his sister to grab hold of his shirttails and follow him through the front door. "Then I called the neighbor on the floor below, left Marion and the baby with him, and ran for the policeman on the beat," Curtis told reporters. Curtis Hansen was "the idol of the neighborhood" for his gallantry, the *Chicago Herald & Examiner* beamed. A photo of the Hansen brothers appeared in the paper the next day. The older boy was proclaimed a hero and presented with a silver cup as a reward.

When World War II came, Curtis "the Fearless" enlisted in the Marines and was shipped off to the South Pacific to fight the Japanese island by island. His record was exemplary, and Kenny grew up holding his big brother in awe, although they were never particularly close given their eight-year age difference. Curtis was tough and assertive. Kenny, according to his son Mark, was the polar opposite of his brother. He was nonconfrontational and would avoid entanglements at all costs. Mark Hansen said his father hated hospitals, lawyers, and bloodshed. "He was like that his whole life. A rider gets hurt at his stable? Bang! He's outta there!"

In the late 1940s, Ethan and Lucille Hansen moved north, settling along the lakefront in the Scandinavian neighborhood known to Chicagoans as Andersonville. Kenny enrolled at Amundsen High School, an imposing redbrick fortress at the intersection of Damen and Foster avenues. Within the school's austere corridors, Kenny met and courted his future wife, Beverly Rae Carlson—"red head, radiant, real swell"—or so it was inscribed along side her graduation portrait appearing in the 1951 Viking, the Amundsen High School yearbook.

From the time they were children, Ken Hansen and Beverly were inseparable. "I was probably twelve, and there was an empty store front at 2332 Winnemac, so I rented the store because I was making plaster novelties, and Beverly came in to buy a Mother's Day gift," Ken remembered. They shared a love of horses, and at age fourteen, they opened a pony ride called Hoppy's Corral, after Hopalong Cassidy. A happy couple, they were destined for marriage. "Bev's boy, bold, best line . . . Student Council; Special Chorus; Variety Show; Music Festival; lab assistant; Senior Play; hall guard; LOG staff; Honor Society; Clean-up committee, chairman" was written next to Ken's picture.

By the time his senior year rolled around, horses were in Ken's blood. He gave up his plaster-of-Paris novelty business because he had his heart set on opening a stable and had talked about it to classmates and friends. On graduation day, January 25, 1951, Beverly acknowledged his life dream with simple but plaintive schoolgirl devotion—"Ken: I'll never forget tonite my darling. You looked so handsome in your cap and gown. Hope you get your ranch!! Love Always, Bev."

Kenny advanced his schoolboy livery business by helping his father, Ethan, manage a profitable pony-ride concession at neighborhood carnivals during the busy summer months. He collected tickets and kept a watchful eye on the unhappy mounts as they shuffled aimlessly in circles on a flattened bed of hay in a makeshift corral carrying excited school kids on their backs.

In December 1952, as the Korean War wound down, Ken Hansen was drafted into the U.S. Army. While on furlough, he was married to Beverly, who had been living with her parents, Bernice and Walter Carlson, counting down the days until she could begin her new life.

According to Kenny Hansen, he worked at the Park Ridge Riding Academy with his father now and again before he was drafted. Garrisoned in the Trolon Valley in South Korea for a little more than a year, Hansen was honorably discharged in the spring of 1955. Upon his arrival in the Windy City, Kenny and his new bride moved into a basement apartment at 5056 N. Claremont Ave. on the North Side. The young couple later relocated to 5321 N. Kenmore Ave.

Investigator Dave Hamm spoke to Kenneth Hansen in the 1970s; the now-prosperous stable owner told him that in 1955 he bought a new car that he was especially fond of, a dual-quad-carburetor '55 Chevy (Hansen later denied owning a 1955 Chevrolet). With his affairs decidedly on the upswing, he enrolled as an undergraduate at the University of Illinois. The Chicago campus was then located in cramped quarters on Navy Pier, a narrow strip of man-made land jutting out into Lake Michigan at Grand Avenue. Hansen attended classes for only one semester, but the educational experience was pivotal in more ways than one, for it was in the university setting that Hansen was allegedly introduced to gay sex.

When trying to be ingratiating, Kenny Hansen sternly reminded his closest associates that he was *bisexual*, not homosexual, believing there was much less stigma attached to that. Hansen went to great lengths to conceal his sex life from the possessive Beverly, who didn't much care whether or not he kept company "with the guys"—just so long as he maintained a proper distance from the flirtatious beauties coming on to him at the stables.

In the 1950s, Silas Jayne dominated the Midwestern horse-breeding profession. For an ambitious small-timer looking to move up in the world of show horses, getting to know Si was a prerequisite to any hope of achieving future success as a buyer and seller. Whether or not Kenny knew Si in the 1950s is still a mystery. What is clear is that the chances for a young up-and-comer like Kenny Hansen to land a good job in the horse world without the help of a rich and powerful stable owner like Si were slim to none.

Working side by side with his father tending horses at the Park Ridge

Riding Academy and supervising the pony concession at Hollywood Kiddieland, a corner-lot amusement park at Devon Avenue and McCormick Boulevard featuring water rides and horses, wasn't much of a career opportunity for Hansen but was all he could find in the weeks prior to and following his discharge from the service. He dreamed of the day when he could strike off on his own and purchase a stable with the name of Hansen prominently displayed on the signage.

Curiously, only four years out of high school, Kenny and Bev negotiated the purchase of a stable at Eighty-Second Street and Kean Avenue in south suburban Willow Springs, a close-knit burg steeped in political corruption and described by a handful of angst-ridden residents as "secretive" and "clannish." Ethan knew some people in the horse business who had an equestrian boarding stable and a run-down livery business they were looking to sell. He alerted his son, and a sale was consummated. "My buildings were ancient, made of wood," said Hansen. "In fact, I would haul skids into my barns to make them look presentable." The Hansen horse farm was located across from a Lithuanian cemetery and only a few miles from the eerie Devil's Creek location where the frozen remains of the Grimes sisters would be found nearly a year and a half later. Hansen maintained that his purchase agreement with Robert Denton White and his wife, Minnie, was concluded on June 7, 1955. It was further agreed that Hansen would take possession of the property in October, once the transfer of title was recorded.[3] Apparently happy and content in their new life, the newlyweds relocated to the south end of the county "after the horse season in '55 in roughly October," Ken said, where they renamed the Shetland horse farm and livery business the Bro-Ken H.[4]

"We bought it on contract," Hansen told the authors. "And we bought the apartment all furnished. We were there thirteen years at that stable and were paying Bob and Minnie all that time, but then I had an opportunity to get the big stable on Ninety-Fifth Street."

There are discrepancies to Hansen's version of events. In the fall of 1955, the Illinois State Toll Highway Commission held the title to the property at 8214 Kean Ave. in Willow Springs, which suggests that Hansen either subleased the property from the lessor White or did not take actual possession until several years later. In the office of the Cook County Recorder of Deeds, Torrens property records for Lyons Township, where Willow Springs is, revealed startling information—the Illinois State Toll Highway Commission owned this parcel of land up through 1957.

Neither Hansen's name nor his business is found when the Yellow Pages for those years are examined. The Bro-Ken H Riding Academy Inc. at 8214 Kean Ave. does not appear in any Cook County commercial telephone directory until December 1960, more than five years after Hansen claimed to have moved south to open a livery business. This is very curious, given that in the 1950s, every city and suburban business received a free Yellow Pages listing whether they wanted one or not—unless, of course, the stable was under a different name.

The truth is, Kenny Hansen's exact whereabouts in the summer of 1955 remains shrouded in mystery. And there are no witnesses who saw Kenny in or around the Idle Hour Stables on the evening of October 16, 1955. Judith Anderson said that Hansen was employed as an Idle Hour stable hand in August of that year, despite Kenny's repeated claims to the contrary stating that he had closed on the Bro-Ken H property two months earlier.[5] Anderson was seventeen years old in 1955, and horseback riding was her special hobby. More often than not, Judy and her friend Linda Hoffman went to Idle Hour to ride the bridle path along the Des Plaines River.

What is known is that Ken Hansen was admired by a number of young girls who rode horses at the stables he tended. He was remembered as easy-going, attentive, and always mindful of exercising proper safety procedures inside the corral. He was also regarded by the young girls as charming and devilishly handsome, a good teacher of riding technique, and always very patient and courteous. They could not possibly suspect nor would they choose to believe that his better nature, evidenced by a warm, engaging smile, was often overruled by a darker side.

In the early 1970s, Leila Dempewold and Marie Cassidy were attending classes at the School of the Art Institute in Chicago when their lives intersected with Ken Hansen. The heaviness in the classroom that afternoon contradicted the lively artistic atmosphere that normally prevailed at this time of the day in Room 200. Off and on, young men and women peered out from behind their canvases to look at the naked, muscular male model who posed before them. It was the first time the students had had a live model in the room. Leila leaned in towards Marie and whispered, "Not bad!" The two girls giggled softly. "Hey," Leila continued, "do you want to go horseback riding? Sky Hi Hopes has great horses and even better looking instructors!" Marie tilted her head to the left, so she could see the model as well as her drawing and nodded. "That sounds good."

Over the next few months, Leila and Marie took both art classes and English-riding lessons together. After the semester ended and just as

Chicago's scorching, humid summer began, Marie, now smitten with riding, procured a summer job at Ken and Beverly Hansen's stable. "It was the summer of '73, and I had nothing to do," Marie recalled. "The Hansens were always looking for help, especially during the summer because there were more kids and more trail rides."

Although she rarely saw Kenny or Beverly and never saw Danny, Mark Hansen was "kind" and "cute," and Marie got to know him quite well. "I'd drive him to see his girlfriend in Bourbonnais, Illinois. We talked about a lot of things. I liked him a lot. He had a cute little squint when he talked."

Marie did odd jobs around the stables, from feeding the horses to putting on and taking off the saddles before and after trail rides. According to her, the horses were well taken care of. "Lightning was my favorite quarter horse. He was a beautiful brownish-red and had the best disposition." Marie sighed before relating an ugly incident at the stable that colored her opinion of Ken Hansen and his wife.

"One day I was putting something away in the tack room and this guy, about my age—twentyish—came in and slammed the door behind him. He grabbed a crop (a short riding whip) and said, 'I'm going to rape you.' I backed away. I was petrified. Then I started pushing him. He shoved me back and somehow, during the pushing and shoving, I got away." Marie ran for the aid of one of the other young women who had worked at Sky Hi Hopes for a long time. "I told this rough-and-tough butch girl about what happened and she told me, 'You'd better get used to that stuff. You're working at a stable, not Kiddieland.'"

Marie pondered that reality over the next few weeks, but it wasn't the sexual advances that forced her to quit. It was Ken and Bev Hansen. "I was leaning next to the corral fence watching kids learning to ride when a small Ford pickup truck backed into me. For a few minutes I was lodged between the fence and truck. I screamed out in pain. The driver, an older fellow who worked at the stables, pulled the vehicle forward, got out, and began yelling at me."

Mark was nearby and came to her rescue. Marie said,

He helped me to my feet. I was limping and in pain. Mark brought me into the kitchen of their trailer so I could call home and get a ride to the hospital. Once inside the trailer, Mark called for his parents. They didn't like . . . run into the kitchen. They strolled in and stood a good distance away from me. They looked like they had just gotten up. So-and-so backed up and hit her, Mark told them. Ken and Bev said nothing. I made a couple of calls to family and friends but nobody was home. Mark gave me a glass of water and after about ten minutes, I limped out of the trailer, into my car, and drove myself to the hospital.

Marie never returned to Sky Hi Hopes again. She said, "You'd think that at least Beverly would do something to help me. But neither of them did anything. They just didn't care."

Ken Hansen seems to be a Dr. Jekyll and Mr. Hyde. Alternately, he was Kenny the charmer and doting father of two growing boys and Kenny the accused serial pedophile taken to task by the Hooved Animal Humane Society (HAHS) for mistreating his stable horses. Hansen was accused of starving his animals before selling them for slaughter. The practice allegedly went on for years, despite numerous attempts by HAHS investigator Donna Ewing to compel the courts to sign an impoundment order. No such order was ever issued, however, suggesting to Ewing that Hansen's association with the influential "horsey set" helped shield him from prosecution.

Mark Hansen, who owns a sixty-two-acre spread in Crete, Illinois, believes that the portrayal of his father as a horse abuser is inaccurate and unfair. "First of all, horses are expensive. That's why we would buy the skinny ones, fatten 'em up and try to give them a second chance." Ewing and her colleagues, according to the son, mistook the appearances of malnourished horses at his stable as wonton examples of Ken Hansen's deliberate cruelty. "You have three choices—send them off, find homes for them, or kill 'em." Horses that are "sent off" end up in rendering factories where they are slaughtered and packaged as horsemeat. "There is a big market for horsemeat up in Canada and in Japan," Mark Hansen said. "We [Mark and his dad] preferred to restore them to health and find a good home for them."

Nine generations of Jaynes inhabited the far Northwest suburbs of Chicago at one time or another. About fifty miles northwest from the city limits of Chicago, well up into McHenry County, the Jaynes' neighbors there remember them as a roughhousing lot, prone to bad behavior and occasional acts of violence. Townspeople shuddered each time Silas and his brothers paraded through Main Street on their way to the railhead to herd to their ranch nearby the range horses shipped in boxcars. Horses of value were steered to the family ranch and trained for riding. Glue-factory candidates were shipped to Rockford to be slaughtered, processed, and packaged as dog meat. And every time the Jaynes galloped into town they were like a bunch of drunken cowboys on a roundup, pretending it was Dodge City circa 1880. "The Jayne Gang rides again," shrugged one of the locals who found the Wild West antics rather unsettling.

Silas, the orneriest of the brood, was one of twelve children (eight girls and four boys) born to Arthur and Katharine Jayne, owners of a plot of farmland up in Lake County.[6] George Jayne, the youngest boy, was Si's half-brother, born fifteen years after Si. Things were never right between them. By the time the first Jayne stables were opened for business in the 1930s, Si already had a rap sheet following a rape conviction in 1924. He served a year in the state penitentiary at Pontiac before returning to the ranch to launch the family business.

Recalling the character of this big, raw-boned brute destined to become her brother-in-law, Marion Jayne, George's wife, said, "You have to understand that Si was a very unbalanced man from day one."[7] As unbalanced as he may have seemed, few doubted Jayne's business acumen. Crime reporter John O'Brien called Jayne "a ruthless competitor" who bought and sold horses on a cash basis. "His customers included well-heeled business people who sent their daughters to him to become equestrians," wrote O'Brien.[8] "Silas fawned on the parents by telling them their daughters had natural talent but needed better (and more expensive) horses to progress. The proud parents would invariably ante up."

Si opened his first riding stable in 1932, at the southwest corner of Dee Road and Touhy Avenue in Park Ridge. He called his layout the Park Ridge Stables, but early settlers knew it better as the Clay Hole because of the abundance of rich, thick clay dug out of the earth and used for the manufacture of brick. According to local historian Dr. Stanley Borchers, "reports of suspicious activities" were common throughout the eight years of Si Jayne's stewardship. The Park Ridge Stables was an immediate hit with the younger folk, and the village officials considered Jayne a "sound businessman." Once a year, he would bring his prized horses to the Des Plaines Valley Equestrian Association's annual Gymkhana event near Touhy and River Road. The young horseman dazzled the crowd of spectators with an exhibition of riding that only a circus daredevil would even attempt. As the crowd roared approval, Jayne stood astride two horses (with one foot firmly planted on the back of each of them) and raced around the corral "Roman style." In 1940, he sold off the Park

Ridge Stables to land developers who turned the old Clay Hole and the surrounding grounds into quasi-resort area called Park Lane. Jayne made the first of several fortunes. "Money is my religion!" he boasted.

Greed and a lust for profit fueled the rise of Chicago's so-called Equestrian Mafia. And while Si Jayne was recognized as the founding "godfather," he was not alone in his treachery. From the mid-1970s until 1991, fifteen horses were maimed and electrocuted so their owners could cash out in a massive insurance swindle that would result in the indictment of nineteen horse trainers, veterinarians, and owners, among them Richard Bailey.[9]

Others who possessed inside knowledge of the shady dealings involving the Jayne Gang and low-level operatives like Bailey were understandably fearful of going public with disclosures. Everyone was afraid of Si and what he might do if a confidence was betrayed. "The horse world," according to veteran horseman Bob Breen, "is a world you wouldn't understand. It's a closed community, and word gets around fast.

The trail of fraud always seemed to lead back to the doorstep of Silas Jayne or one of his minions. Said one horseman in the know, "If Si Jayne liked your horse and made you an offer, you'd better let him have it, or he'd get it somehow, even if he had to kill it."

Arson fires at horse stables in the Chicago suburbs are not a recent phenomenon. In the early 1900s, cliques of gamblers were in the habit of burning down racetracks when one rival group gained a trackside-betting concession over another. By the 1940s, however, the arson menace had spread to the riding academies and the world of show horses. Police in River Grove, Illinois, investigated a 1940 blaze that wiped out one of Si Jayne's properties, Green Tree Stables, and with it ten horses.[10] It was a tricky business trying to establish proof of arson. But with so many stables burning down, then re-opening under new names with the same cast of characters signing the insurance check, it suggested to police that this was not mere fate or an act of God.

Police in the surrounding suburbs of Chicago paid closer attention to Silas's antics after a family spat with his half-brother George Jayne erupted into a cycle of violence that dragged on for years.[11] "Si Jayne was an amazing piece of work," said Dave Hamm, a former Illinois State Police lieutenant and now retired Du Page County Sheriff's Police officer. He was under no illusion about the sinister nature of Si Jayne. "You would have to encounter him like I did to truly understand that he was just plain evil. That is the only way I can describe him."

In contrast, George Jayne was handsome, articulate, and even-tempered with a polished demeanor and courtly manner, though not without a shady side to his character. From time to time, the younger Jayne engaged in petty frauds and deceptions common among the men of his profession.

Silas and his first wife, Martha, gave George his start.[12] "Silas is the older brother, you know, and he taught George all he knew and then gave him financial backing as well," an acquaintance told *Chicago Sun-Times* columnist Tom Fitzpatrick. "The feud began because George didn't show Silas any gratitude and then started cutting into Silas's business and hiring away Silas's people."[13] From time to time, there would peace offerings followed by a temporary cessation of hostility.[14]

Silas Jayne acquired the Idle Hour Stables, 8600 Higgins Rd., Park Ridge, when he sold his interest in the nearby Happy Day Stable to his brother George. At the Idle Hour, horses were boarded, and young equestrians were trained in the formal English style of riding. He bought the property in 1952 and provided lodging for a dozen grooms and the caretaker, Ralph Fleming, and his family. "Ralph came out of St. Louis and ran the business," recalled Bob Breen. "He booked the hayrides and attended to everything else that needed looking after. He'd bring these young boys in to do odd jobs from time to time. He'd buy them cigarettes or something. Some of them were delinquents or living in homes." Fleming would bring in a "load of horses" from out of state. Some of the animals were potential prize-winners. Others were half-dead, worthless, and ready for the slaughterhouse. The condition of the animal didn't matter.

Si had six to eight stalls down the side of the barn, and that's where he showed off his horses for sale. "You see, that's all he *ever* did was sell horses," Breen added. "Si was a clever businessman."

In November 1965, ten years and one month after the Schuessler-Peterson murders, Jayne sold the Idle Hour Stable and the surrounding land for suburban redevelopment. With contented smile on his face and a fat purse, Si moved his operations to Elgin to open Our Day Farms and continue as always.

Si's brother Frank Jayne Sr., rated the sixth leading trainer in Illinois, ran thoroughbreds at Arlington Park and Washington Park for many years. He aligned himself with Silas in the ongoing spat with their half-brother. Meanwhile, George hired all the right people, collected blue ribbons, and kept expanding his business to the detriment of Si and his fragile ego.

In 1962, about the time there was a second fire at Idle Hour, George added to his considerable holdings Tri-Color Stable, a hundred-acre spread with three barns in Northwest suburban Palatine. Tri-Color grossed $400,000 a year and was a showplace for the top hunters and jumpers.

Between 1959 and 1965 when private differences between the brothers escalated into an all-out feud and a deadly car bombing at the Tri-Color Stable on June 14, 1965,[15] neither Frank nor Silas uttered a friendly word to George. But neither brother appeared willing to leave him alone either.

In 1963, a sniper fired at George with a high-powered rifle, but the sniper's aim was well off the mark. A year later, a George Jayne horse named Schottzie was injected with a dose of turpentine and died. The steed was valued at $25,000. Another horse named Wildcat took sick at the same time but was saved by a team of veterinarians. George Jayne blamed Frank and Si, but the police took no action.

Assistant State's Attorney Alvin Morse stated that George Jayne contacted the Internal Revenue Service to accuse Silas of income tax evasion, but as it turned out, George was the one who ended up being audited. Turning to a dejected George Jayne, a lawyer in the know offered a sobering bit of advice: "The only way this will end is if you kill the sonofabitch."

Sometime after his life was threatened in or around 1965, George wrote down information that he felt would in the event of his death wreak revenge on Si. Knowing that he was a marked man, George confided to his wife, Marion, that he was in possession of certain incriminating information: "If Silas gives us any more trouble, I have the evidence to put him in the electric chair."

"Marion held fast to her belief that her husband '*knew* that murders had occurred inside of Si's [Idle Hour] barn,'" said ATF agent James Delorto. "George prepared a letter to be opened upon his death, and he told Marion to take it to the police if anything happened. 'This will cook Si's goose,' George had said, but the letter was never found, and Marion had not actually read the contents. Marion tore the house apart looking for it. She gave Dave Hamm this information." The investigators believed that the missing letter spelled out the grisly details of the abduction-murders of Tony and John Schuessler and their friend Robert Peterson by one of Silas Jayne's key operatives. George never went to the authorities with his information. It was the only trump card in his deck should the random acts of intimidation escalate and threaten the safety of his family and him. As Delorto explained, "George understood that if Si knew that Marion was in possession of the information, he would have to kill her, too. The whole group was out of control." If true, how did George cobble up the pieces of information to pin the Schuessler-Peterson murders on his obstreperous half-brother?

Delorto said George "knew about the mud floor, the discovery of the metal shavings on the victims' bodies, and the testimony of neighbors who said they had heard the screams of children. He also knew that Kenny Hansen worked at the Idle Hour from time to time."

"You would think that decency and common sense would have dictated to George that he should go to the police at that moment in time, but he didn't," Dave Hamm declared. "Marion believes that he disposed of it in the intervening years because he knew that its publication would only bring universal shame and disgrace upon the family." Hamm sighed and shook his head. "You can't apply logical acts to illogical people. I'm always amazed by what people often do."

The revealing letter remains missing. Delorto remains convinced that George indiscreetly revealed the existence of the letter to Si. What passed between them at that emotional moment can only be surmised.

On April 10, 1967, Cook County Sheriff's Police Officer Ralph Probst was assassinated in the kitchen of his suburban Hometown, Illinois, duplex. A gunman armed with a rare .41-magnum pistol fired a single shot through the pane of the kitchen storm window, dropping Probst to the floor. The police officer was rushed to Little Company of Mary Hospital where he died from his head wound twenty minutes later. The killing was cold and professional and classified "unsolved," though a team of veteran detectives who refuse to give up the hunt for the murderer of their fallen colleague have come up with their own theory.[16]

At the time of his death, Probst, a county police officer since April 20, 1964, was assigned to a special task force investigating high-profile crime. He once boasted to his colleagues that he was on the verge of cracking a "big case," one that would earn him a fast-track promotion to the rank of sergeant. The thirty-year-old father of three never divulged the details of this sensitive investigation to either his wife or partner, and his case files disappeared shortly after his death. This last bit of intrigue fueled considerable speculation in cop land. Ralph Probst, it was whispered, had been poking into the stables, searching for evidence of horse-related crime. Allegedly, Probst stumbled into bits and pieces of sensitive information that would help unlock the secrets of the Cherie Rude murder mystery and by extension illuminate a path that would lead towards the resolution of the Schuessler-Peterson murders.

"Everything I was able to uncover about Probst prior to his death did *not* point in that direction," said Art Bilek, the former chief of the Cook County Police who in 1997 was part of a special task force assigned to unravel the tangled threads of the officer's death. "There is, however, plenty of evidence that Probst visited one of Hansen's stables. It was part of his jurisdiction and a matter of routine."

By 1965, Kenneth Hansen was successful and well known throughout the southern suburbs. He owned and operated two riding academies specializing in Shetland ponies—the Sky Hi Stables at 17201 S. Central Ave. in Tinley Park and the High Hopes at Ninety-Fifth and Kean. He had divested himself of the Bro-Ken H much earlier.[17]

"Hansen used women to lure boys to the stables. The women were of legal age, and a lot of cops would go there as well for the free sex," disclosed Jack Reed, a thirty-five-year veteran of the Cook County Sheriff's Police, whose case files inspired Hollywood to cast actor Brian Dennehy as the fictionalized Reed in a series of made-for-TV movies.[18] Kenny's women allegedly accepted the "hospitality" of the stable owner, though the women recruited for these illicit activities were not likely to view their situation as prostitution. The women attracted to the stable all shared one thing—a love of horses. While most were content to pursue their passion for the equestrian world legitimately and above board, a certain percentage were willing to do *anything* demanded of them, according to Reed and others. "This was a time long before the rock-star and sports 'groupie' phenomenon we know today," Bilek adds. "But it was analogous, and the stable owners profited from it."

The Bro-Ken H Stables was centered in the middle of a thriving corridor of vice and gambling controlled by the Chicago Mob and protected by Mayor John "Doc" Rust, the thoroughly corrupt Willow Springs Police Department, and a handful of Cook County Sheriff's Police who considered the vice-mongers "clients"—and not potential targets of a crackdown. Suburban riding stables like the Bro-Ken H and the subsequent properties Hansen owned in the 1960s and 1970s became magnets for organized-crime hoodlums and their progeny. According to one report, "Mad" Sam DeStefano, the monosyllabic killer, donned Western attire and spent his happiest hours in the company of his daughter and galloping around Kenny's corral.

"You see, it all starts with the kids," said Delorto. "The hoods had the money to pay for riding lessons and the means to stable a horse, so they brought their children out and saddled up." Even Tony "Big Tuna" Accardo, the ruling don of the Chicago Outfit, availed himself of the bridle path and back barns of George Jayne's Tri-Color Stables in Palatine. He privately thanked George for his warmth and friendliness.

After years of digging, Bilek is convinced that Accardo henchman DeStefano ordered the murder of Ralph Probst to extract revenge. In his capacity as a Cook County police officer assigned to a special task force investigating organized crime, Probst had managed to ruffle the feathers of this professional killer, who had no compulsion about putting a man to death over the slightest provocation. Tom Hampson, one of America's best-known private investigators, questions this scenario. "Until the Colombians [and their drug cartels] came along, organized crime did not assassinate honest cops for 'slight provocations,' even if the suspect *was* Sam DeStefano.[19] I have to wonder what Probst was *really* up to."

Soon after the execution-style murder of Probst at the northern end of Cook County, according to the theory advanced by Dave Hamm, George Jayne felt the viselike grip of Silas Jayne slowly tightening around his neck. To safeguard his life and to protect the lives of Marion and the four children lest they suffer the same fate as Cherie Rude or Ralph Probst, George hired former Inverness, Illinois, Police Chief Frank H. Michelle Sr. as a personal bodyguard. "Marion was scared shitless of Si Jayne," said Delorto. "She was [for a while] a stay-at-home wife and was very fearful for the lives of her children."[20]

Kenneth Hansen, the gentleman horseman making a name for himself in Chicago's southern suburbs, had his own part to play in the final chapter of the Jayne-versus-Jayne blood feud. If George Jayne did, indeed, know who killed the Schuessler-Peterson boys and if Kenny Hansen was involved, then Hansen would certainly have a reason to want George dead.

On October 28, 1970, George and his immediate family gathered at their five-acre Inverness estate on Banbury Road to celebrate sixteen-year-old George Jr.'s birthday. After dinner and cake, George and Marion repaired to the basement recreation room of the redbrick Colonial to play a game of bridge with daughter Linda and her husband Mickey Wright. The George Jayne family was close-knit and enjoyed doing things together. George was shuffling the deck of cards when the sharp crack of gunfire shattered the calm. The shooter had silently crept up to the basement window at the northeast corner of the house. He rested the high-powered rifle on top of a thick hedge two feet from the window and took careful aim. The bullet, fired from a scoped .30.06 Savage rifle, settled dead center in George's chest. The hired assassin raced back to the getaway car, described by witnesses as a late-model red Oldsmobile with a black vinyl top. The vehicle sped off into the night moments ahead of the arrival of the Palatine Police Officer Michael J. McDonald. McDonald's efforts to resuscitate George Jayne failed, and death overtook the embattled horseman minutes after his arrival at Northwest Community Hospital.

When informed of his brother's passing, Silas Jayne stared incredulously at reporters and feigned deep anguish and sorrow. "This is terrible!" he exclaimed. "I realize the bad light this thing puts me in." He said he had no idea who would want to shoot his dear departed brother but implied rather spitefully that George's gambling habits might have put him in a tight spot with juice-loan racketeers. The death notice appearing in the newspaper the next day listed the six surviving sisters of George Jayne, his wife and children, but no mention was made of either Silas or Frank Jayne Sr.

The assassins turned out to be sloppy and careless—an easy mark for law enforcement. Si engaged "hit teams" to vie for the privilege of killing George. "Red" Wemette and Kenny's brother, Curtis, the pathological syndicate hit man, were allegedly promised a reward totaling $50,000 by Silas if George was brought back alive, according to statements made by Robert Lee Brown, a Michigan horse trainer and convicted perjurer. Brown opened a thirty-five-horse stable on Steunkel Road in Frankfort, Illinois, with Ken in November 1970.[21]

Though he was never officially listed on the Chicago Crime Commission's who's-who organizational chart of ranking Mob figures, Curtis Hansen, the heroic little boy who rescued his siblings from the house fire in 1936, was a syndicate associate with important underworld connections. He had a stake in the Old Town porno bookstore managed by and partly owned by William "Red" Wemette and ran a saloon on the South Side that was little more than a front for prostitution.[22] He even dabbled in politics, helping to elect Sheriff Frank Sain in 1960.

Kenny, not nearly as tough and unflinching as his brother, confided some of his darkest fears and deepest apprehensions to Brown, his live-in guest after he launched Sky Hi Stables in Tinley Park.[23] Over cocktails and dinner at Jardine's Restaurant one night, Hansen complained to Brown that Beverly was "running the business down" and revealed bits and pieces about horse deals gone bad and old arsons. Brown was not surprised or shocked to learn of any of this. It was the nature of the horse business, after all, and in his younger years, he had witnessed worse

things. There was one aspect, however, that troubled him about his erst-
while business partner and after-hours drinking chum. Seven months
after George Jayne was murdered, Dave Hamm and officers from the
Illinois State Police and the Illinois Bureau of Investigation (IBI) were
closing in on the trail of the killers. It was a nervous time, and Kenny,
perhaps speculating his arrest and indictment on a charge of solicitation to commit murder was imminent, weighed his options. Should he
betray Si and risk deadly retribution or keep his mouth shut and accept
serious prison time?

Brown suggested that Ken go to the state's attorney and reveal everything he knew about Si Jayne's intricate operation. After all, what was
left to lose? Si had already reneged on a promise to pay Kenny's team and
had hung him out to dry. Kenny played it close to the vest. Something
terrible had happened a long time ago that he just did not want to talk
about. "Ken, what could be worse than murder?" Brown wondered. The
reply came, "You don't even want to know."

Armed with arrest warrants, Hamm, accompanied by two other agents,
appeared at the Robert Brown Stable in Will County on June 5, 1971, inquiring after Kenny. Moments passed before Hansen sauntered forward and
surrendered meekly to the IBI agents. Off to the side staring intently at
Hamm was Roger Spry. The IBI men removed $462 in cash from Kenny's
pockets and certified cashier's checks totaling $155,000, but Hansen was
unable to post a $10,000 bond. The mysterious checks, his attorney Arthur
J. O'Donnell patiently explained to the court, were not made payable to
him. Hansen pleaded not guilty and was incarcerated in the foul Cook
County Jail pending a formal arraignment hearing in front of Judge
Joseph A. Power of the Criminal Court.

The secret indictment charged Kenny with conspiring with Lawrence
Smith and Ancil Earl Tremore to abduct and murder George Jayne. It
was alleged that the three men carefully plotted their moves from July
30 through August 2, 1969 and had actually approached the Jayne residence on Banbury Road with weapons drawn. "Lawrence Smith initiated
contact with us," Hamm recalled. "He lived in Kankakee, and Tremore,
his cousin, was in the Army at the time. They were just a couple of unso-
phisticated farm boys in their late twenties who hung out with Hansen at
the stable in Tinley Park." With an eye on collecting the $25,000 reward
money, Smith told how they were solicited by Kenny to kill George. "After Hansen made the solicitation, Joe LaPlaca, a member of one of the
competing hit squads, and Silas went to Hansen's stable to meet Smith

and Tremore," explained Hamm. Jayne supplied them with an Enforcer, a cut-down carbine with a pistol stock. "He had a bunch of them in his collection," Hamm said. "The Enforcer was Si's favorite weapon."

Although Jayne, the compulsive swindler intent upon murdering his half-brother, had three teams of hit men on the job, none were particularly skilled at their craft. Kenny's group proved to be the most inept of the three. "They were a trio of bumpkins," chuckles Hamm. "Tremore and Smith bought a case of beer and drove up to Crystal Lake where they rented a room and got drunk. They blew it and gave up."

A month after George Jayne was killed, Dave Hamm took the time to review the Schuessler-Peterson case files gathering dust at Eleventh and State with Thomas J. Drury, an IBI investigator on administrative leave from the Chicago Police Department. Hamm read with growing interest the old reports describing the accounts of screams emanating from a field in the vicinity of Si Jayne's Idle Hour Stable the night of the murders and came away believing they were sex crimes.

Up to that time, few in law enforcement had paid attention to the Idle Hour Stables or Ken Hansen. But Hamm had a funny feeling about the man. Call it a lawman's intuition or sixth sense, there was more to Kenny than met the eye. Hamm was so convinced of it that he began asking around, "Who in this circle of people is a pedophile? Who had access to that barn? The only guy I could come up with was Mr. Hansen."

The relationship, if any, between Ken Hansen and Si Jayne varies according to who is giving the story. Frank M. Jayne Sr.[24] claims to have introduced Kenny Hansen in 1961 to his older brother Si. According to Frank, Kenny "wanted to buy this horse. And kind of a cheap horse but still worthy to get more than fifty or one hundred dollars. Horses were selling cheap at the time, and good livery horses, you could buy a good livery horse for $100." As the story goes, Si was selling a horse for Mrs. Marzano, a "widow lady," whose departed husband had owned bowling alleys and had a show stable in the area. "His widow asked my brother to dispose of the horses. And that happens to be one of the horses he sold to Kenny Hansen" for $500.

Hansen said he knew Si's third wife

better than I did him because you know we talk about horses and stuff but Si was not a friendly, friendly person. I mean he'd do his business, and it was, he'd be gone. Frank Sr. was the friendly one. I mean he was the one that would take the time to do all of the amenities that are proper and socially acceptable and stuff like that. Frank Sr. was far closer, we played polo and everything. He would come to my stables like once a week and I would, we'd drive up to Elgin once or twice a week and play polo. We did that for like a year or so. And that's the way Frank Sr. was. But Si, you never would see him. You'd get into his office, and you'd talk for whatever business and poof, he'd be gone, you know.

Kenny also said he knew Si only as an interested spectator at horse competitions: "We would see him and his brother George at the horse shows but sat up in the [International Amphitheatre] balcony."

Kenny also described his dealings with the Jaynes as strictly a business arrangement—buying a broken-down horse or two from Frank Jayne Sr. on occasion. Hansen's dealings with Si were friendly, and Si knew perfectly well what Kenny was all about. After all, Si Jayne fancied himself as a liberal thinker. Young boys were not exactly his cup of tea, you have to understand. He much preferred the company of pretty young girls in makeup, flouncy dresses, and high heels. But he wasn't going to kick about another horse trader's sexual preferences—he would transact business with the likes of Ken Hansen just as long as it did not interfere with his business or put him on the spot in some awful way.

At the behest of Assistant State's Attorney Nick Motherway, charges against Hansen were quietly dropped so the case against the second squad of hit men, who had succeeded in carrying out the bloody deed, would not be clouded by the presence of additional suspects likely to confuse the jurors. "Nick wasn't overly excited about them anyway," Hamm said. "Tremore was off in Europe, and the witnesses were not good." Kenny, his pride injured and his pocketbook picked clean by lawyers, retreated into the shadows of his Camelot Stables, wanting nothing more than to be forgotten about by the cops. Law enforcement unwittingly obliged.

After being informed that an arrest warrant had been filed against him, Silas Jayne strolled into the Elgin Police Department and casually asked what all the fuss was about. He was informed of the charge and ignominiously removed to the Cook County Jail to await State's Attorney Edward Hanrahan, a tough law-and-order man, who filed the necessary indictments. Jayne was held without bail from May 23, 1971, until May 25, 1973.

The case against Silas Jayne and his coconspirators charged with the murder of George Jayne went before Criminal Court Judge Richard J.

Fitzgerald on April 2, 1973, and for the next four weeks, the famous F. Lee Bailey, defense counsel to Silas Jayne, dazzled and captivated the spectators in the packed courtroom. Throughout the trial, Silas Jayne stared menacingly at the jurors. His bluster gone, Jayne resorted to a form of psychological terrorism in a final effort to sway the twelve courageous citizens impaneled to decide his fate. The jury deliberated for nine and a half hours before returning guilty verdicts on conspiracy on April 29.

Ignoring Bailey's plea not to "bury" his client, Judge Fitzgerald ordered Jayne to serve his sentence in the downstate Vienna Correctional Facility. Shaking his head, the famed defense attorney called the verdict "confused and illogical."

"It is absolutely impossible to be guilty of conspiracy and not be guilty of murder," Bailey said to reporters. "If you accept the evidence, you have to go all the way."

Emerging from the courtroom with her two daughters, Linda and Patricia, moments after the verdicts were read, Marion Jayne indicated that she wasn't through with Si, at least not yet. Flushed with emotion, she added, "Now maybe George can rest in peace. I think the law should be changed, however. It's not enough for conspiracy to commit murder."

Unaccustomed to losing, F. Lee Bailey considered the outcome a moral victory . . . of sorts. After all, the jury said that Silas Jayne had not committed murder. He had only *conspired* to commit murder, and that, Bailey gloated, "is a relatively minor felony."

"I have not had a major criminal trial in the Midwest since 1973," he later wrote. "It is probably just as well. The trial of Silas Jayne would be a very hard act to follow."

A few minutes past 5:00 AM on May 24, 1979, the doors of the Sheridan Correctional Center, to which the prisoner had been transferred, swung open, and out stepped Silas to greet his faithful wife, Dorothy McCloud Jayne, and his brother Frank Sr. They had waited eight years and two days for this reunion. Looking fit and tan, the seventy-two-year-old horseman smiled warmly at his closest kin. "Come on, Frank, let's go home!" he chirped, clapping his brother on the back in show of brotherly affection. The irksome George was at last out of Si's hair, and the unpleasantness of the past—the swindles, the arson fires, the murder of the three boys, and Ken Hansen—were now all behind him. What a sight for sore eyes his little ranch would be! Si could almost smell the hay and the horse dung.

  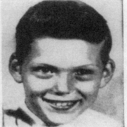

| JOHN SCHUESSLER | ANTON SCHUESSLER | ROBERT PETERSON |

THE DAILY ✪ BULLETIN

HON. RICHARD J. DALEY, Mayor

VOL. 2.   OCTOBER 20, 1955   NO. 206

| ATTENTION | ATTENTION | ATTENTION |

John Schuessler
5711 N. Mango av.

Wore a brown shirt with a ranch design, blue zipper satin jacket with slit pockets trimmed in red; lettering on left side of jacket "CUBS" blue lettering with red trim, blue jeans, black gym shoes trimmed in white with white shoe laces. The above clothing is old and well worn.

Anton Schuessler
5711 N. Mango av.

Wore a white flannel shirt with mixed black design, blue sating zipper jacket with slit pockets trimmed in red; tear on right pocket pinned together with a safety pin; lettering on left side of jacket "CUBS" blue lettering with red trim; letter "U" missing, blue jeans with stiching on right knee, black gym shoes trimmed in white with white shoe laces. The above clothing is old and well worn.

Robert Peterson
5519 Farragut st.

Wore a dark satin zipper jacket with red elastic bands at wrists and waist; red line down each sleeve; White Sox Emblem on left side of jacket white on black, blue jeans, black gym shoes trimmed in white with white shoe laces. The above clothing is old and well worn.

THE ABOVE CLOTHING WORN BY THE VICTIMS WHEN LAST SEEN HAS NOT BEEN LOCATED. ANY INFORMATION

RELATIVE TO THE ABOVE CLOTHING, AS PICTURED AND DESCRIBED, SHOULD BE TRANSMITTED AT ONCE TO

Chief of Detectives, John T. O'Malley
Chicago Police Department, 1121 S. State St.
Telephone: Wabash 2-4747, Extensions 253 and 299

Hours after the disappearances were first reported, a deluge of police handbills showing the images of the missing boys and the description of clothes they were wearing was distributed citywide, and information also was dispatched citywide via the teletype system. Local law enforcement hoped that someone might turn up who had seen the missing boys.

Photo from the Chicago Police Department News Affairs Division

Anton Schuessler Jr. (second row down, third from right) poses with classmates for the sixth-grade class picture five months before his death. Photo courtesy of Paul Garland

Front and side views of
the Garland Building,
111 S. Wabash Ave.
Physicians, dentists
and eye doctors have
made up the bulk of
the tenancy in this
vintage office building
since it opened in
1915. Robert Peterson
signed the register here
on October 16, 1955.

Photos by Lawrence Raeder

The route of the Northwest Side streets traveled by the Schuessler-Peterson boys on the last day of their lives is depicted in this map reconstruction. Stop number #4 was the Stanton Hobby Shop. It would have been impossible for the boys to have reached this location by 3:30 PM. *Chicago American* map, October 19, 1955.

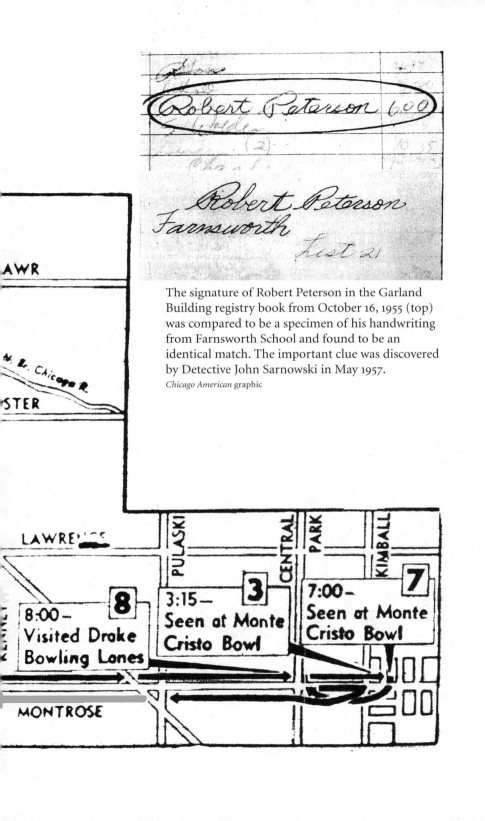

The signature of Robert Peterson in the Garland Building registry book from October 16, 1955 (top) was compared to be a specimen of his handwriting from Farnsworth School and found to be an identical match. The important clue was discovered by Detective John Sarnowski in May 1957.

Chicago American graphic

The Schuessler-Peterson boys were spotted inside Monte Cristo Bowl, 2236 W. Montrose Ave. (top), and Drake Bowl, 3550 W. Montrose Ave., in the early evening hours of October 16. Photos by Lawrence Raeder

The Jefferson Park Recreation alleys at 4747 N. Milwaukee Ave. were full-up when Bobby and his friends entered the building shortly before 9:00 PM looking to bowl a game or two. Turned away by the owner, they walked a block north to Lawrence Avenue. The former ten-pin parlor is today a banquet hall. Photo by Richard Lindberg

The Schuessler-Peterson boys possibly hitched their fatal ride on the southeast corner (to the lower right of the automobile) of the intersection. The photo is of Milwaukee Avenue, looking north at Lawrence Avenue circa 1957. Until the 1970s, this was a thriving neighborhood shopping district. Photographic print ICHI-35512 courtesy of Chicago Historical Society

This is the scene where the bodies were found as it appears today. On October 18, 1955, liquor salesman Victor Livingston found the remains of the Schuessler-Peterson boys at this location in Robinson Woods, south of Lawrence Avenue between River Road and East River Road. Photo by Lawrence Raeder

This is the way the bodies were positioned when they were first discovered.

Photo courtesy of Dr. Richard Ritt

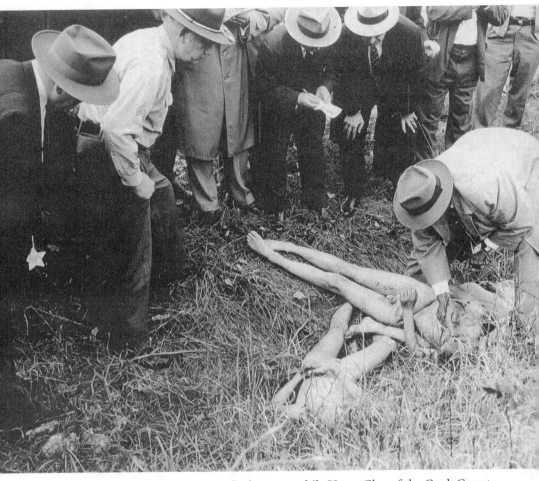

The men in the fedora hats trample the scene while Harry Glos of the Cook County Coroner's office takes a closer look. The bodies of the boys were rearranged, the ground contaminated, and trace evidence obliterated. Photo courtesy of James Delorto

Detective James Lanners (far left in the light sports coat, with his hands behind his back) was one of the first Chicago Police investigators to arrive at the scene but was ordered to stand away from the bodies of the victims and to keep his hands firmly secure behind his back. Cook County Coroner Walter McCarron and his deputy Harry Glos (hovering near the remains) made it clear that they were in charge and did not want the Chicago PD or any other rival agency "horning in" on (and possibly claiming credit) for their findings. This was typical of the jurisdictional turf battles between law enforcement officials so common in those days but often with disastrous consequences to a murder investigation. Photo courtesy of James Lanners

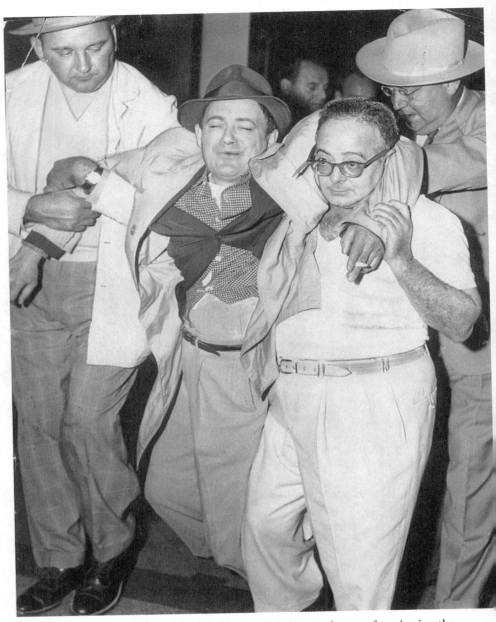

His world shattered and his last vestige of emotional control gone after viewing the battered remains of his two sons on October 19, 1955, Anton Schuessler Sr. collapses into the arms of Deputy Sheriff William Greenberg (left) and Cook County Morgue attendant Frank Sariano. *Chicago Sun-Times* file photo. Grieving father Anton Schuessler. Reprinted with special permission from the Chicago Sun-Times Inc. © 2003. August 13, 2002.

On October 20, 1955, Chicago Police Detective Michael Ricci (on the stairway) questions a Jefferson Park neighbor in the 4900 block of Lester Street, while a motorcycle officer asks passers-by if they had observed anyone suspicious lurking in the neighborhood on the night of the triple murder. The house-to-house canvass was the largest in Chicago PD history up to that time. *Daily News* file photo. A motorcycle patrol officer. Reprinted with special permission from the Chicago Sun-Times Inc. © 2003. September 7, 1955.

The Petersons mourn the loss of their son Robert moments before interment.
Life magazine photo

St. Joseph Cemetery is a scene of grief as the Schuessler brothers are laid to rest. In a state of collapse, Anton Schuessler Sr. and Eleanor Schuessler sit in front of the twin caskets.

Life magazine photo

Lieutenant Patrick Deeley (left, holding papers), head of the Chicago Police SIU, briefs members of the detective command staff. Captain John Ascher of the Chicago Crime Lab is shown third from left. Photo courtesy of James McGuire

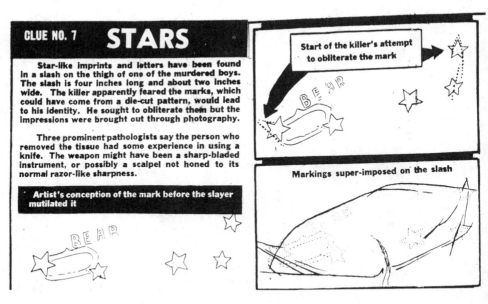

CLUE NO. 7 STARS

Star-like imprints and letters have been found in a slash on the thigh of one of the murdered boys. The slash is four inches long and about two inches wide. The killer apparently feared the marks, which could have come from a die-cut pattern, would lead to his identity. He sought to obliterate them but the impressions were brought out through photography.

Three prominent pathologists say the person who removed the tissue had some experience in using a knife. The weapon might have been a sharp-bladed instrument, or possibly a scalpel not honed to its normal razor-like sharpness.

Artist's conception of the mark before the slayer mutilated it

Start of the killer's attempt to obliterate the mark

Markings super-imposed on the slash

The "mysterious marks" on the skin surface of the murder victims, shown here in diagrams, were found by Frank San Hamel of the *Chicago Daily News*. The marks were chilling clues first published in the paper the week of December 5–9, 1955. At the time, they only deepened the mystery, until ATF agent James Delorto uncovered their significance forty years later. *Chicago Daily News* illustrations

Mike Spiotto took over day-to-day supervision of the Special Investigations Unit in January 1956. Before calling it a career, he rose to the rank of acting superintendent of police. Photo courtesy of the Chicago Police Department News Affairs Division

Timothy O'Connor was Chicago Police Commissioner from 1950 to 1960. Photo courtesy of the Chicago Police Department News Affairs Division

Sheriff Joseph Lohman (left) was well meaning but ineffectual. He is shown with members of his staff in 1955. Photo courtesy of James McGuire

Detective James Lanners looks for a possible lead in the score sheets from the Monte Cristo Bowl, where the boys were seen shortly before their rendezvous with the killer.

Photo courtesy of James Lanners

Sketches Show Similarity

Sketches by Adolph Valanis, police artist, showing similarity of rapist (left) hunted for almost year and new suspect in triple slaying drawn yesterday from description by woman eye technician in downtown building.

Is this the infamous John Wayne Gacy or an older North Side rapist? In 1957, the *Chicago Tribune* published a copy of the Valanis sketch of the Garland Building loiterer who accosted Bobby Peterson. In 1995, Ken Hansen's defense attorneys tried to convince the jury that this sketch was an accurate likeness of Gacy, only thirteen years of age at the time of the triple murders.

Perrue Bauer—reserved, righteous, refreshing . . . Office helper; hall guard; College Day committee; intramurals; German club; G.A.A.

Corrine Becker—"Corny," chatterbox, cunning canary . . . Sigma S.G.C.; Lettergirls; intramurals; library assistant; Honor Society; biology newspaper; College Day committee; Special Arts club; Fashion club.

Margie Bezin—Taylored, talkative, transportation . . . National Honor Society, vice-president; senior correspondent; Quill and Scroll; Omega S.G.C. secretary; Graduation committee; Lettergirls; gym leader; intramurals; bowling league; Chicago Press Guild; Variety Show.

Nick Bilder—lanky, lean, likeable . . . intramurals; Greek club; hall guard.

* * *

Marshall Black—garrulous, go-getter, gagster . . . associate editor, LOG; Letterman; football team; hall guard; swimming team; Pin and Ring committee; Prom committee; intramurals; 4B Social committee.

Bruce Bower—fun-loving, fashionable, flirtatious . . . intramurals; Lettermen's club; Variety Show; Social committee; Senior Play; drama.

Russell Brandenburg—blonde, bold, baffling . . . intramurals.

Dornjean Buch—Deejay, delightful, darling . . . intramurals; Executive committee; Prom committee; Omega S.G.C.; Senior Play; drama; Variety Shows; Fashion Shows; Girls Chorus; Music Festivals.

* * *

Constance Buss—friendly, freckled, forgiving . . . Mixed Chorus; Special Chorus; 219 worker; office worker; Alpha S.G.C.; G.A.A.; Lettergirls; LOG; intramurals; Nominating committee; Student Council.

Beverly Carlson—red-head, radiant, real-swell . . . Office worker; intramurals; hall guard; lab assistant; biology newspaper; library staff; Student Council; Spanish club; G.A.A.

James Carlson—quiet, quick, qualified . . . Honor Society; bowling league.

Ross Carswell—tall, "Texan," true shot . . . Intramurals; Art club; assistant Latin Club; Honor Society.

HERE WE LEARNED OUR A, B, C's

Deane Chapin—wow, whee, wham . . . Omega S.G.C. past president; 4B Social committee; Senior Play; Fashion Show; 4A Social committee; GAA Board of Control; Variety Shows; LOG representative; intramurals.

Georgiana Clacson—little, lively, lovely . . . President of G.A.A.; chairman of Social committee; Variety Shows; Field Day; Student Council; Posture Contest; office helper; Fashion Show; S.G.C. past president; intramurals; Lettergirls; 4B Social committee.

Willa Colvett—reserved, refined, resourceful . . . Sigma S.G.C.; G.A.A.; Lettergirls; Chorus; intramurals; chemistry lab assistant; Music Festival; biology newspaper; LOG representative; National Honor Society, president; Program committee; Latin club; bowling league.

Bill Davis—hoy, best-shot . . . intramurals.

* * *

Bobbie Mae Dutton—aggressive, accomplished, a versatile girl . . . Variety Shows; Zeta S.G.C. president; drama; G.A.A.; office worker; lab assistant; intramurals captain of Majorettes; Fashion Show.

Gloria Edge—small, sauce, office worker; Spanish club; Art club; intramurals.

Joan Efting—cheery, chatty, charming . . . Omega S.G.C.; College Day committee; Variety Show; intramurals; Music Festival; Latin club; National Honor Society; Girls' Chorus; biology newspaper; Fashion Shows.

John Efting—tall, thin, "the thing" . . . Social committee; Variety Show; Senior Play; intramurals; Music Festival.

* * *

Nancy Eversole—author, amiable, attractive . . . Graduation committee; Variety Show; Fashion Show; Music Festival; office helper, Sigma S.G.C.; Program committee; hall guard; Spanish club; intramurals.

Phyllis Faust—devastating, delightful, dangerous . . . 4A Social committee; Zeta S.G.C.; hall guard; intramurals; G.A.A.

Lois Gibbs—popular, pretty, personality . . . Cheerleaders; Service Girl; Social committee; Nominating committee; office helper; Posture Contest; intramurals; Fashion Show; Variety Show; hall guard.

Michael Ginakakis—gentlemanly, good guy, Greek . . . Greek club; intramurals; Latin club; lab assistant.

* * *

Gerald Goldstein—genial, generous, "Ger" . . . Honor Society; Program committee; intramurals.

Athina Gregory—courteous, cooperative, congenial . . . G.A.A.

Ken Hansen—Bev's boy, bold, best line . . . Student Council; Special Chorus; Variety Show; Music Festival; lab assistant; Senior Play; hall guard; LOG staff; Honor Society; Clean-up committee, chairman.

Larry Hauber—tall, tow-head, tops . . . swim team; baseball team; band; intramurals; bowling league.

Amundsen High School yearbook photos in January 1951 show Kenneth Hansen, "Bev's boy," bottom row, far right. Ken's future wife, Beverly Rae Carlson—"red-head, radiant, real swell"—is in third row from the top, second from left.

Image courtesy of Mark Hansen

Ken Hansen, around 1955, shows off his collection of competition trophies.
Photo courtesy of Mark Hansen

Curt Hansen (left), his wife, Sally, and Ken Hansen in the 1970s.
Photo courtesy of Mark Hansen

Silas Carter Jayne, the "godfather" of the Equestrian Mafia, was in custody in 1979. Photo courtesy of James Delorto

Bev and Ken Hansen, the high school sweethearts, in middle age.

Photo courtesy of Mark Hansen

James "Jimmy-boy" Delorto is fourteen in 1955. Photo courtesy of James Delorto

James Delorto in 1991 is on duty in the office of the ATF. Photo courtesy of James Delorto

James Delorto poses on the street in 1985. Photo courtesy of James Delorto

Sky Hi Stables, shown here in July 1966, was owned by Ken and Bev Hansen; in 1970 they merged it with High Hopes Stables and renamed it Sky Hi Hopes Stables. Photo courtesy of Mark Hansen

Jack O'Malley stirred considerable controversy during his term of office as Cook County state's attorney. Photo by Joel Longmeyer

Ken Hansen was sixty-one years old at the time of his arrest August 11, 1994, for the three murders. Photos courtesy of James Delorto

Roger Spry was a chief prosecution witness.

Photo courtesy of James Delorto

This 1955 photo is believed to be of the Bro-Ken H Stables in Willow Springs.
Photo courtesy of Mark Hansen

Joseph Plemmons (left), Ken Hansen, and one of his prized Dobermans at
Sky Hi Stables in the early 1970s. Photo courtesy of Mark Hansen

Arthur O'Donnell, the "gentleman" (left), and Jed Stone, the "street fighter," answer reporters' questions following the verdict in the first Kenneth Hansen trial. Photo by Robert A. Davis. Defense lawyers. Reprinted with special permission from the Chicago Sun-Times Inc. © 2003. September 7, 1995.

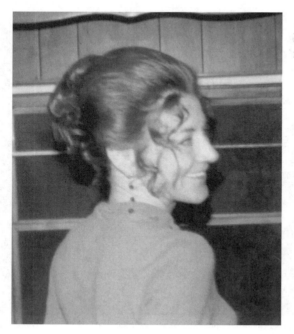

Beverly Hansen is caught in a carefree moment.

HAYRACK RIDES

"WE GO RAIN OR SHINE"

- HAY RACK PARTIES
- COVERED OR OPEN WAGONS
- HORSES BOARDED, BOUGHT & SOLD

RIDING INSTRUCTIONS
PRIVATE OR GROUP
LARGE INDOOR ARENA

TA lcott 3-0100
IDLE HOUR STABLES
RALPH FLEMING, PROPRIETOR
8600 HIGGINS ROAD — PARK RIDGE

An Idle Hour Stables newspaper advertisement in 1955 offers hayrack rides and riding lessons in the large indoor arena.

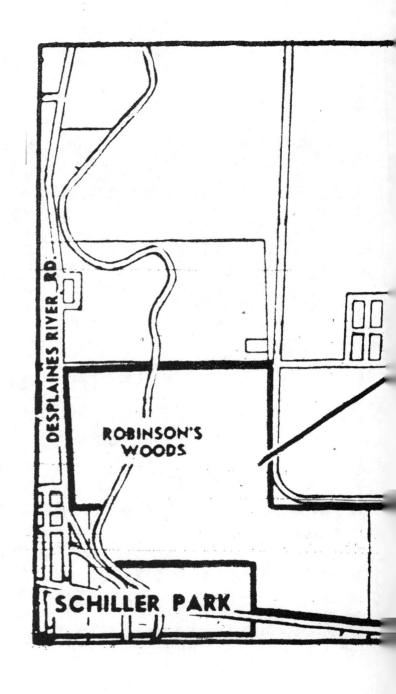

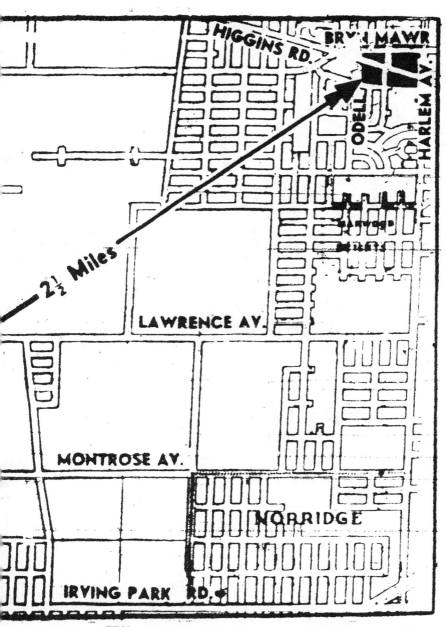

The 1955 map connects Robinson Woods to the vicinity of the Idle Hour Stables in Park Ridge, where the neighbors claimed to have heard boyish screams. Much of the adjacent area was prairie land at the time. The possibility that the boys were killed out on the open field and not inside the stable must be carefully weighed against the testimony of the nearby residents and Bob Breen, who was living on the premises at the time. *Chicago American* map. October 27, 1955. Copyrighted 1955, Chicago Tribune Company. All rights reserved. Used with permission.

Judge Michael P. Toomin of the Cook County Circuit Court presided over the first trial of Kenneth Hansen.

Attorney Leonard Goodman took up the cause of Kenneth Hansen in the belief that the wrong man had been convicted. His work has been pro bono.
Photo courtesy of Leonard Goodman

Helen Voorhees is pictured at the time of her marriage to Frank Brach.

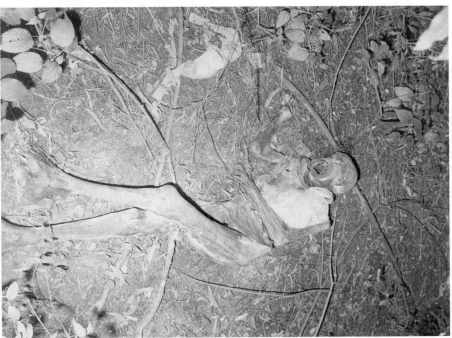

Is this Helen Brach or Helen Doe? The remains of this unidentified female murder victim were found on 159th Street about ten months after Helen vanished.
Photo courtesy of James Delorto

Requiescat in pace. The boys are laid to rest. Photos courtesy of Lawrence Raeder

10

Till Death Do We Part

WITH THE GEORGE JAYNE fiasco played out, the murder-conspiracy charges filed against Kenneth Hansen in 1971 faded from public memory. His long reign as stable boss, master of the trail ride, and horse seller nearly over, Kenny melted into the backwash of the distant southern suburbs of Cook County. For the first time in his life, he was free to indulge his sexual fantasies without always having to be mindful of his wife.

By 1987, the former Amundsen High School sweethearts were divorced, and the Camelot Stables, their last horse ranch, was gone. "That divorce," Ken Hansen said, letting out a sigh. "Her mother talked her into it. Her mother was never happy with me . . . " Real estate taxes had tripled, forcing the Hansens to sell the entire property to a developer to pay off the taxes. "The land becomes valuable," their son Mark said. "People don't want horses. They want *houses*."

Strip malls, townhouse developments, and acres of asphalt covered over the fields of tall grass that had flanked the two-lane country highways snaking southward through Cook and Will Counties. The same patterns of urban sprawl that devoured the virgin prairie land near the Idle Hour in the 1960s now threatened the livelihoods of the remaining stable owners at the other end of the county. Changing popular tastes caused the livery business as it had been conducted in the previous decades to decline sharply. A generation of kids who had never heard of Spin and Marty, Roy Rogers, or Paladin showed little interest in participating in slow-paced hayrides in the age of electronics. Haunted Halloween rides and pumpkin carving are still popular in late autumn and reflect the seasonal nature of the today's livery business. But it is not nearly enough to keep up with the overhead of feeding and lodging horses and paying rising property taxes.

After shutting the gate on the old corral one last time and with the ink still drying on his divorce decree, Ken Hansen moved his belongings into a white frame house at 18761 Cicero Ave., the main thoroughfare of County Club Hills, the Crossroads of Opportunity, an integrated, middle-income suburb located twenty-five miles south of Chicago. Invisible in this out-of-the-way suburb, Hansen sold litters of Doberman pinschers once a year to roadside customers, battled the ravages of diabetes, and, according to investigators, continued to carry on with a succession of young boys and men that no one seemed to care much about. Many stories of this irredeemable pedophile's sexual escapades emerged. Fairly typical was an incident that occurred in 1975 when Steven Rycraft was in his early twenties. According to Rycraft, he was tricked into going to Hansen's apartment, where Hansen got drunk and savagely attacked him. The forced penetration caused rectal bleeding for several days afterward. "Stop whimpering!" growled Kenny to his unwilling victim, who was forced to endure the deep and painful humiliation for many long minutes.

"What a piece of trash he [Hansen] was!" Jack Reed, the former Cook County Sheriff's Police detective, exclaimed as he describes the lifetime of pain and suffering Kenny inflicted on one underage victim, whose identity remains closely guarded. "We talked to this young man that Hansen drugged, sodomized, and finally dumped near 159th Street and the Rock Island Railroad tracks. He [the youth] never got over it. Today he's an alcoholic bust-out who can't sleep through the night, hold a job, or function normally in society. When you talk to this guy today, it's like talking to the victims of the pedophile priests we hear so much about."

Reed said that Ken Hansen used horses as the lure to entice victims into his car and was successful because "He always read people better than most. He was an astute psychologist, if you will. I don't know how many lives he ruined, but I think he should be buried in the deepest hole in the earth," the retired detective quickly added with bitterness in his voice.

Unable to reconcile as husband and wife, Bev managed, for a time at least, to strike a common ground with Ken, who continued in the day-to-day management of the stables. Bev had managed to keep her little family housed, fed, and clothed amid the profligacy of Ken's secret life. Later, during his prison-cell interview, when asked if Bev knew that he was bisexual, Hansen replied, "Oh, no, no, no. I hope not! It was certainly something that you kept quiet about. I hope Beverly didn't know but I don't think she did. I was not promiscuous, you know. . . . But any affair I ever had [with a man] was consensual I have never forced myself on anybody, ever."

Bev was "the bean-counter of the family, and that stable was her life," said her son Mark, a forthright and hard-working husband and father who bears the scars of years of emotional turmoil and an inner-directed conflict towards a father he both loves and reviles. Bev supervised the family business and remained on cordial terms with her ex until the livery business began to drop off, and she was no longer able to keep the business running on a profitable basis as she had before.

Coupled with a succession of devastating financial reversals, including the theft of valuable farm equipment by a dishonest stable hand, the situation grew increasingly desperate and may have provoked a failed suicide attempt by Beverly. "Her brother was institutionalized from the age of twenty until he died," Kenny explained. "He definitely had serious problems, and she [Bev] had several nervous breakdowns, and we brought her out of it [her depression]." Consumed by an overwhelming sense of displacement and slipping deeper and deeper into despondency over the loss of her beloved stable, Beverly Hansen committed herself to a psychiatric treatment center in Tinley Park.

Her slow deterioration was painful for Mark to watch because he loved his mother very much. Mark also related that his father seemed concerned about her plight. Though divorced, she continued to live on and off with Hansen in a separate trailer next to his Country Club Hills residence. She was also living with Mark and his future wife, Debbie, and seemed to perk up when performing the mundane chores of farm life. "Baling hay was her therapy," Mark recalled.

On June 12, 1989, the last day of her life, Bev did not appear to her son to be overly despondent as compared to her earlier bouts of depression. In a conversation with Mark the night before, she seemed surprisingly buoyant and upbeat—not what one would normally expect from someone contemplating the unthinkable. Beverly Hansen was looking forward to the arrival of the department-store deliveryman and a roomful of new furniture purchased only two days before.[1] She had her heart set on brightening up the house in Country Club Hills, having waited a long time to do it up right. Despite the financial quandary Beverly was in at the time, "she was *not* a person contemplating suicide," said Jim Delorto, bothered by the obvious contradiction. "Would a person planning to kill herself go out and buy furniture?"

Mark and Debbie were working at Glenwood Stables, their five-acre horse farm, when Kenny telephoned. "Have you seen your mother?" he asked with mild urgency. Beverly was back with her son and his girlfriend but had held on to a set of keys to the Country Club Hills residence and from time to time would drive over there to putter in the garden, check the mail, or just pass the time of day. When she failed to show up for breakfast with Kenny at the Calumet Restaurant on Sauk Trail

Road close to Mark's farm that morning, Hansen placed another call to his son. "I was supposed to meet her here. Do you know where the hell she is?" Mark said he had no idea where she might be and hung up the phone. His dad called two more times. "I'm going back home," he said with mounting irritation.

The next call was placed from Country Club Hills, where Kenny had allegedly just made a grisly discovery. Beverly's lifeless form was suspended from the base of the trapdoor leading up to the attic crawl space. A vacuum-cleaner cord was wound tightly around her neck. Kenny had reached for his pocketknife and cut her down. Then he called his son one more time.

As terrible as the news of Beverly's apparent suicide must have been to Mark, his father, agitated and upset, asked that his son keep his wits about him and follow precise instructions. Kenny ordered Mark to go to the Country Club Hills house and look after things but said that he wouldn't be there by the time Mark arrived. "Be sure to bring a pocketknife with you. And you must tell the cops that *you* found her, do you understand?" Kenny explained that "he couldn't handle it" and had to leave.

Mark's only explanation for his dad's strange reaction to Bev's death goes back to his father's personality traits acquired early in life. Kenny was ill equipped to handle trauma or face up to personal crises in a responsible manner. "He is one of the smartest people I know—but also one of the stupidest. He reads three hundred novels a year and is a reservoir of knowledge. He could have been a great CEO . . . " It is pointless for him to say anymore on that subject.

Mark, age thirty at the time of this tragedy, complied with his father's odd request and for his trouble ended up in the crosshairs of an investigation. He found his mother sprawled on the floor just as Kenny described and waited twenty minutes before calling long-time family attorney Art O'Donnell, who advised him to call 911 right away. When the Country Club Hills police arrived on the scene minutes later, Mark lied to them, as instructed. "I cut her down," he said.

"Did you check to see if she was alive?" an officer asked.

"I touched her. I knew she was dead," shrugged Mark. The death of Beverly Rae Hansen was officially classified as "death by hanging"—an obvious suicide. Close the case file. End of story or so it might have seemed.

Dave Hamm's intuition told him there was more to it than an attractive, depressed, middle-aged woman killing herself on a cloudless summer morning in June with the furniture men soon to arrive. Kenneth Hansen was in a tight spot. With the miseries of old age staring him directly in the face and without visible means of support, he had to carefully weigh his options and chart a course for the future. The house and almost every other item of value, according to Hamm, were in Beverly's name following the divorce. For years, Bev had held the fragile threads of their marriage together, despite Kenny's "ways" and his constant carping about her "running the business into the ground." Was it suicide or murder? The circumstances of her death are cloudy and disputed.

Debbie Hansen does not believe her father-in-law could have done such a terrible thing as that. She believes his concerns for his ex-wife at the time that Camelot Stable was coming down belie the actions of a murderer. "Over the Christmas holidays [prior to Beverly's death], Ken suggested the family go to Florida in order to take Beverly's mind off the tearing down of the barn," Debbie said. "Ken didn't want to see her so depressed, and he knew that leaving town was a good thing. I'll be honest with you when this happened, I actually was not surprised because she had committed herself into Tinley [sanitarium] for a couple of weeks."

Hansen certainly had the motive and ample opportunity to kill her. "He wasn't going to be included in her will, and he knew it. She was going to leave it all to Mark, and Ken didn't have a pot to piss in," Delorto explained. "He knew he could work on Mark once Bev was out of the way. All of Kenny's old-age needs would be taken care of with his ex-wife gone." Hansen would finally have had a place to call his own.

"I knew she had a problem," Mark said. "Did I think she would kill herself—the answer is no. If I thought *for a minute* that my father had killed my mother, I would have gone to the police. Besides, you don't murder a person by hanging them."

Neither the tiny, under-equipped Country Club Hills Police Department nor the Cook County State's Attorney pushed for an investigation.

Jim Delorto and others in law enforcement are at odds with the suicide theory. Delorto is convinced Beverly Hansen was strangled to death on the first floor and then dragged upstairs to be strung up and cruelly displayed—Kenny's coup de grace to a woman who had tried and failed to inculcate the milk of human kindness into her husband. "She was a very thin woman, and a series of unexplained bruises were visible on her backbone—bruises that are consistent with being dragged over a bumpy surface, or stairs," Delorto said.

"Women who commit suicide do not do so by hanging themselves," observed Art Bilek, who has seen enough of these horrors to know. "In all my years of police work, I cannot think of one suicide I have *ever* investigated involving a woman who killed herself with a rope. That is simply not how a woman goes about ending her life. I'm surprised the police bought into it."

Homicide investigators call this deliberate deception "staging a scene." "In some situations, the police have been too quick to classify a case as suicide based on their initial observations at the scene," writes Vernon J. Geberth in *Practical Homicide Investigation*. Too often, a police investigation that fails to collect necessary evidence at the crime scene results in prosecutors not receiving enough information to justify the filing of an indictment.

Dave Hamm said he believes that "Ken was absolutely capable of murder. He had a sociopathic personality. *He* killed his wife." Classic sociopsychopaths are utterly manipulative, devoid of normal guilt feelings, and without fear of consequences.[2] Their capacity for cruelty is often disguised by an engaging personality and surface charm. They employ this charm to manipulate, intimidate, and control others in order to satisfy their own selfish needs. Hamm said Hansen meets all the established criteria.

"Sexual psychopaths learn to manipulate and victimize early," writes Jonathan Kellerman in *Savage Spawn: Reflections on Violent Children*, "sniffing out vulnerability and weakness with the agility of heat-seeking missiles. They begin with victims who can't complain—animals—and hone their skills tormenting, killing, and mutilating before moving on to human prey." That Hansen was intentionally cruel to the horses and animals he took care of while working for his father years earlier is probable but as yet unproven. His mistreatment of the stable horses at Camelot and Sky Hi in later years is well documented by the Hooved Animal Humane Society (HAHS), which charts and investigates complaints phoned into their offices.

Questioned by a *Tribune* reporter, HAHS investigator Sally Bradley Milo, who worked for Donna Ewing, characterized Hansen's attitude as "defiant" after she threatened to impound his animals when she found out that he had sold off malnourished horses for dog meat. "We'd go in there, and he'd say, 'What horses do you want me to send to the killers now?' We were an annoyance to him, and he played with us. He knew if we got a call, we had to check it out, and he had his way around it. He always won."

In his assessment of criminally violent psychopaths, Dr. Robert Hare states that about two-thirds of their victims were male strangers, whereas two-thirds of the victims of nonpsychopaths were family members or acquaintances.[3] Ken Hansen's victims were drawn from a mostly anonymous pool of adolescent and postadolescent males picked up along the highway. According to Geberth, the sociopsychopath

> selects a victim which he considers the 'right type,' someone he can control (either through manipulation or strength), usually a stranger. Most of the victims will share some common traits. He uses his verbal skills to manipulate his victims and gain control over them until he has them within his comfort zone. He is excited by the cruelty of the act and may engage in torturing the victim. He is aware of police procedures. The body is often removed from the crime scene.

Why the strange death of Beverly Hansen was not fully investigated reflects poorly upon the peculiar brand of politics and the tug of war between police and prosecutors in the Chicago region that to the layman seems as visible and yet as mysterious as fox fire. "Half the battle we face as investigators is convincing the prosecutors," sighed Hamm, who thinks back to Beverly Hansen with much remorse.

As for Hansen himself, in an interview for this book, he was asked if he killed his wife.

> Absolutely not! If Herb Hollatz thought that I had hurt the woman that he loved, yeah, he would do anything to put me where I am. I mean that was the crux of the thing. And I, she was under psychiatric care, and she was suicidal, and she was a manic depressive, and I thought she was on medication. No, I didn't kill my wife. I loved Bev.
>
> Selling the stables was unfortunately the straw that broke the camel's back. You know, we were behind in the taxes, and they'd double our taxes and tripled our taxes, and we couldn't make enough money just to pay our taxes, so, I mean, it was either lose the place to the government or sell it.

11

The Long Road Home

TRAFFIC STARTED MOVING AGAIN, the blaring horns stopped, and the cursing came to an end. Jim Delorto gently pressed his right foot to the accelerator, easing the light-blue 1993 Chevy Impala forward. He managed to keep pace with the glut of rush-hour traffic jamming the Eisenhower Expressway, a ribbon of congestion connecting the city to the Interstate 88 tollway and the western suburbs. His destination was the Aurora-Batavia exit in remote Kane County, but on this day, his mind wandered. Thinking back to his childhood days, Delorto heard himself say, "C'mon, let's go fishing!" The sound came from deep inside, a cry from that time in his life when he answered to the name "Jimmy-boy." Other vivid scenes from his past flashed through his mind, images as fresh as if they had happened yesterday. William "Red" Wemette's frank and revealing admission had kindled these thoughts.

After a nearly two-hour commute, he finally pulled into his own driveway. Delorto unhooked his seatbelt and opened the car door. As he sat in his car, he thought about his second-hand Schwinn bike, a gift from his parents prior to his fourteenth birthday in 1955. He remembered feeling as invincible as Superman when he was astride that shiny silver bicycle.

The carefree good ole days of lookin' cool and ridin' 'round Robinson Woods with his buddies at his side abruptly had ended with news of the triple homicide in October 1955. His life dramatically changed, as did the lives of so many other children throughout the Chicago metropolitan area. Fearful parents laid down strict rules for youngsters to follow. A generation of Chicago kids was curtly informed that they could no longer play outside after sunset. Doors were to be locked at all times, and there was to be no hitchhiking under any circumstances. Life as they had once known it changed not only for the children but for the grown-ups as well.

Delorto and his schoolyard chums Ralph Ciangi and Harry Fulk did not care much about what their angst-ridden parents had to say or the conflicted emotions their parents were experiencing in the wake of the defining tragedy. The boys confidently believed they were big enough, strong enough, and smart enough to outwit the bogeyman if such a sinister presence even existed.

Fishing in Robinson Woods or one of the other forest preserves scattered across the county ranked high with boys age ten to fifteen. "The fish didn't bite if the sun was shining," Delorto mused. "All of us in the neighborhood fished after dark, and two of the best places to camp out were near the Des Plaines River in Robinson Woods or the pond in the Elmwood Park Cemetery." But now, the young Delorto was suddenly under constant parental surveillance, even if he was in the company of his brothers or friends. The bogeyman, they were warned, was out there, and every child was a potential target. "What bogeyman?" Jimmy wondered.

As a general rule, Delorto didn't like to waste time reflecting on childhood nonsense. He had a habit of walking away when anyone asked him questions about his past, and he made it a practice to assiduously avoid engaging in those kinds of conversations. In private moments, however, childhood memories occasionally flickered up from his subconscious.

Jimmy grew up contented and relatively free from strife, with his three brothers in the middle-class surroundings of Elmwood Park, just over the city limits of Chicago, west by northwest. James M. Delorto Sr., Jim's dad, managed a group of workers at the Israel Hat Company, a manufacturer of ladies' hats during a time, not so very long ago, when the well-dressed woman would not dare to venture out of the house without an appropriate head covering.

The elder Delorto and his bride, Maria, began married life in the Italian quarter on the Near West Side, at Loomis and Lexington, a crowded ethnic ghetto brushing up against the Greek Delta to the immediate north and the Jewish Maxwell Street to the south. James Sr. and Maria soon had four spirited boys. For much the same reasons as the Schuesslers had for abandoning Logan Square apartment life in favor of Jefferson Park and the Petersons had for leaving Swedish Andersonville, the Delorto family had for leaving the Italian neighborhood. They had outgrown the confines of the cluttered Little Italy. In 1947, the Delortos followed many other Taylor Street Italians by moving west to Elmwood Park, a 1920s' planned community. The family settled into a modestly appointed brick bungalow at Eightieth Avenue and Westwood in the Parish of St. Celestine, not far from Harlem Avenue, Chicago's new and emerging *Corsa Italia* or Italian Boulevard.

In 1955, Jim was an eighth grader at the local Catholic school but already looking forward to beginning his freshman year at Elmwood Park High. His mind flashed back to a frightening incident that had occurred not far from the grassy ditch where Victor Livingston found the corpses of the murdered boys in Robinson Woods. "So why did I become so spooked by it? Did I think it could happen to me?" he now wondered. The other question he asked himself was just *when* exactly was he forced to take his mother's fears to heart and concede that she was probably right. Delorto thought long and hard.

Although he didn't admit it to himself or his friends at the time, he had observed the same bedtime rituals as every other little kid who nervously glanced under the bed and into the closet before retiring. Other teenage boys slept with the nightlight on in the bedroom, Delorto recalled in a moment of self-justification.

Old and distant images of a cold November night in 1955 appeared in his mind's eye. Weekend camp-outs under the open skies in the company of his friends were now relegated to "girlish sleepovers," as Jimmy called them, on Friday or Saturday nights. From the time the three boys were killed, Delorto's parents were constantly checking up on him and his brothers. Delorto shared a bedroom with his younger brother Frankie, a room that was small and cluttered with schoolbooks and fishing and camping equipment. The two twin beds were covered with matching hand-crocheted spreads. On the night Delorto hosted his first sleepover, two sleeping bags were spread across the floor in between the beds. Frankie, who was four years younger, loved hanging around with his older brothers and was always willing to become a "partner in crime," that is, if they asked him.

The day before, Delorto and his two chums Ralph and Harry had pitched a small tent in the woods bordering River Grove's Elmwood Cemetery, a burial ground adjacent to St. Joseph's Cemetery and near where an older couple said they believed they saw Anton Schuessler Jr. in the company of Charles Dahlquist earlier that summer. The plan called for the three of them to sneak out of the house at a strategic moment when mom and dad were preoccupied downstairs and go fishing in the woods. In hindsight, it was a stupid idea, but when a kid is fourteen, he feels invulnerable to all earthly dangers. Uncharacteristically, Frankie expressed no desire to tag along, although deep down he probably wished he was older. There was no percentage in asking to go. His brother would have definitely said no.

Delorto reran the events of that evening. "We turned off the lights, except for the one on the nightstand, sat cross-legged in a tight circle on top of the camping equipment, and told scary stories. Frankie sat on his bed, wrapped in the spread Mom had made, and listened."

Frankie inched closer to the circle of teenage boys as they spoke of Blackie, the crazy cemetery caretaker who devoted his entire life to protecting the dead and hunting down trespassers. Blackie's clothes were always dirty . . . and his large hands looked as if there was blood on them. The cemetery custodian was a fearsome-looking man, who drove around in an old, gray Nash Rambler and patrolled the cemetery, "shagging everybody out." When the neighborhood kids saw him coming, they would yell "Blackie!" and then run for their lives. If they were caught, would Blackie turn them into the cops or worse—try to kill them?

"Remember Gary?" asked Ralph knowingly. They nodded solemnly. Gary was an eleven-year-old boy who wasn't a friend exactly, just a punk kid they knew from school who flaunted authority by vandalizing gravestones in the cemetery. It was common practice in those days for Catholic parishioners to pay the caretakers to affix embossed or laminated photos of the dearly departed to the headstones. Juvenile pranksters, like Gary, made a sport of racing in on their bikes and clenching a screwdriver to pry loose the mounted photos. And it was up to Blackie to catch them by whatever means available.

One Saturday afternoon, Gary had been at it again, when suddenly Delorto heard a horrible scream. "Help!" a boy cried out in the distance. It was Gary, as plain as day. Jimmy and his friends, who were just outside the cemetery's chain-link fence, stopped their baseball game to see what all the commotion was about. They stared wide-eyed as the red-faced, sweating boy on a bicycle made a beeline for the hole in the cemetery fence, desperately trying to escape the clutches of the crazed caretaker. Blackie's beat-up Nash was just too fast and was closing the gap. The car bounced noisily over the graves and flat headstones, knocking down flowers and shrubbery standing on the way, hell-bent on killing the trespasser. Jimmy had no doubt about it. Then they heard the sickening sound of crunching metal. The young boy flew off the old Huffy and with a dull thud landed headfirst in a thorny bush.

"Stay out of this cemetery, you damn whippersnapper! Do you hear me, boy?"

The youth was banged up pretty badly, and scratches covered his body. He pulled himself to his feet, wet pants and all. The bike was crushed.

Because of Blackie, Jimmy decided at the last minute that it made sense to leave little Frankie home this time. It was a chilly Saturday night, almost three weeks after the murders. Jimmy and his friends sat around his bedroom waiting for just the right moment to slip out. Jimmy's father relaxed on the couch watching *Gunsmoke*, while his mom washed the dinner dishes and prepared the kitchen for breakfast. Frankie was fast asleep. Finally, the moment had arrived. "Let's go!" Jimmy whispered and followed as the other two boys gingerly crept out the bedroom window and descended the two-story trellis to the ground. Jimmy, Harry, and Ralph jumped on their bikes parked nearby and zipped through the shadows in the alley. Within minutes, they crossed the intersection at Belmont and Cumberland. Enjoying an exhilarating rush of freedom, they streaked by the southern end of the forest preserve.

Out of breath, they finally reached the small tent sequestered in the woods less than fifty feet from one of their favorite fishing holes. After an hour or more had passed, the young adventurers gathered up their big catch and headed back to the patch of dense grass where their discarded bikes lay. They planned to camp out for a few more hours, for the time being forgetting about Blackie and the person or persons who killed the three boys.

Thinking back to these boyish, foolhardy escapades in the cemetery woods, Delorto stifled a smile and reached across and gathered up the office paperwork that lay helter-skelter on the passenger seat next to him. He realized that in some mysterious way, he might even be longing to return to those days of yesteryear.

He glanced towards his house. As much as he enjoyed his two-story, blue-gray brick residence in Batavia, it was the oversized garage that delighted him the most. With three young boys who enjoyed the space as much as he did, a three-car garage was a luxury akin to owning a Beverly Hills mansion. The Italian boy whose folks came from Taylor Street was every inch a prosperous suburbanite. He had come a long way. Funny sometimes, how things turn out.

As he sat in the quiet of his car, parked in front of that beautiful garage, Jimmy's thoughts raced back to the to the words of his friend Harry on that chilly November night. "Boy, it's creepy out here," he mumbled. The comment broke a ten-minute silence and was punctuated by Jimmy's announcement that he wanted to go back home. Evidently, he had not explained his actions clearly enough to his friends, because he was met with blank stares.

"Go home? We just got here!" The boys' sense of new-found freedom was short-lived, suddenly disrupted by the rustling noises of an advancing figure in the woods. "It's Blackie!" exclaimed Harry breathlessly. The oncoming footsteps, the crunching of leaves, all of the sounds made by the approaching figure scared the shit out of the boys. Ralph was certain it was "the man who killed the boys." Whoever it might be, none of them wanted to hang around a moment longer to find out. They scrambled, haphazardly dropping their catch along the way. Jimmy took cover behind a fallen tree. Harry fell by his side just as Ralph tripped and landed on his face. Ralph screamed for help, the terror in his voice sending a chill through his companions. Jimmy said his prayers. As the sound of the footsteps came ever closer, Jimmy made an Act of Contrition, reciting the prayer that Catholics reserve for times when death is imminent. At this terrible moment, his heart pounded. *Shit, why did I do this?*

He had never been as afraid of anything as he was now. Whatever happened beyond this point, he would have to accept the responsibility. The unseen presence suddenly grabbed Ralph by his left ear and the collar of his jacket and lifted him to his feet. To his enormous relief, it wasn't the forest preserve murderer or the imaginary nighttime ghoul. Instead it was two plainclothes police officers. Jimmy and Harry stood up, very much relieved but shaking and apologetic. After the police escorted him home that night, Jimmy faced his mother's full fury. "I was worried sick!" Maria cried, holding the door open. "I called the police!"

Later that night, Frankie confessed to his big brother what had happened. "Mom came in to check on you guys, and the pillows you put under the covers didn't work. She got all upset and called the cops, and I got scared. Mom kept saying, 'Frankie, you know where Jimmy-boy is. Tell me.' And so I did. You're not mad at me, are you?" "Naw," shrugged Jimmy, "I would have done the same thing." With those last words, the boys fell into a deep sleep. The following morning, they awoke to face the terrible wrath of the old man.

"Are you crazy, boy?" James Sr. said, glowering at his oldest son, who sat bolt upright in bed, his eyes wide open. "Stay out of those damn woods! That's all I have to say! Do you know what happened out that way just three weeks ago? Do you have *any* idea? Or do you want the same thing to happen to you?"

And so the adventurous young boy, who dreamed of becoming the real-life incarnation of Sergeant Joe Friday on TV's *Dragnet*, found himself grounded for the next two months. But he came away from the ordeal with an elemental truth and a valuable lesson learned. When you don't heed warnings or fail to tell your parents what you are up to, something bad is likely to happen in an unguarded moment. The thought of the Schuessler-Peterson kids was etched in Jimmy's memory, an example for how bad things can be if you exercise poor judgment.

Immersed in thought, Delorto continued to sit in his car and for a moment had forgotten the present. He wiped his brow, and his eyes darted from left to right. "Damn, what a time that was," he muttered. "Was I this same person back then?" So much time had passed, and so many bridges had been crossed. And now, through one of life's stranger coincidences, it was all brought back in sharp focus.

"I'm going to get the motherfucker who killed those boys," he muttered as he pushed the car door wide open. Jimmy was stiff and tired from fighting the expressway traffic. He thought about buying a Metra commuter rail pass and avoiding all of this grief. Maybe the train ride to and from the suburbs would afford him a few blessed moments of R&R or, at the very least, another chance to flip through the pages of his memory and piece together the fleeting fragments of a past that seemed so strangely distant. Delorto had to admit, however, that forty years later, the terror of the murders was still there. Delorto was now home safe and sound and intact, although a slight tension tugged in his chest. It was yet another reminder that if he continued like this, he would likely die before seeing his sixtieth birthday. He didn't like to think about his dad dying of a heart attack in 1982 at the age of seventy-two. With feigned cheerfulness, he called out, "I'm home."

Debbie greeted him with a hug, as was her custom. She recognized the odor of cigarettes clinging to her husband's person, but because he looked so tired, she didn't nag at him about the dangers of smoking. Jimmy lovingly kissed his wife on the forehead, took a pass on dinner, and headed straight up to bed.

12

"Oh, by the Way . . . "

IT WAS ANOTHER OVERCAST, dreary autumn afternoon. Nadia Martinez greeted Delorto with an end-of-the-day smile and mumbled,

"Rotunno's coming in tonight so I guess you'll be working late." Burdened by an exhausting day, Jimmy replied in his best loyal-soldier voice, "Good agents, like good secretaries, work late."

Nadia shook her head. "Good agents also have heart attacks," she said sarcastically. "I'll visit you in the hospital!"

Delorto ignored her good-natured chiding. "If you see Rotunno on your way out, let him know where I am."

"How do I know what he looks like?" Nadia muttered as she left the room. "Besides, how can he miss you? You're the only one left in the office!"

John Rotunno carried himself with authority. He stood six feet tall and had grown up on the Northwest Side of Chicago. After college, he locked in on a job with the federal Drug Enforcement Agency (DEA). Assigned to San Francisco, Rotunno was at the epicenter of one of the Justice Department's most controversial and harshly criticized investigations in the drug war—the closing off of the Nicaragua—San Francisco cocaine pipeline and the arrest of kingpin Norwin Meneses and eight members of his "family." In 1989, nearly six years after Rotunno penetrated Meneses's insulated world, the overlord of the cartel was convicted and incarcerated—not in San Francisco but in Nicaragua.

When an opportunity to transfer to the Chicago bureau of the ATF surfaced, Rotunno packed up his family and headed home. He was assigned to a task force investigating the Black Gangster Disciples (GDs), the largest and most imposing inner-city street gang in the United States. It was another drug conspiracy case, and Rotunno was looked up to as something of an expert because of his fine investigative work for the DEA. His name came up during one of Delorto's "circle jerk" meetings with staff (as these monthly management bull sessions were called) to compare leads and share sensitive intelligence about pending cases. Invariably, one group would possess key information that another could use. John Rotunno was the talk of the meeting. His team was credited with taking down 125 GDs—the hand-to-hand traffickers infesting the streets of Chicago.

At the next bull session, Delorto sought approval from the other seven key supervisors before adding Rotunno to the team. "I like this guy's tenacity. He's no bureaucrat, he's pure investigator," Jimmy said, as his eyes scanned the room looking for a favorable response from his colleagues. "I need someone with his own internal engine, an agent who likes his work and gets the job done." The supervisors obliged. Delorto had hit a homerun during his Horse-Mafia investigations, and Wemette's disclosures encouraged them to move forward with this latest exploration.

What I really need are a few more Red Wemettes, Delorto thought. He also needed to establish a link to one of the stable fires so his group could legitimately push the case. Murder wasn't within the ATF's jurisdiction. Delorto conveyed the news to Rotunno a week later, "I've got something really good for you and will tell you more about it if you want to come over."

His curiosity piqued, Rotunno expressed interest. "I'd like to get out of the ghetto for a while."[1] Arson sounded pretty good to him.

In recalling the conversation, Delorto said, "In the DEA, the only things you ever work on are drug cases and more drug cases. There is absolutely no diversity in the type of investigations you are called on to work. John wanted variety and new challenges. I respect that."

Arson was only a small part of the equation, the younger agent soon learned. The rest of it—a forty-year-old unsolved murder case as well as the incredible threads tying this guy Hansen to Helen Brach and Si Jayne—was incredible. But it would be another three to four months before Rotunno was freed up, forcing Delorto to bide his time on the Schuessler-Peterson investigation. But Jimmy also knew it was well worth the wait, and now that wait was finally over.

His eyes darted from the clock on the wall to a dog-eared, greasy-looking cardboard box resting on the floor next to his desk. The box was marked "Hamm." *Where the hell is Rotunno?* Delorto leaned over, grabbed the top file, and spread the contents across his desk. Not long after George Jayne's murder, Tom Drury of the IBI turned over the entire Schuessler-Peterson file to Dave Hamm, hoping that Hamm could make some use of it. And now Hamm had graciously extended the same courtesy to Delorto who remembered what Dave had told him that night on the phone, "I know Kenny is good for those murders."

Examining the documents, Jimmy came across a collection of old police reports dated October 18, 1955, along with signed statements of witnesses. Certain phrases jumped off the page, "screeching of tires . . . young voices screaming for help . . . sounds coming from the stable . . . loud dual-exhaust." Delorto fidgeted in his chair, thought for a moment, and murmured to himself, "Whatever happened to those boys *must* have happened in Jayne's stables."

With a sudden jolt, he stood straight up. "Damn!" He scribbled a few phrases on a memo pad to remind himself to alert the other agents. He remembered that many years earlier, Dave Hamm had been the first to voice suspicions about Ken Hansen and the three murdered boys. Delorto turned and opened the top drawer of his file cabinet and located a document labeled "Idle Hour Stables–1956." Weeks before, Delorto had managed to track down a tiny captioned photo of a stable fire in a *Chicago Tribune* article at the Chicago Public Library's microfilm reading room. He had stared at the screen for many minutes and wondered, *Why did the Idle Hour burn down on that day? Why on May 15, 1956?* Delorto had asked himself those questions over and over again. He backtracked through the newspaper archives for other relevant articles that give him answers. Through meticulous searching, the veteran street agent located a *Tribune* story from 1956 spelling it all out. The article described Coroner Walter McCarron's determination to convince the Schuessler and Peterson parents to allow his staff to exhume the bodies. A final check for trace evidence might uncover some bit of overlooked forensic clue about where the murders occurred. It wasn't long afterward that the Idle Hour Stables burned to the ground. Delorto suspected that if he could ferret out enough information from these old case files and newsclips to make a case for the ATF's arson division, there was a good chance the government would consider reopening this forty-year-old mystery to see *what else* lie hidden.

At first blush, the evidence appeared solid. The loose collection of strange facts was compelling, but the investigation would languish without the expertise of a Rotunno. Still Delorto had to wonder, *How was it possible that no one in law enforcement at the time connected the fire to the murders of the Schuessler-Peterson boys?* If just one of them—Lohman, Gutknecht, Deeley, or O'Connor—had threaded the needle, the case would have been closed in 1956. Delorto was certain of it. The sheer volume of dead-end leads was numbing: 43,740 people were interviewed, another 3,270 had been questioned as suspects with 244 given lie-detector tests. Over 3,000 investigators had worked tirelessly, many on their own time, but it yielded nothing. Was it just a case of bad luck, or was it inflated egos or incompetence?

"Hey, Jim, what do you say?" A rough voice broke the silence. It was Rotunno finally reporting for duty.

Delorto got right to the point. "I found what may be a break in a huge case. I need your hundred percent attention."

"You got it. I'm ready to go. So, what do you have?" Rotunno eased back in his chair, crossing his legs.

Delorto asked if he had ever heard of the Schuessler-Peterson murders.

The younger man frowned. "Wasn't that the case from the fifties? The three boys that got killed?" Rotunno added that he wasn't alive back then, and suddenly Delorto felt as old as Methuselah. "I remember my dad talking about it," Rotunno continued. "He knew all about it."

"Here's some material I want you to read," Jimmy said, picking up a sheaf of papers and pushing it into the agent's hands. "Oh, by the way, we're going out of town next week to meet with this CI that I happen to know."

"Who is it?"

Jimmy was coy. "You'll see." Delorto arose from his chair, motioning to Rotunno that it was time to go home.

That night, after Rotunno put his eight-year-old daughter to bed, he rang up his father, who filled him in on the lurid details of the 1955 child murders.

On their way to the airport a few days later on a dark and dreary Chicago morning, Jimmy briefed his new partner about the confidential informant they were scheduled to meet and interview on his home turf—Red Wemette.

"The porn guy?" Red was known by his reputation and the company he kept.

"Yep . . . the porn guy."

Delorto and Rotunno said little else to one another until their vehicle approached the crowded O'Hare lot. The flight was on time, and that afternoon, the ATF agents flew towards an undisclosed location in the south. Two hours later in a nearly empty terminal, they rented a four-door sedan. "One of those cheapies," Delorto said to the Hertz clerk. After a few more minutes, they reached the rent-a-car lot and were soon on their way to the Quality Inn nearest the rendezvous point with Red.

As they passed through the languid southern countryside, Delorto felt relaxed and completely at ease for the first time in weeks. By the time they reached their destination, the sun had already set, but the sky retained an orange hue, and the air was humid. It was a comfortable evening, and Delorto was less than impressed by his lodging. "Welcome to the Ritz!" Jim said, with no attempt to hide his sarcasm. He turned into the Quality Inn parking lot. Part of the neon had burned out on the motel's sign. Just across the parking lot, the agents spotted a bar. The government pays agents a sixty-dollar per diem. It is barely enough to cover the nut, and it remains a lingering bone of contention between the bean counters in Washington and the men and women trying to make do out in the field. "Let's meet in fifteen minutes in the bar," Rotunno said as he lifted his gym bag from the back seat of the car and walked toward the small, no-frills lobby of the motel.

That night over steaks and a beer for Rotunno and two fingers of scotch for Delorto, the agents covered all the bases in preparation for meeting Wemette in the morning.

"Hamm said he likes Hansen for this crime," Delorto said softly. "Red has always been upfront with me, but he said they were both stone-cold drunk the first time he confessed to the murders."

"How do you want to do this?" John interrupted. "He's your CI."

Delorto paused to swallow a piece of sirloin steak before answering. "Let Red talk. You'll see that he likes to ramble. When we need to redirect him, we will but otherwise let him finish. Let's find out exactly what he knows. I'll start with something like, 'What do you know about Kenny Hansen?'" Delorto took a sip of his scotch, paused, then said, "And look for any of his *oh-by-the-way*s. They're probably the most important part of the interview, when you get down to it."

Morning came much too early. The sun glared through the crack in the drapes, cutting across Delorto's face. He woke up with a jolt, and after a brief moment of uncertainty as to where he was, he peered at the clock radio. "Six! Shit!" he mumbled as he dragged himself out of bed and into the shower. The pressure was weak, but at least the water was hot. Delorto let the water drip down his back for several minutes before reaching for the soap. And, of course, the very moment he picked up the bar of soap, the telephone rang. Delorto turned the water off and stepped out of the shower. "Parking lot in fifteen. Did you call Red?" John Rotunno asked, sounding chipper.

A light flicked inside Wemette's medium-sized, vinyl-sided home. Two menacing Doberman pinschers bounded from the screened-in front porch, tails aquiver. They raced toward the agents in attack mode.

"Holy shit!" Delorto said under his breath.

"Fuck!" Rotunno exclaimed and stepped back. "Those are the biggest Dobes I've ever seen!"

As the two agents stepped back toward their rental car, a tall, thin, red-headed man strode out the front door, smiling broadly. "Don't worry. They won't hurt you as long as I'm here."

"You're full of shit," Delorto retorted. "I'm not coming up there until you call them off."

But before Red gave his dogs the command to retreat, the closest dog, in a playful gesture, stood up on his hind legs and dug his large front paws into the frightened, five-foot-eight-inch-tall agent's shoulders, planting a sloppy Doberman kiss on Jimmy's face. Delorto's nose was mere inches away from the Doberman's sharp canines. "You know, Red," Delorto said, "if your dogs had come through the screen door without you standing behind them, I would have popped 'em both."

"You know," snickered Red, "if they came through the door and were going to attack you, Delorto, you wouldn't have had time to open your briefcase and get your gun."

Red called the dogs off, and, like dutiful children, they retreated to his side. "You should have seen the look on your faces when you guys saw the dogs! You're both pussycats!" The former Chicago stable hand and Mob informant greeted the supervisor like a long-lost friend but smiled cautiously at Rotunno. "I'm so glad you're here, Jimmy. I've got a lot to say."

As the three men walked toward the house, Red seemed relieved to have the chance to unload by telling everything he knew. "I can't tell you how many times I mentioned it to FBI agents, but nobody would listen," he said in a weary, frustrated tone. "Nobody cared. It was at the Canterbury Farms in Gainesville, Florida.

"That's where Tommy Burns got busted for killing a horse," Red confided as he escorted the two agents to the rear of the house, where an iron table and four chairs rested on a patio next to a large swimming pool. A lot of scummy people were involved in racketeering and insurance-fraud schemes in the horse world.

"What do you know about these people and what they do?" Delorto probed.

Wemette rattled off the names of the trainers caught up in the investigation. "Bobby Lee Brown, Lee Ryder, Jerry Farmer, Frank Jayne, and Ron Mueller . . . there are others."

"What do you know about Lee Ryder?"

"Ryder is a copper from Skokie who was on Frank Jayne's payroll. Bob Brown is a Si Jayne horse-racket groupie. They would bring their horses to each other's shows. Their nags won medals, and then they'd take out a lot of insurance and then kill 'em."

"And that guy Ken Hansen?" Rotunno asked.

"That's a complicated story in itself," chirped Wemette. "Ah, Curtis Hansen, Kenny's brother . . . Uncle Roy used to date Marion Hansen, sister of Curt and Ken. Curt was a hit man for the Mob, and I went with Marion to see him at the Valley View YAC, and Ken always showed up. They used to play gin rummy all the time and eventually . . . well, that's where I met Hansen. I met him through Curt, and I met Curt through Marion."

The agents were familiar with the Curt Hansen and his terrible reputation.

"No horse dies of old age, not when you have insurance on them," Red said flippantly. "Marion? Well, she died many years ago. They kept her out of the limelight. In fact, I used to stay at her house over on Claremont Avenue."[2]

"How old were you when you met Curt?" Jim asked.

"I had to be eighteen. Maybe nineteen." Red stared at Jim for a moment. Then his eyes quickly darted over to Rotunno. "Mind you, I looked *very, very* young. I could pass for a fifteen- or sixteen-year-old. I had a baby face, red hair. I got carded until I was twenty-five."

Wemette continued. But this time he began to refer to himself in the third person, as if he were out of his body or talking about somebody else. "Red was a guy who felt very upset about what happened as far as the arrest. He was trying to vindicate himself for what he had done. He was out to change the world. Red left high school in his junior year and joined the Marines." Wemette paused, allowing his words to sink in. "Red was arrested while he was in the Marine Corps." He collected his thoughts before switching back to using the first person. "That's why I was discharged from the service. I felt very bad about it, and I felt I had let my country down. You see, I was a very carefree kid, and at that point, I realized that I had done something really wrong. And I wanted to try and make up for it in a big way." In 1970, Wemette was arrested for the transportation and sale of an M14 rifle, a military gun. "I was picked up across the street from the Magnum Chateau in Lyons, Illinois . . . case number 67CR603," he rattled on, chuckling nervously. "I was just a kid back then. The judge gave me six months of suspended probation."

Red paused and looked off in the distance. The sky was a crystalline blue, and the air thick and moist. The lights on the patio swayed gently every time a welcome breeze swept across the yard. "That was in '67," he continued. "I met Hansen a year later." He interrupted to explain his fascination with automatic weapons. "It was a different kind of thing because I had played with machine guns before. Actually, it was exciting to me because it didn't just go bang. I liked handling them. Two of the other guys collected those heavy eleven-pound M1 rifles from World War II, and I was really fascinated with all of it."

Delorto stood up, stretched, and walked to the edge of the pool and gazed out at the rolling green pastures. "Okay, so what about Kenny?"

"That's what I was getting at," Red shot back. "I found out about Curt through my uncle, who was a cabdriver. And so, on my own, at that moment, I decided to make Curt my first target for arrest. I had gone out with an agent by the name of Leaky for a few undercover buys."

"So am I to believe that right out of the Marine Corps you became an informant?"

"Yeah, that's about it, Jimmy," Red smiled. "In order to keep close to Curt, I hung with Kenny." It was another few minutes of awkward silence before Red blurted out, "It's not like I wormed my way into Kenny's home. He wormed his way into *mine*." The words coming out of Red's mouth were precise and cautious. "He wasn't a very likable person, but he had this phony charm that tricked people into liking him. The first time I met him he was over at the YAC, Curt's place. He had everything out there . . . a swimming pool . . . everything a person could want.

"Procol Harum and all of those rock groups that were big in the late 1960s, early '70s went to Valley View YAC. I met Buddy Rich and his daughter. I met a lot of celebrities."

"I seem to recall you mentioning that. Oh, yeah, very exciting," Delorto said impatiently.

"Curt was a terribly dangerous guy. On the other hand, Kenny had this high squeaky voice and seemed very feminine to me. He was not the kind of person I really wanted to know. However, one day after playing cards, he came to me and said, 'I have horses, too. I have stables.'" Wemette continued to relate his story as the agents took notes. "So I said to him, 'That's nice,' and I remember walking away from Kenny, and he followed me like a puppy dog. 'Would you help me carry something over to the stable?' I hesitated, and then said, 'Okay.' Then he said, 'I need a lift,' so I drove him in my car. I think he had an accident or didn't have a driver's license or maybe didn't have a vehicle." Red slowed down so the agents could keep up with him. "We got to his place, Sky Hi Stables. When we arrived, the car was immediately surrounded by twenty, maybe twenty-five, of his Dobermans." Certain that he had the agents' attention, Red stood up, circled behind his chair, and recalled, "There were people there, lots of customers, kids, whatever. I was still afraid to get out of the car.

But I did get out and unloaded his stuff. That was the first time I had an extended conversation with Kenny Hansen."

By 1968, Kenneth and Beverly Rae Hansen were in the middle of their marriage and raising two young boys, Danny and Mark.[3] Over the ensuing months, Red and Beverly became very close. "I liked Bev. Mark would sit on my lap and fall to sleep. He craved a father figure. He was a darling kid." Red's face saddened as he recalled his friendship with Kenny's pretty red-headed wife. "She'd drink Courvoisier, and once when we were at Jardine's, it must have been in the winter, out of the blue she said to me, 'Everybody knows that you replaced Roger Spry as Kenny's boyfriend.'"[4] Wemette hotly denied any implication that he was gay. "'Hey,' I told her, 'I did *not* replace him, and I have *no intention* of replacing him.'"

Roger Spry had started living with Ken and Bev when he was almost eleven. As an adult, he became a party to the horseman's arson and fraud schemes.

Leaning closer, Delorto told Red in a low voice, "I know Roger. He cooperated with us in the Helen Brach case."

Red had no special fondness for Spry, but he had concerns about Hansen. "The first day I met Kenny, I sensed there was something wrong with him. I also believed that I was very capable of handling myself, and I didn't have to worry about him. He was a short guy and not tough at all. He wasn't like Curtis. I watched Curt beat people at blackjack and then bust them up for losing."

Delorto sensed that Red was embarrassed, awkward, and uncertain of himself.

"Kenny was a con man. Very docile. And Curt had a motel on Route 30 in Frankfort. So one day Marion called her brother Curt and said, 'I want you to give him [Red] a job, and I want him to live out there.'"

Delorto looked puzzled. "So you were living at Curt's place. May I ask why?"

"To get close to him because I was an informant and I wanted to see him busted."

Delorto was confused by Red's odd living arrangements and was growing impatient. "What does all of this have to do with Kenny?"

"I lived in the motel. Curt had a lot of different people living there. He had a big place to manage, and he needed people—lifeguards at the pool, stable hands, you name it. He had to have a staff of thirty to forty people." Wemette was a self-professed jack-of-all-trades. He trimmed hooves, forged shoes, cleaned up horseshit—just about any demeaning task Curt asked him to do around the stables, and he did it with a smile. "I did what I was told to do. I worked in the kitchen. I'd saddle up the horses . . . whatever. But all of a sudden, Curt tells me to 'Get out,' so I got out!"

Red's life choices were poor, and now years later, he had to live with that. In a voice tinged with bitterness and remorse, he reflected on his tragic mistakes. "I was trained to fight in Vietnam, and I had orders to ship out, and, boy, was I ready to go. I was supposed to report to Travis Air Force Base. I was on leave, and I came home to pick up $500 extra money from the machine-gun sale. I was stupid. That was the end of my military career, and now, once again, I was homeless."

"You weren't afraid of Curt?"

"Afraid of Curt? Yes, who wasn't? Hell, yes, I was afraid of Curt. I watched him put a guy through a window. So one day I go over to Kenny Hansen's place," Red said, picking up the thread of his story. "He lived in a house trailer on the property. There was a stable and a barn, too, and his whole family lived there with him. The trailer had three bedrooms, two baths. Beverly had a dog kennel where she raised dogs. Anyway, I told Kenny what happened, and he said, 'Why don't you come in and have a drink.' It wasn't a question. He pulled out a bottle of Cutty, and we started drinking. I drank a lot of scotch in the Marines so I wasn't worried. I remember him getting up from the table and leaving the room. When he came back, he had a small bag of marijuana. 'Do you want some of this?' he asked me. 'No,' I said. 'I don't do that stuff.' And he said, 'Okay.' I was carrying a .45 in the small of my back. I always did in those days, so if anything went down, I was certain I'd make it out alive."

John wondered if that kind of talk was just part of his tough-guy bluster. "Were there any other drugs in the house?"

Red shook his head no. "So I went to the bathroom. I knew he was up to no good, but I also knew that I wanted to keep close to Curt and staying at Kenny's place was the best place for me to be. Curt's wife, Sally, Beverly, and the two boys were in Las Vegas."

Red repositioned himself in the chair. "Kenny hung up my keys up high on a wall in the trailer and said, 'I don't think you should drive tonight. You've had a lot to drink.' I agreed and felt a wave of relief. I never expected what happened next to happen."

According to Wemette, Kenny led him into one of the boys' bedrooms. As they passed the bathrooms, Red could hear the whimper of puppies. "There were a lot of Doberman pups in the third bedroom," he remembered. "Anyway, I sat on the lower bunk bed in the boys' room. My head was whirling, and I was beat. I took off my shirt and jeans and was in my skivvies. It wasn't long before I fell into a deep sleep. Later on, I don't know how long it was, but I woke up to find Kenny trying to pull down my underwear for Chris' sakes!"

"'You don't even want to think about that,' I said to Kenny. 'I'm a Marine, and I'll go to the police.' That's when he backed off." In spite of what happened that night, Red moved his gear into the Sky Hi Stables. Roger Spry also lived at Kenny's ranch. "He was Kenny's lover, his homosexual lover. And the boy was hostile about it! He came to me once and said, 'Why are you calling me a queer?' He asked me what I was doing in the trailer with Kenny at night."

Wemette finally volunteered the information the agents had come looking for. "Oh, by the way, I remember Roger once asked me if Kenny mentioned the Peterson boy. I told him I didn't know. I told him we had a lot to drink, and I wanted him to understand that I didn't want anything to do with Ken . . . in that way. 'I don't want any problems with you, Roger,' I said. 'So just go your own way.'"

Upon hearing the first "Oh, by the way . . . ," Delorto's and Rotunno's eyes widened.

"Did Kenny tell you about the Peterson boy?" probed Delorto.

"Yeah," Red stammered. "Well, the one time he told me amongst many other things that night he was bragging about, um . . . about him killing these Peterson boys in '55."

"What did he tell you?"

"He told me it was a very famous case, and then he held up his hand and with his index finger and thumb about a half-inch apart said, 'I came about this close to being in the headlines.'"

"That's it? That's all Hansen said?"

"I thought he said it to impress me. He told me about a lot of other things that he had done, like burning down barns."

Jim interrupted, "You were drunk at the time, right?"

"Yep, we were drunk," Red replied, smiling wryly. "But Kenny said to me, 'I killed those two boys in '55, but I didn't mean to do it.' He said that." The agents let him continue. "I don't know why he told me, but he did." For a moment, Red was silent, thinking hard. Then he added, "Curt told me . . . he always referred to Kenny when he wasn't around as 'my fag brother.' Once, after I moved back into Curt's place, he asked me what happened the night I went over to Kenny's, and he said, 'I had to clean up after my fag brother. I always wanted a brother and, instead, I got a sister.'"

Rotunno interrupted, "Curt told you he cleaned up after his brother?"

"No, Curt said he had to clean up after his fag brother when he killed those kids."

Delorto leaned back in his chair. Red sat motionless as if he was holding something back, a tidbit of information that might blow things open.

"Did you ever read about the murders in the newspaper?" Jim wanted to know.

"I was ten years old at the time," Red answered. "I never heard the Schuessler name and only knew about the Peterson boy because of Kenny."

Red parked himself on a padded bench.

"So why didn't you tell this story to one of the federal agents you were working with earlier? Why did you wait until now?" John asked. It was a logical question.

"Every time I mentioned the murders to the FBI agents, they'd cut me off right in the middle of the sentence and say something like, 'We're not interested in murders. Murders are a local offense. I don't want to hear it, so don't bring it up again.' In fact, I had mentioned *several* homicides."

"Well, we're going to talk about this again," Delorto announced. It was getting late, and Rotunno wanted to get back to the motel to write up a report. The ATF men arose from their chairs and shook Red's hand. They were uncertain about some of the more troubling aspects to the story. The issue to mull over was Wemette's motivation for coming forward at this time, apart from his personal crusade to rid the world of its mobsters. Red's words played over and over again in Delorto's mind. *Yep, we were drunk. But he said, 'I killed those two boys in '55, but I didn't mean to.'* Jimmy unlocked the door on the driver's side and slid behind the wheel.

"You know, we're gonna need help," Rotunno said. He had in mind another crackerjack ATF agent working out of the Chicago office who had worked on many sex-related crimes. "We should get Jim Grady in on this." Rotunno scribbled down a few key words—"pedophile, arsonist, and murderer?" and then tossed the notebook in the back seat of the car. Back at the Quality Inn parking lot, Rotunno reiterated, "Grady's our guy."

Later that evening, after writing up their notes and making the obligatory call to the wives back in Chicago, the agents returned to Red's home for round two of what was likely to be many interview sessions in the months ahead. They spent much of the evening rehashing the frauds and schemes hatched by the Equestrian Mafia. Conjuring up these old stories pained Red because deep down he loved animals, and the thought of stable horses perishing horribly in arson fires was terrible for him to contemplate. Just what goes on in people's minds, anyway?

Ken Hansen's name never came up that night. There were no further "Oh, by the way"s from Wemette. Over the years, Delorto had developed a genuine affection for Wemette. As odd as Red's motives were for co-operating with the government in a score of Mob-related investigations, Jimmy did not question them.

"I need to go over our report and make sure we understood everything you said," Delorto told Wemette as the agents left his residence. It was just after midnight when Delorto's head hit the pillow. Images of past arsons, charred horse carcasses, and a child murderer running around loose played over and over in his mind until sleep finally overtook him.

Jim Grady, an investigative specialist focusing on crimes against children, transferred into the Chicago field office of the ATF from the detective division of the Du Page County Sheriff's Police in 1989. "He was perfect for us," Delorto recalled. "He understood the psyche of both victim and violator. We knew we were going to be talking to adults who as children were victims of a serial pedophile. Jim could penetrate the protective barriers these men had put up. You have to understand that a person suffering this kind of abuse early in life may not be inclined to be a hundred percent forthright. Grady *knew* how to breach a subject's defense mechanisms." With the blessing of Joe Vince, special agent in charge of the ATF arson squad, Grady was added to the Schuessler-Peterson team. Not long after, he was given his first opportunity to pour through the reams of yellowed paper stored in the cardboard boxes of the long-dormant case file. Delorto and Rotunno were emptying the contents of those boxes when Grady poked his head in the doorway and asked, "What's all of this?"

"We've got a lot of reading to do," Delorto sighed, thinking to himself that he must be crazy to get involved in am ice-cold, unsolved murder case just one year before retirement. With a capable investigative team finally in place, the beleaguered ATF agent was hopeful that in another year, when it came time for the formal good-bye dinner, the wall plaque, and all the rest of the happy horseshit, he could ride off into the sunset without regrets.

Rotunno, according to Delorto's master plan, would take hold of the nuts and bolts of the day-to-day casework: developing and examining the physical evidence (such as they could come up with) and coordinating witness interviews. His work would dovetail into Grady's side of the investigation—the unraveling of motives, opportunities, and the complex psychological threads tying "Kenny's boys" to a raft of barn burnings and frauds, pedophilia, and a murder cover-up.

Delorto opened a bulky folder, and a collection of five-by-ten photographs of the three boys taken moments after the discovery in Robinson Woods spilled out, spreading across the floor. He picked up an enlargement of a close-up shot of the curious markings found on John Schuessler's thigh—markings identified by Dr. Kearns during the postmortem and publicized by Frank San Hamel of the *Chicago Daily News*. Grady flicked on a desk lamp. He squinted his eyes and frowned. "Hum. . . . It looks as if somebody neatly cut off a few layers of the kid's skin to cover up something."

"So we've got a Hannibal Lecter–like murderer out there," Delorto said flippantly. "My son Tony is almost the same age as Anton Schuessler Jr. was at the time of the murders."

All three men gazed intently at a poignant image of the Boy Scout honor guard carrying the casket of thirteen-year-old John Schuessler past a throng of mourners at St. Tarcissus towards the waiting hearse that would convey him to the cemetery. The room was silent as the agents reflected on the senseless tragedy and tried to imagine the private hell the parents must have endured throughout that horrible ordeal. Lost in their private thoughts, there was nothing more to be said just now.

13

Born into Misery

THE STENCH INSIDE THAT SMALL, arid room was unbearable. The blond-haired boy, Roger Spry, picked up dog excrement and disposed of it and arranged himself on the dirty, flea-bitten mattress that passed for a bed. Above him was a small window. Spry often slept sitting up with his face turned towards the tiny opening so he could breathe clean air. Roger passed the night sleeping on the "ground floor" of Kenny Hansen's dog kennel at the Bro-Ken H.[1] The boy loved animals. Next to Beverly Rae Hansen, the pretty lady living in the house, animals were about the only creatures in this world that had shown him affection of any kind. Spry sat on his mattress thinking about his crummy life and wondering when Mr. Hansen would be kind enough to let him come inside his home again. As bad as it was, this new arrangement was better than the life he had known with his alcoholic father and prostitute mother.

Born into a world few people could imagine, Roger Spry lived the first ten years of his life in a small West Virginia coal-mining town. When the mines closed down in 1959, his father traveled to Illinois in search of employment. After six months had passed, he sent word back to his wife to pack up the car, Roger, and the six other kids and join him in Calumet City, near the South Works steel mill.

The vice district of Cal City was a savage and lawless strip festering along the ragged edge of the Indiana-Illinois state line. Since the earliest years of the twentieth century, the town had been under the thumb of one rackets boss or another. Gambling, prostitution, and other adult entertainments ran wide open. Stag films were peddled in the back alleys and doorways of the town back in the days when pornography was commonly known as "smut," and possession of the same carried stiff fines and prison sentences. At the Penny Arcade at 114 State, a large, secret room in the back accommodated up to thirty patrons who paid $10 a piece to view a four-hundred-foot-long stag film. The local politicians were up to their eyeballs in graft and on the dole of organized crime. They were powerless to prevent any of the illicit goings-on. Conditions had remained much the same from the horse-and-buggy days up until the early 1990s when commercial redevelopment and changing societal tastes rendered the last of the gaudy sin-and-sleaze palaces obsolete.

Young and good-looking, Roger's mom went to work as a stripper after her husband, a chronic complainer, alcoholic, and general loser, proved incapable of caring for his sons as he drank himself into oblivion. The gambling dens, peep shows, and sex clubs lining Strip Row opened for business in the early-evening hours and remained open until six the following morning. In this Dickensian half-world, this mere wisp of a boy was compelled to sit quietly on the barstools inside the dives while his prostitute mother sold herself to the barflies and johns who worked in the steel mills nearby. Half-naked girls hustling patrons at the bar for drinks and sexual favors winked at him suggestively while the jukebox droned in the background.

After a few months, his mom made other arrangements. She kept the two younger brothers, who were five and six years old, and the other five children were sent to live with relatives in the area. Roger, the eldest of the shirttail brood, was compelled to go to work. But there was one problem—there were no help-wanted signs posted for ten-year-old boys. In desperation, Roger's mom hired her son out to an uncle's gas station at Narragansett and Archer avenues on the Chicago South Side. There he met Wally Ososki, an ordinary-looking fellow who dropped in from time to time. But, oh, the stories Wally would tell about the exciting times he had working at stables most of his life.

"You mean there are places in Chicago where you can go ride horses?" Roger was drawn in.

"Sure, son, would I lie about a thing like that?"

Before the year had passed, Roger quit the gas station and went to work for his buddy Wally. Looking back on his adventures with Wally, Spry recalled, "We used to take the ponies out to the suburbs and saddle up the little kids and take pictures of them with a Polaroid. He gave me $25 for the weekend."

That was a considerable amount of money for a kid in 1959, but Roger Spry's life made an abrupt U-turn the day Ososki drove then-almost-eleven-year-old out to the Bro-Ken H Stables at Eighty-Second Street and Kean Avenue to pick up ponies. That's where Roger met Kenny Hansen, the man providing livery rides and horseback-riding lessons to kiddies. The handsome boy enchanted Kenny. Beverly was deeply moved and saddened by his circumstances. What could they do now to help out the little chap? Certainly, their home was big enough to accommodate him. Food was on the table, schools were nearby, and horses were available to ride out at the Bro-Ken H. No foster parent could ever hope to compete with a wholesome setup like this. It seemed to be a perfect *Spin and Marty* arrangement all around, and the Hansens were most eager to have young Roger come and join their happy little family.

It is alleged that Roger Spry was "sold" to horseman Kenny Hansen in a straight cash transaction when it was obvious that neither of his parents had the interest, time, or inclination to give the boy a proper upbringing. The agreed-upon sum supposedly was $500, although Ken Hansen remembers it a different way. "His uncle had dropped him off and never picked him up. He'd been snitching Coke from people. It ended up his mother had, like, nine kids, and she would entertain her customers in the same bed as Roger. Beverly wanted to adopt a baby . . . it ended up Beverly brought Roger back. I would never bring some kid home and dump it on Beverly without even talking about it. But, anyway, she keeps Roger."

Ken's son Mark Hansen does not believe for a second that the circumstances of Roger's arrival at the ranch were the result of a cash consideration. "My dad took in guys that needed help, he was always that way. Roger came to us after his stepfather tried to kill him with an axe."

Whoever can be believed, the fact stands: Compared to the depravity of Strip Row, the Hansen stables and their second-floor apartment at Seventy-Ninth Street and Harlem Avenue must have seemed like Shangri-la—at least in the beginning. At first, Ken welcomed Spry to his home and taught the boy to care for the horses and ride them with proficiency. The youngster refused Kenny's sexual advances and said he was exiled to the filth and manure of the dog kennel as punishment and forced to sleep alongside the Dobermans until he "came around." In time, Kenny broke young Spry's resolve. He made "Rog" his own "very special boy."

Spry's memories of his early days out at the Bro-Ken H Stables are mostly at odds with Hansen's—Spry's images are of child abuse that he had locked deep in the subconscious. He never forgot the ordeal of abandonment or his surrogate mother, Beverly Rae Hansen. Years later, Roger warmly confessed his affections for Ken's wife. "I loved Beverly. She tried to take care of me. We lived on the second floor of a two-story building, but after I had been with them for a few days, Kenny moved me into the dog kennels." Weeks, then months passed. Roger Spry observed firsthand Kenny's habitual pursuit of young boys. Some, but not many, rebuked Hansen and were fortunate enough to escape. According to Spry, others protested the abuse in anguished tones but eventually were forced to succumb.

Late one afternoon, Roger listened intently as Kenny and an adolescent named Mike Burns shouted at one another on the other side of the kennel wall. Spry stood up and walked over to the door to listen. His body was tense, and he shook uncontrollably. "You motherfucker! Leave me alone!" Burns blurted out. "Spry's been running his mouth about you to everybody." Roger's heart stopped. Hansen snarled, "You're a damned liar! He wouldn't do that." From behind the wall, Spry heard an angry commotion—low curses and the sound of pushing and shoving. "Leave me alone!" The boy kicked and screamed. His cries were followed by a painful moment of silence. Spry backed away from the door and swallowed hard. He pushed aside discarded pop bottles and began stacking wooden pop cases in front of his door, hoping Hansen and Burns could not penetrate the makeshift barrier. Then he sat himself down on the mattress and sobbed uncontrollably. Suddenly, with great fury, Burns pounded on the door. "Open up, Goddamn it!" "Please don't come in! Please don't come in here!" Roger wailed. Burns crashed through the door, spilling the pop bottles across the floor. A spray of glass particles and Coca-Cola spattered across the bed. Gritting his teeth, Burns grabbed the cowering boy by the throat and dragged him off the bed.

"What are you doing?" Kenny asked Burns as he approached from outside.

"He's been running his mouth about you," Burns replied angrily. He did not release his grip on Roger's neck.

Kenny boiled over. "Leave him alone! Let him go, do you hear me!" Hansen separated the two boys but glanced at Spry in a way that made him feel very queasy.

Burns patted Roger's head in a show of mock affection and exited the room. Spry bolted off the bed and ran toward the yard, ignoring the broken glass embedded in his foot. He felt no pain; for the moment, he felt he was safe. He stormed around the backyard until the pain set in and then sat down on a broken barn stool next to the garbage cans and inspected his right foot. The young boy grabbed a dirty towel from the trash and wiped away the blood.

Spry kept a watchful eye out as Kenny and Burns climbed the stairs to the second floor of Hansen's residence. Once they were safely out of sight, the child retreated, gritted his teeth, and limped across the lawn to the front of the house. Like a cat, he squeezed through an open window into his so-called bedroom. He cleared the shards of broken glass from the top of his mattress and swept the floor clean so the dogs would not hurt themselves. Then he lay on his bed and looked out the opened window. Ten minutes passed before he saw Burns get into his car and drive off.

Spry drifted off to sleep. The next thing he remembered that night was awakening to Kenny's gentle nudge. The horseman was sitting on the edge of his bed. "You know, it's all right," he said in a soothing voice. Kenny allegedly pulled down Roger's trousers and performed oral sex. That chilly night, the soul of a young boy whose last name was an ironic metaphor of vivacity, died and was never reborn. *It's all right, Roger. Everything is going to be okay.*

In the middle of the second Helen Brach murder investigation, Jim Delorto and Dave Hamm first learned the intimate details of Roger Spry's squalid existence and his apprenticeship to Kenny Hansen. Joe Baumann, a sergeant in charge of the Glenview, Illinois, investigative bureau at the time, remained an important conduit for Hamm during the long and frustrating Brach case. At one point, Baumann suggested that Hamm interview Spry, by now a construction worker in Morton Grove, Illinois. The retired cop agreed to arrange a meeting. Baumann, who had coordinated local efforts at the time of Helen's disappearance in February 1977, introduced the candid and oddly impressive Spry to Hamm and Delorto. They were ushered into the kitchen of Baumann's cream-colored bungalow. There they spent the next few hours discussing the incredibly bizarre parade of characters Spry had observed passing in and out of the Bro-Ken H and the other stables Hansen operated over the years. They poured over events from the turbulent 1960s and the changing 1970s. Names of grooms, stable hands, flimflammers, society hangers-on, and champion riders at the various south-suburban stables drifted in and out of conversation and were recorded for future reference. Spry also spoke of his recollections of Kenny's other property—Sky Hi Hopes (Hansen merged two stables, the Sky Hi and the High Hopes into one operation, then later renamed it the Camelot Stables).

Waxing poetic over the joys of riding, Spry told them about all the horses and riders he had trained over the years. Despite the hardships and cruelty of his fractured childhood years, it was becoming quite apparent to the agents that it was a price Roger Spry was willing to pay in order to gain acceptance into the horse world. Why didn't he attempt to escape after experiencing so much suffering, sexual torment, and humiliation? Or could it be the stories he was telling these agents, as Hansen suggests, were tainted by exaggeration?

While attending Argo Community High School, "I lived at all of the stables," Spry remembered in a low voice.[2] "There were other young boys around who would clean stalls and horses and lead [the horses] out of the barn when we were putting up riders."

Delorto studied this diminutive but roughhewn man with a sporty crew cut. "He had been rolled real hard," Jimmy would later confide to Hamm. It was clear by the appearance of Spry's leathery skin that he had spent considerable time under the sun.

"How did you meet Helen Brach?" Hamm wanted to know.

"Frank Jayne and Kenny Hansen brought her over to Sky Hi Stables, and I met her again at Richard Bailey's stable in Morton Grove, you know the one at Harms and Golf Road," Spry responded. "They'd ride up in a flashy big Cadillac, and everybody knew she was a pigeon; everybody who worked at the stable knew the whole thing was a scam." Laughing, Spry added, "No horse bought from Hansen or Bailey ever died of old age!"

Roger had a strange sense of humor. "I rode the nags they were trying to sell her. I knew it was all a scam, but I didn't get involved. I was a very good rider and could make a lousy horse look good if they wanted me to, unless, of course, I had too much to drink." Spry chuckled before continuing. "Sometimes they would shoot up the horse with dope to cover up its lameness or injuries, but I did what I was told. I was just a stable hand."

The information Roger was supplying to the law-enforcement agents that evening was not terribly revealing, but it confirmed that they were at least on the right track. After Brach realized that she had been swindled, the candy heiress threatened to file lawsuits against Frank Jayne and Richard Bailey, Spry said.

Delorto interrupted, "Did you know Silas Jayne?"

"Yes," Spry responded without batting an eye. "I was about fifteen or sixteen when I met Si."

"Did you ever meet Silas Jayne anywhere else beside that one particular stable or farm in Elgin Township?"

Spry paused to gather his thoughts. "I met him at Idle Hour Stables at 8600 Higgins. I was with Kenny at the time."

"When was the last time you saw Silas Jayne?"

"The last time I saw Si was at a horse show at Oak Brook Stables . . . in the late 1960s."

That was a long time ago. Delorto wondered what else Roger remembered, but he sensed that the interview was coming to a close.

"We'll probably see you in a few weeks," soothed Hamm. "By the way, are you still riding?"

Spry looked down at the half-empty coffee cup and said softly, "No. I'm doing construction." He took another sip of coffee, leaned back in the chair, and added a final twist that gave them pause. "Once when we were preparing saddles in the tack room, somehow or another Si's name came up . . . and I said, 'You know, one of these days I'd like to ride with Si,' and Kenny tells me, 'You don't want to ride for that man. You don't want to have nothing to do with him. He's crazy!' I said, 'What do you mean he's crazy?'"

Back at his office the next day, Delorto flipped through an assortment of old case files. He spotted a matchbook advertising the Monte Cristo bowling alley retrieved not far from the spot in the woods where the boys were found. He thought about it for a few moments, and it occurred to him that maybe the matchbook was on the floor of the trunk when the naked bodies of the boys were tossed into the car. There is a natural tendency for a piece of paper to stick to skin, Jimmy thought. In the haste to dump the bodies in the woods, it was conceivable that the crusty, water-logged matchbook stuck to the skin of one of the kids. As the bodies were tossed into the ditch, the matchbook likely flew off, landing in the grass beyond the ditch. At that moment, Jimmy realized that there had to be two men, not one, involved in the murder and cover-up. It would have required at least two people to load and remove the bodies from the trunk. There were no scratches on the skin suggesting otherwise.

Spry met with Delorto and Hamm for a second round of interviews on November 14, 1991, at a restaurant on Waukegan Road in Glenview—a block from the police station where the first reports of Helen Brach's disappearance were filed in 1977. By now, the government had gleaned a lot more information about Horse Mafia scams. The two agents looked to Roger for independent corroboration of what other witnesses had told them as well as other interesting tidbits he could share with them about the horse killers. But by this time, the government even had names of specific horses the young horseman rode. "We knew Bailey, Frank Jayne, and Hansen were involved; Bailey and Jayne were the big players," Delorto said to his peers during another one of his staff meetings before he drove out to meet with Spry. "The horses they owned didn't die of old age," Delorto said, remembering what both Red and Roger had told him.

"I knew Bailey was wining and dining not only Brach but other women who he ultimately scammed. I don't remember the names of those old broads, but from time to time, Hansen or Bailey would put the call out that they needed horses to sell. They'd practice their scams on anybody who was fool enough to believe them. . . . There were big players like Jerry Farmer, Bobby Brown, and Dr. Ross Hugi [a Mundelein, Illinois, veterinarian] who knew that there were a lot of other people in on the scamming." Spry's memory was vivid.

Hamm and Delorto looked at each other knowingly.[3] Roger said he was introduced to Frank Jayne, Richard Bailey, Jerry Farmer, Wally Holly, and Lee Ryder in the early 1970s when he worked for Hansen at the Sky Hi Stables at 17201 S. Central Ave. He spoke freely about insurance scams and stable fires—arson-for-profit schemes that destroyed barns and horses and drove competitors out of business.

The agents learned for the first time that on August 14, 1970, Roger Spry and a man named Michael "Chicken Coop" Cooper burned down the Forest View Stables, a competitor's operation undercutting Kenny's livery profits. Reveling in the danger, Spry doused a hay truck with gasoline, resulting in the destruction of the stable and thirty-five healthy horses.[4] Firefighters from five south-suburban departments struggled to contain a blaze threatening to rage out of control. Losses were pegged at $100,000. Roger Spry was allegedly paid $300 for the job, a notion Kenny's youngest son Mark dismisses as total fabrication.

"It had nothing to do with my father," Mark Hansen said, insisting that Roger Spry could not be trusted to tell the truth under any circumstances. "Ed Thomas, a buddy of Roger Spry, got into a barroom fight with his girlfriend. Soon after, she transferred her horse from Sky Hi over to Forest View Stables, owned by Bill and Joanne Cummings." The night of the fire, Mark said Ed decided to get even with the girl by torching the hayrack on the rear of the truck. Spry went along for the "fun of it." After the brakes burned off, the truck rolled inside the barn igniting the inferno. Mark added, "Ed had a beef with his girl, and my dad was really pissed off."

According to Spry, Hansen had once paid him a few bucks to burn down a neighbor's barn. "You know, I screwed up the first time, and the barn didn't catch on fire so I went back and doused it with gasoline."

If Kenny was, in fact, involved in one of the many barn fires, the ATF could step in and arrest him. Spry's confession could be enough information to lock Hansen up long enough for them to gather more information about the boys' murders.

Spry described Hansen's involvement with Frank Jayne Sr. and an unusual conversation at Sky Hi during the spring of 1977, when he overheard Frank reveal hidden details about Brach's death to Hansen.[5] "I remember Frank Jayne telling Kenny that Richard Bailey had set up a bogus land deal with Mrs. Brach which involved a large amount of cash."

For decades, Ken Hansen roamed free and unhindered. But from the information extracted from Spry and Wemette, the ATF agents managed to effectively isolate Kenneth Hansen from the omnibus of horse trials winding their way through federal court. Subsequent interviews with Spry zeroed in on Kenny's alleged involvement in the Schuessler-Peterson murders. One of the most troubling aspects was the rationale that guided healthy, robust, and otherwise intelligent young men. Why would they allow themselves to become so cruelly degraded without complaint?

"Roger and Red were satellites in Ken Hansen's constellation, but we soon realized that they didn't care much for each other and didn't get along very well," explained Delorto. Living like orphans with precious little to call their own, they would from time to time steal from one another and engage in petty games of one-upmanship in order to curry their benefactor's favor. "Each of them in their own way depended on Kenny, and they were willing to put up with just about anything because of their love of horses." And although Mark Hansen admitted that his father could have been more generous with what he paid these boys and saved himself a whole lot of aggravation down the road, he said, "Spry was hardly the indentured servant. They all wanted to take the easy road in life. Joe Plemmons, for example, was a *great* horse trainer, but he always looked for the easy way . . . the path of least resistance."

Reputed to be a small-time horse defrauder, in 1992 Plemmons was sitting behind bars in the Folsom State Prison in Sacramento, California, ready to divulge what he knew to FBI Agent Peter Cullen and Delorto—and he seemed to know a lot, appearing well versed on the world of horse swindlers and the Brach murder.[6] Joe Plemmons met Hansen in 1970 while attending a horse show at Peacock Ridge, a large riding facility located in Flossmoor, Illinois, not far from the Sky Hi Stables. The two young men appeared to have a lot in common, and Plemmons took a liking to the rugged-looking stable owner. Three months later, he was at Sky Hi negotiating a lease deal with Hansen. "I did not work for him," Plemmons said. "I leased part of his facility." In February 1971, like a proud papa, Plemmons hung out a shingle at Sky Hi and imagined himself on the way to great success, or at least that is what he thought at the time. "I used to live at Kenny's barn," he said, moving on to the Brach disappearance. "And one day, Richard Bailey called me up and said it was urgent that we meet. He was acting kind of wacky, so I asked Hansen to join me." The three men met at Hackney's Restaurant in Glenview, Illinois. Over coffee, Bailey asked Hansen matter-of-factly, "Will you take care of Mrs. Brach for me? I'll pay you $5,000." According to Plemmons, Hansen was indignant—"No way I'm not getting involved." The horseman excused himself from the table to go to the bathroom, and Joe and Bailey sat at opposite ends, quiet and feeling awkward.

"What about you, Joe?" Bailey said, breaking the silence.

Plemmons shook his head and said, "I'm a lot of things, but I'm not a killer."

The story Plemmons shared with Delorto and Cullen seemed believable. Bailey was out hunting. *He couldn't do it himself. He doesn't have it in him to commit murder*, Delorto thought. *He could con you out of your shorts, but he couldn't kill.*

John Rotunno and Jim Grady, seasoned investigators attuned to the deep psychological overlays of this case, met with Spry again in the summer of 1993. They were trying to draw out of Spry an accurate reconstruction of the triple homicide, based on what Hansen had confided to Roger in a careless, unguarded moment.

"So he said that he [Hansen] was having sex with the two younger boys inside the Idle Hour barn and that the older boy [Bobby Peterson] showed up and caught him and that the younger boy [Anton] said that he [Bobby] was going to tell his parents?" Grady asked in a soft voice.

Spry ran his fingers through his hair and drew a deep breath. "Kenny told me this when he was half in the bag. He said, 'I picked up three kids, and my thing was to have sex with the two young boys at the same time.' That was his fantasy, you see.

"Kenny said he took them to one of the back barns, and he sent the older boy [Bobby Peterson] somewhere out of sight to do something like brush horses or whatever, so he could have sex with the two younger boys."[7]

"When Ken Hansen told you [how he killed the boys], did he show you how he did it?" Grady asked.

Spry replied that Kenny told him that he grabbed Bobby around his throat with one arm. Spry paused to raise his right arm parallel to the ground to illustrate a choke hold. He said Kenny had done that so that he would have the other arm free if the other two boys tried to get away.

"What did he tell you happened after he had them in his grip?" Grady interjected.

"He said that the other two boys were trying to get away. He said because the other kid was screaming so loud, Kenny grabbed a hold of him. The other two were trying to get away, and while they were struggling, he had accidentally choked one of them to death."[8]

"Kenny said he accidentally choked the Peterson boy?"

"Yes. He said he had no other choice, so he said he killed him."

"Did Ken tell you he killed the other two boys?"

"He said that Si showed up. Si was wild, he was crazy, and he was really mad," Spry said without pause. "Kenny said that Si argued with him, 'Why do you have to get me into this stuff? This could ruin me!'"

Horse trainer Bob Breen, living with his family at the Idle Hour in the fall of 1955, disputes this scenario. A witness to Jayne's frequent tirades, Breen said that Si was very strict (to the point of obsession) about keeping up proper appearances at the stable. "Si Jayne was a businessman and did not tolerate any foolishness. Si wouldn't permit drugs or prostitution at Idle Hour . . . but at the Northwestern Stables, they were doing that kind of thing." Refuting the contention of Roger Spry and other young men who were told essentially the same story by Hansen in moments of unguarded candor, Breen said, "If he [Hansen] was doing that kind of thing, Si would have shot him dead." Decades later, Breen, age ninety-eight, acknowledged that Jayne was an arsonist, a swindler, and perhaps many other unsavory things but told the authors that he seriously doubted that Si was a child murderer. Breen's grudging admiration for the craggy, curly-haired boss of the Horse Mafia runs against the grain of law-enforcement thinking and the statements of Spry.

"Anything else?" Grady moved his chair closer, listening to Roger attentively.

"He said that Si helped him load the kids in the trunk of the car, because Si figured to protect himself, you know. He'd *have* to help Kenny out. So they dropped them in the forest preserves."[9]

Grady looked at Spry evenly, trying to decide if his story was plausible or not. "How old were you at the time when you first heard this?"

"About fifteen." Spry became defensive. "I was there, you know . . . all by myself at the Bro-Ken H barn. What happened is that when someone comes out to go riding, Kenny had me sign them up on this log sheet he kept. He never gave me any money or anything, so every so often, I would take a few bucks for myself and stick it in my pocket. . . . So I was there one day by myself. Nobody was around. Two people came out to go riding, and I put them on horses and kept the money."

"How much money?" Grady asked.

"I think it was about four or five dollars." Spry appeared distracted. "They hadn't quite made it out of the forest preserve, and Kenny pulled up in the car, and he saw the people, and as soon as he got out of the car, he walked over to the sign-up sheet, looked at it, and said, 'Rog, why didn't you sign the people up?' I told him that I forgot, and he said, 'Rog, if you keep it up, you're going to end up just like that Peterson kid!'" Spry said that Kenny "scared the hell" out of him. "I knew that he'd kill me, too." Then Spry proclaimed, "The last time I had sex with Ken was sometime in the 1970s. I was maybe eighteen or nineteen."

Rotunno ordered a round of coffee. The chatter from the other customers echoed throughout the restaurant, and Grady wondered if his conversation with Spry had been overheard. He lowered his voice. "Do you know Red Wemette?"

Spry nodded his head. "Oh, yeah. Absolutely. According to Ken, he was his other boy."

"Were you jealous?"

Spry seemed shocked. He expressed his outrage, "If Kenny had somebody else, he let me alone! Why the hell would I be jealous?"

According to Spry, Ken Hansen surrounded himself with young boys and adolescents who were agreeable to carrying out his bidding. In the nature of his relationships with young boys, Hansen shares striking similarities to the fictional character Fagin in *Oliver Twist*, Charles Dickens's novel of slum life in Victorian London and the scheming arch criminal who lured a gang of underage street urchins into a life of petty crime, thievery, and debauchery.

Not long after Grady conducted his first interview with Roger Spry, the investigators reached consensus with their government superiors that it was in the best interests of everyone if the horseman moved across the country with his current girlfriend, Colleen Quinn, to ensure their safety and protection. Grady and Rotunno had both agreed that Spry would be a credible witness they would likely call upon to testify once the case went to trial. Following her daughter's graduation from high school, Colleen and Roger decamped to the south after Spry received a job offer in Texas. It was enough of an incentive for him to move. He was paid $3,700, enough to cover his rent and out-of-pocket travel and relocation expenses.[10] As he raced down old Route 66 in the direction of El Paso, Spry confided details of his checkered past to Quinn who would later recall, "He told me a story, and the one thing that was very, very clear in my mind was Roger said that he [Ken] put his hands on his [Roger's] shoulder and looked at Roger and said, 'If you ever do that again, you will end up like the Peterson boy!'"[11]

After a brief spell in Texas, Roger came home. He went to work as an itinerant construction laborer before settling in with a family up in Mundelein, well north of Chicago. There he gave riding lessons and attended to the horses. Roger Spry subscribed to the stable man's old adage, "Horseback riding is life; the rest is just details."

By summer 1994, Jimmy Delorto was burning the candle at both ends. Cigarettes, cheeseburgers, scotch, Helen Brach, and one-too-many late-night strategy confabs with Dave Hamm, Jim Grady, and John Rotunno at the Seven Dwarfs restaurant in Wheaton exacted a terrible toll on the veteran ATF man, engaged as he now was in a mental chess game with Kenny Hansen. Now that Richard Bailey was down for the count and the other members of the Horse Mafia were scurrying for cover lest they become the next target of RICO (the anti-racketeering law Racketeer Influenced Corrupt Organizations), Ken Hansen became the primary target of the widened investigation. Indictments were certain, but Delorto wondered what direction Steve Miller of the U.S. Attorney's Office intended to go with this. "So there we were in the middle of the Brach case, and Wemette dropped this bombshell on me. I knew I wanted to prosecute Hansen on federal kidnapping charges in conjunction with murder," Delorto said. "But would they go for it? The answer was no."

Steve Miller was excited about Wemette's disclosures, but he declined to prosecute the case at the federal level. Realistically, it was better suited for the state level. The Bailey prosecution drew repeated criticism from defense attorneys, civil libertarians, and the press for pushing the limits of the RICO statute far afield. The Justice Department and the federal courts have long maintained that the prosecution of state crimes is the primary responsibility of the state where the felonious act had allegedly occurred.[12]

In 1992, Jack O'Malley, a Charles Evans Hughes Scholar from Cornell University, won election to his first full term of office as Cook County State's Attorney. A strong supporter of tough truth-in-sentencing legislation requiring that certain violent felons serve 85% of their sentence, O'Malley was lashed by old-guard Democratic politicians because he was the lone Republican to hold a major county office during the flowering of the second Daley Machine.[13]

Dave Hamm inadvertently had launched the Ken Hansen investigation years earlier in the midst of the George Jayne inquiry, but the timing had not been right for prosecution. But now O'Malley rolled the dice and gambled that he could weather the sniping criticism of his opponents and indict Hansen after Jim Delorto and his team completed their preliminary interviews with Spry, Wemette, and Plemmons. Two of O'Malley's best, Assistant State's Attorneys Patrick J. Quinn and Scott Cassidy, were assigned to lead for the prosecution. Quinn was a capable and thorough prosecutor. He had joined the state's attorney's office in 1981 and would remain on board until his elevation to the Appellate Court in 1996. Cassidy had been appointed an assistant state's attorney in 1986.

Justice had taken *many* hits since 1955, but after so many false starts and dead ends, shadowy suspects quizzed and released for want of evidence, and the total abandonment of hope, the moment of vindication for the families of the victims was at hand. On August 10, 1994, an arrest warrant, issued in the south-suburban Markham courthouse, charged Kenneth Hansen with the crime of arson, what could be the prelude to the final resolution of the thirty-nine-year-old mystery. Hansen's arrest for arson would be pave the way to the three charges of murder. Delorto said that the ATF first "needed to substantiate" its involvement in Hansen's case, so "We hung our hats on Spry's testimony. . . . It was a strong case of arson because we had the arsonist." Spry as Hansen's victim had done whatever Hansen had told him to do, Delorto said.

Detective Richard A. Schak from Area 5 Headquarters on Chicago's Northwest Side was dispatched to Country Club Hills by his lieutenant to give Kenny an early-morning wake-up call. Less than a month had passed since Richard Bailey's arrest in Gurnee for fraud and conspiracy. Things were moving in all sorts of strange and unexpected ways for Jim Delorto, who needed time off to collect his thoughts and recoup his energies. Determined to retain control of the investigation, Delorto pressed on, oblivious to his rapidly deteriorating health.

Ten days before Kenneth Hansen was taken into custody and charged with the crimes of murder, Delorto and Rotunno called on Malcolm Peterson at his suburban home, where he and Dorothy had moved in the early 1970s after their youngest child had graduated high school. The agents were faced with a difficult and most unpleasant task. Neither one relished the thought of resuscitating the Petersons' nightmarish ordeal and forcing the family to live the memories of 1955 all over again. The agents wanted to complete this assignment as gently and quickly as possible. Common courtesy dictated that they should drive out to the suburbs and inform the Petersons so they would not hear of Hansen's arrest for the first time during the morning newscast. The rightness of their courteous gesture did not make their duty any more palatable. During the drive to the Peterson home, Rotunno and Delorto haggled over who was going to do the talking. Neither of them wanted to do it. Back and forth they went, but in the end it was Jimmy who spoke up.

Malcolm Peterson, reserved and dignified in old age, answered the door. He escorted the men to the laundry room where they could speak out of the earshot of his wife, Dorothy. Malcolm walked with a cane, the result of a recent stroke.

"What took you so long?" the father asked.

Rotunno and Delorto exchanged nervous glances and shook their heads uneasily. What could they possibly say to him now?

Peterson struggled to find the proper words to convey his innermost thoughts, but in the end, he just stood silent.

Because of his uncomfortable and awkward meeting with Malcolm Peterson, Jimmy was more motivated than ever to gather as much hard evidence as possible. Some of the important details of Delorto's investigation resulted from the time he spent with his son at the public library. "I brought Michael with me to the library, and together we took out every book on the constellations," he recalled. For two hours, father and son flipped through textbooks attempting to match star patterns with the markings found on John Schuessler's flesh as they had appeared in Frank San Hamel's drawings in the *Daily News*. Delorto believed that the star images and the word *BEAR* were significant and could lead them to the doorstep of the killer.

"This is Ursa Major, Dad," Michael said pointing to the picture.

Delorto's shifted his gaze to the text. *Ursa Major* is Latin for "greater she-bear." In Greek, *arktos* is the word for *bear*, hence the name Arctic, which means *bearish* and describes the far northern parts of the Earth where the Great Bear constellation, also known as the Big Dipper, dominates the heavens. Delorto repeated the word *bear* several times until he remembered that Hansen had a horse named Bear.

Not long after his trip to the library, Delorto ran into Roger Spry at the Chicago ATF offices and handed him a photocopy of the markings found on John Schuessler's thigh. Spry, having now returned to Chicago, stared at the copy of the newspaper photo for a few seconds. "Let me get back to you on that," the tanned horseman said and headed toward Rotunno's office. Two hours later, Spry dropped by Jimmy's office. In an excited tone, he said, "That's what was drawn on Kenny's stool!" Spry took the pen out of the agent's hand and leaned over the desk. He meticulously drew a picture of a three-legged stool. "The legs collapse," he said. "Kenny could carve any picture in leather. He had all the tools. He was really good."

Hansen had admitted that he was handy with leather, and from time to time, he made his own bridle and saddles. He recalled carving a stool top for his nephew, but he denied ever owning a three-legged wooden stool honoring "the Bear" and used to sit on while shodding riding horses because he said he never a horse by that name. "I had Tom Collins, and Beverly had Bull Gen, and then I had a horse named Blackjack.

Delorto believed Spry, who said that when Hansen traveled from stable to stable across Cook County, he conveniently stored the "Bear stool" in the trunk of his prized Chevy. Hansen's failure to empty the contents of his trunk before tossing in the trussed-up naked bodies of his victims was an enormous blunder.

Eyewitnesses from the stables repeated essentially the same story. They all agreed they had observed Hansen lugging his stool around on many occasions. Accurate descriptions from the old police files of the stool's appearance and construction were provided to the ATF investigators, who compared the rough sketches drawn from Spry's memory to the 1955 newspaper account. There was one big problem. The only solid piece of physical evidence linking Hansen to the crime scene could not be found.

On August 6, just days before O'Malley ordered Hansen arrested, Jimmy suffered a heart attack, though he didn't suspect what was happening to him at the first hint of pain. "I was on the firing range when I felt something funny stirring in my chest. So I asked my partner, John Mazzola, what he thought it could be," Delorto recalled. "He said it might be indigestion and told me to burp, but that didn't help at all. I didn't know any better, so I stayed on the target range and kept firing away when I should have been on my way to the ER." Before the end of the day, Delorto was lying prostrate in Elgin's Sherman Hospital, rigged up to a heart monitor, and counting his blessings that he was still alive. With the arrest of Hansen looming on the calendar, Delorto was out of commission. The ATF agent was laid up for two weeks, enduring a painful angioplasty followed by quadruple-bypass surgery. "Well, at least I lived through it and got to see our case unfold." He tried for the longest time to dismiss this period of inaction from his mind but couldn't. He wanted a smoke, but none were to be found.

Shortly after 6 AM on August 11, 1994, Detectives Schak and Ronald Koncz, accompanied by Assistant State's Attorney Quinn, two federal ATF agents, and three Chicago Police officers, cautiously circled Ken

Hansen's house in Country Club Hills and looked for signs of activity. A light burned in the kitchen. Several of the men went to the side door, which was a sliding glass door in a screen porch or covered patio on the north side of the house, Schak later testified. But Kenny was not at home. It was possible, of course, that Hansen, on to something, was hiding under a bed or in the crawlspace.

In the house next door, Jim Tynan was preparing to go to work when his roommate spotted a tow truck and a suspicious white car parked across the street. Tynan had lived next door to Hansen for the past five years, and while he was not a close friend of Hansen, the two men agreed to look after one another's dogs when either of them was out of town.

"Someone was looking in his [Hansen's] patio-door windows. I put my head out the door," Tynan recalled. "There were people by his front door. I went in and called out at the stable to Debbie." Mark Hansen took Tynan's phone call soon after his father had left Mark's house and seconds ahead of the arrival of Schak and his men at the Tynan's place. The next-door neighbor barely had time to explain to Mark the flurry of strange activity he had observed going on at Kenny's property when he heard the knock at the door. "Where is Kenneth Hansen?" they demanded.

"I told them he was down south. He has a farm down south in Southern Illinois by the Shawnee National Forest." Tynan said that the last time he had spoken to Kenny was on August 4.

Schak and Koncz left him to feed the dogs and take his early-morning shower.

Frustrated, the team of detectives and police officers tramped back to Hansen's shabby abode for a second look. To Schak's surprise, the side porch door was unlocked. Hearing a noise coming from inside the house, the detective slipped inside to take a look. There was no sign of Hansen, just one of the lonesome and hungry dogs waiting for his master to return.

Schak scoured the premises for a full fifteen minutes, pausing to examine photographs, an address book, and a telephone directory lying on the dresser. Without a search warrant, he was powerless to confiscate these items, but they looked interesting, and Schak made a mental note of them.[14] The task at hand was to get a search warrant, return to the house, and confiscate a current photograph of Hansen from the dresser to aid in the arrest. All they had to work with up to this point was a faded black-and-white of a more vigorous-looking Kenneth Hansen snapped in 1971 when he was pulled in for plotting the murder of George Jayne.

Schak went through procedures and received the search warrant on August 12 at the courthouse in Markham, Illinois. Later on that warrant, certain things were seized.[15] Although Hansen was not at home when the cops showed up the second time at his door, Tynan identified his neighbor from two snapshots removed by Schak. He said that Kenny was dieting and had lost considerable weight since the photos had been taken.

Late in the afternoon, Kenny confirmed to Tynan by phone that he was on his way home from his pack trip to Brown, Illinois, and would be stopping off at a neighbor lady's house a few doors south. By now, the police were poised to make an arrest. Hansen, traveling in the company of his son Mark, dropped him off at the farm in Crete and continued home, unaware of what awaited him. He was to rendezvous with Mark in another hour or so and continue to Lake County, after putting on a fresh change of clothes and attending to the dogs.

It was at around 5:00 PM when Hansen eased his truck into the driveway. The night before he had crashed in Joliet and was looking gaunt and haggard in a worn jumpsuit he had thrown on for the drive back to the Chicago suburbs. Tynan invited him in for coffee but said nothing to Hansen about the presence of police detectives in his house earlier in the day.

In his last few moments of freedom, Kenny rambled on in generalities. "He was telling us about this trip down south, and [then] he called Mark," Tynan said. "Mark put him on hold, and he [Ken] went to his truck to get a phone number, and he came back in and sat down. Then the police came in with their guns—I mean they came from everywhere." The startled Tynan remembered it as a scene straight out of a Western movie. The excited screams and shouts of Lieutenants John Farrell and Lou Rabbitt of the Chicago Police Department, who made the actual arrest, were enough to awaken the dead.[16]

"I mean everything was just going crazy," Tynan said. "I know he [Hansen] asked if he could put his shoes on, and they let him put them on, and I think they took him out then."

The stooped and slightly built horseman said he was in shock. "I thought my neighbors were doing dope or something. They wouldn't tell me what I was arrested for."

Handcuffed and humiliated in the presence of his neighbors, Hansen was marched to an awaiting car and taken to the downtown headquarters of the ATF at 300 Riverside Plaza—the same office where Jimmy Delorto received Red Wemette's telephone confession nearly three years earlier.

Detective Fleming "told me we were going to the precinct, but he drove me around for five or six hours," Hansen said. "It was nine or ten o'clock at night when I arrived downtown."

Kenny had already had an inkling that the police were surveilling his property, and, in the weeks leading up to the arrest, he made discreet inquiries among the neighbors as to whether they had observed strangers prowling the grounds near his house. Believing that all of this unsolicited attention had something to do with the ongoing Brach-Bailey investigation and nothing more, Hansen made mocking reference to the police spies as his own personal Keystone Cops. At the time of the arrest, he was already under a subpoena to testify before a grand jury. In fact, Hansen readily agreed to sign an affidavit on Richard Bailey's behalf denying that Bailey had solicited him to kill Helen Brach.

In the next few hours, Hansen was subjected to an intense round of interrogation. He was held incommunicado, allegedly refused his Miranda rights, and repeatedly denied permission to telephone his lawyer. Chicago Homicide Detective Mike Fleming, according to Hansen's version of events, laughed at him and said that his attorney "was not going to serve time" for him, "so what good would it do?"[17] Fleming, who retired from the department in 1996 after twenty-three years in the trenches at Area 5 Detective Division, categorically denies the raw accusation that his fellow officers and he employed coercive tactics against Hansen: "That's not accurate at all. I absolutely never said anything of the sort. We Mirandized him [in the car] and never denied him access to a lawyer."

Fleming said he "spent hours" talking to Hansen, a lot of it just good-natured BS about the horse world. Kenny was relaxed, voluble, and very much at ease. The two men got on well. "I'm a city boy, so I don't know much about horses," Fleming said. "But I remember him telling me that horses and rats have something special in common. They are the only creatures incapable of regurgitating. That is why a horse will always examine every morsel of food before putting it in his mouth.

"Hansen said that if you place an item as small as a tack into the feed, the horse is smart enough not to swallow the tack. He also said that horses are the only animals with pores. But he turned out to be all wrong about that."

In the interview room, Fleming questioned Hansen before he was turned over to Assistant State's Attorney Barbara Ann Riley of the organized crime section.[18] Kenny spoke in a calm and rational tone but lowered his gaze in deference, avoiding direct eye contact with his inquisitor. It is a natural tendency for people with something to hide. He remained low-key throughout, and his manner was placid. He spoke of early hardships, running his father's pony concession, his college days out on Navy Pier, and the vexing labor issues he was forced to confront with the employees of his stables. On his sexual preferences, he was quite emphatic in telling Riley that he was bisexual and not gay. Off-handedly, Hansen had admitted to Detective Fleming that he had routinely picked up "hundreds of runaway boys" for the purpose of having casual sex with them. As a means of attaining sexual gratification, oral sex was fast, anonymous, and without complication. Ken revealed Beverly's bouts of irrational jealousy that were shown to women she suspected of "coming on" to him in the stables. Hansen was surprisingly candid about his personal life, but he disavowed any connection to the Schuessler-Peterson murders or involvement with the Idle Hour Stables.

Concerning his dealings with Silas Jayne, he told Lieutenant Farrell that he had been to Si's stable on Higgins Avenue "two or three times" in the 1970s.

Then he called Mark to solicit comfort and support. Dazed and confused, the young man desperately wanted to believe in his father's innocence. "I asked him if he confessed to the crime and he said 'Are you kidding? I didn't confess to something I didn't do.'" Mark said that his dad was a "nice person" who wouldn't hurt anyone. Regarding the Forest View arson fire that destroyed thirty-six horses, Mark contradicted his earlier statement and said, "It was a case of disposing of an old livery barn. It was just a little, old, dilapidated building. He would be doing them a favor if he torched it." As to the darker possibility that his dad was a murderer, Mark was insistent in his father's innocence: "Whoever would have done a crime like this would have had to be a monster or something, and that's not my father."

Mark's wife describes an entirely different kind of man than the one accused of serial pedophilia and murder. "Kenny would come by the Glenwood Stables all of the time. He was very helpful with the horses," Debbie said. "He spent a lot of time with my son, and he was so gentle with animals and kids. I just don't think it's true. I've never seen him in a gay act or trying to pick up a boy or man. Unless Kenny had a secret life and had me fooled, there was no way he killed those boys."

"We had enough on Kenny regarding the 1970 arson but needed more," Jimmy said. "When the call came in from Cheryl Hollatz [the daughter of another of Hansen's victims] after Hansen's arrest, we were able to move on murder charges."

Hansen gained the quasi-notoriety ordinarily reserved for celebrity criminals with hubris and daring. Cable television carried the news of Hansen's arrest to nearly every corner of the country. After thirty-nine years on the backburner, the Schuessler-Peterson case was a national story all over again. Chicago's best-known journalists clamored for whatever salacious details the cops and prosecutors were willing to share about this withered, sullen-faced, little man accused of committing one of the city's most heinous crimes. When Kenny appeared before Judge Gilbert Grossi for a bond hearing on August 13, 1994, reporters were shocked by how just how unassuming and average he appeared. The man standing before them was hardly the portrait of a monster.

Defense attorney Arthur J. O'Donnell, a veteran Chicago barrister well up in years, argued that there was "no direct evidence" linking his client to the thirty-nine-year-old murders. Hansen's hopes rested on the tired shoulders of O'Donnell, a gentleman farmer from northwest Indiana, a Jesuit-trained attorney, and a veteran colleague whom lawyers in the Midwest greatly admired because of his integrity, intelligence, and polite courtroom demeanor. However, at the time of Kenny's arrest, O'Donnell's health was precarious. He had been recently hospitalized because of heart problems. But he believed in Ken Hansen and had represented the horseman through thick and thin, including his 1971 arrest on suspicion of planning the George Jayne hit. O'Donnell was there for him following Beverly's death in 1989, and now, five years later, it was déjà vu all over again now that Kenny had been dragged downtown to answer for additional serious crimes.

"The sheer length of the delay has necessarily dimmed the memories. The passage of four decades makes the defense an impossible undertaking," protested O'Donnell, who seemed to be conceding defeat before a trial date could be scheduled.

O'Donnell and the Hansen family went back a long way. He was a close friend and legal advisor to Curtis Hansen, when Kenny's older brother was active in Park Forest, Homewood, and other suburban locales, engaged in his own peculiar adventures. O'Donnell had some personal issues of his own to resolve, and during some particularly troubling times, he had agreed to work for Curtis Hansen as a bondsman, eventually branching off into private practice. "Art was a dear friend of mine. But he lost more cases that he should have won," remembered colleague Bob McDonnell.

State's Attorney Jack O'Malley admitted that the links his team would establish between Hansen and the Schuessler-Peterson boys *would* be indirect: "After forty years go by, you don't solve a case by physical evidence."

Judge Grossi promptly denied Hansen's request for bail.

Sensing that he needed expert help with the case, O'Donnell phoned a colleague, the well-known Chicago criminal defense attorney Jed Stone. Stone, a legendary litigator known for his flamboyance, wit, and daring, is always in the public eye, it seems, for his controversial stance against the death penalty and ardent defense of mobsters, murderers, and the assorted castoffs of society who would otherwise have to rely on overburdened, overwhelmed public defenders for legal representation. After catching up with his colleague for a moment, O'Donnell came right to the point.

"Ken Hansen is my client," he said to Stone. "He's being held at the Cook County jail on murder charges. I could use your help."

Stone was familiar with the case and eager to join in. "Count me in. When can I meet with Mr. Hansen?"

As he reviewed the state's case against his new client, Kenneth Hansen, Stone said, "Over the years, I've grown increasingly suspicious of snitch testimony. And this is a snitch case. Essentially, they are trying to make their lives better by making someone else's a living hell." Stone admits he has little respect for law-enforcement officers who rely on informants to build their cases. "Some of the ATF agents tried to shape their facts around the testimony of snitches. That's how innocent people get convicted."

The next day, O'Donnell sent via messenger a batch of old news clips and case files for Jed to digest in his office, including articles originally published in 1955. Stone's preliminary read-through of the case convinced him that the boys were slain by a pedophile. On that point, there seemed to be little dispute between the defense team and the prosecution. "The secrets [to unraveling the mystery] of their deaths lie not in the words of snitches repeated forty years later," Stone said, "but in the science of the case."

Stone suggests that the greasy substance found on the soles of the boys' feet did not come from the horse stable. "Seems to me it might be petrol stains. Perhaps they were killed where cars were kept or near a grease pit."[19] Stone studied the autopsy report and decided for himself that the boys were attacked inside a garage and not a stable. He shook his head and wondered, "In the first place, why would these boys be in their bare feet?"

The lack of physical evidence against the defendant Hansen greatly troubled Stone. It was the best reason in the world to take up the cause. Nobody could ever accuse Jed Stone of backing away from a challenge, even when the odds were so heavily stacked against him. It didn't take long for the famed attorney to formulate an opening strategy. First, however he would solicit the opinions of experts—members of the Chicago Police department.

Intrigued by Detective John Sarnowski's highly published but mostly far-flung notion that the teenaged John Wayne Gacy killed these boys, Stone and O'Donnell produced a copy of Adolph Valanis's identikit drawing of the "potato-head" boy spotted inside the Garland Building by Maria Gonzalez in the months leading up to the October 1955 murders. With the illustration in hand, Stone paraded into the cafeteria of the Criminal Courts Building on Twenty-Sixth Street one afternoon to confront some of the cops he knew who were eating lunch and batting the breeze.

Stone stood for a moment in the middle of the crowded dining room examining the men and women in blue. For dramatic effect, he positioned himself in such a way that every person in the immediate vicinity would be sure to notice him. Then he spotted a table nearby, strolled over, and held up the sketch, fully exploiting the opportunity. No introduction or explanations were necessary as Stone asked the cops a simple, direct, question, "Does this person look familiar?"

"Yeah sure! That looks like a young John Gacy," one detective chimed in, with a chuckle to his voice. "No doubt," agreed another. "It sure looks like Gacy." Courthouse personnel crowded around the drawing to take a closer look.

Satisfied with what he was told, Jed Stone turned and walked away from the curious cops. At least now he had an alternative theory to work with, a long shot to be sure but quite possibly it would likely be enough to receive the support of law enforcement.

Stone has not wavered in the opinion that Gacy, a boy from the Northwest Side like the murdered boys, was responsible. "I don't know what happened to these three boys, but my theory is that they were John Wayne Gacy's first victims."

Days later, Kenneth Hansen tapped his fingers on the metal table in front of him and waited impatiently for his attorneys to arrive. Dressed in a dowdy Cook County jumpsuit, the horseman looked haggard and spent, twenty years older that his real age.

He had become a semipermanent resident of the Cook County Jail and was becoming accustomed to its brutal ways, having spent time here once before.

An attorney sat down only a few feet from the man in the prison fatigues. "Mr. Hansen, I'm Jed Stone. I'm going to be working with Mr. O'Donnell on your case."

Hansen nodded sullenly, never losing eye contact with Stone.

"Tell me a little about yourself, your background and all," Stone said as he took out a pad of paper and a pen from his briefcase.

Hansen was candid about his lifestyle and sexual preferences. Young men were to him like catnip to a cat, but he categorically denied he had anything to do with the killings of the Schuessler-Peterson boys. "Why would I kill them?" he asked, not expecting Stone to supply the answer. Then, in a soft voice, Hansen made a startling admission. He said he was HIV positive, a diagnosis he would later deny making.

Unsure if Hansen was making a plea for sympathy or just had it in him to confess the wretched circumstances of his life, Stone made no comment. He just listened and jotted down a few notes. Hansen continued to speak openly about his life, at times almost apologetically in subdued tones.

Explaining that his lifestyle choices in 1955 were "experimental," Kenny spoke freely about a man named Herb Hollatz, admitting that they had had consensual sex. In the Pontiac prison interview for this book, Hansen talked about sex and that he "didn't even know there were homosexuals. . . . In '55 we were . . . back in those days, we didn't even talk about sex when we were growing up. We didn't even use the words in the house. My mother was [laughs] . . . it was a different approach. Nothing like it is today." About same-gender sex, "No, it wasn't going on in the military. Like I was saying, I never thought there . . . it was not a thing to talk about. I never talked about sex in those days. Bev would be wearing a nightgown from her neck to her toes every night. My mother would slap my face if she knew what I was doing. It was not something you talked about. My mother was a Catholic. All of my friends were Catholic."

To Stone, Hansen said he was honeymooning in Texas when the boys were killed and that he could provide photographs to prove he wasn't lying. "I have a buddy in Texas who will tell you I was there with Beverly." Unfortunately, the only thing the Texas buddy could remember was that Hansen and his wife were there sometime that fall. Conceivably, the visit could have occurred after October 18.

When pressed for details about his grown sons, Hansen was less direct. "I have two boys," he said. Since his arrest, he said that this oldest son, Danny, has become increasingly distant and cold toward him; however, his son Mark, and Mark's wife, Debbie, put up their farm to pay Hansen's attorneys' fees.

"I don't judge clients," Stone said dismissively. "My job isn't to make judgments about any of them. I treat each person with dignity." The first conversation with his client convinced Stone that Hansen was resolved to spending the remainder of his life behind bars. "It was not because of anything Hansen has said. It was what he didn't say." Hansen desperately hoped that his new hotshot attorney would provide assurances, that everything was going to be okay, that burden of proof was on the prosecution, and that there was absolutely no evidence against him that would hold up in court. When Stone provided no such assurances, Hansen's optimism evaporated.

That Kenneth Hansen was an admitted bisexual was enough in Stone's mind to encourage the state to move forward and prosecute. By the same token, Kenny's past sexual misdeeds were likely inside the courtroom to foster prejudice against gay lifestyles. Jed Stone counted on it and plotted his argument accordingly. "It's my job, if not my calling, to stand in front of the judge and say, 'Stop! You can't convict a man because you're a homophobe. It's wrong, and I won't let you do it.'"

Stone ended his preliminary meeting with Hansen. He stood up and filed his notes back into his briefcase. The corners of his mouth turned up slightly as if he was trying to smile, but he couldn't. As far as he was concerned, this frail, scared man was wrongfully accused.

Jed Stone met with his client several more times in 1994 and 1995. The case against Kenneth Hansen was pushed to trial over the objections of the defense. Struggling to find the right words to describe his lack of confidence in a criminal justice system he believes convicts innocent people, Stone had this to say about Ken Hansen, "I don't think a person should be judged by the worst ten minutes of his life."

14

A Man Without a Horse

WITH KEEN INTEREST, a stout young man watched as the pitch-black quarter horse, reminiscent of the famous Black Beauty,[1] moved gracefully over a snow-packed, fenced-in pasture. As the magnificent animal cantered in the distance, snorting and showing off, Herb Hollatz puckered his lips and attempted to whistle, hoping to draw the beautiful horse closer. A rush of frigid air stung Herb's face. It was early winter 1952, and the twenty-one-year-old man reflected on the irony of his present situation. He was enjoying the woodland surroundings and the horses going through their paces at a stable in a remote corner of Park Ridge,[2] one of the more prestigious, upper-income suburbs in Cook County.

Just a few days earlier, he had moved out of his parents' home because of old, festering resentments directed against his father, a Chicago Police officer who had voiced one too many objections about Herb's reckless lifestyle and lack of ambition. With no real profession, Herb was nervous about his immediate prospects, and so the young horseman launched his job search at the Park Ridge Riding Academy. He hoped the stable owner would give him something to do. In the early 1950s, less than seventy-five businesses in the Park Ridge area served the needs of its residents.

Herb shuffled through the fresh snow until he reached the first building that looked like it might be occupied. He turned and glanced up at the glaring afternoon sun. Kicking the snow out of his way, he made his way to the weather-beaten building. A sparely built young man, whom Hollatz judged to be Ken Hansen, emerged from one of the hay barns shouting, "Shovels? Here, boy! Shovels!"[3]

Unbeknownst to Hansen, the visitor was sizing him up as he maneuvered a leather strap over Shovels's head. Then Hollatz spoke up. "Hi," he said in a quiet voice so as not to spook the horse. "You have your hands full with this one, I see."

Surprised, Hansen spun around, "What was that?"

"Spirited horse," Hollatz replied.

"Actually, he's quite gentlemanly, he is. What is it I can help you with?"

Hollatz said he was looking for work.

Hansen's expression softened. "Kenny Hansen here. I'm in charge. C'mon inside and warm up." Hansen slapped the horse on his backside in an attempt to show who was boss. "Doesn't like the stall much," he said. Shovels nipped at Hansen's hand and leapt upward, arching his back. "Heck, he gets a little stir-crazy trapped inside all winter." Suddenly, Shovels bolted forward, shying away from something on his right. "Easy boy," Hansen said, as he closed the stall door. "Gotcha."

The visitor bantered with Kenny, but Hansen pretended not to hear. Hollatz was silent for a moment, and then breaking the uncomfortable silence, he announced, "The white patch on his forehead looks like a perfect diamond. You should've named him Diamonds, don't you think?"

Hansen walked to the corner of the stall where he picked up a small wooden stool with a leather cover on the seat. Hollatz noted a pattern of some kind etched into the leather, but he couldn't quite make out the detailing.

"You got a horse of your own, Mister?" Hansen inquired.

"Naw, not right now."

"Well, I got to clean his hooves if you don't mind. Say, do you know how to clean horses' hooves?"

Hollatz forced a smile but was uneasy. "Yeah, I could do it, that is, if you wanted me to."

"Good. You can hang your hat in the bunkhouse." Hansen needed help, and this fellow looked as good as any. That's how stable hands were hired in the old days—I'll ask you no questions, and you tell me no lies. Without bothering to reiterate the specific terms of employment outlined by his father, Ethan Hansen, Ken pointed Hollatz in the general direction of a one-story building across the corral. "That's where you'll sleep. Does that suit you?"

Hollatz correctly sensed that Ken Hansen possessed a deep understanding of horses, but years later, he would say that there was something about the stable manager that struck him as a little off-kilter. Hansen finished up with the horse without so much as uttering one word to Hollatz. Then Hansen exited the barn, leaving his new man to his own devices.

The long, one-story wooden building attached to the main house was reddish brown. Hollatz kicked away the blown snow piled up by the entrance and opened the door. As soon as he stepped inside the bunkhouse, he removed his old woolen pea coat. Looking down a long corridor, he felt a momentary exultation. He thought, *How easy was that?* The place he would call home for the next few months was sparsely furnished and cold. There were few amenities provided—a stove, a refrigerator, a sink, and a bathroom. That was all. The noisy, rusty floor radiator whistled on and off, emitting small blasts of warm air. As he sat on the bed and folded the meager items of clothing he brought with him from home, Hollatz looked forward to better days. His optimism was short-lived, however. Within a few weeks, Herb was forced to reevaluate his situation as his gratitude to Hansen gave way to a lingering dread.

For the moment, Hollatz was the only stable hand actually living on the premises. The darkness and the quiet of the bunkhouse apartment both frightened and comforted him. He felt like a child being held after school in a dim, quiet classroom. One particular night, not long after he signed on at the stables, Hollatz was lying awake in his bunk. The steady drumming of the falling rain against the roof made it hard to sleep. Finally, after many minutes had passed—he wasn't sure exactly how many—he drifted off. Some time later, he was roused from his dreams by the presence of someone hovering over his bed in the darkened room. The intruder was fondling his privates. As Hollatz trained his gaze on the shadowy presence, however, he was startled to realize that the figure leaning over him, kissing and massaging his genitals, was not some gorgeous woman he might have imagined. In an instant, Hollatz sprang to his feet. The phantasm was Kenny performing oral sex on him.[4] Hollatz said he was repulsed by the idea of a man touching him in a private way, but at the same time, he had to admit that what Hansen was doing aroused him. It was a moment of brutal revelation.

So often in his life, Hollatz perpetuated his own miseries. In a strange and perverse way, he seemed to savor psychic torment, as the victims of repeated emotional and physical abuse are known to do, replaying the hurts over and over again in the back of their minds, each time magnifying the old injustices many times over. As the days rolled into weeks, Hollatz deliberately avoided Hansen. There were times, however, when he couldn't escape Hansen's attentions, and even more troubling, there were times when he had to admit to himself that he *really didn't want to*.

Other complications and distractions arose. Over the past year, Hollatz had been dating a young woman from the neighborhood named Arlene Zielke. As he struggled with his sexual identity—balancing his mixed feelings for Zielke against what the people in the "silent fifties" commonly referred to as "perversions and unnatural desires," made real by Kenny—Herb's life was further complicated when the enchanting Beverly first caught his eye. One afternoon as Hollatz shoveled horse manure into a wheelbarrow, he watched Hansen chatting with his girl-friend, Beverly Carlson. Herb asked no questions and kept his head low to the ground, focusing on the manure pile and not the pretty young woman. Quite honestly, he didn't care to know much more about Hansen. Keeping his mouth shut at crucial times, even though his curiosity was peaked, kept Hollatz out of harm's way, a valuable lesson that his daddy had taught him early on. There were set rules for him to follow—codes of conduct, decency, and honor that were enforced by his father, a straight arrow, who always reminded Herb that his dad was "a Chicago cop."

But Beverly was a woman he wanted to know better, and, for the moment, he began to feel a little better about himself and his manhood.

"Hey, Herb, c'mon over here!" Hansen shouted across the corral as Hollatz laid down his shovel. "I want you to meet somebody." The stable hand bounded across the field to where the pair was standing. "This is Bev," Hansen announced, beaming.

What man wouldn't be proud to have this lovely red-haired enchantress for a girlfriend? Hollatz thought and sighed. The young woman with the pretty red hair was framed against the background of the snowy woods and the corral. *She's one of the most beautiful women I've ever seen,* Herb thought. Then, in a faltering tone, the flushed Hollatz shyly greeted her. "My hands are dirty," he apologized, tucking them into the pockets of his jeans. His head pounding, he quickly turned and loped off. *She's too good for him,* he thought before resuming his chores.

On the plus side at the Park Ridge stable was his beloved quarter horse Shovels that he purchased from Hansen for the sum of $50, and there was Beverly. But he wondered if that was enough to anchor him at the stable, where he was forced to put up with the leering Ken Hansen and his sexual innuendos and sexual abuse. *Where can I go?* he asked himself over and over again, but there just wasn't anywhere to go and not one person he trusted enough to talk to about Ken's repeated harassment.

He certainly couldn't go back home and discuss matters with his parents. His dad would most likely want to kill him because he failed to measure up. Hollatz had in his mind that his dad already considered him a weak sissy-boy and a terrible embarrassment to the family and its good reputation. Shamed, the young man took a hard look at his life and concluded that he was ineffectual and a failure, just like his dad had said.

Hollatz wanted nothing more from Hansen than a roof over his head, occasional mentoring, and the use of the riding ring. He yearned for springtime to arrive, vowing to flee the stable and find a more desirable situation at the earliest opportunity. He couldn't understand, however, why he never fought back or why he allowed Hansen to have his way sexually. Was he afraid of losing his job or being separated from the black horse? The answers were slow in coming. The situation was perplexing—move back home to oppressive conformity and stern lectures or continue in a reckless way with Hansen and be tormented by feelings of guilt and shame. Hollatz was unsure of his feelings for Arlene and Beverly and pondered the question of whether he was a gay man living in a straight world or vice versa.

Hollatz bought himself some time by deciding to remain in Park Ridge, " . . . for the time being." There were, however, some unexpected rewards for sticking around. In December 1952, Hansen was drafted into the military. Prior to leaving town, Kenny proposed to Beverly, but even that disappointing bit of news didn't matter much to Herb. For now, he enjoyed Bev's company on a fairly regular basis and driving Ken's new car around the area. There was something richly sensuous in her nature, and she had an artistic temperament. Over Christmas, they became fast friends, but never was there the hint of a sexual relationship. While Bev worked at the Lakeview Trust Bank in Chicago, Hollatz hung around the stables biding his time.

Mark Hansen believes that while his father was in Korea, he penned a letter to Hollatz advising him in strongly worded terms that he did not approve of the budding friendship with his fiancée and that it was in Herb's best interests to "get lost."

Deciding that the company of the horse people at Park Ridge Riding Academy wasn't so special after all, he transferred his horse to the Rancho Russell Stables at 5301 Cumberland Ave. in River Grove and returned to a dysfunctional family in what amounted to an admission of defeat. "My Dad might have asked my Uncle Curt to go 'speak' to Hollatz about my mom," speculates Mark. A visit from Curt Hansen always seemed to produce the desired result. For the time being, Hollatz settled back in with Mom and Dad, pining away for Beverly and imagining what it would be like to become intimate with her.

On a weekend pass during basic training, Hansen returned to Chicago, fetched Beverly from her parents' home, and got married. That was June of 1953, according to Hansen's recollections. The honeymoon had to be delayed until 1955, given Ken's military obligation. Bev's nuptials effectively crushed any glimmer of hope Herb might have entertained for taking his schoolboy crush to the next level. Resigned to his disappointment, Herb temporarily drifted out of Hansen's orbit.

A chance meeting in October 1955, not long after Ken's hitch was up, stirred up troubling self-doubts for Hollatz. He instantly recognized the voice. "Hey, Herb! It's good to see you!" Hansen smiled agreeably.

"There were other people around," Hollatz said, "and I just happened to spot him, or he spotted me. I don't know which."[5] During their brief encounter, Kenny "performed oral sex [on me] again." Herb's memory was cloudy on the details.

"I need to tell you something, and you can't tell anybody else," Hansen mumbled to Hollatz after he had finished zipping up his pants. Herb wanted to run away and forget about what had just happened, but he did not move. "Curiosity killed the cat!" his father always cautioned, but this time, Hollatz failed to pay heed. What new scheme was his former boss up to now?

"You promise you won't tell anybody, because if you do, my brother, Curt . . . well, you know what he's like . . ."

Sweating, Herb Hollatz nodded his assent. He had heard about Curt's reputation and knew what to expect. "I promise," he said. In a casual, nonchalant tone that belied the horror of the deed, Hansen allegedly confessed to killing the Schuessler-Peterson boys. He supplied the little details that left no doubt in Herb's mind that the story was true. The Peterson kid was sent off to another part of the stable leaving Hansen alone with the two brothers. When Bobby stumbled back into the barn ten to twenty minutes later and witnessed Kenny engaged in a lewd act with his friends, he put up a terrible row. "I'm going to tell my parents!" he threatened. Hansen panicked. So much shit would come down on him that he might has well dig his own grave. Worse, what would Bev say? A brief but violent struggle ended when the horseman (or someone) chloroformed the boys. This is what Hollatz was made to understand as he huddled with Kenny on a darkened Chicago street corner in the late fall of 1955.

Herb tried to speak, but his nerves were jarred, and his lips could not form the proper words. He stood there like a cigar-store Indian, frozen with fear and thinking of the newspaper stories and television newscasts describing the chilling murders. In his mind's eye, he could easily picture Kenny doing the bloody deed. The Schuessler-Peterson case was the only crime people were talking about just now; men like Hollatz who were living underground lifestyles were spooked by the presence of cops shadowing their known haunts.

"If you tell anybody, my brother, Curt, will take care of you. Do you understand that, Herb?" repeated Hansen.

Hollatz felt his hot breath and nodded. He did not know now what he should do. He was frightened by the new moral dilemma. If he told his father or the police about it, he would risk retribution at the hands of Curt Hansen and permanent estrangement from his future wife and family, or if he kept silent on the matter, he would have to deal with the guilt caused by his inaction. Knowing that a terrible weight had been thrust squarely upon his thin shoulders, he began to cry. What would the old man say to him now?

Why would a child murderer take such a terrible risk by volunteering this information to *anyone*? At a deeper, more subconscious level, Kenny might have succeeded in convincing himself that this heinous crime leveled the playing field with his older, more menacing brother. Curtis, who took particular delight in deriding Ken as his "fag brother," had maybe done it one too many times. Maybe now Curtis would finally accord him the brotherly respect he felt entitled to. The element Kenny sought from his stable hands and the "throwaway boys" was the pleasure and satisfaction derived from their all-consuming fears. That these young men stood in awe of him and he commanded respect through force and intimidation was part of the sexual narcotic. It was all about control and power.

Approximately two weeks after Hansen's confession, investigators approached Hollatz as he stood under the covered walkway in front of the main bunkhouse at the Rancho Russell Stables. Outside, it was drizzling and chilly. He lit up a cigarette as the two plainclothes detectives began their interrogation. Nervous but not to the point where he would arouse undue suspicion, Hollatz responded to the policemen's questions in clear and steady tones. "I know nothing about anything." He explained his whereabouts on the night of October 16, 1955; an uncomfortable silence followed.

A week before Thanksgiving, Hansen mysteriously turned up at the Rancho Russell Stables inquiring after Hollatz. He found him in the tack room perched in front of a black-and-white TV. The stable hand slowly placed his cup of coffee back on a small wooden table and gazed up at his former lover with apprehension. "What do you want, Kenny?"

"I know the cops were over here asking a lot of questions. What did you tell them?" Hansen demanded. "Have the police been coming around?"

Hollatz was defensive. "Nothing. Absolutely nothing. I kept the promise. I've said nothing!"

"You sure about that, Herb? You absolutely sure?" Hansen drew closer.

Hollatz arose from his chair and backed away. Slowly turning around, he made his way for the exit. Hollatz did not want to discuss the matter, struggling as he was with his inner voice prodding him to do the right thing for a change, his overwhelming fear of Curtis Hansen, and his instinct for self-preservation. Hollatz could almost feel Hansen's piercing stare burning a hole in his back. He just kept walking.

Christmas passed, and Herb was deep in the throes of depression. He spent the holidays alone pondering his next move, never quite sure what to do. A beer or two after work was an antidote for the blues, but then it all came back to him the moment he tossed his car keys on the nightstand and was alone with his thoughts in his father's home. The cover-up and the physical threats escalated a problem with alcohol. He was consuming as many beers and shots as his system could tolerate.

There were times when he was drinking heavily and bantering with other horseman to the point where his mind became fogged and his words sounded nonsensical. "Forgive me, Father, for I have sinned," he murmured before reaching for the next glass of lager.

The barflies wondered if he had taken leave of his senses. "What was that you said, Partner?"

Without explanation, Hollatz would smile uneasily and walk away.

Two weeks later, Hollatz loaded up his horse in a trailer that had seen better days and headed out to Phoenix where he figured he could work the ranches, ride horses to his heart's content, and live the life of an unconcerned cowboy. In a car borrowed from Arlene, the man and his horse headed west to escape Hansen and the storm cloud of guilt. Most of all, he looked forward to new beginnings. But it proved impossible. After failing in his job search, Hollatz frequented the bars of Phoenix. His only true pleasure in life was caring for Shovels, his devoted horse, but paying for the upkeep on the beast was quite another matter. Apart from the time he spent on horseback, this wasn't much of a life for him after all. Thoughts of suicide crossed his mind. According to statements made by his daughter Cheryl years later, Hollatz made the attempt on at least one occasion.

His thoughts often drifted back to Chicago and the whereabouts of his girlfriend. Herb wondered how much better off he would be in the state of matrimony. Maybe family life and the responsibilities of child-rearing were the ticket out of this wraithlike existence. He brooded over the matter for days, wondering if Arlene would grow impatient and marry someone else if he didn't make a move soon. As quickly as he had fled from the Northwest Side, he returned to Chicago to fetch Arlene and move her back to the desert for a whirlwind wedding, with a promise to care for her elderly parents thrown in. The impressionable girl was only nineteen. On January 4, 1956, the young couple exchanged vows. Over the next ten years, Arlene gave birth to six children—three girls and three boys—but Herb was not a stay-at-home dad. His Phoenix neighbors rarely saw him. Hollatz was busy crisscrossing the southwestern highways, living a nomadic life, and leaving the kids and the wife to fend for themselves as best they could. The dutiful mother believed her husband was gambling or carrying on with another woman. She had no idea just how wrong she was, nor would she have really cared by this point. Phoenix to Chicago and back again and so it continued like that for the next several years.

In Chicago, Herb was teased by the other horsemen about his hillbilly ways—a real down-home, *rednecked peckerwood*, as he was so cruelly taunted. He made a fistful of money in Chicago doing what he pleased, but Arlene and the kids saw little of it. According to rumors filtering back to the wife in Arizona, Herb was living the high life, spending all of his money on booze, boys, and horses. As their twentieth wedding anniversary approached, the couple agreed that the sham marriage had gone on long enough. Divorce followed.

The wandering horseman, uncertain of his identity but afraid to pursue an openly gay lifestyle, was not seen nor heard from by his family until August 12, 1994, when a cable-news report emanating out of WGN television in Chicago caught his attention. Kenneth Hansen had been arrested on an arson charge. As the image of the balding, physically impaired horseman flashed before him on his TV screen, Herb knew in his heart he couldn't let this go on any longer. He would have to tell someone.

After a long period of estrangement from his family, Hollatz, with old age approaching, had settled down in Tucson. He had joined Alcoholics Anonymous, sworn off gambling and booze, and successfully completed the ten-step program. Memories of Kenny had gradually faded. The nocturnal fear of Curtis Hansen sticking a shiv into his back on some dark, moonless night had eased.

That Kenny was still alive and active in the horse business back in Chicago (let alone that he was covering his tracks for an old and forgotten crime) had not occurred to him. Nearly four decades removed from Hansen's admissions, Herbert Hollatz battled throat cancer and other assorted ailments. The prolonged illness and the other vulnerabilities of old age had softened him. He wanted to get his deadly secret off his conscience and live out his senior years in peace. At last, he picked up the phone.

Herb tearfully confessed to his oldest daughter, Cheryl, all of what he knew about the three slain boys and pointed a finger at Kenny Hansen.

"Why?" she demanded. "Why did you wait all this time before you told me? How could you let this happen?"

By now, Hollatz was the grandfather of three boys. By his calculations, they were only a few years younger than the Schuessler and Peterson boys at the time of their deaths. "I wish I knew," he drawled.

Cheryl was confused, scared, and humbled by the knowledge that her father failed to lift so much as a finger. "How could he do this?" she asked her husband, who held her close as she tearfully rocked back and forth. "My God, how could he live with himself?" she wondered. She promised to keep this revelation to herself, but in her heart, she knew that she could not aid and abet this distant and aloof man who tried and failed to be a decent, caring father. Cheryl stared at the telephone knowing what she had to do. Directory assistance provided her with the number of the Chicago office of the Bureau of Alcohol, Tobacco, and Firearms.

Nervously, Cheryl jotted down the phone number. It was the hardest thing she had ever had to do. Within forty-eight hours, ATF investigators and assistant state's attorneys from Chicago swarmed around the doorstep of the Tucson trailer park where Herb was living, eager to hear what this man had to say after finding his name and address penciled into Kenny's little black book of friends, lovers, associates, and other personal contacts.[6] The investigators and state's attorneys carried inside their file-filled briefcase a photograph of Curtis Hansen's gravestone.

Herb Hollatz had kept his promise for thirty-nine years and told no one. His reasons are understandable given the moral climate of the era and his fears for his personal safety. "I guess I was afraid, or embarrassed, of having a homosexual affair with Ken," he admitted, and besides, "Curt Hansen would kill me if Kenny wanted him to."

15

Showdown at Twenty-Sixth and Cal

THE DRIVE OUT FROM the office canyons of Chicago's Loop to the Cook County Courthouse is a depressing excursion into the heart of urban poverty. Boarded-up storefronts and graffiti-marked buildings paint a portrait of inner-city hopelessness. The West Side neighborhoods of Douglas and Lawndale are among the poorest in the nation. Twice in the 1960s, various sections of the commercial district along Roosevelt Road were set ablaze during massive urban rioting, leaving brick-strewn empty lots in their wake. Economic redevelopment has been slow and haphazard.

As Judge Michael P. Toomin looked out his car window as he made his way toward the courthouse complex on Tuesday, September 5, 1995, he couldn't help but reflect upon the miseries of life in these slum neighborhoods. Juxtaposed against this thought was the massive structure of the courthouse, the "justice mill" located at Twenty-Sixth Street and California Avenue. Within its somber walls, he had decided the fate of many unfortunates, many of whom had lived most of their lives nearby. Toomin was a former assistant public defender and criminal defense attorney for much of his career before he was elevated to a judgeship in 1980. Still lost in his musings, Toomin slowly crossed over Twenty-Sixth and turned his Cadillac onto a long driveway in back of the criminal courts building. Toomin was privileged. Trial lawyers, state prosecutors, jurors, and guests parked across the street from the courthouse in a massive three-story parking garage or had the option of turning right onto Twenty-Sixth from California and making a quick right into a large lot.

With a sense of urgency, defense attorney Jed Stone walked across California from the garage, where he routinely parked his car. Today, he was lucky; his law clerks had already delivered three jammed-packed file boxes to the courthouse. Stone walked quickly up the twenty or so steps to the courthouse doors. Just before he reached the revolving doors, he stopped momentarily and listened. He heard birds chirping, a sound that always cheered him.

Stone always looked forward to engaging in the compelling drama of average people responding to random questions put to them about their private lives, relationships, and attitudes concerning social problems likely to impact the dispensation of justice. There was always something new to learn as the opposing camps went about the business of assembling a panel of twelve from the venire facias.[1] He expected that most of the jurors who survived the final cut would prefer to have been excused. This is especially true of people called upon to serve in high-profile murder trials. Stone knew from experience, however, that once impanelled, the jurors were likely to prejudge his client based upon their own experiences and acquired attitudes. It was human nature, and Stone understood better than many of his younger colleagues the serious psychological impediments he must overcome.

In his well-thumbed copy of Emerson's *Essays*, Stone had underlined, "It was a high counsel that I once heard given to a young person, 'Always do what you are afraid to do.'" Selecting twelve objective jurors was usually a very difficult task. If they were being honest, defense attorneys would admit that they feared jury selection because they were never sure what people really thought or the nature of their prejudices or what pushed their buttons. The most difficult task before Stone would be to convince the jury to view Kenneth Hansen not as a monstrous pedophile and child murderer but as an ordinary human being guilty of bad judgment.

Stone was deep in thought as he passed through the security gates. The noise made by the heels of his shoes striking the tiled floor echoed loudly in the empty hall. Suddenly, he remembered one of Winston Churchill's epigrams, "Courage is rightly esteemed the first of human qualities . . . because it is the quality which guarantees all others."

Arriving at the courtroom, Stone pushed open the heavy door with great force. His intensity evaporated as he realized that jury selection would not begin until 10:30, and he was early. The red leather chair behind the bench was empty. Stone walked to the front of the room and placed his briefcase on the defense table. He spread his hands flat on the table and recited his opening arguments, delighted that for the moment no one else was around to hear him. In about thirty minutes, pretrial motions followed by jury selection for the murder trial of Kenneth Hansen would begin.

The ceiling of Toomin's courtroom, room 400, was painted with rich pastel colors in an organic medley of circles and flowers, which lent the room a touch of the fantastic. The chairs, tables, pew-like benches, jurors' box, and all of the woodwork had recently been sanded and stained a deep mahogany. For the past nineteen years, this decorous, intimidating setting had served as Judge Toomin's exclusive bailiwick.

Slowly, lawyers, bailiffs, interested spectators, and the press filed into the courtroom; prospective jury members were not allowed in to hear the motions. On the long, wooden table used by the prosecution, Assistant State's Attorneys Scott Cassidy and Pat Quinn placed face down three-by-four-foot, black-and-white photos of Bobby, John, and Tony's naked bodies lying in the ditch and an aerial survey of the Idle Hour Stable taken in the 1950s. Arthur O'Donnell, the other defense attorney, sat down next to the three file boxes on the table at which Jed Stone sat about twenty feet from the jurors' box. Both men were collecting their thoughts.

As if on cue from a stage manager and walking with the aid of a cane, Ken Hansen, escorted by a sheriff, hobbled into the room and slowly made his way to the defense table. He wore a 1970s'-vintage, baggy, ill-fitting, dark-gray suit. His hair was unruly, and he appeared to be in poor health. Judge Toomin opened his chamber door, and everyone stood as he approached the bench and sat down. The bailiff, a rugged-looking middle-aged man, quieted the visitors and press. "People versus Hansen," he said laconically.

Toomin, a hard-working and reliable jurist, knew the history of the crimes of which Hansen was charged. At the time of the murders, Toomin was living on the North Side of Chicago and attending high school. The crimes and their aftermath evoked powerful memories. Glancing first at Hansen and then turning his attention to the prospective jurors seated in the box, he introduced himself and delivered his opening remarks.

The Hansen case was originally placed on Judge Thomas Cawley's calendar, but when he retired in 1994, Toomin replaced him. Later, Toomin, in answer to question about how he felt about the trial, said, "Well, I thought it was a high-profile case with some interesting issues."

One of the key issues the judge had to carefully weigh in the pretrial section of Hansen's trial was the admissibility of Hansen's history of pedophilia. This point was persuasively argued by the prosecution before Judge Cawley in 1994. It boiled down to whether behavior unrelated to the Schuessler-Peterson case had direct bearing.[2] Acknowledging that a jury would likely be prejudiced against the defendant by hearing this kind of testimony, Cawley nevertheless allowed the state to explore Hansen's sexual history as a probable motive. The search for truth was the over-riding consideration, Cawley advised counsel, but he also recognized the legitimate arguments of the defense team and granted a motion to limit testimony and bar the prosecution from bringing up other criminal investigations in which Hansen's name might have surfaced, specifically Hansen's 1971 arrest for plotting George Jayne's murder. O'Donnell and Stone were most concerned about the climate of homophobia in the courtroom likely to be kindled by the testimony of people who would accuse Kenneth Hansen of sexual molestation in the 1960s and beyond.[3] Stone's contention was that the testimony of one or more witnesses citing a history of sexual abuse would light the way for a guilty verdict, one based not on "evidence" per se but tainted by the prejudices of jurors against gay lifestyles and gays themselves.

A second key issue for the Hansen trial was testimony of four men. The state's case was built entirely on the claims of these four individuals Stone denigrated as "government snitches." They would testify that Hansen confessed the killings to them individually and at different times over a twenty-one-year period from 1955 to 1976. "None of the four ever went to the police with the alleged confessions until 1991 when one of them, a paid government informant using several aliases, allegedly told Special Agent James Delorto at the Bureau of Alcohol, Tobacco, and Firearms, that he could 'solve the Peterson and Schuessler murders,'" Stone said. Toomin allowed the testimony, saying later in an interview, "Judge Cawley had already entered an order admitting the testimony of these people, and both the prosecution and the defense relitigated it in front of me. I read everything, and I said, 'It sounds alright to me.'"

Another sensitive matter passed over to Toomin for review was whether to bar all references to Silas Jayne, the godfather of the Horse Mafia, in court. "The only reason that Silas Jayne's name would be mentioned is to titillate [the jury] and convict the defendant," Stone insisted. "It's the same reason [the prosecution is] talking about [Hansen] picking up hitchhikers in 1965 and having sex with them. That's inadmissible because [it] has nothing to do with 1955."

However, prosecutor Scott Cassidy argued, "The defense didn't argue it [until] Judge Cawley's ruling [switched on] the light bulb in their head. I respectfully submit, Judge Toomin, if they thought Silas's name should stay out of this, and there was a good legal basis to do so, they would have included it in their original motion, but they did not."

"This [is] a specious argument," O'Donnell interjected. "Silas Jayne's name adds nothing by way of making a fact true or false in this case."[4]

Toomin thought for a moment and then said, "There are statements attributed to Mr. Hansen, some third-party admissions where he names

Silas Jayne as the person who helped him move the bodies. He [Jayne] was aware of the murders."

As Toomin pondered the issue, Hansen thought back. *In '62 I bought a horse, Pandora, from him* [Silas Jayne]. *We would see him at horse shows and stuff like that. Si was not a friendly person. I mean he'd do business, and then he'd be gone.... I didn't know him in '55. I never in my life worked at anybody's stable doing stable work but my own. But when it was my father's* [stable], *it was like my own anyway."*

O'Donnell again interrupted Toomin. "Are you also aware of the oral admissions supposedly made by Hansen at the Fifth District Police Station? It says right in there at the conclusion, 'Hansen has *no* knowledge. He states that he has no knowledge of the Schuessler-Peterson killings.'"

Annoyed and increasingly agitated, Judge Toomin tapped his pen on his desk. "I said that I was going to allow it in because how far do you go to sanitize a case? That's what his name was—Silas Jayne. What are we going to call him, Mister X? Idle Hour was after all *his* stable." Toomin refused to be swayed by O'Donnell's persistent badgering. "Having reconsidered the ruling of March 30th, I will modify it to the extent that witnesses may be allowed to refer to the stable owner by his own proper name, Silas Jayne. By the same token, you will be attacking the testimony of your own witness, Frank Jayne Sr." All evidence relating to murder victims Cherie Rude and George Jayne, however, was excluded.

The well-known and respected O'Donnell glanced nervously over at Stone as the next matter on the docket, the next of the key issues, was the admissibility of the defense that the real killer of the Schuessler-Peterson boys was convicted serial killer John Wayne Gacy. "We want to bring in Lieutenant Sarnowski, who was one of the primary investigators on the case in the 1950s," Stone announced.

Toomin listened attentively to their arguments. The judge had searched for legal precedent and had studied old case files. "All the cases I found supported the state's position that this was totally inadmissible." Toomin considered the Gacy angle a far-fetched diversion. He also knew that the mere mention of Gacy's name would fire up the attention of the media. He told the defense attorneys, "Of course, there is a principle of law that the defendant should be able to introduce evidence of another offender who might be responsible. But," he cautioned, "there has to be evidence, not just conjecture and speculation."

The judge again tapped his pen on the top of the bench. It was a familiar signal that he was impatient and ready to move forward. This idiosyncrasy contradicted his otherwise placid courtroom demeanor, leaving attorneys, defendants, and jurors occasionally on edge.

Toomin adjusted his glasses and looked over at the prospective jurors. "I'd like you all to rise to be sworn."

After the task was completed, Toomin turned and faced the defendant. "You may stand, Mr. Hansen."

Hansen pushed himself up with one hand on the table and the other on his cane. By the time he was on his feet and at attention, Toomin was already ticking off the charges.

"Count one alleges that on or about October 16, 1955, Kenneth Hansen committed the crime of murder in that he, without lawful justification and with malice aforethought, killed John Schuessler by strangulation."

The judge read the same wording for the count of murder against Anton Schuessler Jr. and against Robert Peterson.

Hansen leaned back in his chair and thought, *As God is my witness, I didn't kill those children. I would not, I could not, and I didn't.*

As Toomin finished his recitation of the criminal indictment, a neatly dressed middle-aged woman in the back of the courtroom winced. A few jurors—and many of the spectators—spontaneously turned and looked in her direction.

Toomin continued with fortitude, "Counts four, five, and six allege the same offense of murder as to the three persons alleged in the first three counts. The allegations, however, are somewhat different in that it is alleged in all three counts that the defendant, without lawful justification, killed John Schuessler by strangulation during commission of the offense of indecent liberties with a child. The same allegation is made with respect to Anton Schuessler and Robert Peterson, as well."

The judge spoke to the prospective jurors in a dispassionate tone, "The indictment that I have read in part and summarized for you, ladies and gentlemen, is, of course, not to be taken by you as any evidence of the guilt of Mr. Hansen." As he spoke, he thought to himself, *Jurors are not predisposed to acquit people, and many of them will admit to the belief that 'We wouldn't be here if he wasn't guilty.'* For the next few minutes, Toomin defined the presumption of innocence[5] and covered in its entirety the manner in which the verdict must be made.

Although Toomin kept absolute control over his courtroom, it was Stone who had occupied the center stage for much of the pretrial motions. In another life, the artful criminal attorney might have played Falstaff in Shakespeare's *Henry IV*. Like Falstaff, the proselytizing Stone scorns the world of moral imperiousness and sanctimonious judgment. "Judge, the next motion is a motion *in limine*?"[6] Stone continued. Over the next thirty minutes, Stone argued against the credibility of a witness who delivered adhesive tape to the Idle Hour Stable: The "People intend to call a witness who will say that he may have delivered adhesive tape to the Idle Hour Stable." On the faces of the murder victims were found traces of adhesive tape. In 1955, a reference was made to "adhesive tape." The tape was a common variety. "If you opened up any medicine chest, certainly my own medicine chest in our Farwell Avenue apartment in 1955, you'd find a roll of adhesive tape there," Stone said with a hint of jest in his voice. "Adhesive tape isn't peculiar to the equine industry."

"Your Honor," Prosecutor Cassidy interjected, "several witnesses will testify that it was common practice to use adhesive tape to tape up horses' legs. Also the state's evidence will show that it was a routine matter in the equine industry that the horse's lead from the bridle was approximately two centimeters wide [almost an inch]. It's apparent that once you see the postmortem photographs, [showing] the wound on the neck of Bobby Peterson—you can visibly see a strap-type wound around his neck. It's clearly indicated on the postmortem that it's two centimeters wide.

"There's a witness named George Orose who will testify that in fact he delivered products to the Idle Hour back in 1955 including adhesive type tape," Cassidy continued. "He's provided us with tape that is similar to the type he delivered to the stable. We've shown that tape to Mr. Stone and Mr. O'Donnell, and it is adhesive-type tape. So I believe there is a sufficient nexus based upon his testimony."

Stone attacked the prosecution's arguments. "If there was a witness, let's say a police officer who came back and said, 'I recovered the adhesive tape,' then perhaps we could say that there was a legal nexus between tape being found on the bodies and tape being found in the barn; but there is no evidence that there was tape in the barn." Stone cast a contemptuous glance at Cassidy as he sat down.

The tape, the tack (stable gear, i.e., reins and bridle), Silas Jayne, and the coroner's original medical reports consumed much of the judge's time that first day. The debate was at times tedious, bitter, and contentious.

"The tack is even a more powerful argument, if you will," Stone said. "No one is going to say that the kind of tack the People intend to use as demonstrative evidence was found at the barn or even *existed* in the barn or was *in* the barn at Idle Hour. They're going to say that a two-centimeter ligature was found on the bodies—the body of one of the boys. That ligature was noted by [pathologist] Dr. [Jerry] Kearns as marks around the neck just as easily the result of a belt or necktie that had been twisted."

"Objection, Your Honor," interrupted Cassidy. "*That* is not evidence."

To support their argument, the defense produced copies of medical reports filed by Drs. Kearns and Hirsch in 1955. The discussion began with a reexamination of the photocopied documents and the signatures of Drs. Hirsch and Kearns. "Now the fact is that they lost or mislaid the original of that document, the signed copy," Stone affirmed. "Our problem is that we've got a forty-year-old murder case where there is clear exculpatory evidence in the police files and in the coroner's files, and now they're saying somehow we can't use it."

To the astonishment of the defense team, Toomin sided with the prosecution. "Well, just because it's in the file doesn't mean it's going to be used. I don't know what they intend to use to prove up the cause of death," Toomin said. "That obviously will be an element that they will have to prove up."

Cassidy returned to the implement of death used to strangle the boys. "We're not trying to fool anyone. We're not trying to fool the fact finder by saying this had to be it. No. We're not trying to do that. We're just saying that these boys were murdered in the Idle Hour barn, and I believe we're allowed to put this type of evidence in and allow the jury to determine what type of weight they want to attach to it."

Toomin was blunt, "I understand that you have no witness who will be able to testify that the exhibit that you're going to bring into court—the bridle and the reins—were present at the Idle Hour."

"No, I don't."

The judge ruled the adhesive tape inadmissible because it was "a classic example of circumstantial evidence"; the tack was also not deemed admissible.

Nobody in the court could read the face of the accused to get clues as to the thoughts swirling through Kenneth Hansen's mind as he sat implacably up to now. But listening to the judge strike down Jed Stone's objections one by one, he increasingly looked tired, scared, and without hope. Kenny's lips moved ever so slightly, "I didn't kill those boys."

For the next hour the debate was over jury selection, or voir dire.[7] The men and women sitting in the box listened closely as Toomin narrated the rules of the court and the methods by which they would be chosen as jurors.

After a brief recess, defense lawyers took one last stab at keeping certain evidence out of the trial, specifically Silas Jayne's name, recognizable and likely to influence the jurors. Toomin reiterated his decision. Because Frank Jayne Sr. was being called upon to testify, it was absurd to think that Si's name would not come up at some point.

The rain subsided, and sun peeked through the heavy gray clouds, casting yellowish patches on the floor of the courtroom. One swath of light cut across the table where Kenneth Hansen was seated. He kept his poker-faced expression, whispering a few words to Art O'Donnell, asking what would come next. But Ken knew the answer to that question. As soon as the jurors were impanelled, the trial would commence, and his fate would be decided.

When the time came for the defense to interview the prospective jurors, Toomin asked Stone to submit the questions for review. Jed Stone was irked, and later in an interview, he said, "I really hadn't considered giving the state or the court my questions in advance or that I was going to be subjected to sort of a prescreening. I wrote up the questions as a courtesy to the court because the court asked for our questions pertaining to issues of homosexuality." Stone respected Judge Toomin but considered his handling of this phase of the trial less than professional. *This is bullshit,* he thought to himself. *Homophobic bullshit!* He told the judge, "I'm a little reluctant to have to go through the process of having my voir dire receive a stamp of approval is what I'm saying."

Toomin was becoming increasingly frustrated. "A lot of your questions are just not going to be asked. And, you're going to run the risk of having objections made [to your arguments] and sustained. You could make your record here, but I can tell you that much of what you have got here I find extremely objectionable. And there's no way I would allow you to ask these questions."

He reviewed each question. The first was repetitive, about publicity about crime in America. Question two asked about personal views on the criminal-justice system. "I would not allow you to go into that," Toomin snapped at Stone, who did not have the time to respond as the judge scanned the last questions.

"Question eight deals with bumper stickers. And nine, personalized auto license plates." Toomin leaned back, suppressing a chuckle. Counsel seemed to be straying pretty far afield. "May I ask what the relevance of *that* is?"

Stone cleared his throat. "Judge, it's been my experience that you can learn an awful lot about a person's tastes and judgments, their prejudices and biases by what they put *behind* their cars and the message on their license plates. A function of voir dire is to explore the interests and biases of people [to find those] who will keep an open mind and be fair." He added that he wanted to know if any prospective juror was homophobic or a member of the American Horse Show Association (AHSA), which could be indicated on a bumper sticker.

Toomin allowed the bumper-sticker questions but vetoed all questions about prosecution for political reasons even though innocent and any experience that might cause bias against a murder defendant.

The most controversial line of questioning Stone intended to pursue had to do with opinions about homosexuality. "There's some discretion that can be allowed there," Toomin said. "I think you should be allowed to ask something, but I'm not sure when I look at these questions, that I agree with the way they are worded or even the scope of them."

Stone approached the bench. "I would ask the court to treat the subject of homophobia in the same way it treats the subject of racial bias or anti-Semitism. I think it's good practice to say to [an all white] jury that African Americans will be witnesses for this case. Can you judge the believability of an African American witness the same way? Do you have any prejudice against African Americans?" A younger, less-experienced attorney would likely be more circumspect in his or her choice of words, but Jed Stone seemed unconcerned. He challenged Toomin when he thought it was appropriate. "With all due respect, can you be fair? You're going to hear evidence that Mr. Hansen has engaged in homosexual acts. Can you put that out of your mind?"

"The courts have been very guarded in allowing this type of inquiry. I'm willing to allow some inquiry," the judge replied. "But I'm not, as yet, convinced as to how extensive it's going to be."

O'Donnell cut him off. "You will hear evidence of homosexuality in this case. Can you set that aside? There are really two issues here—homosexuality and pedophilia. In our society, people feel very strongly about these issues. More than treason, you know, or anything else."

Quinn said the question was whether the jurors' feelings would influence their ability to be fair and impartial.

Stone cited an earlier legal appeal involving the condemned serial murderer John Wayne Gacy, whose spectral presence loomed large in this case. Gacy's attorneys said the judge had refused to ask potential jurors to describe their feelings about homosexuality, whether between adults or an adult and a juvenile, and because of this, their client was doomed from the start if any juror was prejudicial to gay men.

Dealing with this sensitive issue was not something Toomin wanted to focus on to the exclusion of everything else, but it had emerged as the predominant theme this first day.

Question forty-three asked about a juror's feeling towards a person being HIV positive. Stone said there was reference to Ken being HIV positive and that the prosecution meant to use that in evidence. Quinn shot back that they did not, and again there was a moment of awkward silence.

Toomin sided with the prosecution and said he would not allow questions about the jurors' feelings or their moral judgments.

Blood rushed to Jed Stone's head as he stood in front of the bench. He felt as if he were about to explode. *This isn't fair,* he thought. The room was quiet as Stone glanced back at his client. Later, Hansen said that in prison, he'd been tested; he was adamant that he was not HIV positive:

Stone said the judge's limitations on defense questions were "unreasonable, forcing us to exercise preemptory challenges in a way that is not meaningful and, therefore, in violation of the fifth, sixth, and fourteenth amendments of the United States Constitution. That's my feeling about what you have just said." Jed Stone collapsed in his chair next to Hansen, convinced that the trial ahead would be a whitewash against his client. Stone freely admitted in an interview that he was in the unenviable position of representing a less-than-ideal defendant. Hansen's "a homosexual, yes, a bisexual, yes. He was upfront about that. I agree we're not going to pin father of the year or Scoutmaster on Ken."

Hamstrung by the limitations imposed upon them, Stone and O'Donnell used the questions they had left in their voir dire of prospective jurors. Many of the candidates expressed hesitation, doubt, and in some cases extreme reluctance, fearing that being on the jury would take them away from their families and jobs for a long time. Others cited health issues or deeper conflicts they were forced to wrestle with in their personal lives. One individual admitted that because of an earlier encounter with a pedophile, he would feel uneasy about sitting on "a jury such as this." He said he had been "approached as a young man," and "I cannot put that event out of my mind."

A panel of twelve jurors plus four alternates was finally assembled.

On a calendar, the clerk put a large red *X* over September 5, 1995—the first day of the trial was over.

The next morning, surviving members of the Schuessler family waited patiently outside room 400. From time to time, an anxious spectator would open the door and peek in. With the door slightly ajar, the people milling about the corridor watched as the clerk reserved the first two rows on the right side of Toomin's courtroom by taping a small sign to the wall: PRESS. At the entrance to the courthouse, media cameramen positioned their Sony 400 video cameras on tripods. A reporter from Fox News Chicago paced the area, checking his notes and awaiting the arrival of the attorneys. Scott Cassidy and Pat Quinn tried to sneak past the phalanx of reporters, but five journalists shoved microphones in front of their faces and badgered them with questions. "What is your take on the trial?" the TV newsman called out. "No comment," Cassidy responded in an icy tone as the two prosecutors pushed on to the entrance of the building. A *Chicago Tribune* reporter managed to keep up with their brisk pace. "Are you happy with the jurors?" The assistant state's attorneys ignored the seemingly innocuous question and quickly disappeared behind the marble pillars dividing the main entrance from the rest of the first floor. Federal and state prosecutors generally are tight-lipped in their dealings with reporters, preferring to deflect questions (whenever possible) to the designated press spokesman downtown.

The cameramen hastily redirected their equipment toward the front entrance to videotape the arrival of Stone and O'Donnell as they passed through the security gates. It was not the sexiest or most compelling video, but it was required all the same. Producers call these short clips "B-rolls." "Mr. O'Donnell, what are your feelings going into the trial?" the Fox newsman wanted to know. Before he could answer, a woman's voice chimed in, "How is Mr. Hansen doing?" The two veteran defense attorneys paused to respond. Unencumbered by the gag orders and protocol constricting government attorneys, Jed Stone was much more forthcoming in his responses. He recognized that maintaining good media relations was an essential part of the process. Playing to the press sometimes worked to the advantage of his clients. With a firm grip, Stone shook the reporter's hand, and with a hint of optimism in his voice, he stated, "Mr. Hansen is in good spirits. We're prepared to present a case that will prove his innocence."

Except for the area reserved for the media, nearly every available seat in the courtroom quickly filled in. A constant buzz of conversation permeated the room until the bailiff called for order. The defense team rose from their seats. Stone, wearing a deep-gray wool suit, announced their presence, "Jed Stone and Arthur O'Donnell on behalf of Kenneth Hansen before the court."

A plump, middle-aged woman, her hair swept back into a severe temple-tightening bun held in place with a black band, entered the courtroom with a chubby, balding man. The judge and the attorneys paused momentarily to observe Gary Kujawa and Nancy Kujawa Rauscher, the stepchildren of Eleanor Schuessler, as they made their way toward their seats.

Toomin briefed the jurors on the procedures in a criminal trial. "The duty and obligation of counsel is to make objections when they are warranted." Toomin told the jurors that they "need not be concerned with the legal reasons behind the admission or rejection of evidence that is placed here in court."

Patrick Quinn followed with his opening statement. "Ladies and gentlemen of the jury, let me start by telling you what this case is not about. This case is *not* about homosexuality," the prosecutor said with exaggerated emphasis. "What this case is about is child molestation and murder."

Agitated by the remark, Stone looked up at the ceiling. He ran his hand through his hair, sweeping a stray lock back into place. Quinn leaned over the prosecutor's table, opened a file, and again faced the jurors. "He [Hansen] admitted to picking up many children who were hitchhiking over the years, taking them to stables, and having sex with them. He admits offering them jobs and room and board to entice them." Quinn continued to focus on Hansen's repugnant behavior, and when he saw that his words were having the desired impact on the jurors, he phrased a provocative question in the form of a statement. "One thing I would ask is why would anyone say they had killed somebody. If you're in danger and you want to be a tough guy in a bar or people—"

"I object!" Stone cut him off, saying that Quinn's rhetoric wasn't allowed in opening statements.

The judge agreed. But Quinn knew that the jurors would remember what he said and that the men and women in the jurors' box liked him— he thought. "Lastly, ladies and gentlemen, we are operating under an old statute, a 1955 statute involving malice aforethought, the purposeful killing of children, and we'll prove that beyond a reasonable doubt."

O'Donnell gave the defense's opening statement. "Ladies and gentlemen of the jury . . . Mr. Quinn's opening statement told you that this is not a case of homosexuality. I ask you, because it's fresh in your mind, to review what you've just heard. If ninety-five percent of it did not deal with the question of homosexuality and pedophilia, then I didn't hear the same thing you did, and that is one of the real problems of this case." O'Donnell's strategy was aimed at convincing the jury that this case was corrupted by the homophobic attitudes of the prosecution. O'Donnell was troubled because he could not gauge the jury's attitude in this regard. "We will not deal with the question of homosexuality in the same sense that Mr. Quinn does," O'Donnell added. "We will deal with the question of a murder that took place forty years ago, and you will see the emphasis between the defense's case and the state's case.

"I agree with Mr. Quinn in one respect—that this is a very important case. . . . It is also extremely unique. I challenge anyone within the sound of my voice to tell me about one murder case in this country that was tried forty years after the event. . . . The only situation comparable to this is the Holocaust cases involving concentration-camp guards in Treblinka, Auschwitz, or Dachau who were spotted in Cleveland or Detroit and were charged with war crimes many years later."

O'Donnell could see it in the eyes of the reporters that the gravity of his words had taken hold. "I have to beg you to not make this a case based solely on homosexuality. Do not make this a case of pedophilia even though the bulk of what Mr. Quinn talked about was dealing precisely with that issue."

O'Donnell summarized the highlights of Ken Hansen's life. After he graduated in 1951, he worked for William A. Lewis, a men's clothing store. Ken helped out at his father's business of pony rides at carnivals and church functions In 1953 Hansen was drafted into the army and served until January 1955. On June 7, 1955, he and his wife, Beverly, bought a stable, "not up on the Northwest Side where there was a great variety of them, on the Southwest side near a town called Willow Springs," O'Donnell said. "They called it the Bro-Ken H Stable. He went into business there in June of 1955, that's four months before October 1955, when this [tragedy] occurred."

O'Donnell then proceeded to resuscitate the John Wayne Gacy theory hatched by Lieutenant John Sarnowski and his partner Ed Kocinski. If the defense intended to pin the murders on Gacy, who was thirteen at the time of the crimes, there was precious little hope for an acquittal.

Quinn and Cassidy whispered back and forth, opening and closing files.

"That evidence does not come from the defendant, it comes from Robert Peterson's father, and you will hear that testimony," O'Donnell said, pausing long enough to take a deep breath. "Sarnowski is a witness in this case but unfortunately is currently a patient at Resurrection Hospital [in Chicago, where he had been moved from Lake Geneva, Wisconsin]. Two weeks ago he suffered a relapse of lymphatic cancer, and we asked to continue the case." And without Sarnowski's testimony, the defense knew there was, again, precious little hope for an acquittal.

Because the judge had ruled against the defense on so many motions, O'Donnell wondered if he was managing to reach the jury as he launched into a mud-slinging attack against the federal law-enforcement agency that brought these "spurious charges" and the credibility of their informants. "An unholy alliance was created a few years ago between William 'Red' Wemette and a unit of the Justice Department called the Bureau of Alcohol, Tobacco, and Firearms, probably the most discredited law-enforcement agency on the face of this earth following the Waco disaster and Ruby Ridge.

"Roger Spry also received money and was taken care of by the government after he decided to cooperate and verify Wemette's story. He's a pathetic character." Moisture built up on O'Donnell's forehead as he reminded the court that no physical or scientific evidence, no fingerprints, no actual eyewitnesses whatsoever could be produced—"Nothing but two paid witnesses and another pathetic character by the name of Hollatz." O'Donnell, his head bowed, retreated to his chair as the prosecution summoned forth its first witness.

Beatrice Blane, the elderly aunt of the Schuessler brothers, came forward to be sworn. She searched the audience for her sister's stepchildren, and only after she had spotted them nodding to her reassuringly did she take her place on the witness stand. Mrs. Blane knew all about the Equestrian Mafia. She had read about the crimes of Si Jayne in the newspaper and his involvement with the Idle Hour Stables. And she remembered quite clearly, as if it were yesterday, her beloved nephews John and Tony Schuessler. Her eyes saddened when Cassidy held up a two-by-two-inch, black-and-white photo of her sister's youngest son. "That's Tony, my nephew."

The defense had no questions for her, as her only purpose was to identify her nephews.

"The People call Ernest Niewadomski," Quinn declared.

A family man who still resided in suburban Mt. Prospect, the fifty-seven-year-old Niewadomski testified, "I work at Big Ern's fast-food restaurant. . . . I was seventeen and a senior at Gordon Tech High School in 1955. I was at the Monte Cristo Bowling Alley. I met Tony and John Schuessler and Bob Peterson. The Schuesslers were neighbors of mine. John and Anton were wearing Cub jackets. The other boy was wearing a White Sox jacket. They had jeans on. I later heard they were missing and told my mom I had seen them all together. I told Mrs. Schuessler. Many different police officers came to the house. I was interviewed thirty, forty, maybe fifty times by police and newspaper reporters."

Confused thoughts whirled around in his head. Niewadomski was nervous about being here. Quinn gently guided his witness through the questioning with smiles of assurance.

When O'Donnell stood in front of him to ask the next set of questions, blood rushed to Niewadomski's head, and he suddenly felt a tad nauseated. O'Donnell had one goal: to get Niewadomski to admit that there may have been a fourth person—possibly Gacy—with the Schuessler and Peterson boys. "I'm asking you, Mr. Niewadomski, is that possible there could have been a fourth party?"

"I seen no one else with the boys. The three boys stuck together as a threesome. There was no four." The witness was insistent on that point, forcing O'Donnell to retreat.

"And is it possible they could have met somebody say twenty minutes later, about ten to eight, or eight o'clock, before they left?"

"Objection to what's possible, Judge!" Quinn retorted.

But O'Donnell continued to speak. "If you know—"

"Sustained," Toomin ruled.

Ralph Helm, the fifteen-year-old Lane Tech student walking his girlfriend home the night of October 16, 1955, testified that as he walked north on Milwaukee Avenue near Lawrence, he had observed an eleven-to-twelve-year-old boy on the curb to his left, thumbing a ride.

"So he was actually facing you as you walked north on Milwaukee Avenue?" Cassidy crossed in front of the witness stand and stopped abruptly at the edge of the jurors' box. He never took his eyes off Helm. "Did you have an occasion to look at him?"

"Yes, sir." Helm's voice was soft and his tone protective. "I would estimate eleven to twelve years of age. As I passed the boy, the boy on the curb was to my left; to my right in a doorway, I observed two other boys standing back out of the rain."

When Stone objected, Toomin, who was busy taking notes, looked over at the defense table and said, "I'll sustain that."

After he dropped off his date, Helm said he walked passed the same intersection to take a southbound bus home. The boys were not there. Two nights later, Helm's mother called the police, who showed up to interview Helm the next day.

The teenager was urged to accompany the police to the funeral home and, if possible, help to identify the boys. Although it was extremely difficult to gaze down at the body in the casket—Helm had thought to himself, *He's just sleeping*—he identified Anton as the young boy who was hitchhiking in the rain.

Cassidy presented to the jury four large, black-and-white photos of the storefront at Lawrence and Milwaukee where the boys had loitered in the rain. Helm put his head down, appearing uncomfortable. At that point, Toomin ordered an adjournment for lunch.

Hetty Salerno, one of the Park Ridge residents living close to the Idle Hour Stables in 1955, described the layout of the area back then: "There was nothing there. It was all fields, no expressway, [no] houses, just stables and a farm." Salerno was proud of her home of forty years, a tri-level with an attached garage and an open breezeway. Her neighbors—the Paneks, the Glasscotts, and the Parkers—were all friends. She professed that she had never before heard screams like that in the safe surroundings of Park Ridge. Salerno said she was scared and went into her home and did not go back outside that evening. But she never forgot those awful screams. "One was very loud; the other one was softer. Whether it was the same or two different [children], I'm not sure." Two days later, her husband caught the tail end of a news report describing the crime scene. That's when he called the police, who, in large numbers, perhaps thirty or more, she guessed, marched side by side through the open prairie "looking for something" under tangles of brush, downed tree branches, and dried leaves.

Cassidy took two steps closer to the witness stand. "Just west of that field there was a building, was there not?"

"The stables," Salerno took a deep breath and glanced at Hansen.

"Do you recall the name of those stables? Was it the Idle Hour Stable?" Cassidy's eyes darted in the direction of the defense table expecting an objection, but neither defense attorney said anything. Cassidy presented the large black-and-white aerial view taken April 7, 1955.

"It shows the area we used to live in," she said, "Higgins, Peterson, Grace, and the stables, Mr. DeGraff's property right there, and the farm was over in that direction."

It was the defense's turn, and Stone approached the front of the jurors' box. "Mrs. Salerno, you're not saying that the screams that you heard came from the barn, are you?"

Holding her breath, she was glad that no one could see her hands shaking. "I'm saying that it came from that direction."

"Of course, there were many things between your home and the barn in 1955, weren't there? So you're not suggesting to this jury that the screams that you heard came from inside a barn as opposed to an open field, are you?" Stone wanted her to say that she didn't hear screams coming from inside the Idle Hour barn.

"I'm saying that Mr. Panek, my husband, and I heard it directly down Peterson [Street] from that area, not from the side where the fields were."

"Can you tell us with accuracy how far away the screams were from you?"

"About a block and a quarter from our house."

Stone hammered away at Salerno. He suggested that the screams could have come from the houses on Grace. Or the area behind Grace in a large open field. "How is it that you know [you heard the screams] between nine o'clock and ten o'clock at night?"

Salerno's voice softened. "We had four small children. They went to bed at eight o'clock. Nine o'clock every night, whether it was rain, hail, or snow, we'd go out on the breezeway, enjoy our coffee, and just talk alone. We'd put jackets on if it was cold. So I know it was nine o'clock. This went on for a year or two—we always did the same thing."

Stone then asked about the police officers walking abreast in the open field. "Did you ever think to say to them, 'No, gentlemen, don't be walking over here in the field, go further south towards the stable.' Did you say that to them?"

"No, because my husband handled it at that time, I didn't."

"Okay. I'm asking you if you ever directed the police who were searching in the field for evidence to the area of the stable? Is that a no?"

"That's a no, sir."

Then the prosecution asked her about her wartime experiences serving in London. "Following the bombings in London, there were screams?" Cassidy asked in a voice that was low but clear.

"I was an ambulance driver during the war," Salerno replied before Stone voiced yet another objection.

"Were these the loudest screams you ever heard before when you heard them on that night?" Cassidy continued.

Again, Stone objected, which the judge sustained.

Next on the stand was Violet Sable, who moved in 1953 with her family to 1024 Peterson, near Idle House Stables. Quinn needed the seventy-three-year-old Sable, who still resided at that address, to corroborate her memories of that time. He showed her an aerial photograph of the neighborhood and pointed to a building. The bespectacled woman leaned closer, "It was a stable."

"And directing your attention to what I would call the back barn area, is this also part of that Idle Hour Stable?"

"Yes."

Stone asked, "You were at a cookout that night, weren't you?"

"At a barbecue next door." Sable said that she was home by ten o'clock and was certain that she did not hear any screams. "It started raining, and I closed all the windows" in her house.

"Of course, that would have been after ten o'clock?"

"Approximately."

"Right. But while you were at the Panek house, you heard no screams?"

"No."

Stone was pleased.

Next to testify was Roger Hammill, the former news photographer who lived less than a mile from Robinson Woods in 1955. He said he was at lunch when he got the call about the bodies being found. Hammill knew all of the local landmarks, including an Indian burial grave just south of the woods. Hammill described the crime scene. "I took a photograph to show how the bodies were positioned and the area where they were found. And then later on, the assistant coroner, Harry Glos, came on the scene and then, well, he took over."

The prosecutor unveiled the crime-scene photos. A couple of the jurors winced at the sight of the naked, battered remains of the boys and turned away. The prosecutor drew the witness back in, "People's exhibit number seventeen for identification?"

"You're looking north," Hammill said, "and you can see the three lying down there and Harry Glos pointing to them. One of the officers as I recall was Peters, Sergeant Peters, but the man in the black coat, I don't know who he was."

Quinn held up additional images for Hammill to identify, driving home the point that the crime scene had been trampled with no regard to securing evidence.

"We didn't have anything like yellow tape in those days," the witness said. "We just hoped that the police would keep the people out of the way. But, no, as you can see, a lot of people got in there that had no right to even be there."

Quinn produced a photograph showing Glos's shocking disregard because he had, quite clearly, flipped over Bobby Peterson's body and rearranged the positioning of the other two boys. "To the best of your knowledge, did the police recover any physical evidence from that crime scene besides the boys' bodies?" Before Hammill could answer, Stone objected, but Hammill responded quickly, "No, not to my knowledge." The Chicago Police crime lab was equipped with state-of-the-art technology and had capable staff in the 1950s, but, in the main, good old-fashioned detecting and instinct were still viewed as the surest way to solving homicides.

Cassidy handed jurors the enlarged photos of the crime scene. "If you would, sir, pass it on after looking at it. No further questions, Your Honor." The prosecutor watched closely as each juror in turn absorbed the full impact of the frightening images. Cassidy wondered how many of these good people had children of their own.

Patrick Mason, a fifty-one-year-old Southsider who had ridden horses at the Bro-Ken H in his youth, appeared to be hesitant to share his memories. He said that starting when he was eleven, his sister, a friends of hers, and he took the Bluebird Bus south on Cicero to Sixty-Third Street every weekend for about a year to Willow Springs. In exchange for doing some work—mucking stables, feeding the horses, and taking groups of riders out as a guide—"we were allowed to take livery horses out and ride for free."

On the last day he was at the stables, "I went into the smaller of the two barns to get a horse to take out a group of riders, and halfway through the barn, I looked to my left and in an empty stall, I saw Mr. Hansen performing oral copulation on a boy."

"Object!" O'Donnell barked. "Move for a mistrial, Your Honor."

Low whispers echoed Toomin's courtroom. The bailiff quieted the audience.

"Objection overruled. The answer may stand."

Cassidy requested that the witness repeat his answer. Mason said the boy was Gene McCoy, fifteen years old. Hansen was performing oral sex on the boy when Mason interrupted them.

"I went into the attached barn, the large barn that had horse stalls on both sides of the aisle. I went to the rear of the barn to get another horse out," he said, beginning to stammer, "and I was in the process of saddling it when Mr. Hansen came up behind me and grabbed me by the crotch."

Again, a low murmur echoed across the room.

"I turned, spun around, and shoved him away with my elbow. He told me that I had to go along with the program that he had going there or I would not be allowed to work there anymore." Mason sat back in the chair and gazed across the rows of people listening to him. "He stuck his finger in my face and told me that if I told anybody about what I saw him doing, I'd wind up in the woods like those other boys. I told him he could have his job, and I was leaving, and he told me that I'd better not say anything because he also knew who my brother and sister were."

The then-twelve-year-old had held back his tears. "You better not put a hand on my brother or sister. I'm leaving now."

Patrick Mason never again returned to the Bro-Ken H. Cassidy asked him if he could identify Kenneth Hansen. And now, thirty-nine years later, Mason sat on the witness stand in a Cook County courtroom and pointed to the defendant. "That's the man sitting in the middle over there."

Stone reviewed his notes and asked the retired Chicago policeman about his meeting in Las Vegas, his new home, with ATF agent James J. Grady on August 19, 1994. Mason said he told Grady that Hansen had never approached him in a "sexual manner." Without hesitation, Mason recited the names of three horses housed at the Bro-Ken H in 1955 to 1956—Sarge, Hong Kong, and Blackjack. According to Mason, there was no horse named Bear at Hansen's stable in 1956. For many years, Mason suppressed the memory of the traumatic and frightening events of 1956. He kept it to himself, refusing to discuss it. Who could fault him for that?

The next witness was arguably one of the prosecution's stars—Roger Spry, Ken's throwaway boy.

Spry recalled the first time Kenny had bothered him at the stables. "Initially I lived with Kenny and Bev . . . and their kids . . . in the house," he mumbled, "but after spurning Kenny's sexual advances, I was forced to sleep in the dog kennel." The forty-eight-year-old man sighed. "I was eleven or twelve when Kenny performed oral sex on me."

"Sir, after this first molestation, how long did Mr. Hansen continue to molest you?" Quinn asked.

O'Donnell pounded his hand on the table. "I'm going to object to the characterization of molestation."

"I'll sustain the objection," Toomin said.

Quinn ignored the directive and asked the question again.

Stone objected and called for a sidebar. "If we're talking about acts of sexual intercourse with a minor, then we're talking about other crimes," Stone said. "This is clearly inadmissible unless it goes to prove a pattern. They can't develop a pattern fifteen years after the crime."

Quinn replied that Judge Cawley had already allowed this type of testimony. Toomin said he was not going to reexamine the issue again.

Frustrated, Stone appealed one more time, "Judge, this court has the duty to make sure reversible error isn't committed. . . . I don't believe Judge Cawley's opinion or ruling gives [the prosecution] carte blanche to bring in acts of sexual molestation or anything as a consenting adult. Therefore, I respectfully object and move for mistrial. I think this is far beyond Judge Cawley's ruling."

Toomin denied the motion.

The jury learned that the defendant had sex with young Spry for "another seven years," and Spry did nothing to prevent future molestations, even after he was of legal age. Spry described graphic scenes of young, male hitchhikers brought back to the stables for free riding lessons and trail rides in exchange for sexual favors. According to Spry, Hansen's customers paid big dollars to board their horses, and to them, Kenny was a charming family man.

Spry was asked to outline as best as he could the gruesome last moments of the Schuessler-Peterson boys lives, based on what Ken Hansen had confessed to him years after the boys' deaths. Spry talked nonstop, "So he said that he was having sex with the two younger boys and that the older boy showed up and caught him and that the younger boy said that [the older boy] was going to tell, so Kenny said that he grabbed him, and he had a hold of him around his throat, and that he was watching the other two boys so they couldn't get away. He said the other two boys were trying to get away. He said he grabbed [Bobby Peterson] like this with his right arm to hold him so he could have this arm free so the other two boys couldn't get away."

Spry supplied small but important details of just how Hansen said he "accidentally killed" Peterson. "He said he had no choice but to kill the other two boys." In a dark, reflective whisper, Spry added, "He said Si showed up and was wild and really mad! He said that he and Si took and loaded the kids in the car and dropped them in the forest preserves."

O'Donnell asked the court to adjourn for the day. Obviously, he needed time to regroup and build a strong response during cross-examination.

"We have a strenuous objection," Quinn interjected. "You have known him for many, many years. I cannot imagine why the defense might not be ready to cross right now."

"He's covered a relationship spanning thirty-five years that I have to go into exhaustively," answered O'Donnell. The aging defense attorney glanced at Spry and thought, *He's a liar by his own admission. There's no way the jury's going to buy into his testimony.*

Hansen sat quietly, dismally reflecting on the testimony of Roger Spry. In a later interview, Hansen said, "I would never bring some kid home and dump him on Beverly without even talking about it. We had Danny, and Roger slept in Danny's bedroom when he was there. I never molested him as a child, and he never slept in any kennels." Regarding the sexual relationship with Spry, Hansen mused, "Roger and I were showing horses. . . . He was showing, and I was with him. We were drinking, and we had, we started our affair because we were sleeping in the tack room, and we started having an affair. I don't know why he'd say that stuff."

Toomin checked his watch. It was almost five o'clock. "It might be a good time to recess."

16

Memories and Nightmares

NO ONE—NOT QUINN, Cassidy, Toomin, Stone, O'Donnell, or Hansen—appeared to have had a restful night when the trial resumed at 10:15 the next morning. A cousin of Robert Peterson discreetly slipped into the courtroom and took her place in the unreserved seating area in the rear of the courtroom.

Roger Spry emerged from the back of the courtroom with an enthusiastic look to him. He was a man with a story to tell and damned if he wasn't going to let it all come out.

In an attempt to paint an unflattering portrait of Spry, O'Donnell got right down to it and reminded the jury that the witness was a self-admitted liar and a thief. "Yesterday you indicated on direct examination that you had stolen money in the stable, is that correct? And when Mr. Hansen confronted you, you told him the reason you didn't put people's names [who had paid for the trail ride] down on the registry was that you forgot?" O'Donnell asked, the timber of his voice rising.

"Yes, sir."

"That wasn't true, was it, because you indicated to us you took money because he hadn't been paying you anything, is that right?"

"Right," Spry answered wearily.

"And you're also a liar by your own admission because you told [Hansen] that you forgot to put the names down, but you didn't forget. You did it deliberately, is that correct?"

Spry was cocky to the point of defiance as he also admitted to stealing a Palomino horse and money from Ken Hansen.

O'Donnell leveled a question that was undoubtedly on everyone's mind—"Are you a homosexual, Mr. Spry?"

"No, sir."

"Have you ever been?" badgered O'Donnell.

"No, sir."

"What do you define yourself as?"

"A heterosexual."

"But you occasionally do homosexual acts, is that it?"

Spry said nothing for a few seconds.

"Participate in homosexual acts?"

"Yes."

"And there's a big distinction in your mind about that?"

Spry nodded but had a more difficult time framing a convincing response to the question of why he didn't—or couldn't—leave Kenny's stable when he was old enough to strike out on his own. "Well, when you don't have an education, you don't have any money, you don't have any clothes, and you don't have no place to stay, it's kind of hard to find a job," he said.

"Yesterday you indicated on direct examination that you had stolen money in the stable. Is that correct?" Hard of hearing, O'Donnell moved in close.

"Yes, sir," acknowledged Spry. He was unctuous to the point of sarcasm.

"So, by your own admission then, you are a thief, is that correct?"
Cassidy sprang to his feet, "Objection!"

Toomin gestured for him to sit down and responded, "Overruled."

"And you are also a liar by your own admission," O'Donnell charged.

Spry was caught off guard but composed himself. "Yes, sir."

O'Donnell paused and switching subjects requested Spry to repeat Hansen's confession inside the Bro-Ken H Stables saddle-repair shop. O'Donnell faced the jurors and scrutinized their facial responses as Spry reiterated the story.

"When you heard this story, what did you do?" the defense attorney asked.

"Scared the hell out of me," Spry leaned back in the chair. His eyes darted up toward the judge and then toward Hansen, before he ran his left hand through his hair and settled his attention on O'Donnell.

"Did you say anything to him like, Oh, my God?" O'Donnell asked.

"No," Spry replied nervously. "I just kept my mouth shut."

"You are fifteen or sixteen years old, and a man just told you he killed three people. . . . Is that correct? Now at any time after that did you call the police?"

"No." Spry looked at the prosecutors, waiting for an objection to this line of questioning. Quinn and Cassidy, who sat next to one another and from time to time would lean in and whisper in the other's ear, gave no objection.

"As a matter of fact, Mr. Spry, you have a case pending in the Circuit Court of Cook County, don't you? And the charge is what?"

Spry knew it would get around to that sooner or later. "Arson. Burning a barn down," he replied softly.

"And when they told you they were going to arrest you, I'm sure that scared the hell out of you, too, didn't it?"

"Not really." Spry, who was living with his girlfriend, Colleen Quinn, at the time of the arrest, admitted that his attorney, Marie Lapinski, "came to an agreement" with the people in the state's attorney's office. For his testimony in this trial, he would receive eighteen months probation for criminal damage to property in that 1970 arson case.

O'Donnell changed tactics. "Have you ever had sexual encounters with other persons?"

"No, sir."

O'Donnell smiled. "Never? So you never had any sexual encounter with Mr. Hansen?"

Spry was forced to admit the truth. "Yes, sir."

"Well, do you look upon that as being different? I asked you if you had sexual encounters with any other persons. You said no."

For the next thirty minutes, O'Donnell went over Spry's circumstances. "And the Hansens took care of all of your medical needs? In fact, you were managing [one of Hansen's] stables as recently as 1986, weren't you?" By the end of the cross-examination, O'Donnell believed he had succeeded in demonstrating an altogether different side to Spry than the prosecution's image of the abused little waif who suffered at the hands of a pedophile.

Upon redirect, the defense team requested a sidebar in order to discuss the possibility of impeaching Mr. Spry. Quinn suggested, "If they cross-examine him regarding any deal, we would be allowed to go into the details of the arson, which means Ken Hansen paid him three hundred dollars to burn down a competitor's barn." The prosecution wanted desperately to bring this information in as testimony but was precluded.

Spry watched with interest as Quinn postured in front of the jury box. Answering the prosecutor's questions, Spry again told that the first week he lived at Bro-Ken H Stables, he was in the apartment. After Hansen approached him, and Spry refused his advances, Spry said he was exiled to downstairs in the dog kennels.

"When was the last time you had sex with Ken Hansen, sir?"

Spry said nothing.

"Were you afraid of Curtis Hansen?"

"Scared to death of him," Spry mumbled.

Mark Hansen said he believes that his father's notorious cheapness fostered deep and lasting resentment among Spry and the other employees. Kenny worked these boys hard but paid them very little, and they never forgave him. "With my mom gone, the disgruntled ex–stable hands extracted their revenge against Kenny, by agreeing to testify against him. If my mom was alive today, there is no way Wemette would have started all of this. None of them would have done it!" he adds emphatically. "They loved my mother and would not have wanted to hurt her in this way. He was hardly the indentured servant," chuckled Mark, who knew Roger well during the years they lived together under the same roof. "My dad sent him to school. He lived with us upstairs. Roger is the kind of guy who likes to make up stories."

Next up was Colleen Quinn, who told the court that she met Roger in June of 1992. She knew little about his background, but a ride across the country gave the couple an opportunity to share stories. She said, "Roger got a job opportunity in Texas so we sold things and packed up the car and drove to Texas. During the drive, I remember very well we were headed towards El Paso, and Roger was telling me a little bit about when he was small about how his mother had left him, and he was working on a ranch with ponies and with horses. He mentioned to me that while he was working at the stable, he was told of a story about three young boys' deaths in Chicago." The woman admitted that she was not familiar with all the sordid aspects of Roger's troubled childhood, but she said she loved him all the same.

Meanwhile, in a hotel bar not far from the Criminal Courts Building, Herbert Hollatz broke his vows of abstinence. "Bud and a whiskey back," he told the bartender. He was supposed to be at the courthouse at least thirty minutes before the scheduled time for his testimony, but at the moment, his mind was on other things—not on keeping appointments. As he gulped down his brew, it occurred to him that this was the perfect time to race off to Mexico and avoid testifying against Hansen. As he drew a picture in his mind of how he would accomplish something so bold, he knew that he was just bullshitting himself. Herb lacked the courage to attempt to defy the government that way. Herb was a coward. He had been all his life. A small boy, awkward and timid, he felt slighted by his father, a Chicago Police officer. Desperate to win his father's or for that matter any man's attention, Herb pretended to be hardened, without sensitivity or empathy. Before long, he exhibited a carapace of arrogance—except when he was around Kenny Hansen. Flushed with embarrassment, Herb mulled over his testimony. The prosecution would paint him as an unwilling witness who had no intention of snitching on Ken Hansen. Herb, a father of six children, had spent most of the past thirty-nine years wandering between Illinois and Arizona. During those years, he had had little to do with his family and nothing to do with Ken Hansen.

Herb's mind flashed to the night in October when Hansen had confessed. "I just killed the three boys," Hansen had said as if he were anesthetized. Hollatz had asked, "Why?" Hansen replied, "I was told to kill them."

Herb paid the bartender and, with a heavy sigh, returned to his car and drove off in the general direction of Twenty-Sixth and California, noting with quiet dismay the dilapidated storefronts and the scent of poverty along the route. It was a different kind of squalor than his trailer in Arizona but squalor all the same.

Colleen Quinn was wrapping up her testimony at the same moment Herb stepped off the elevator on the fourth floor. A sheriff was waiting and escorted him to a private room where the witnesses stayed prior to their testimony. Minutes later, he heard his named called. Herb approached the bench dragging a psychic ball and chain behind him. His voice cracked as he swore *to tell the whole truth and nothing but the truth,* and his legs nearly buckled as he stepped up behind the witness stand.

Herb scoffed at the accusations that he was a homosexual predator. During the investigation, the ATF agents had ruled him out as a coconspirator in the boys' deaths—though it must have crossed their minds at some point that Herb might have owned or driven the white flatbed truck witnesses claimed to have seen moments before the boys were picked up. None of this came out in court, but the prosecutors all agreed that Herb was a good witness. As he sat there staring out at the spectators, he didn't want to worry about what people thought. His health was fragile, and he had recently been hospitalized for heart problems. On top of that, his throat-cancer surgery forced him to speak slowly and deliberately. His trip back to the Midwest had required a doctor's approval.

Herb recalled that when Hansen seemed anesthetized when confessing, "I just killed the three boys." When Herb asked why, Hansen replied, "I was told to kill them."

Quinn asked Hollatz how long after the murders had the conversation with Hansen occurred.

"About a week," he answered. "I said why? And he said that somebody had told him to do it. He said that if I said anything, his brother would kill me."

"Did you believe him?" Quinn asked.

"Definitely."

O'Donnell began his questioning, getting out of Herb that during the two to four months he was at Hansen's, they had had sex and that Herb's father had died in 1980. "So after that you didn't have to worry about what your father would think," O'Donnell said. "It didn't occur to you to go to one of his friends on the police force and tell them that you knew who killed the Schuessler-Peterson boys?"

Hollatz did not respond, but he could feel his temples pounding as the blood rushed to his head.

O'Donnell persisted, "Didn't you know this man, this murderer, was loose on the street? Mr. Hollatz, again, I don't want to pry into your personal life, but you were very fond of Beverly, weren't you?"

"Yes."

"Would you say you might have been in love with her?"

Hollatz stared anxiously at the jurors, and his voice rose as he responded, "I could have been, yes. Real easy." He said that he had been dating Arlene Zielke on and off for a couple of years before getting hitched in Arizona. (Several family members insisted that the marriage took place in Chicago because Arlene's ailing mother wanted to attend the ceremony.) He coaxed the young girl into marrying him with a promise that he would take care of her parents.

"You came back and lived in Chicago for a period of time after you moved out of state, didn't you?" O'Donnell asked. "How long did you stay here?"

"About seven, eight years," Hollatz said. "You know I came back twice for my parents' funerals."

The prosecution had crafted an image of their witness as a principled man of high moral rectitude who was repeatedly victimized by the degenerate named Kenneth Hansen. But on cross-examination, Herb admitted that the sex was "consensual." When he was twenty-one, he had begun his homosexual affair with Kenny, and it had continued off and on again for the next three years. The admission was both painful and embarrassing for Herb.

O'Donnell supplied a moment of unintentional levity when he asked Hollatz how many grandchildren he had.

"Fifteen and two on the way."

"You beat the heck out of me," cracked the elderly attorney. Then O'Donnell disparagingly asked, "Did you drink today?"

Hollatz looked at his feet, then said, "On and off."

Quinn jumped to his feet. "Objection! Relevancy?"

"Answer may stand," Toomin concluded. "He said on and off."

The prosecution then attempted to preserve the credibility of the witness: "Sir, were you afraid of Curt Hansen?"

Herb replied in the affirmative.

"When did you learn that Curt Hansen was dead? When were you told that?"

"I was told April 8th. I guess it was when you came out there."

"Has the government ever given you money to come into court, sir?"

"Objection!" Stone demanded but was overruled.

Quinn reminded the court that the government was paying for Herb's airfare and food and lodging while in Chicago.

On the third day of Ken Hansen's trial and before the jury was brought in, defense attorney Jed Stone told the judge that the prosecution intended to call Glenn Carter. Stone's understanding was that Carter, who was fourteen in 1954, would say he'd seen Bobby Peterson at Idle Hour Stables at some point in either 1953 or 1954.

Quinn said the correct years were 1954 and 1955.

Thinking about what Quinn had said made Stone grit his teeth. "I submit that that is not probative[1] of any issue in this case. Remember the state's theory is not that these children were customers of the Idle Hour but that they were picked up while hitchhiking, specifically by Mr. Hansen and taken to the Idle Hour." *If I am wrong, Stone thought, it qualifies as a balls-to-the-wall career fuck-up.* "So the fact that somebody claims they saw somebody there on an earlier occasion doesn't come close to answering any questions. It creates an Idle Hour nexus in the evidence. That isn't probative of any fact or issue but is highly prejudicial."

"It's very probative. Would a child go to a place where he's been before or where there are ponies? It's probative. It's much less than we initially intended to use him for," Quinn argued. "Much less, indeed."

In statements in pretrial testimony on August 19, 1994, Glenn and Bruce Carter said they had bumped into Bobby Peterson and his buddies John and Tony Schuessler the day of their disappearance. Later, Toomin recalled in an interview that he thought this issue was brought up in order to introduce the conversation of the five boys at a certain time and place, with one of the boys commenting about a car that had gone by, "Oh, that's Hansen, we're going to see him later at the stable." The judge commented, "I don't think [the prosecution] tried to get that in."

Stone and O'Donnell were very much aware of the potentially damaging testimony against their client and were delighted that the only "true piece of evidence" linking the Schuessler-Peterson boys to Hansen was ignored by the prosecution.

Glenn Vernon Carter was a sober, retiring schoolteacher in 1995, approximately fifty-four years of age. He, too, was baffled by the prosecution decision to overlook the information about the happenstance meeting with Bobby, John, and Tony on October 16, 1955. Shadowy memories of the conversation had been buried deep inside his head, but there wasn't a day that went by when Glenn didn't recall little Tony's girlish voice, "Is that Hansen?" He never understood why John didn't want Tony to talk about Hansen. "Be quiet. You've said too much already." He did, however, remember the fear his entire family experienced for nearly forty years—until Kenneth Hansen's arrest.

The jury was brought in, and testimony began for the day. Carter took a deep breath as he waited for the first question. A slight smile crossed his face as he remembered that during his freshman year of high school, he had visited Idle Hour at least "ten to twelve" times. Accompanied by his younger brother Bruce, he had enjoyed trail rides in Robinson Woods. Glenn and Bobby were in Boys Scouts but were in two different Boy Scout troops although the troops did things together at church.

Quinn showed Carter a photograph of Bobby and one of the stable. Carter used his right forefinger to point out the path where his brother and he had liked to ride.

Stone approached the witness stand and smiled. "You and your buddies went to other stables as well?"

"No. There again for us, transportation-wise, Idle Hour was the easiest and cheapest to get to. Whenever you could save a dime or nickel, you saved it."

It was strange that no one bothered asking the witness if he had observed Kenneth Hansen working at Idle Hour in 1955 or about his chance meeting with the Schuessler-Peterson boys, though he had recalled during the grand-jury testimony quite intensely that his brother and he had told their parents about the brief conversation with Bobby Peterson. The parents ordered their boys to remain silent on the matter—not because of physical threats but because their parents feared that if they told the police, the fiend who killed the boys would hunt them down.

According to one source, Bruce Carter wept openly when he first told investigators about the oath of silence his mother had forced him to take. The Glenn Carter questioning was a wash. Why the prosecutors did not ask Judge Toomin to allow them to compel the witness to reconstruct the chance meeting in the street is puzzling. Five boys rendezvous on a Sunday afternoon, but only two of them return safely home. The prosecution apparently did not consider the matter important enough to bring up in court. Even the judge had to admit that he was mystified by their decision, because he would have allowed it had it been introduced.

What followed next in court were the sworn statements of several young men who had engaged in sexual activity with Hansen going back to the 1960s. The prosecution proved, through the testimony of Roger Spry and then Robert Stitt, that Hansen lured young boys into his arms with the help of other young lads.

The forty-three-year-old Stitt spoke with passion about his childhood years. His grandmother took care of the children because his mother worked up to nineteen hours a day. "I didn't see my dad at all because he was in the service," Stitt said. "About eleven years old, eleven or twelve in 1963 I started working at the stables"—Hansen's Sky Hi Hopes Stable.

A neighborhood carnival also had pony rides, where Stitt and his friends could make a couple of dollars. "We made enough money to take a bus out to the stables," he testified, and the friends would ride horses for an hour.

Cassidy asked how often the friends went riding when they were eleven.

"Lots. One day we missed the last bus coming back. A gentleman came out and asked us if we knew how to bridle horses and help close up the barn, work out there," Stitt recalled. "We didn't know that much but from that point forward every weekend we would go out there. Sometimes we cut school Fridays and be there Friday, Saturday, and Sunday. They had a bunkhouse on the facility where we would stay. I did everything from shoveling manure to bringing shavings in, feeding horses, saddling them, doing everything there was to do."

"And what did Mr. Hansen give to you or what did he give you in exchange for the work you did?" Cassidy asked.

"At the time, we didn't get anything but being able to ride the horses, and then when I was about twelve or thirteen years of age, he put a title of manager or assistant manager on me," Stitt said with a weak smile. "He paid me like twenty-five dollars a week, gave me a room of my own in the bunkhouse."

It was only after Stitt had settled in at the ranch that Hansen made his opening move. "And, it was like a Friday or Saturday, I'm pretty sure about it. It was about two in the morning," Stitt said. He told how he was awakened by Kenny, who had just returned from a day of polo. "He had been drinking." Stitt could still remember the smell of alcohol on Hansen's breath. "He had been drinking, and he had his hand on my testicle trying to kiss me, and that—"

Stone flew to his feet and bawled, "Objection!"

But the witness kept talking. "I pushed him away."

"Overruled," Toomin said as he leaned toward the witness, hanging on the young man's every word. Stitt was neither a paid government snitch nor an alcoholic. What he said had merit. "I kind of pushed him away. He tried one more time within a matter of two minutes, and that was the extent of that. I kind of just said, 'You know, I don't feel comfortable.'"

"Did that kind of conduct ever occur again between yourself and Mr. Hansen?"

Stitt frowned. "Maybe two or three, one or two more times. There was probably an attempt, but, you know, that was about it."

"Eventually you went to live with the Hansens, did you not?"

Stitt nodded and then said that he began having problems in school. "I was thirteen at the time because I was just going into the seventh grade. I mean I must have cut 286 days out of a 300-day school year. My parents suggested that maybe I would be better off in St. Charles[2] or somewhere like that, so I ran away. I took off."

Stitt hitchhiked to Los Angeles where he found that life in Tinsel Town was even more unpleasant than what he had experienced in Chicago. After a few months, he moved back to the Windy City. "I came back, and I don't know how, how or why Kenny decided to find me. But I was at 111th and Hale, and we were kind of milling around out there when a car pulled up, and it was my cousin. And he said, 'Bobby get into the car.'

"I jumped in the car, and as we drove off, I glanced back and saw that Kenny was in the back seat. He said that he had sent my cousin and a few other friends out to look for me, to pick me up off the streets. Then on the way out to the stables, we had a long talk about me going back to school and things like that."

According to Stitt, his parents agreed to grant Hansen protective custody of the delinquent teenager. "Beverly was as close to me as my mother and, in some ways, closer," he said. "I mean Beverly was always concerned about me. I was one of the few that actually lived in the house with Danny and Mark. I didn't live in the bunkhouse. I don't remember anybody else living in the house with Danny and Mark besides myself."

Cassidy asked if Stitt had ever met Roger Spry. He had.

"Can you describe the relationship between Roger and Ken?"

"Roger was—"

Stone lurched forward and raised his right arm. "Excuse me. Objection. It's a continuing objection."

Toomin gestured for him to sit down. "Objection is overruled. You may testify."

"Kenny and Roger were having a relationship," the witness stammered, "a sexual relationship. We referred to Roger as Kenny's boy, you know. Roger was Kenny's right-hand person at the time. He was stuck to Kenny."

Bob Stitt told the court that he had signed up for military service but returned to the stables when his hitch was over. "Kenny and I talked about a lot of things. One time when I asked him about Roger's jealousy and everything, he said [Roger] was getting too old and fat for him, you know."

On one occasion, in 1974, Stitt called Hansen from Alabama to tell him that he had found two fifteen-year-old boys who needed jobs. Hansen told Stitt to bring the boys to the stable. Later, Hansen told Stitt to bring one of the boys to his apartment because he wanted "to do" the boy. Stitt told the court that during the years, he picked up thirty or more boys who were hitchhiking and took them to Hansen's stables "for that purpose." By the time Stitt was fifteen, he was driving one of Hansen's farm trucks.

From Stitt's vantage point on the witness stand, Hansen appeared agitated.

"Judge, objection on the grounds of relevancy," O'Donnell said. "We're talking about unemployed soldiers that needed a job in 1974. How is that relevant?" The defense team was irritable and concerned that Toomin had allowed prejudicial testimony.

Stitt told the court that Hansen rewarded him for introducing him to young men who happened to be "great kids as well as lovers."

Stone and Cassidy approached the bench; the attorneys had trouble keeping their voices low so the jurors couldn't hear. Stone argued, "We haven't established that they were eleven- or twelve-year-old boys. I don't think they were if they were in the Army and looking for a job. It's only prejudicial. Judge, I would urge the court to grant our motion for a mistrial based upon the improper testimony of Robert Stitt."

There would be no mistrial.

For her first court appearance, Anne Movalson's fingernails were carefully manicured and her hair recently styled. As she waited for the prosecution to begin the questioning, Movalson was aware that the only reason she was there was to stipulate that Kenneth Hansen knew Silas Jayne. In the 1950s, she had spent most weekends at Idle Hour Stable where she met Hansen. She was thirteen at the time and noted that he was "muscular and cute." "One day I heard Kenny talking to some other people about high school," she testified. "He said he went to Amundsen." Movalson had recently completed a report about the Norwegian explorer Roald Amundsen, the first person to reach the South Pole, and decided to use it as an ice-breaker. Hansen was polite to the thirteen-year-old but indifferent.

"So as a thirteen-year-old girl, how is it that you came to know who the owner was at that stable?" challenged Stone.

"My parents paid the board [for her horse], and my father always referred to it as Si Jayne's place."

"So really what you are telling this jury is based upon something you learned from your dad. You *think* the stable might have been owned by Si Jayne?"

Movalson remembered that like many of the teenaged girls who rode horses out that way, she, too, had a crush on the older stableman Kenny Hansen. Stone asked if they had talked much or traded phone numbers, and Movalson said no to both questions.

Movalson said she wasn't certain if she would have accepted a date with "an older man" or not. The woman's response bothered Stone. He thought for a long moment and then said, "I know when not to ask certain questions. And *that's* being a gentleman and a lawyer. I will sit down now, Judge."

Witness Donna Ewing said she was only eleven years old when she observed first-hand the terrible cruelty and inhumanity directed toward animals, and it changed her life forever. A neighbor boy had invited her up to his tree house to take a look at some new puppies. To her shock and horror, the bitch's collar was nailed to the floor so the pups could eat whenever they wanted. Without thinking, she freed the mother dog, and it ran into the forest preserve that bordered the boy's property. The dog abandoned her pups and was never seen again. Ewing always had trouble describing the terrible scene to others because recalling the incident brought on waves of sorrow. When she became an adult, Donna Ewing became an advocate for animal rights.

She organized the Illinois-based Hooved Animal Humane Society (HAHS) to protect horses from abusive owners. The Emmy Award–winning actress Loretta Swit, who has a long history of involvement with animal rescue, is a strong proponent of Ewing and her organization.[3] "I am strongly supportive of any animal protection effort that has Donna Ewing's involvement," stated Swit. "Donna Ewing and her investigators have performed hundreds of rescues over the last three decades. Ewing brings more than her years of experience and hard work to HAHS—she brings a strong sense of vision, a total commitment to the animals, and unshakable ethics and integrity."[4]

After she was sworn in at Hansen's trial, the tall, thin, blonde-haired Ewing smiled gently and took the stand. Dressed in an expensive beige suite, she looked more like an attorney than an adventurous horsewoman. She recalled with vivid detail the time her sister, Elaine, invited her to go horseback riding at Idle Hour Stables.

Prosecutor Quinn asked why she would remember the defendant from back in 1955.

"Well," Ewing replied hesitantly, "my sister and her girlfriend both had a crush on him. They were talking about this adorable riding instructor, so I took special notice of him." Ewing remembered that he was about her height and "had piercing eyes. I'll never forget his eyes."

"Did you have an occasion in the early 1970s to run across Ken Hansen again?"

"Yes," she said, "about 1972."

"Pursuant to your duties with the Hooved Animal Humane Society?"

"Yes, it was." Soon after Ewing established HAHS, she received a telephone call informing her of mistreated livery horses at Camelot or Sky Hi Hopes. She wasn't exactly sure because "the name kept changing back and forth." Ewing personally went out to investigate the Tinley Park stable where she found a dozen or so livery horses near death. She reported the neglect and abuse to the Department of Agriculture, suspecting that Hansen was planning to sell the animals to international slaughterhouses disguised as horse ranches somewhere in the U.S.A.[5] The thought of inflicting needless suffering on these old and tired animals haunted her because she believed that most of Hansen's horses could be spared and, in time, become great companions to a kindly owner. According to Ewing, charges against Hansen were dropped. He threw some feed into the stalls of the livery horses to appease outside investigators who could have interrupted his lucrative business.

Later, in an interview, Mark Hansen recounted a completely different tale. "Horses were expensive back then, so my dad would buy thin, sickly horses off a killer buyer, fatten them up, and keep them as trail horses. Donna came along one day, and so did Roy Mayhem [a killer buyer], and my dad said to her, 'You tell me which horses to get rid of, and I'll sell them back to him. Then they'll have no chance of survival!'" Mark was noticeably upset. "We kept horses even if they were old."

Stone continued questioning Ewing. "Did you meet Ken Hansen [in 1971]?"

"Yes. He had aged a little, but I said, 'Are you the same Kenny Hansen I took riding lessons from at Idle Hour?' 'Yeah,' he said, 'I gave lessons there.' He didn't remember me, but I certainly remembered [Hansen's] name."

Stone rigorously questioned the woman leaving little time between her response and his next question.

"Do you remember the name of the horse you rode?"

"No. I don't remember the color or name. I just know I was there." She didn't remember much of anything about what she wore or the name of the horse.

"Can you describe the schooling ring of the Idle Hour in 1955?"

"It had a dark surface. The walls, I believe, were light, and we just took little jumps along the edge of the arena. It had some dark brown stuff on the ground. I don't know what it was." Nor did Ewing remember very much about the look or size of the stables, but she was almost certain that Hansen was wearing rust-colored riding britches, black boots, and a polo shirt.

"When did you think you learned for the first time Kenny's last name was Hansen?"

The horsewoman recalled her sister's voice as if it were yesterday. "This is Kenny, our instructor," Elaine had said as she mounted her horse. Ewing's sister had been dead for many years, but, oh, the wonderful memories Donna had. "His name was bandied about. 'We're going to see Kenny Hansen. He's the darling instructor. You have got to meet Kenny.' I mean, it was embedded in my brain."

"And you remembered that sixteen years later when you talked to someone at the Camelot Riding Stable in Tinley Park?"

Ewing responded patiently, "Yes, I did. It was kind of ironic. I thought that name was so familiar. And he resembled the Kenny I had known. He had curly, kinky, wavy kind of brownish hair, kind of a widow's peak, was about as tall as I am now. He had very piercing brown eyes; he just had something about him that I remembered. When he gazed at you, you knew it."

Donna Ewing felt that same stare from Hansen now. She tried to avoid eye contact, but after one glance, their eyes locked. Later, Hansen remembered his first encounter with Ewing. "It had to be in the '70s; she had the Hoofed Animals Society, and she was out to inspect my stables. She didn't have anybody with her. I would buy ex–race horses that were slow, you know, and bring them from the track. I had probably one or two recent purchases that were gaunt; I mean their ribs were showing and stuff like that. We'd fatten them up and . . . run them slow."

Joe Plemmons walked into court knowing that he was squealing on Hansen, and that sent a chill up his spine. He met Kenny in 1971 at a horse show at Peacock Ridge, a stable close to Camelot. He testified that he was most eager to further his own aspirations in order to be welcomed into the equestrian in-crowd. For this reason, he leased one of Hansen's barns at Camelot and hung out a shingle. He said his only interest in the horse business was selling hunters and jumpers. "I'm sure everybody has seen the Olympic competition on television. The jumps are relatively wide. And then you also have hunter classes, where the horses would jump eight jumps, and you are adjudged accordingly to how good the horse's form is."

In June of 1972, Plemmons posted a classified ad in the *Chronicle of the Horse*—"Hunters, jumpers, show ponies, boarding, training, showing, horses taken on consignment." He included his phone number and name.

In 1971, he competed in jumping against a man named Wally Holly, Plemmons mumbled after a long quiet second. It was at Sky Hi Stable in Tinley Park, Plemmons said, and he had conversed with Holly. After the event was over, a group of riders replayed the day over cocktails at Jardine's Restaurant in Tinley Park. "To my knowledge, Noel Wall, Jackie Justice, possibly Joanne Perrot, Beverly and Ken Hansen—there might have been a couple more. This was an after-the-horse-show party," Plemmons said.

"During the party, did Wally Holly's name come up?" Quinn asked.

"Yes, it did." Plemmons looked at the sketch artist. "He [Kenny Hansen] was bragging about how good a rider and horse trainer Wally was."

The same group got together again about a week later, the witness said, and Hansen brought up the name again but this time asked Plemmons why Holly didn't seem to like him very much. According to Plemmons, not being liked by someone greatly agitated Hansen. "He told me that I would either be loyal to him or he wasn't going to be loyal to me, and we weren't going to be friends. Basically, we were going to stick together, so now tell me what he said, and I did."

With a sense of urgency, Stone objected to the line of questioning. "The witness is relating what someone else said to him. It's hearsay."

"No," Toomin disagreed, "It's being offered as a response to Mr. Hansen. That's the relevance of what's being offered here . . . Mr. Hansen's response. It's part of the same conversation. Overruled." He turned and looked at Plemmons. "You may answer."

Plemmons looked down for a long, hard moment. "Wally Holly told me that Ken Hansen had killed three boys."

"Objection! Objection! Objection!" Stone's words went unheard.

"I would ask you, sir, to please tell the ladies and gentlemen of the jury what you told Ken Hansen," Quinn said, satisfied with himself.

Stone objected and was granted another sidebar conference in chambers. The attorney paced the small room and argued ferociously, "I warned you this was coming. It's objectionable. Hearsay. It's being offered for the truth of the matters asserted. It's an out-of-court declaration by a non-party declarant—Mr. Holly. It's rank hearsay, and it's objectionable."

Quinn jumped in, "Again, what he would say, I believe, is 'Wally Holly said he [Hansen] killed three kids, and Si Jayne owns [his] butt.'"

Toomin sided with the defense on this one. "Certainly not an admission." The judge, who was two-thirds the height of the towering Stone, looked up at him and said, "I will sustain your objection." The defense asked for a mistrial, and, once again, it was denied.

Toomin offered an explanation for his decision. "It's the same thing as a police officer coming in and saying 'So-and-So just finished interviewing, and he says you did this and that,' and the defendant says, 'Yeah, I guess I did.' That's what I assumed the purpose of this conversation was. Apparently it is not, and I agree that it is improper, and I will strike his statement as to anything that Wally Holly told him. I will instruct the jury to disregard it."

Stone and O'Donnell both knew that the men and women of the jury had already logged the comment deep in their memory, if not in their notebooks. They would not forget what Plemmons had told them.

In 1976, Plemmons said he and Hansen left a party around three in the morning. While Plemmons drove them back to Camelot (Hansen was intoxicated and couldn't drive), Hansen confided to his friend that he "hated his brother Curt and that Curt held those boys over his head like a club."

"When he said that," Quinn asked, "what was Ken Hansen referring to, what three boys? What did he tell you regarding the boys?"

The witness was stone-faced. He took a deep breath. "It was either him or them. In 1955, to be gay was unacceptable, that society wouldn't take it." He added, "Kenny started ragging on me that I had wasted my life, made a shambles of it. I said my life had been bad but you killed three boys, you did George Jayne—"

Stone again pushed for a mistrial, reminding Toomin that in an earlier, pretrial ruling, he had barred any mention of Silas Jayne's alleged solicitation to Kenny to line up a hit-squad and murder George. Toomin denied the motion.

The defense grilled Plemmons about his criminal past, complete with a dramatic reading of documentation from a federal trial. It was noted that on two separate occasions, he changed his name. When he lived in California, he was known as Travis Passmore, and he acquired about one hundred thousand dollars from the People of the State of California by fraudulent means. Plemmons, who had been leaning slightly forward, now leaned back in the uncomfortable, wooden chair. "That's correct," he said.

After defrauding the people in California, he moved to Pennsylvania and used the name of Kenny's youngest son, Mark Hansen.

Angered by Plemmons's frequent interruptions, Stone admonished the witness. "You know, Mr. Passmore, Mr. Plemmons, Mr. Hansen, or whoever you are, if you would wait to answer the questions that were posed, this would go a lot better for both of us."

Plemmons watched as Stone backed away, observing Plemmons with utmost seriousness. Before he could reply, the defense attorney added, "You knew that Joe Plemmons had a terrible reputation for telling the truth?"

"Or something like that, that's true."

"Do you remember being asked this question and giving this answer," Stone said as he opened the transcript to page 269. His right forefinger slid down the page until he reached line six. "'Joe Plemmons had a very bad reputation for telling the truth, didn't he?' And your answer was, 'That's true.'" Stone turned quickly and walked back to the defense table and tossed the file on a small stack of other files. Plemmons followed him with his eyes. "Now about the 1976 conversation [with Kenneth Hansen]. Anyone on the planet earth can come in and say Joe Plemmons is telling the truth about this?"

"No."

Stone paced back and forth in front of the jury box, certain that he had thoroughly discredited the testimony of the horseman, as of late from North Carolina, whose sentence for criminal fraud was cut from three years to seventeen months in prison in return for his earlier assistance in the Helen Brach investigation. "So the ladies and gentlemen of the jury have to believe you, a convicted felon as you say, a convicted fraud, and a convicted liar, about that conversation as well?" Stone suggested that Plemmons was testifying "only to get himself out of hot water."

"That's correct," he conceded.

Thunderous clouds moved in from the west on the fourth day of the trial, and the weather turned cruel as the attorneys inside room 400 once again haggled over last-minute motions. Bobby Peterson's cousin entered the courtroom after everyone was seated. Eleanor Schuessler's stepchildren were sitting in the second row. They had already caught the attention of the reporters sitting across the aisle and had indicated that they would be available for interviews after the sentencing.

Judy Anderson, one of the riders who remembered Hansen working around Idle Hour in 1955, was summoned to the stand. As the round of questioning began, the press feared another long day of repetitious testimony. The reporters' interest perked up immediately when the middle-aged woman told about her first meeting with Hansen. Anderson had been accompanied by her friend Linda Hoffman Trivers, now married. "I had just come back from a month's vacation in California with my parents, and it was at the end of August that we went there [Idle Hour Stable]." She admitted that her memories were fuzzy of what had happened up to that moment Linda had tumbled off her horse.

"After you went to the Idle Hour, where did the two of you ride?"

"We, first of all, rode down Higgins to a bridle path and then took that . . . it paralleled the Des Plaines River. We were coming back to the stable when the strap that held her saddle broke, and she just fell, sprawling into the cinders, scraping her hands and knees. We both walked our horses back to the stable. When we got back to the stable, we turned in the horses, and my girlfriend paid for her time, and we turned around and walked, started to walk away." Anderson and her friend were almost to the road when she remembered that she had not paid for the trail ride. "I asked my girlfriend if she would wait for me, and she said, 'Yeah. I'll sit right here.' She sat down by the side of the road. I turned around and went back to the stable and wanted to pay this fella that was standing over by . . . that was there standing in the yard."

Anderson moved anxiously to the edge of her seat. "I asked him, you know, would he take the money. I forgot to pay. He said, 'Well, I can't take your money, only Jayne can take your money.'"

"What happened after that?" Quinn spoke softly trying to help the witness remain calm.

"He said that Jayne would be back in a few minutes, [I'd] have to wait. He was waiting, too. I had seen him there before, a very good-looking man, and I asked him his name." The young man introduced himself as Ken Hansen. "Well, I told him my name, and we talked about working there. I asked him how long he had been working there, and he said off and on, maybe a year. I asked him how you go about getting a job like this. I was interested in doing something with horses I thought at the time. So I was really interested in talking to him about how you go about getting a job. I had never worked before. He told me that he, in effect, that he and Jayne go back a long way and that he'd been riding since he was a little kid, you know, like eleven or twelve years old."

The fifty-seven-year-old woman blushed as she recounted the harmless flirtation. "I was interested in him, and I said something about getting together sometime. I'm in the phone book, and my father's name is Robert J. Anderson, you know, and I indicated the sign-in book, that you had to sign in before you took a horse out."

Prior to the trial, Anderson had met with ATF Agent John Rotunno. Employing her artistic skills and a vivid memory, she had molded a clay bust of the handsome young man she had met at Idle Hour Stable in 1955.

"We're talking about a high school girl meeting a guy forty years ago and having a three minute conversation with him?" Stone sounded incredulous.

"It was more like ten to fifteen minutes."

"And then when you were shown some photographs by the ATF agents you weren't able to identify any of the photographs?"

According to Anderson, the photographs were unrecognizable to her. So she constructed a clay bust of the young horseman she believed to be Kenneth Hansen. "So you decided to make this bust of the man you remembered from forty years ago?"

"That's what I recall he looked like." Anderson was nervous. "I looked at about forty different photographs that day, and I couldn't identify Ken Hansen. Whoever these other people were, I don't know." The look in Anderson's eyes bespoke her mounting anxiety. But she was telling the truth, and the next witness corroborated her testimony, at least halfway.

The next witness, Linda Hoffman Trivers, corroborated Anderson's description of the riding accident. She said the cinch (the belt that goes under the horse) came loose, and she got hurt, scraping up her arms and knees and "I think some on my face. I can't remember. I might have protected my face, but I know I [hurt] my arms." Trivers remembered the extent of her injuries, but to the dismay of the prosecution, she could not recall the name of the stable where the mishap occurred.

Pat Quinn asked, "How is Judith Anderson's memory?"

"Phenomenal" came the reply.

With a crew cut and manicured nails and attired in a smart-looking Brooks Brothers fall suit, Cook County Medical Examiner Dr. Edmund Donoghue stepped forward to present expert testimony.[6] Toomin accepted Donoghue's credentials as an authority in the fields of anatomical and forensic pathology, determining that he was "duly qualified to render opinions as to the cause and manner of death." Working with enlarged black-and-white photographs positioned on three easels and using a rubber-tipped pointer, Donoghue enumerated every bruise, cut, and scratch on the boys' bodies with precision and without emotion. Some of the graphic images were taken by news photographers in Robinson Woods, others at the County Morgue.

With certitude, Dr. Donoghue declared that each of the boys had "died of strangulation." Throughout the gruesome narrative, stifled gasps could be heard coming from the rear of the courtroom. One juror covered her mouth in shock.

"Doctor, if you would take a close look at the photograph, do you also see what I think you identified previously as adhesive tape marks on there?" Cassidy pointed to one of the large photos of Tony Schuessler.

"Yes, there are adhesive tape marks on here," Donoghue said, glancing at his wristwatch. Fifteen minutes of scheduled testimony had turned into forty. Donoghue continued his testimony after Cassidy drew his attention to the wound on John Schuessler's left thigh. The jurors' faces registered shock when the doctor described "a gaping defect where part of the skin of the left thigh had been cut out" on John Schuessler. The wound measured ten by four centimeters (about four inches by one-and-a-half inches).

"The final photograph, this is the left thigh of John Schuessler, and it shows the incised wound. The incised wound means that it was made with a sharp instrument. Pieces of tissue were actually cut out here, and it appears that that was done after death because there is no evidence of any bleeding or vital reaction."

As certain as he was that the boys were strangled, however, Donoghue was less sure as to whether or not they were molested, which Drs. Kearns and Hirsch's 1955 autopsy reports could not determine either, saying only that penetration had not occurred.

Jury members and spectators leaned forward to hear more.

Stone tapped his foot gently on the wooden floor before he stood up and walked around the defense table. "Dr. Donoghue, are you aware that Dr. Kearns and Dr. Hirsch set the time of death as 9:30 PM on October 16, 1955?" Stone asked.[7]

"Well, I'm not sure that I am aware of that."

"Well, let's not be coy," Stone said "Are you aware of the fact—"

"Well, I don't know that. Let me just check." Donoghue opened up a file and flipped through the fifteen or so pages. When he couldn't come up with the information, he drew a deep breath and said, "No. I'm not sure that I am aware of that."

Stone handed the witness a seven-page summary of the 1956 exhumation of the three boys.

The defense played rough, throwing one question after another at the medical examiner, and for the first time since he took the stand, Dr. Donoghue showed visible signs of strain. "Well, yeah, that's maybe where we're getting the struggle. I'm not sure that this is the position of Dr. Hirsch and Dr. Kearns because this document has never been signed."

Satisfied with the answer, Stone moved on, asking Donoghue about what kind of adhesive was found on the boys, but the medical examiner did not know. Asked if he was aware that those stains on the boys' feet were analyzed by researchers at the Armour Research Foundation at the Illinois Institute of Technology, Donoghue said he was, but he didn't know the origin of the stains.

"Now did anybody from the prosecution's office bother to show you the Standard Oil report of those black stains before you came to court this morning?" Stone asked.

Cassidy flew off the chair, "Objection!"

"Objection sustained," Toomin growled. "May I see you for a minute?"

"Sure." Like a naughty child, Stone tightened his shoulders and cautiously approached the bench.

Toomin exercised patience as he explained his views. "The whole purpose of utilizing this hearsay is to modify, explain, or discredit opinions that he may have as to the cause and manner of death. He did not on direct examination go into anything about the time of death or the absence of stains. I mean, you can ask him about the significance of this, but to suggest that something is being withheld at this point, I think is improper. I don't think that's the purpose of why I allowed you to do this."

"Let me try it another way," Stone said matter-of-factly.

He tugged on his beard and smiled as he resumed his questioning. "You could analyze those stains to determine where they came from?"

"Well, theoretically it's possible. I've never seen it done."

"You are aware, are you not, that diatomaceous earth was found in the wound of one of these boys?"[8]

"Well, that's what it says in this report, yes."

"Are you aware of what diatomaceous earth is?"

Dr. Donoghue sighed, "Well, it's a form of earth. I'm not too familiar with it, no. I presume it has diatoms in it."

"Do you know what grade 209 diatomaceous earth is?" Stone asked, but Donoghue did not know. Stone read from page four of the coroner's report, "It says, diatomaceous earth, bone meal, insecticides, finally divided top soils, and pollen granules from certain fall flowers were found in the wounds of one of the victim's heads. A survey was made of all places that practice horticulture. The survey included greenhouses, florists, cemeteries, golf courses in the Northwest Side of the city and adjacent suburbs. Now, Doctor, based upon your experience, would this kind of information assist you in arriving at an opinion as to the cause and nature of the death of these children?"

"Well, no," Dr. Donoghue said. "I had already arrived at an opinion without ever having seen this report. So, no. I don't think it adds anything."

"Did you find any evidence that any of these children's bodies bore any evidence of hay?"

"No, I didn't find any evidence of hay."

"Straw? Manure, horse manure specifically?"

"No." Again Donoghue ruled it out, as well as knowing about trace evidence of oats, barley, and horse feed.

"But it's your opinion that the presence of diatomaceous earth wouldn't assist you in determining the nature, cause, or place of death?" Stone turned and faced the jurors.

Dr. Donoghue clung to the belief that the information would not be of much value in determining the cause and manner of death but conceded, "It might assist in locating the place of death, but I suspect that you're going to find that diatomaceous earth occurs in a lot of places."

Stone nodded. "Let's try and move into something closer to your area of expertise." The defense attorney showed the witness Defendant's Exhibit

5, a three-page document entitled "History of the Murders of Robert Peterson, John Schuessler, and Anton Schuessler."

The M. E. said he had seen it before.

Even for an experienced defense attorney like Stone, the next line of questioning was difficult and embarrassing.

"And you are aware that it states on page one, 'it was further noted that no semen was found in the sinuses, teeth, or palate which would indicate a sexual act.' Are you aware of that?"

Donoghue said he was.

"Are you aware that the Chief of Detectives reported that nothing was found in the rectums of these boys and that in his words there is no evidence of any sexual molestation?"

"Well, that's what the Chief of Detectives said, yes."

"Sir, do you have any evidence that you can give to this jury that these boys were killed in a stable?" Stone asked.

"No," the medical examiner admitted.

A quick cross by Cassidy concluded with Dr. Donoghue's opinion, "There's at least evidence that's suggestive of a sexual nature of this attack because the deceased were found without any clothing."

Stone was back up on his feet. "Dr. Donoghue, clothing might be removed and destroyed because it contains evidence, yes?"

The expert witness replied in the affirmative.

The courtroom stirred restlessly. Schuessler family members were visibly upset with this line of questioning, and for a second, it appeared as if one of them might speak out in protest. Sensing a disturbance brewing, the bailiff stood up and quieted the audience down before that could happen, allowing Stone to continue.

"And, of course, that has nothing to do with sex?"

"If it's . . . well, it could. That might be the evidence you'd want to get rid of."

Stone tilted his head to the right and grinned. "And it may not have anything to do with sex?"

Reluctantly, Dr. Donoghue admitted, "Well, it also might not."

"And you are not suggesting with forty years of hindsight that you are in a superior position to determine whether this is a case of sexual molestation [against] the doctors who did the original autopsy or the Chief of Detectives who investigated the case, are you?"

"Objection, Your Honor." Cassidy approached the bench. "Counsel is not offering that as substantive evidence."

"Sustained."

As the trial progressed, Jed Stone changed his wardrobe from stylish suits to dress pants and sports jackets. The change to more casual attire was part of his normal trial routine, and he wasn't going to break old habits for this case. Stone's thirty-odd-year court ritual was his way of telling the jurors that he was confident of his client's innocence; the trial was going his way. Stone spent his entire lunch hour reviewing grand-jury testimony, before the judge returned, and the bailiff summoned Lance Williamson, the next witness.

In 1974, Williamson said, Joe Plemmons introduced him to Kenneth Hansen at Sky Hi Stables. Williamson was a professional rider, who would subcontract his services (training horses, teaching riding lessons, and the like) to stable owners. According to Williamson, over a three-month period in 1974, he was at Sky Hi Stables five to six times a week. During a morning coffee break, Hansen told Williamson that while working at Idle Hour Stables, he met Si Jayne in the 1950s.

Stone asked if anybody else would have been present for that conversation, and Williamson, thinking for a long minute, mumbled, "Yes, his ex-wife, Beverly."

Quinn moved slowly towards the desk, gathered up a file, and hesitated. He carefully thought about his question as he fumbled through the papers. "Did Ken Hansen ever have a conversation with you regarding his sexual preferences?"

Williamson had done things in his life that he probably knew were wrong, and as he sat there gazing out at the crowded courtroom, he thought about something he had once heard: *Life, it's not an easy thing. To those who have shall be given, from those who have not shall be taken away even that which they have. The Lord invites us to see what it is that we have.* "He liked to have sex with young boys."

Stone nodded and drew a long, deep breath. "I don't say this to embarrass you, but I believe it is your position that at some point when you were a teenager, Mr. Hansen made an advance to you?"

Nervously, Williamson admitted that was true. He also said that when he turned Hansen down, he was neither fired nor was his life threatened.

"Obviously, he didn't kill you?"

Williamson tried but couldn't prevent a slight smile. "No."

Guarded by two federal agents, William "Red" Wemette fretted and paced about the small witness waiting room processing his thoughts and practicing his testimony. *He never molested me*, murmured Red over and over again in his head. The tall, stocky, forty-six-year-old man had spent hours going over his testimony with prosecutors. He had been a snitch for years but testifying about his own sexual preferences, well, that was just too embarrassing. Wemette also didn't like the idea of being escorted in and out of Chicago, but he knew that his life would likely remain in peril until the day he died. He was a protected witness, and somehow he had to make the best of the situation. That was the price one had to pay for being a hero or a snitch, depending on one's point of view.

Wemette testified that he lived at the Sky Hi Stables off and on between the years of 1968 and 1973. He loathed Kenny Hansen for reasons he didn't completely understand. What was vividly clear to him was that his one-time friend had killed the Schuessler and Peterson boys. Of all of the witnesses paraded before the jury that week, Red Wemette provided the most detailed and chilling account of Ken Hansen's admission of murder.

Cassidy asked, "In regards to these conversations, can you please continue with what he said to you that first time?"

"He said that it was a very famous case, and it was in the headlines, and *he* almost made headlines himself. He says, 'I came that close to getting caught.'" Wemette raised his right hand and spread his thumb and forefingers about a half-inch apart, mimicking Kenny's gesture. This information came to him in the summer of 1968.

Remorsefully, Red confided that Hansen "said he strangled the boys. He said he picked them up hitchhiking" and "took them to a barn on the Northwest Side of Chicago called the Idle Hour Stable." Wemette spoke with contempt in every syllable. He leaned forward and turned his head to the left. The witness could feel Hansen's piercing gaze. For a split second, the federal informant looked like he was going to overheat and melt. "He said that his brother was there, and he asked him to help him."

It was dead quiet in the courtroom. Wemette occupied center stage and seemed to be enjoying the limelight. "I believe he said his brother injured one of the victims with a blunt instrument of some type."

Wemette described the setting and disclosed the incriminating conversation with Kenny when the murders were first brought up. According to Wemette, Hansen was seated on a piece of lawn furniture under a large umbrella and was reading his newspaper. It was one of the first times Hansen was not drinking. It was a pleasant, still morning at the Sky Hi Stables. "Yes, he told me that he had picked up the boys, and one boy, the youngest boy, he had taken into a separate room, and the two older boys were on a horse or a pony. I'm not sure which."

Wemette's face was white with anger. "And he sent them riding in an arena or whatever, and the other boy he had sexual relations with, fellatio, he performed fellatio on the younger boy."

"Did he say what happened next?" Cassidy asked politely.

"And then he told me that he sent the younger boy back in, and the other boy came out, and he went with him, and the older and younger boys interrupted them while they were . . . I was told that he said the older boy—"

Stone defiantly objected to the witness' rambling. "He was told?"

"Mr. Hansen told me," Wemette said, looking sourly at the defendant.

"He was told by Mr. Hansen?" Toomin asked.

"Please continue, Mr. Wemette," Cassidy finally said.

"That the older boy [Bobby Peterson] and the younger boy [Anton Schuessler] . . . the younger boy had told the older boy what had happened and said, 'Come on, let's get my brother [John Schuessler] out of here; let's go. Let's call our parents; let's call the police.'"

His voice rising, Red recalled Hansen saying, "There was a scramble . . . a scramble-type situation, and he [Ken Hansen] asked for assistance from his brother [Curt] to help him." According to Wemette, "Curt botched the job, and when he disposed of the bodies, there was a piece of evidence left behind that could connect him to the murder. He [Kenny] seemed plagued by that and feared of getting caught."

Wemette clasped his hands as if he were praying and set them on the top of the witness stand. "He told me he moved to the South Side of Chicago and low-balled himself, just trying to stay mediocre where he wouldn't be noticed."

Regarding the barn where the boys were allegedly murdered, Wemette said, "He told me it was burned, somebody had burned it for him." Wemette still felt the heat of the fire. He stretched his fingers. "He told me the case was heating up in the newspapers. He asked me a lot about the case and said did I know anything about it, and I said no."

The men and women of the jury stared at him, trying hard to fathom this strange world of horse slaughter, barn fires, deceptions, and "riding in show." So little of the horse world with its criminality makes any sense to people who live their lives by the rules.

"He mentioned a third party that might be a forest preserve . . . "

Wemette paused uncomfortably. "He said a forest preserve employee, possibly a ranger was also involved."

The witness snickered.

Stone reprimanded him for making light of the proceedings, "Mr. Wemette, there is nothing funny here. Am I mistaken about that as well?"

"The only humorous part is you're trying to confuse me." Wemette was flippant.

"No, I'm not, sir. I'm trying to get the truth from you." Stone's courtroom semantics were familiar to reporters who had observed him in action over the years. The attorney scowled. Wemette asked him to repeat the question. The court reporter, Fay A. Robertson, read back the question from the tape.

"Mr. Wemette, did you tell this jury not twenty minutes ago that Ken had the barn burned down?" Stone asked.

"Yes, I did."

"Now, did you tell this jury that the reason that you think he said this to you is because there was some evidence in the barn that was going to convict him?"

"He said the case was heating up."

"Well, this was supposedly some years after the Schuessler-Peterson deaths?"

"I thought it was a matter of months."

"Matter of months?" Stone shook his head.

"Yes."

"And you think that the reason [the barn at] the Idle Hour, a barn that Ken didn't own, [was burned] because the case was heating up?"

Wemette shrugged, and his face was hard. "That's correct."

"Did you know that he [Hansen] and his wife bought their barn on the South Side on June 7, 1955, five months before the Schuessler-Peterson boys were killed?"

"Objection!" Cassidy bellowed. "Relevance!"

"I don't know where he—" Red tried to continue.

Toomin laid down his pen and leaned forward. "Wait a minute. I'll sustain it. It assumes a fact that is not in evidence at this time."

Hansen tried to ignore the anger he was feeling toward Red. *Evil, evil, evil,* he repeated over and over again in his head. Later, in prison, Hansen said, "I believe that Red choreographed the entire affair. He became a snitch for the FBI. Any affair I ever had [with another man] was consensual; I have never forced myself on anybody! I taught riding lessons to children my whole adult life, and nobody ever filed a complaint. If Bev was alive, Red, Roger, Hollatz, Bobby . . . none of them would have said what they said about me."

Glancing toward the jury, Stone questioned Wemette about the $14,500 he had received from the government between 1971 and 1989 in return for his cooperation as a federal informant. "Well, while you were receiving money from the taxpayers as a mole, you were in the pornography business?"

"Yes," Wemette said. His wide smile showed his large teeth. He added that he was also involved in a restaurant business.

"In fact, you wanted to buy some property that was owned by Beverly Hansen, didn't you?"

Wemette did not respond. He looked up at the judge, who gestured for him to answer. "Yes, I did."

"And the purpose of buying this property was so you could run some kind of liquor establishment?"

The informant shook his head. "No. I was going to build my home there," adding that the deal never went through.

"In fact, you resented the fact that it didn't come together, didn't you? And you bore a grudge against the Hansens for that, didn't you?"

Stone showed a contract between Beverly Hansen and William Wemette. "And who is Robert R. Wemette Senior?" Stone asked.

"He's deceased. He's my father."

His anger and excitement rising, Stone pounded away at the witness. "So you changed your name in the mid-seventies to adopt your father's name?"

"That is correct."

"Well, when you were introduced to the jury about an hour ago and swore to tell the truth, you told this jury your name was William."

"That was my birth name."

"I'm sorry. I'm confused. What is your name as you sit here now?"

Toomin asked in a low tone, "Isn't his name Wemette?"

"No, it's not," Cassidy whispered.

"You mean today he goes by a different name?" Toomin was puzzled.

"He uses a different name altogether right now. He goes by a different name other than William Wemette."

The judge turned away from the attorneys and quickly said, "I don't know if it's that big of a deal, to tell you the truth. What's the point that he uses a contract name or another name when he introduced himself in court? That's going to be cleared up on redirect. I mean, it confused me. It could deceive others. I don't know what his new identity is. Obviously, that's not relevant."

The jurors were in a state of confusion. The judge recessed the proceedings until 10:15 Monday morning.

17

Dog Days of Testimony

ON THE MORNING OF the fifth day of the trial, September 11, 1995, the sun cast bands of light across the courtroom. The humidity in the room started out brutal and continued to climb throughout the day. The prosecutors and the defense recalled Red Wemette's testimony from Friday.

The strategy of Hansen's defense team was to undermine the prosecution's evidence concerning motive. They tried to demonstrate that Hansen was physically incapable of committing the crime. Their goal was to raise doubts about the prosecution's timeline and finally to suggest that the key physical evidence against Hansen had been compromised at the crime scene in 1955, lost, or both.

"The case was heating up, and therefore Hansen burned down the barn to cover up evidence," Wemette professed.

Over the defense's strong objections, Judge Toomin allowed the captioned photo from page ten of the May 15, 1956, *Chicago Tribune*, the one found by Jimmy Delorto in the library. The photo was of a back barn at the Idle Hour Stables in flames after the Schuessler and Peterson families agreed to have the children's bodies exhumed for further trace-element analyses. The information appeared to be a direct corroboration of the CI's testimony. But was it prejudicial? Toomin felt he had no choice but to overrule the objection. He had a hunch that his decision would provide the defendant's attorneys fuel for an appeal, but Toomin also believed that testimony from the next few witnesses would justify his decision.

Chicago Police Lieutenant John Farrell, who had arrested Hansen, was called to the stand and answered questions about that day, August 11, 1994. Suppressed evidence was information from Farrell listening in on a telephone conversation between Hansen and his neighbor, Jim Tynan, when the defendant was overheard saying, "The police are looking for me." Whether or not Hansen had advance notice has yet to be determined, but what was curious was that, according to Farrell, after his prisoner was read his Miranda rights, Hansen spoke freely about his life and his sexual preferences.

The lieutenant stated that just before the arrest, Hansen got out of the pickup truck and walked to the front door of a neighbor. Farrell followed him into that home, told him he was under arrest, and placed him in the back seat of the unmarked squad car." In a later interview, Hansen gave his version of the arrest, which is remarkably different from Farrell's. "They wouldn't tell me what I was arrested for. They handcuffed me and put me in a little, tiny red car in the back seat where my knees were hitting against the seat. It was about four [o'clock], and he drove all the way. . . . I had a heart attack before, but he drove around until eight and, uh . . . or 9:00 at night and then took me to the precinct. He told me that we were going to the precinct, but he drove me around for four or five . . . six hours. It was nine or ten o'clock at night when I arrived downtown to one of those big tall buildings. . . . And they didn't even tell the truth abut that." Hansen said he agreed to take a lie-detector test "but the detectives said it wasn't necessary. I had nothing to hide. I was willing to take a lie-detector test, but they were concentrating more on Roger and whether or not I had an affair with Roger all of those years. And, uh, I had no idea Roger was connected with them."

Farrell recalled that after the defendant was arrested, "He started out by stating he had been a homosexual his entire life." Hansen told the police that from the 1950s through 1974, he had picked up numerous male hitchhikers during his life for the purpose of having oral sex with them, at times offering them jobs as stable hands. Hansen specifically stated that they were "between the ages of twelve and twenty-two."

"Did he specifically mention a person by the name of Roger Spry?" Cassidy inquired.

"Yes, sir, he did," Farrell said. "He stated that he had a relationship with Roger Spry. He described it as a good relationship. He stated that he started out with Roger Spry when Roger was about nine years old."

A couple of people in the audience gasped; some others bowed their heads, not because they were shocked but because for the first time during the trial, they accepted Spry's testimony as fact and found Hansen's behavior utterly impossible to comprehend, they said later.

According to Farrell, while at the ATF office, Hansen told his story. Prior to the Korean War, he had worked at the Park Ridge Riding Academy with his father. When he returned to the Chicago area, he worked at the Hollywood Kiddieland at Devon and Lincoln avenues and then moved from the North Side to the South Side sometime in October of 1955.

Kurt Voderberg, the owner of Kiddieland, spoke with the authors a few years before his death on April 19, 2004. He recalled what he called "subsidizing" the Kiddieland pony rides to "old man" Hansen in 1955, Hansen running the pony rides, collecting the money, taking his share, and paying Voderberg his. "To me, they were just people who owned the pony rides. They took the tickets in and got so much for each rider." Mr. Voderberg chuckled, "I remember this good-lookin' red-head; she would bring me the money every evening. It was a cash business. We didn't keep records." Without any encouragement, he added, "Honest men drove Fords, slightly dishonest men drove Oldsmobiles, and very dishonest men drove Cadillacs. Hansen [the father] drove an Oldsmobile, so he was only slightly dishonest!"

In an interview, Kenneth Hansen recalled vivid and fond memories of Kiddieland. "I was at the Bro-Ken H in '55, and I would come up north to see Bev, who was helping my father at Kiddieland after she got off work at the bank at three o'clock."

An interesting note is that before Hansen was told by police officers that Spry and Wemette had squealed on him, he repudiated their charges. Farrell testified, Hansen "stated that he had had a sexual relationship with Red Wemette. He stated that they had a good relationship. He stated that Red was with him at the stables in those years. I told Kenneth Hansen that Roger Spry and Red Wemette were both cooperating with the police on this case, and he explained to me that they would do that because he eventually spurned their sexual advances." Hansen "stated that Spry and Wemette were not friends because they constantly were both striving for his attention."

Quinn slowly approached the witness stand, stopping in front of the jurors. "Did you ask the defendant anything specifically regarding the murders of the Schuessler brothers and Robert Peterson?"

"I asked him what he knew about these murders. He stated he only knew what he read in the papers, didn't know anything else about it." Farrell nodded and appealed to the jurors. "He stated that he knew the police were following him because of all of the recent publicity regarding this case in the papers."

An investigation of Hansen's truck yielded only a couple of pieces of luggage, Farrell said. In a subsequent interview, Toomin said about the luggage found in Hansen's pickup truck and the earlier suggestion that he was going to leave the area, "I think the evidence of flight was very remote especially given the fact that Mr. Hansen came back into the area that day." Mark Hansen said that his father had luggage in the vehicle because they were about to drive to Indiana for a horse show.

According to Hansen's lawyers, no one bothered to check the employment records of the Idle Hour to confirm or refute their client's assertions that he had never worked at the Idle Hour Stables in 1955. The chances that these records still existed in 1995 were extremely remote. As Voderberg, the owner of Hollywood Kiddieland, explained, "Doing business in 1955 was on a handshake and cash basis. Nobody kept receipts."

What appeared to be sloppy police work in that Farrell did not record the interview, Stone contended, could be grounds for a mistrial—or at least that is what he hoped. "And, in fact, officer, I think you do know when Hansen moved to 5056 Claremont and when he moved out. You know that he got out of the service in January 1955, you know that, don't you?"

"I didn't know the exact month, no, sir."

"And you know that October is the tenth month of the year?"

Farrell's facial gestures said, *F-you*, but he checked the temptation to say what he was thinking.

"Is it fair to say that Mr. Hansen denied any knowledge or participation in the homicides of Robert Peterson, John Schuessler, and Anton Schuessler?" Stone snapped.

"He denied participation and personal knowledge. However, he did say he read about it in the papers."

Judge Toomin broadly and playfully wagged his finger at Stone as the defense lawyer took his seat.

Assistant State's Attorney Barbara Ann Riley was the next witness for the prosecution. She related what Hansen had told her: while in the army, he came home on a weekend pass and married Beverly, "whom he had known for quite some time." Among other things, during Riley's interview in the wee hours of the morning on August 12, 1994, Hansen had talked at length about his sexuality. "He described himself to me as a bisexual. He did not like the term *gay*; he appeared to have some distaste for what that connoted. He told me that he had his first homosexual encounter when he went to the [University of Illinois] at Navy Pier." She looked at the defendant and sighed, "He stated that this was a typical thing; that many people in the horse business were bisexual." Later, Hansen said that back in 1955, many men were experimenting with their sexuality.

Riley's memory of her extended conversation was remarkable. According to her, Hansen said he often picked up boys hitchhiking and described these boys as "throwaways"—boys with problems and no homes, boys whom nobody wanted.

"He spoke of Wemette in contrast to the type of relationship he had with these other stable boys. He said that with the stable boys, the sex was quick. It was mostly oral sex. It didn't take long. He specifically said there was no romance involved, no wining or dining. His relationship with this man Red Wemette, he told me, was different and lasted longer. It wasn't just a casual sexual encounter like he had with these other boys." Riley forced a smile, feeling strangely pleased with her response and, at the same time, fervently wishing that whoever killed the three boys was at the bottom of the Chicago River.

Quinn looked at the witness in amazement, his brows drawn together in a long dark scowl. "Did you speak to Mr. Hansen about Silas Jayne?"

"Yes, I asked him about Silas Jayne, and he was not comfortable at all talking about—"

"Objection, Judge!" shouted Stone, leaping to his feet. Toomin sustained the objection only as to the way the question was asked. Stone sat back down in his chair and cried, "Objection!" a second time over the prosecution's line of questioning. The judge frowned and leafed through his notebook looking for information that would help him with his ruling. "Overruled," Toomin said, much to Stone's chagrin.

After all of the objections and over-rulings were made, Quinn chimed in, "Ken Hansen about Silas Jayne?"

"He became nervous. His answers were short." Riley's face softened. "He told me that he knew Silas Jayne only on a business level. I am not sure of the exact year, but during this period of time, Silas Jayne ran a horse barn that was higher class [with English-style riding] than the type he was running."

During the cross-examination, Stone chastised her for not running a tape recorder or having someone else present in the room during the interview with his client. Over the next five minutes, with Stone's questioning, Riley recalled that Hansen said he had nothing to do with the deaths of Anton, John, or Bobby. Stone thanked the witness and nodded at the jurors.

Then the prosecution presented two stipulations.[1] The first was that if called, Park Ridge Deputy Fire Chief John Lamar would testify that the Park Ridge Fire Department responded to a call at the Idle Hour Stable on May 15, 1956.

Then Quinn announced he would read the stipulation about testimony from one of the parents of the murdered boys. The courtroom was quiet. Bobby's cousin was anonymous to the other spectators, just as she had been the first four days of the trial. Gary Kujawa, Eleanor Schuessler's stepson, reached over and took his sister's hand. He and Nancy both sat with their heads bowed.

"And it will be stipulated by and between the parties if Malcolm Peterson were called to testify, he would identify Group Exhibit 2C, 5A, and 5B, and People's Exhibit Number 6, as being photos of his son Robert, which truly and accurately depict how he looked when he was dead."

Robert's cousin let a whimper escape before she covered her mouth with her right hand. She had kept her composure for four full days of trial, but finally the prosecution evoked a response. For forty years, she had grieved Bobby's death, and the photos were a horrid verification of what she had buried deep in her child's heart so long ago.

Quinn looked over in her direction and waited a few seconds before he continued, "If Malcolm Peterson were called to testify, he would identify People's Group Exhibits 1B and 1C as being photographs of his son Robert Peterson, which truly and accurately depict how Robert appeared in or about 1955, when he was alive and in good health."

Heavy black clouds rolled in during the lunch hour, and the temperature remained in the high 70s. John Rotunno ran up the stairs of the courthouse and hurried through the revolving doors, past security and the press without being recognized.

The men and women of the jury returned from their lunch break and sat quietly in the jury box, their faces showing no emotion. As Special Agent Rotunno took the stand, his ATF colleagues thought, *Heaven help anyone who has to go up against Rotunno.*

Rotunno testified that during a conversation with Robert Leroy Stitt on February 8, 1994, Stitt had said Hansen had approached him sexually one time. In a March 10, 1994, meeting, Joseph Plemmons had "remembered one occasion where he caught Hansen having sex with young boys at the barn," Rotunno said, his testimony given matter-of-factly.

Rotunno's testimony of what Stitt and Plemmons had confessed to him maximized the effect of their confessions.

Then the prosecution rested its case.

Frank M. Jayne Sr., a rugged-looking horseman wrinkled from years in the sun, entered the room. All eyes were fixed on him as he confidently strode towards the witness stand. He was articulate, farm-wise, and nobody's fool. His voice was low, barely above a whisper, forcing O'Donnell to continually ask him to speak up.

"How old are you?" O'Donnell asked the first defense witness.

"Seventy-four going on seventy-five," Jayne said with doubt. "Oh, my, nuts! I am eighty-four."

"Eighty-four?" O'Donnell asked.

Jayne smiled, "I was thinking of your age. You mentioned it."

Jayne related how for over fifty years, he'd owned and operated a horse farm. He trained and sold thoroughbreds with his brother Si and often boasted of his accomplishments.

O'Donnell and Jayne kibitzed like two old guys playing checkers in the park, one always completing the other's sentence.

"Well, they didn't follow in my footsteps," Jayne said, "but my brothers were—"

"—were in the horse business," O'Donnell said. "The Idle Hour Stable?"

"Yes, I'm familiar with that."

"And were you familiar with it during the years of 1950 through 1960, that period of time? Did Kenneth Hansen ever work at the Idle Hour Stables?"

"No way." The witness glanced over at Hansen and then up at the judge. "He wasn't that kind of horseman. We had . . . maybe it would sound foolish to you, but we had high-class horses. And we taught English riding and hunting and jumping, so that customers when they graduated from that, they could go in better competition. I don't want to brag, but we always had the best show place around."

"And Kenneth Hansen, what type of operation did he run after you met him?"

"Well, he was just starting off, and he didn't have no expertise in taking care of horses good. And that might sound funny, but I am not looking down my nose at anybody, you understand. You have got to work hard to be successful."

O'Donnell put his right hand up to his right ear, gesturing that he couldn't hear what the witness was saying, so Jayne raised his voice, so much that he startled a few people who had been lulled into a stupor by the interrogation.

"Can . . . you . . . hear . . . me . . . now?" Jayne asked loudly.

The old horseman claimed that he met Hansen in 1961 "or two or three." "I'm not real sure, but that's the first time I met him. And I rode up with my son. He was selling hay to Mr. Hansen."

"Do you know whether or not Kenneth Hansen knew Silas Jayne? Do you know the circumstances of how they met?"

"That was after." Frank thought long and hard. "I don't remember when it exactly was, but my son was with me, and we went up. . . . He had a horse, and he wanted to sell it. It was kind of a cheap horse but still worth more than fifty or one hundred dollars. Horses were selling cheap at that time, you could buy a good livery horse for one hundred dollars." The witness cleared his throat. "But this horse, he wanted five hundred dollars for it." Si was selling the horse for the widow of a man who had owned bowling alleys. During this transaction, Frank said he introduced his brother to Hansen. The name of the horse was Pandora and according to Si a real good jumper.

Frank Jayne boasted about the "extreme security provisions" at Idle Hour Stable. "There was a night watchman . . . and he would turn the dogs loose after everybody was gone, and then he would patrol around." There was a tall fence with locked gates. In addition to the watchman, "Big John," other people lived on the property from time to time. "There was a family by the name of Lucas . . . Billy Lucas. He rode and escorted rides for my brother Si. And there was a mother and a father and a daughter, and Billy. I know Billy." With a hell-I-know-I'm-right attitude, Frank Jayne continued, "There was Ralph Fleming and Marie Fleming, who cooked the food for the grooms, and they came and ate there. They ate their breakfast, lunch, and supper there."

"So, even when the place was closed, there were still ten or eleven people on the property?"

"Oh, yes. Absolutely!"

"Mr. Jayne," O'Donnell leaned close, "has any member of the law enforcement, the Chicago Police Department, the local police, county police department, any federal agents, FBI, ATF, ever contacted you with respect to this case?"

Shaking his head, Frank said, "No, sir!"

"Just one moment," O'Donnell said as he thumbed through a legal pad full of trial notes. "What kinds of dogs were on the premise?"

"Dobermans."

Quinn didn't spend much time cross-examining Frank Jayne. "Sir, when did you get out of the thoroughbred horse race business?"

"1955. I sold all of my horses, and I went out to my farm."

"Now, at the Idle Hour back in 1955, they were teaching English-riding lessons, right?"

According to Frank Jayne, the Idle Hour Stables in 1955 was famous for their lessons in English riding, not Western riding, considered lower-class by many horse people. Ralph Fleming ran the livery and boarder businesses.

O'Donnell was certain that the jury understood that Idle Hour was a more upscale operation. "Now, even in the jumper/hunter business, your brother Silas was a pretty famous guy, wasn't he?"

"Yes, he was."

"And it would be fair to say that if somebody were involved in the jumper and hunter business, they would know Si?"

"Yes."

"And you say that Mr. Hansen never worked for your brother?"

"That's right. He didn't have the expertise, I tell you."

Barbara Beitzel Ashbaugh, the next defense witness, testified that she worked at the Idle Hour Stables in the summer of 1954 and began teaching there full-time in 1955. "I never saw Mr. Hansen there during the years 1954, 1955, or 1956," she said. According to Ashbaugh, a former neighbor of Hansen, there was a night watchman at the stables, and the gates and doors to the barns were locked at night. She testified that there was a fire in one of the barns in May 1956.

Dan Strong, a friend of Hansen, looked over at the defendant and smiled gently. "I served in the military with Kenny," he said, and after he was discharged from the military in 1955, "Kenny and Bev visited me in Texas." He could not recall the exact dates.

Edwin P. Thomas Jr., an automobile mechanic from Culver, Indiana, smiled bravely as he took the oath to tell the truth. "I met Kenneth Hansen probably around 1957 or 1958, somewhere right in there. I can't be exactly positive, but I was a young kid then." When Thomas was nine or ten years old, like so many youngsters, he rode horses at the Bro-Ken

H Stables. At the time, he was living with his parents in Justice, Illinois, and "as often as I could get a couple of dollars to ride," he said, "I would walk three, maybe three and a half miles to the stable."

The courtroom was so quiet, that even Bobby's cousin, who sat in the last row, could hear the witness breathing. "The only person I know that I seen every day who signed people up and took their money at the stables was Terry Legenhaven."

"What about Roger Spry?"

Edwin said that about a year after he started riding at the Bro-Ken H, Roger started helping out. They played together. About a week later, Roger's dad told Ken and Bev to raise Roger, which the youngster "seemed very happy about." Edwin helped Roger do morning chores during the summer. When it was the school year, Bev picked the boys up at school and dropped them off at the stables. Around dark, she would give Edwin a ride home.

O'Donnell turned toward the jury. "Where would you see Roger?"

Thomas arrived early in the morning, before school, but he never saw Spry sleeping in a dog kennel. "Sometimes he was outside. If he wasn't, I would have to go upstairs into the house to get him."

"The house," O'Donnell emphasized. "Where is the house in relationship to the stable?"

"Well, there was a building in front by the road, and it was like a storage area in the front, and then there was a sign-up room; a little tack room, and the old section above it was where they lived."

The defense attorney relaxed and shrugged his shoulders. "Calling your attention to 1965, did anything unusual happen with regard to your relationship with the stable?"

"Well, I had just joined the service for a four-year hitch, the United States Marine Corps." Following two tours of duty, Edwin returned to Chicago and caught up with Kenneth Hansen at his new stables. That was in May 1969. "I spent quite a bit of time at Sky Hi," he said. "There were about seven or eight of us that would get together Wednesdays and Saturdays and play polo. I helped out at the barn there, and Kenny fed me and gave me a place to sleep, a roof over my head, and I stayed there until I located a job." In exchange for room and board, Edwin worked at Hansen's stables during the day. At night, he was an order picker at Consolidated Foods in Maywood Park, Illinois. In 1970, the Viet Nam veteran got married, and once again his life changed dramatically. He spent less time at the stables and more time on the road driving a truck for

Car Carriers Incorporated, delivering new Fords to dealerships throughout the Midwest. His wife filed for a divorce in 1975 (an all-too-familiar occurrence for veterans) and was granted custody of their two children. Edwin remarried in 1976.

"Now, Mr. Thomas, when was the first time that you suspected or believed that Mr. Hansen might be a homosexual?"

"In 1969 when I got out of the service."

"Had you ever seen anything to lead you to suspect that he was a homosexual during the period prior to that? Did you ever see him pick up boys hitchhiking on the roads or streets and bring them to the stables?"

"No, no."

Thomas remembered Robert Stitt because the two boys became buddies. "I was going to school for motorcycle repair in Daytona, Florida, and he lived in West Palm Beach, and I spent the weekend there with him."

"Did you ever have a conversation with Mr. Stitt with respect to sexual advances by Mr. Hansen while you were in the West Palm Beach home of his?"

"Yes," Thomas said. "He asked me if I had ever been approached by Kenny, and I told him no. He said, 'Are you sure?' I said, 'Well, I am positive.' Then I said, 'Have you?' and he said no."

As the years rolled by, Thomas drifted between Florida and Chicago. Every time he was out of work, he ended up back at Hansen's stable. "Kenny was there, Bev was there, and about ten thirty, eleven o'clock, Roger would come in." The witness sighed. "And one day, Kenny just looked at Roger and said, 'You're fired.' Then he looked at me and asked me if I would like to take over the place. And, I said I wouldn't." Later that evening, Spry and Thomas downed a few beers at the bar at the 159th Street Inn. "I haven't seen him since," Thomas said.

Regarding Joe Plemmons, Thomas saw him around the stables but had no memory of who he was or what he was all about. Ditto for Red Wemette. O'Donnell looked down at a note pad he had in his hand. "Mr. Thomas, based upon the association that you had with Mr. Spry, working with him, living with him, going to school with him, [do you think] Roger Spry is a truthful person?" The defense attorney paused, expecting an objection, and when none came, he said, "Are you familiar with his reputation?"

"Yes," Thomas said, looking at each member of the audience as if to make sure Spry wasn't there. "Very bad. Nobody trusted him. Nobody believes him. Nobody even wants him around."

"Would you believe him under oath?"

"No—"

Before the witness could finish the thought, Cassidy bounced to his feet—"Objection!"

"Overruled. His answer may stand." Toomin looked at Quinn and back at the witness.

O'Donnell took a deep breath. "I have no further questions."

Before the jury could ponder Thomas's last words, Quinn said the witness was involved in an ongoing civil matter, and O'Donnell was representing him.

Then prosecutor Cassidy asked about a visit he had made to Thomas's home. "Your mother said, 'The police are here.' Then you said, 'I know. I smelled them as I pulled in.' Right?"

Thomas held back a smile. "Yes."

"Is that the way you feel about the police and the state's attorney's office? Did we really smell?"

Members of the jury and several people in the audience lowered their heads and chuckled.

Thomas put his hand in front of his mouth and pretended to clear his throat. "In some cases, that's the way I feel."

Cassidy walked back to the prosecution's table and whispered something in Quinn's ear, who nodded and smiled slightly. Cassidy took two steps forward and asked, "Mr. Thomas, how many conversations have you had with Mr. Spry in the last twenty years?"

"I couldn't really count how many times I have talked with him," Thomas scowled. "Probably two or three."

"What is Mr. Spry's reputation today as you know it today, Mr. Thomas? What is Mr. Spry's reputation for telling the truth?"

"I don't know anybody that trusts him."

"Okay," Cassidy said without a pause. "I believe you testified you had three more conversations with Mr. Stitt, and he asked whether or not Mr. Hansen had any relationship with you? Right? And you couldn't believe Hansen was that kind of person?"

"Yes."

"I believe, you said you've never seen Roger Spry sleep in the kennel, is that what you said? Are you saying that he never did or you just never happened to see it?"

"I never had any knowledge of it," Thomas said. "In the summertime, almost every morning, I was there, and I never saw him in those kennels."

On redirect, O'Donnell's questioning made it clear that Hansen had never mentioned anything to Thomas about the Schuessler-Peterson boys and that Thomas answered every one of Cassidy's questions the day they came out to interview him. "And what was the last thing he asked you?"

"That was on the edge of the driveway. He turned to me and he said, 'Did you ever pick up anybody for Kenny?' And I said, 'No.' He asked if Kenny ever went on the expressway to pick boys up. I said, 'Well, no.' Kenny never went on the expressway. He didn't like the expressway. He wouldn't ride it. And he made the statement, 'Well, he likes the back door. That is his way of doing things, isn't it?' And I said, 'That is a pretty low shot.' And that was it."

On recross, Cassidy asked, "Speaking of picking up hitchhikers, sir, did you pick up a young man by the name of Robert K. Milliken?"

"Yes," Thomas said without hesitation.

"Do you know if Ken Hansen ever had sex with that young man?"

Agitated, Thomas raised his eyebrows, reached out his hands with the palms facing up, and said, "I don't know."

18

Judgment Day

"MR. HANSEN, STEP UP here, please." Judge Toomin leaned forward as the defendant limped towards the bench, his face mottled and his body sickly. "Mr. Hansen, it's been represented by your attorneys, Mr. O'Donnell and Mr. Stone, that it is not your intention to testify in this case. Is that true?"

All of Hansen's carefully constructed, prison-tempered serenity blew up in a white-hot acid rush that seared through the center of his being. He wanted to testify, but his counsel said no. Hansen swallowed hard. His mouth was dry. "Yes, sir."

"The decision not to testify was made last night," O'Donnell noted. The lateness of Hansen's deliberations with counsel had brought chaos to the schedule of arguments and witness participation. "We have an out-of-state witness coming in at three o'clock on American Airlines."

Frustration was evident in O'Donnell's voice as he asked the judge for a delay in the proceedings. It was a moot point. The sixth day's trial agenda was being cut short so a juror could attend a relative's funeral. Proceedings were recessed until one o'clock the next day, Wednesday, September 13. A superstitious individual might have considered it extremely poor timing for the defense to rest on the thirteenth of the month. Others might have equally thought it apropos for the men and women of the jury to begin to decide Hansen's guilt or innocence on that date.

The final witness testifying in the trial was no stranger to the defendant or the courtroom setting. Mark Hansen realized that he was probably his father's last chance. Standing just short of five-feet, eight inches and wearing a plaid shirt and dark slacks, the compactly built young man proved to be a cautious witness. At the time of the trial, Mark, his wife, and son were living in Chicago Heights, Illinois. "I own stables," he responded with pride in his voice to O'Donnell's second question. The thirty-six-year-old looked guardedly at his father, who stared back at him. O'Donnell did nothing to put his witness at ease, subjecting him to a battery of questions about his father's whereabouts, habits, and friends.

"Do you recall what your earliest recollection of Roger Spry is?"

"Roger has been around forever as far as I was concerned."

"Did he ever sleep in the dog kennels?"

Mark was adamant that Roger slept in the house, not in the dog kennels. His mother and father treated him like one of the family. "There was a house that was on the premises and a big, long barn, but he stayed in the house. He would take care of the horses and help feed them and escort trail rides and things like that."

"At any time did Roger make any complaints to you about your father making sexual overtures to him? Did you ever see your father do any of that?"

Mark's eyes widened, and he adjusted his glasses. "No, sir."

"And at any subsequent periods when you saw Roger either as an adult or as a teenager, did you know that he was having sexual relationships with your father?"

Unmistakable anger was in Mark's voice as he said, "No, sir." He gritted his teeth. The young horseman admitted that when he was in his "late teens or early twenties," he learned about his father's promiscuous lifestyle. Mark frowned. It was still difficult for him to accept that his father was interested in men.

"In addition to owning the stables you referred to, do you own any other business enterprise?"

Once again, Mark beamed with pride. "Yes, sir. I have a farm in Southern Illinois. It's about 350 miles south . . . near the town of Golconda."

O'Donnell stood patiently in front of Mark, and once their eyes locked, he asked, "As a matter of fact, on the day he—"the attorney abruptly turned and pointed toward the defendant—"was arrested, he came back from that farm, didn't he?"

Mark Hansen testified that he and his dad would go to the farm in Golconda every ten days or so during the winter to feed the livestock and at least two or three times during the summer, especially when they made hay.

O'Donnell took a long, deep breath before continuing. "Now, do you recall at some point at Tinley Park when Mr. [Edwin] Thomas left his [parents] to stay with your mother and father?"

"Yes, sir."

Even though the line of defense was vigorously objected by the prosecutors, Mark Hansen was able to say that none of the boys ever complained that his dad made overtures of a sexual nature. When asked about the accusation that his father picked up hitchhikers, Mark glanced over at his father and then back at the lawyer. "Now and then he would."

Smiling, O'Donnell said, "I have no further questions."

For the next ninety minutes, O'Donnell, Stone, Cassidy, and Quinn sparred over witness testimonies, finally agreeing to let them be read aloud rather than having the person take the stand.

Stone's deep voice resonated across the courtroom as he read the first testimony, given in 1955. "Malcolm O. Peterson, if called to testify, would state under oath that he's the father of Robert Peterson, deceased. Further, Mr. Peterson would answer the following questions with the following answers."

In the back of the courtroom, Bobby Peterson's cousin composed herself as Stone began reading the transcript.

QUESTION: How long did you know the Schuessler boys?
ANSWER: I guess I knew them since the Schuesslers moved into the
neighborhood. I don't know if they were always in the same
room [at school]. I would say they were pretty chummy for the
last year. Little Tony, I have never seen before, but I had seen
Bobby with Johnny. Bobby had been going downtown for a year.

QUESTION: Where did he usually go when he went downtown?

ANSWER: My little girl has eye trouble as you probably notice when she came in. She had to get eye exercises, and he would go downtown with her. One time, they went to a double-header ball game.

Stone, a father himself, felt Mr. Peterson's pain as he read the testimony aloud. In the chilling quiet of the courtroom, he heard the soft echoes of his powerful voice as he spoke.

QUESTION: Was he with the Schuessler boy?

ANSWER: No. He was with Terry Reilly and Denny [last name unknown]. I think there were three that went together.

QUESTION: Was he ever out with any of the Schuessler boys before at night?

ANSWER: Late at night, no.

QUESTION: Calling your attention to the 16th of October, 1955, can you tell me what transpired that day in your home from the time Robert got out of bed?

The room was unnervingly quiet. Stone's voice softened.

ANSWER: We got up in the morning, and we kept him home from church because I had some work to do on the garage. I made it four feet longer, but the boards were pretty long, and I couldn't hold them myself, so I kept him home to help me. We worked in the backyard until about one or one-thirty, and then we came in and ate.

QUESTION: Did your son ever skip school?

The more Stone read from the transcripts, the more haunting Bobby's father's words became.

ANSWER: Yeah, he played hooky when he was in seventh grade. He had a little trouble, but we went over and spoke to the school authorities and got it straightened out. It was a spell of a couple of weeks.

QUESTION: Did it last two weeks?

ANSWER: No. He would go to school one day and stay home, maybe the next.

QUESTION: Do you know whether or not anyone else played hooky with him?

ANSWER: That, I do not know.

"So stipulated?" Stone requested. He closed his eyes for a second and tried to imagine Mr. Peterson those last few moments he saw his son alive, waving to him from the sidewalk, a big grin on Bobby's face for his mother who stood by the front door as he disappeared around the corner with the Schuessler brothers toward his rendezvous with the killer. It was an emotional moment for the well-traveled defense attorney.

"So stipulated," Cassidy responded.

With the emotional reading of the Peterson transcripts, the crime-scene photos were reintroduced. Anticipating a series of challenges as to what would be allowed to go into the jury's deliberation room, Judge Toomin called for a sidebar in his chambers, the four attorneys following.

Stone took a breath, relaxed his body for a second, and then announced, "I don't have any objection to their taking a look at black-and-white photographs. Blessedly, they are black-and-white and not in color. They [the jurors] may want to look at them. But when you get a repetition of them, you get to the point where—"

Toomin cut him off, "They are all adults."

"Frankly," Stone said, "they remind me of where the Nazis lined up Jews and dropped them into an open ditch. I have a strong visceral reaction to the photographs. Any right-thinking human being would."

"So you are not going to object to anything going back [into the jurors' room]?"

O'Donnell shrugged his shoulders and said, "The morgue photos Donoghue used, I have no objection to that."

"We're offering them all," Quinn growled. "Which one do you have an objection to?"

"My beef is this. What this does is repetitively show something that's not really an issue," O'Donnell argued. "It is all the images of the bodies in the ditch. Why repeatedly show the same thing just because it's in a different position when that's really not an issue in the case at all?"

Over the next forty-five minutes, O'Donnell, Stone, Quinn, and Cassidy squabbled over which one of the explicit death photographs was to be permitted to be shown to the jurors. Back and forth, one argument contrary to the next, and all compelling. Toomin finally said enough. "Well, I agree with you as to fourteen; twenty—no . . . yes to fourteen, eighteen, twenty, and twenty-two, this one is the only one that shows them in that situation. That's number fourteen. They should definitely go back. This one, nineteen, showing the coroner actually touching the bodies and examining them. When I looked at sixteen, I don't think this is prejudicial. I don't know what great probative value it has."

The men were quiet for a few seconds before O'Donnell said, "I'm getting the feeling that the state is going to argue they don't have any physical evidence because law enforcement corrupted the crime scene." O'Donnell came to the profound, but bitter, realization that *if you want justice, don't go into law.*

After the closing arguments, the men and women of the jury filed into their room the early afternoon of Wednesday, September 13, to consider their verdict. They took only an hour and forty minutes to decide Ken Hansen's fate. Though no physical evidence or eyewitness tying Hansen to the crimes was presented by prosecution attorneys, the jurors wasted little time in convicting the stableman, largely because of the testimony of Herb Hollatz, who was presented to the jury as the sole witness not a con man or government snitch. Juror Tony Cristofono revealed that the first poll was nine to one to convict, with two undecided. He said, "One of the witnesses—Herb Hollatz—had excellent credibility," which helped to sway the doubters.

A collective sigh of relief was let out now that the trial was over.

Except for Kenny. He was devastated because, he said later in an interview in prison, he knew he'd be convicted because of the way he was portrayed by the prosecution's witnesses. "If I did everything they said I did," Kenny said, "I'd hate me, too. Whoever killed those boys is an evil person, but it's not me."

Prosecutor Pat Quinn told reporters, "After forty years, the families of these kids have a right to closure. He said he did it [based on the testimony of his "throwaway boys"] because he did do it. Convict him."

"There is a God," echoed Cassidy, as he made his way to the door trailed by reporters.

Beatrice Blane, aunt of the Schuessler boys, wept openly. "I've been waiting forty years. I'm the last of the family. I'm just glad it's over."

Jed Stone accepted the verdict with customary stoicism. He called it a "great mystery," telling the press, "It is made no clearer today than in October 1955."

Meanwhile, Jimmy Delorto was making his way to his downtown office. He made a left-hand turn onto Dearborn Street, then a sharp right into a self-parking garage. His thoughts were focused on another trial already underway in the Federal Building. For the moment, the doings down at Twenty-Sixth and California were no longer center-stage. A familiar voice crackled through the speaker of the car radio. It was his secretary Nadia Martinez, "It's over. Hansen was found guilty." Delorto was overjoyed, but before he could respond to Nadia, his cell phone rang.

"It was a slam dunk," beamed Jim Grady. "How about joining us for a drink at Tracy's on Fifty-Fifth Street?" The neighborhood restaurant and bar was a favorite hangout for many law-enforcement agents in Clarendon Hills.

Delorto checked his watch. "I don't know if I can make it."

Deep down, Delorto wanted to be a part of the trial, but he was never called to testify. His ego was bruised, but the outcome was a wonderful vindication for several years of hard work. "Cassidy and I disagreed over certain evidence, like the stool, but it was his call. The state planned the defense, and they won without it."

Grady, Quinn, Cassidy, and Rotunno would close Tracy's down as they celebrated their victory.

Delorto thought about lighting up a cigarette. As quickly as the thought came, he suppressed it. He smiled knowing he won *two* important hard-fought victories that day. It seemed like a good time to pull the pin and start thinking about that last vacation he had had to put off. So, on September 30, 1995, in the presence of a few hundred friends, family members, and colleagues, Cassidy awarded Delorto his retirement plaque and expressed the grateful thanks of his associates. The inscription, written as a letter beginning "Dear Jimmy," expressed posthumous thanks from Anton, John, and Bobby. Cassidy read aloud the message. There wasn't a dry eye in the room.

Under drizzling skies, reporters and their camera crews, lawyers, and interested observers converged for the final day of what has been called "the most horrific triple-murder–mystery trial in America." The case of *Hansen vs. People of the State of Illinois* was, in fact, the oldest crime in the United States to be brought before a jury.

The sentencing hearing was Friday, October 20, forty years after the boys' unclothed bodies were found in a ditch in Robinson Woods. Kenneth Hansen focused his attention on getting himself together. Supported by his cane, he walked gingerly into the courtroom, desperate for a miracle. He appeared older than his sixty-two years, illnesses had overtaken him, and his facial expression was devoid of any emotion.

First up on the court's agenda was a motion for a new trial based on the defense's belief that their client was innocent.

Defense attorney Arthur O'Donnell spoke first. He looked empathically at his client for a long moment and then said in earnest, "Remember when I was making my opening statement that I had mentioned the fact that I thought this was a unique case. I think the court took issue and mentioned in front of the jury that this is just another murder case or something to that effect. I respectfully disagree with you in the sense that I think this is a unique case. It is the only forty-year prosecution that I'm aware of in this country for that matter or in any other country." He said the defense was asking the judge to set aside the jury's conviction (a judgment notwithstanding the verdict) and declare Hansen innocent because with the thirty-nine-year delay in the prosecution, he didn't receive due process of law.

The defense called other events into question, specifically the search of Hansen's home and the seizure of his little black book of addresses and phone numbers, which, O'Donnell said, were unjust, a violation of Hansen's rights. O'Donnell flashed a here-goes-nothing look toward his client and proceeded, "There was no objective evidence of sexual molestation in any way with respect to these three boys, who were found in Robinson Woods on October 18, 1955; therefore, there was no basis for the introduction of evidence indicating Mr. Hansen's sexual preference. If these boys were not sexually involved in some way or another, then how in the hell do they get into the question of Mr. Hansen's sexuality? The prejudice of that is readily apparent. No objective juror determining facts and circumstances regarding a murder can be unaffected by the presence of evidence of this nature."

O'Donnell likened Hansen's sufferings to that of the victims of the Holocaust. "I can conceive of no human conduct, other than perhaps burning people in an oven in Germany, that might conceivably compare with the disgust and detestability that we have for people who engage in sexual molestation of children. But that was the essence of this case.

We strenuously objected to the evidence regarding that. We were consistently overruled."

The attorney said the defense had proven that on June 5, 1955, Hansen moved from the Northwest Side and bought a stable on the Southwest Side at Eighty-Second and Kean.

O'Donnell continued, "The period of time which he contended that he was on his honeymoon with his wife—we brought a witness from Texas. The man was honest." O'Donnell read the man's testimony from his notes, "'I believe it was October. I know it was in the late fall, but I can't tell you whether it was the first week or the second or the third week.' But we can't ignore that it may have been around the fifteenth, sixteenth, or eighteenth of October. And if that is so, wouldn't that be a profound effect on this case?"

The aging lawyer relaxed his shoulders, and his face softened. "Deals are being cut, sentences are being reduced, and witnesses in this case frankly admitted under oath that they're were liars. But, of course, they're not lying this time. Are we not corrupting the system ourselves by this practice of taking the path of least resistance and the easiest course of treatment?"

The thin defense counsel thought for a long moment. "Mr. Peterson volunteered in his statement to the police that his son was afraid of something. The police asked, 'Well, do you know what it was?' Mr. Peterson said, 'No.'"

O'Donnell's eyes darted across the crowded room. The audience appeared restless; the defense attorneys exchanged glances as if to say, "Children were murdered so somebody had to do it, and it may as well be Hansen." Years of experience had taught O'Donnell to read a jury fairly accurately; he sensed that the prevailing opinion was against his client. Next, O'Donnell singled out the Peterson family for criticism, questioning the intractable wall of silence that they had maintained throughout the trial. "It has bothered me to no end that Malcolm Peterson and no member of the Peterson family ever attended this trial. He was listed as a witness on the state's list, and, therefore, I fully intended to call him. Then I found out that the State was not going to call him. I immediately had him served with a subpoena. Mr. Peterson hired a lawyer to oppose being brought into court on this case. I don't know his reasons. It could be his age; it could be a lot of things. But I think it's very significant that on the night that this verdict was returned, September 13, 1995, a newspaper reporter called him up, and he had no comment."

The attorney turned back, slowly this time, and faced the judge. "Those are the questions that have to be asked. If a man had waited forty years for vindication of his son's death, is this the way he would respond? I don't know. But I sure as hell know that they don't have any more evidence in this case against anybody than they did forty years ago, other than the testimony of people who were told something twenty years after it occurred and then didn't tell anybody about it until fifteen or twenty years after that. Is this the quality of evidence upon which we want to deny liberty and freedom?"

O'Donnell's words fell on deaf ears; Judge Toomin went over his closing speech in his mind as he listened to O'Donnell's final argument. One particular piece of testimony stuck in his mind—that of Herb Hollatz. The judge recalled later in an interview, "The remarkable thing about Hollatz is that he was not one of the guys involved in crime who sold their stories to federal agents. Hollatz was the best witness—the prosecution's top dog. The defense couldn't attack him; he was telling the truth. Spry, Wemette, Plemmons—they're all rogues, there's no question about that. But the jury knew that. They knew what their background was and how they were involved with Hansen. A quintessential function of the jury is to determine credibility. To have this old guy [Hollatz] come in and let it all hang out in front of God and everybody in this courtroom, that was very emotional. And he was the most credible of all of the witnesses because he was not one of those government guys."

O'Donnell, who knew he was playing a losing hand, walked slowly back to the defense table and stood next to Hansen. "Thank you very much," he said and sat down.

Pat Quinn moved about the prosecution's table, sorting through files and gathering up photos. He began his summation, "Counsel harps on the lack of physical evidence. I would point out that the lack of physical evidence in this case, Your Honor, applies to all suspects in the case. The fact that there is no physical evidence linking anybody to the murder of these children does not mean these children were *not* murdered. In the hundreds of murder cases I have dealt with in seventeen years of working for the state's attorney's office, I can tell the court that I am certain that in less than five percent of those cases there has actually been physical evidence linking a suspect to the crime scene or to the murder victim, meaning blood work, fingerprints, or fiber evidence.

"Error in admission of evidence of homosexual conduct by the accused, Your Honor," Quinn said, raising his voice. "The state filed an extremely lengthy motion in response to the defense's *motion in limine.* We filed it on March 14th of 1995. We had numerous side bars throughout this trial as to the evidence of homosexual conduct, and the court ruled correctly."

O'Donnell and Stone had raised ninety-six specific points, but the judge had only commented on a few of them. The most titillating was inadmissible evidence pointing a finger at John Wayne Gacy, thirteen years old at the time of the murders. Throughout the trial, Quinn had done a good job of defusing the Gacy defense with an emotional appeal to the judge.

"The bottom line in this case, Your Honor, is that the defense has asserted that the state waited until John Wayne Gacy was executed and then purposely charged an innocent person rather than clear the case by blaming Gacy. Judge," he continued without taking a breath, "one of the most courageous and honest things I've seen in the state's attorney's office in a long time is when the Chicago Police Department refused to lay the cases off on John Gacy so they could just look good"—Quinn gestured toward Hansen, who met his gaze with an icy stare of his own—"but it wasn't true, and they didn't do that, and, therefore, the case remained open and was solved as a result of intellectual honesty of the Chicago Police Department when the opposite would have been so easy. . . . Simply put, there was no hint, no scintilla of evidence that John Wayne Gacy killed these three boys on October 16, 1955.

"Now they wish to say they want to have a deposition of officer [John] Sarnowski. Well, they could have done that yesterday. They could have done that the day before when I offered to drive up to Lake Geneva [Wisconsin] and be with them when they interviewed Mr. Sarnowski. They refused my request because, again, they don't want to have this heard in a court of law. You should not grant those requests; they should be denied. They are a sham. Nothing further."

Judge Toomin responded, "The court has listened carefully to the contentions of counsel with respect to the motion now before the court for judgment notwithstanding the verdict for a motion for a new trial. . . . I would conclude [by asking] the defense to assume and consider [if] the shoe were to be on the other foot, how they would approach a request such as was made on behalf of Mr. Hansen? Assume that the state sought to offer against Kenneth Hansen evidence based upon investigative steps taken by police detectives with the aim of introducing not only where they [the boys] went and who they talked to but the conversation that they had and that these witnesses with that basic information were never presented in open court, were never subject to cross-examination. How rightfully indignant would the defense be were that scenario to be played out in an American court of law? Justifiably, it didn't, because the law would not permit it for the prosecution nor does it permit it for the defense."

Stone, O'Donnell, and Hansen stood motionless. The color slowly drained out of the defendant's face as Toomin delivered the final judgment.

"With those comments, the motion for judgment notwithstanding, [the motion] for a new trial shall be denied."

Charged with emotion, O'Donnell responded that by not giving Hansen a new trial, "it makes him the Wilt Chamberlain of pedophiles, which is a ridiculous allegation."

The prosecution brought in four final witnesses to reinforce earlier witness testimony about Kenny's violent, debauched behavior over the years.

Lawrence Smith, one of the conspirators recruited to assassinate George Jayne, took the stand and avowed that in 1968 Kenneth Hansen asked him "if I would shoot a gentleman [George Jayne] for him." (In the end Smith's testimony was moot because after nineteen months of federal investigation, the murder-for-hire charge against Hansen was dropped.) O'Donnell asked him if he was a "hired killer." Smith responded indignantly, "No, I'm not. When I read in the newspaper that George Jayne was killed, I called the police."

Steve Rycraft said that he was working in a jewelry story at 195th and Kedzie in Flossmoor, Illinois, in 1975 the first time he met Hansen. "I was making jewelry," he said in a monotone. "And he asked me if I would size a ring for him." According to Rycraft, Hansen invited him to his Oak Forest apartment after work, and "I brought my sizing tools and stuff with me. He offered me a shot of J&B Scotch. It was a very large glass." Rycraft said he was under the influence of alcohol when Hansen started "rubbing my leg and telling me I was a good-looking young man."

O'Donnell bolted from his seat and in a higher than usual voice objected, which Toomin overruled.

Rycraft continued, "and telling me how handsome I was. I was getting very uncomfortable. And then he took me into the bedroom, undressed me, put me on the bed, and put corn husker oil [in] my rectum."

The judge shifted uncomfortably in his chair, as did most of the other courtroom spectators and jurors, upon having to listen to the explicit details of the homosexual rape.

"Did he put his penis in your rectum then?" Cassidy asked.

Rycraft looked down again, his chin almost touching his neck. He placed a handkerchief in front of his mouth and spoke softly, "Yes, he did."

"Did this cause you a great deal of pain, sir?"

"Yes, it did. It caused me to bleed, and I begged him to stop." The witness looked around the room. Horrified at his own admissions, he said, "He told me to stop whimpering."

"Did he tell you at that time that he's hurt kids before?"

"Yes, he did. He finally stopped, and I ran into the bathroom and locked the door."

"You're going to have to take that cloth away from your mouth, sir, so I can hear you," O'Donnell requested, without having properly addressed the judge. After objection by the prosecution, Judge Toomin reprimanded O'Donnell, "If you have anything to say to the witness, say it through me."

Rycraft continued his testimony. He nodded his head up and down a few times and wiped his eyes with the wrinkled, white cloth. "He kept telling me to come out [of the bathroom]. My rectum was bleeding. I finally come out and told him I had to leave. He warned me not to say anything. And I was afraid that it might cause me problems at my job."

O'Donnell made sure it was understood that Rycraft was twenty-one years old at the time of the alleged rape. Then the defense attorney asked him, "Did he force you to have sex with him?"

"He pushed me onto the bed, yes."

"Could you have left then?"

"No, I was a lot smaller then." Rycraft was shamed and humiliated to the point where he was nearly incoherent. "I discussed it with my ex-wife in 1978. I discussed it with my parents recently, within the last couple of months. I called the police before I discussed it with my parents. I've been trying to forget it."

Bobby Lee Brown, a somber and reserved-looking horseman, then took the witness stand. He looked considerably older than his sixty years. Brown, one of the original defendants in the federal Horse-Mafia trials, bought and sold hunters, jumpers, and racehorses. In 1949 at the age of fourteen, he launched his riding career and turned professional. Brown said Hansen badly abused his horses on many occasions. "I wouldn't let Kenny feed a dog of mine. I leased stalls at Sky Hi [from Kenny from 1968 to 1984] and would give him fifty dollars a stall for twenty stalls, and then I put my horses in them. I had my own men care for the horses."[1]

According to Brown, he and Hansen had business dealings going back a number of years. For a time, they were friends who shared many secrets. Brown related the history of Kenny's involvement in the George Jayne murder plot and how Si "stiffed" Kenny for the money he was promised. According to Brown, Si owed Hansen $10,000 and another $20,000 if Brown and Hansen were successful in taking George Jayne to Tucson. "Kenny told me that he couldn't do it, and he wouldn't do it, that Si had something on him from a long time ago, and that he didn't want it to come out at all."

Art O'Donnell enlightened the jurors about Brown's criminal record, which included a wire-fraud charge in connection with a horse transaction for which Brown was to serve fourteen months, pay a $2,000 fine, and do three hundred hours of community service. Brown would begin serving his sentence on December 5 because he had had four operations for a medical problem and in prison would need more help.

"So you made another good deal, didn't you?" O'Donnell said. "Being in a medical facility is better than being in a prison, right?"

"Well, it *is* a prison."

The fourth witness for the prosecution was ATF agent James Grady, who was brought back to corroborate William "Red" Wemette's and Roger Spry's stories of the August 1970 arson at Forest View Stables where thirty-six horses perished. According to Grady, Wemette stated that on August 14, he "saw Mr. Cooper and Mr. Spry running back from the area of the Forest View Stables to Sky Hi Stables, at which time Mr. Spry had a galvanized gas can with him." Later, Spry told Wemette that "Hansen told him to do it."

O'Donnell vigorously objected to the line of questioning. "This is double hearsay," he said. The judge agreed, but the narrative left the jury with a raw, incriminating snapshot of Kenny Hansen, who later professed he had nothing to do with the fire. "The Cummings were my neighbors and friends. I would never do that."

In a hand-written statement Grady procured from Spry on July 23, 1994, Spry claimed that he was offered $300 to burn down the Forest View Stables. "He did not know how much Mr. Cooper, who was also known as Coop and/or Chicken Coop, was offered," Grady said.

The horses killed were privately owned, not by Bill and Joanne Cummings or their Forest View livery business, which, according to Mark Hansen in a later interview, "was almost nonexistent. The scuttlebutt at the time of the fire was that Ed "Junior" Thomas had a beef with a girlfriend who was boarding her horse at Sky Hi Stables. They got into a barroom fight, and in a childish fit of anger, she transferred her horse to Forest View. One night, Thomas and Spry decided to play a "harmless practical joke" on the ex-girlfriend—or, at least, scare her into moving the animal back to Sky Hi. Spry lit a bundle of hay on fire in the back of a truck parked outside the barn. The blaze spread after the brakes of the truck melted down, and it rolled into the barn near the horses and bundles of hay. Mark Hansen said there was never any intention to kill horses or destroy the barn or Cummings business. "My dad was really pissed off," he added.

O'Donnell challenged Grady's assertion that Hansen paid Spry to torch the barn. "So in other words, the information that you got in respect to the fire at Forest View came directly from Mr. Wemette? And you know that William Wemette has been an admitted liar in court? . . . adjudicated as being a liar in a fraud case? You know that?"

"No, sir. I don't know that."

The biggest challenge before the defense was to try to demonstrate reasonable doubt, but Stone and O'Donnell realized the odds were against them. The defense team brought in several character witnesses.

Linnea Sheehan, who resided in Beecher, Illinois, a small downstate farming town, spoke glowingly of Hansen and his treatment of children, animals, and his loyal customers. Kenny was firm but always considerate, she said. "Kenny was strict because the children were riding horses, and horses are very dangerous. So he was, you know, very conscientious about them always having their helmets on. He was always pleasant to be around. I used to stand and talk with him. He schooled my daughter quite often when we bought our second horse." Sheehan looked at Hansen to gauge his reactions. "He was very nice with the children."

"Did he demonstrate any violence or antisocial behavior?"

"Quite the contrary."

Gloria Redmond, a Cook County correctional officer, had taken horseback riding lessons from Kenny and his son Danny in the late 1970s.

"Did you ever see him be abusive?" O'Donnell asked.

"Never. I thought he was great. He was always helpful. You know, always around. He was always involved with the kids, helping out with the horses. He was, you know, very nice."

"Do you believe that based upon your experience with Mr. Hansen, your association with him, under the facts and basis that you've testified to here that he's likely to commit another crime?"

"I don't think he committed this crime," she said. "I don't think he would commit any other one."

Deborah Hansen, Kenny's daughter-in-law, was married to Mark Hansen in March 1995. Tragedy and struggle has marred their time together. It forged a uniquely strong bond between them because they have been forced to deal with the crushing shame, embarrassment, and emotional trauma inflicted upon them by Kenny's sybaritic lifestyle and the daily knowledge that the man they thought they knew is a convicted murderer. Mark and she were living together when, on May 9, 1988, their son Ethan was killed in a freakish accident. "A group of his friends from school came out to go on a hay ride. Before the wagon had stopped, he jumped out in front, and the horses moved up and . . ." Debbie Hansen's eyes welled up with tears as she answered O'Donnell's questions as best as she could before a room full of strangers.

"He was crushed under the hayrack?"

The men and the women on the jury were taken aback. What happened to Ethan, well, this was an unfortunate and tragic accident that obviously weighed heavily on the poor woman's conscience. Debbie lived with the self-inflicted guilt for years. *If only I could have done something. To have stopped him. Something!*

"Did you see Kenneth Hansen conduct himself in any aberrant or deviant manner with regard to children?" O'Donnell asked. "Did you ever see him in your presence commit an act of deviant conduct with any person, adult or child?"

"No. No."

"Did you have any knowledge or information—"

"No!"

"—that Mr. Hansen had ever been convicted of any crime? How would you describe his personality, temperament, and attitude?"

"I think he had a good attitude. He was great with the people. I've never seen him really get mad or upset. I think he was great with children. If I didn't, I wouldn't let him be with my son."

On the stand again, Mark Hansen said he believed in his father's innocence wholeheartedly. Later in an interview, he said that although he felt confident and reassured in the presence of Art O'Donnell, whom he had known for years, the young rancher had lost all of his faith in the judicial system. And while he believed his father was being intentionally railroaded by the state, he held out little or no hope for redress.

O'Donnell continued his questioning. "Now you were in the courtroom today when Mr. Robert Brown testified as to the conditions of the stables. Did you ever see the stable in any such condition?"

"No, sir," Mark said, clearing his throat. "It's always been kept up and maintained. The stalls were clean, and it was real nice."

"How did your father relate to children?"

"Really well!"

"Particularly with boys?"

"I never saw him try and make a pass or anything else at anybody." Mark released the hold he had on himself and rested his arms on his lap.

"How would you describe your father's temperament, his attitude?"

Mark stopped to think for a few moments. "He's very easy going and helpful to people. You know, he never turned down a person with a problem or anything like that. If they had a problem with a horse or something like that, he'd help them out. He's always been there for advice. Very friendly."

O'Donnell turned his attention to Kenny's marital relations. "Your mother and father separated some years ago. They ultimately got a divorce, I believe. But your father still kept very close to the family and to your mother I understand?"

"Yes." Mark narrated a story about a loving family who spent their summers together growing and baling hay and operating a livery concession for the locals.

"Is there anything that you've observed in your lifetime that would indicate that you would have any reservation in coming to the conclusion that your father is not very likely to ever have trouble with the law again?"

"I don't see any reason he would ever have a problem in the first place. I have no reason to believe he would get in trouble again." The young man's face tightened, and without moving his head, he watched O'Donnell walk back to the defense table and sit down next to his father. *Damn*, he thought, *if I believed that my father was responsible for my mom's death, I'd call for an investigation and whoever killed her, even if it were my dad, I'd help put him away for life!*

Cassidy approached the witness stand. "Did he ever send you to go hide out with Joe Plemmons so the law wouldn't catch you?"

"No, he did not send me there. No."

"But you shot your brother and your dad said, 'Go hang out with Joe Plemmons,' did he not?"

It was a childish mistake that's come back to haunt me, Mark thought before answering. "No, he didn't." Mark crossed his arms over his chest defiantly. "No. I didn't go there at all until I talked to William Wemette."

"And William Wemette talked to your dad, right? And you heard the conversation, did you not?"

"I heard one side of the conversation, yes."

For the next ten minutes, the prosecution put the witness on trial in an attempt to impeach his character, with pointed references to a near-fatal shooting in an altercation with his brother Danny and the alleged videotaping of young girls at the stables without their permission. The most irksome and insensitive questions hurled at Mark by the prosecution had to do with his older brother, who had refused requests to attend his dad's trial or sentencing hearing.

"Did your brother, Dan, tell you that your father stuck his tongue down Dan's mouth when he was kissing him?"

Mark winced as the defense team barked out objections.

"No further questions," Cassidy said, satisfied that he had managed to get in that word picture.

"Let's hope so," O'Donnell muttered as he took his seat.

By midday, the reserved seating was full. Most were anxious to hear from Yvonne DeMuyt, the last character witness for the defense. Beverly Hansen and DeMuyt had worked together at a bank in the fall of 1955. DeMuyt described frequent get-togethers at the Hansen stables. "I went to the party one night and subsequently met my [future] husband James DeMuyt. He knew Kenny from about the seventh or eighth grade. We would have gone over there more than them coming to our home, because they had the stable. Probably once a month, once every six weeks, maybe in the beginning."

DeMuyt said the couples saw each other frequently until the DeMuyts moved in 1968 to a little town north of Fort Wayne, Indiana.

When the DeMuyts married in May, 1957, Kenny was in the wedding party. The honeymoon was short, but Tucson, Arizona, was definitely heaven compared to the miserable Chicago winter that had just passed. Jim and Yvonne both rode horses at Saddle Back Ranch, a resort just outside of Tucson that had both English and Western saddles.

"While you were there, did you have an occasion to visit with anyone?" O'Donnell asked.

"Yes, we did. I didn't know the young man. My husband knew him. Herb Hollatz."

"At the time you were there in 1957, did you know what Mr. Hollatz's business or occupation was?"

"It was in law enforcement, but I'm not sure whether he was a Tucson policeman or a state policeman." After the witness first heard about Kenny's arrest, she contacted O'Donnell's office and asked if she could speak on Kenny's behalf because it was important to her that people know about the other side of Kenny's dual nature—the loving grandfather and family man.

She turned slightly to stare out the large window of the courtroom and gather her thoughts. The autumn sun flickered through the few dead leaves hanging on the thin branches.

About twenty minutes into the interrogatory, O'Donnell finally got around to asking the important questions. "Did you see any aberrant behavior on the part of Mr. Hansen with respect to any human being? Did you ever see him commit an act of violence?"

"No. I can't even visualize him even [being] capable of violence."

"Did you ever see him strike anybody?"

"No. He was not a physical person."

"What?" O'Donnell asked either because he honestly didn't hear her response or because he wanted to emphasize the obvious.

"He was not a physical person," DeMuyt repeated. "I don't think he ever committed a crime."

"Do you believe he committed this one?" O'Donnell pointed to the large black-and-white crime-scene photos stacked on the prosecution's desk.

"Well . . . no! I don't believe he committed *this one*."

"You understand that he's already been adjudicated? Is there anything else you would like to say?"

DeMuyt turned and looked at the judge. "Oh, I'd like to say something else, but I don't think it would be permitted."

As Cassidy recited his closing argument more closely resembling a funeral eulogy than a legal summation, Toomin appeared on edge. Years later, Toomin confided that he wasn't pleased with what the state was attempting to do. "I thought his arguments were improper, because it was an appeal to the emotions of the jurors. And it was not objected to by the defense." Toomin recalled that Cassidy used nearly an identical closing during the prosecution of the individual responsible for Cherie Rude's murder in 1965. "He replaced Cherie's name with the Schuessler-Peterson boys. [During the close of the Rude case] the defense attorneys, Sam Adam and James "Jack" Cuttrone, objected, and I sustained it."[2]

At the sentencing hearing, Toomin now had heard enough—"What did all of that have to do with the facts?" For the first time since the trial began, Toomin's voice showed emotion—anger, frustration, and grief for the loss of three innocent boys. He gazed at Hansen for a few minutes before speaking and then summoned him forward. Slowly, Hansen stood up; his hands shook, and his legs felt like rubber.

"Mr. Hansen, at this time the law affords you the opportunity to speak on your own behalf. If you have anything to say, you may say it at this time."

A hush fell over the courtroom. Barely audible and showing little emotion, Hansen expressed polite thanks and said, "Your Honor, I'm an innocent man. I did not commit these crimes. If anybody's a victim, it's me. The character assassination has been conducted with the highest magnitude. I did not kill those children. I did not run a hit squad. I did not burn stables. I did not do any of those things. I'm innocent. Thank you."

Attention focused back on Toomin. Although it appeared as if he had memorized his closing speech, he glanced down from time to time at a yellow legal pad resting on his desk. He outlined Hansen's life, from his "normal and wholesome childhood" to his having "no prior convictions."

The edges of Hansen's mouth quivered, as if he were trying to force a smile. He had wanted to take the stand, but O'Donnell hadn't allowed it.

Toomin lifted the note pad and turned back the top page. He commented that the lives of the three young boys "ended all too abruptly" and that Anton Schuessler Sr. had died from grief and suffering less than two months after his sons were murdered.

The judge took a long, deep breath before he began his list of the effects the murders had on the community, himself included. All of the stuff of the trial, "particularly from the photographs," brought back the year 1955 and the safer time before "[f]or those of us who lived before and during these times, all calling to mind, the sounds, visions of yesterday, muted in detail perhaps by the passage of years gone by.

"Recollections aptly named and described by authors and commentators as an age of innocence that came to a rather abrupt end with these three murders. Recollections . . . of a city where parents such as the

Petersons and the Schuesslers could and did allow eleven-, twelve-, and thirteen-year-olds to roam freely by foot, by streetcar, by bus, through its backyards, lots, alleys, traveling to different places of amusement and education without fear or harm of injury or molestation.

"Recollections of neighborhoods even then populated by people of different races, ethnic groups but nonetheless were places of safety, whether they were in Jefferson Park where these families lived or Douglas Park or Lawndale or Summerdale or any other neighborhood.

"Recollections of an age of unlocked doors, civility, and respect that ended all too abruptly, replaced by an age that we're all too familiar with. Whether these crimes for which Kenneth Hansen stands convicted of are measured or judged by yesterday or now, if I had to select one word that would sum it up, that word would be horrendous, because they truly were.

The judge explained about the trilogy of cases twenty years before that had "resurrected the death penalty in *Gregg v. Georgia*."[3] One of the judges on the U.S. Supreme Court had commented about "the ultimate penalty: 'The decision that capital punishment may be the appropriate sanction in extreme cases is an expression of the community's belief that certain crimes are themselves so grievous an affront to humanity that the only adequate response may be the penalty of death.' One would be hard pressed to deny that the acts and conduct of Kenneth Hansen would not fit within the pronouncement of Justice Paul Stewart."

Hearing a low murmur in the spectators' section, the bailiff called for quiet.

"But as we know, there is no death penalty for Kenneth Hansen.[4] Had his acts, had his conduct, had these horrendous crimes been discovered earlier, there is little doubt as to what his fate would have been. Little doubt that it would have been richly earned and deserved.

"Fate works in strange ways. And because of the passage of time, because of the changes and evolutions in the law, Kenneth Hansen escaped the hangman's noose, and he escaped the electric chair. Though he has beaten the executioner, what lies ahead may not be much better today, tomorrow, or in the evening of his twilight. Nor should it be."

Hansen's eyes deadened. A drop of perspiration appeared on his upper lip, and he unknowingly wiped it off with the sleeve of his recently pressed tan prison jumpsuit. His fingers tapped the edge of the defense table. He looked over at the sullen-faced O'Donnell and nodded his head at the same time.

"A just sentence here must ensure that the defendant will never be given the opportunity to harm those who are incapable of protecting themselves; that he will not again live freely among civilized individuals; he will not again traverse our streets or boulevards. He will not again enjoy freedoms of terror."

Once again, Toomin lifted the yellow pad of paper up and rolled back the top page. His eyes scanned the notes he had jotted down during the trial. Everyone was silent.

"Aware of the parameters of the law as it existed in 1973, Kenneth Hansen must be sentenced to a minimum of fourteen years, up to a maximum of any term in excess of fourteen years. Under the law as it was then in force, those sentences may be ordered to be served concurrently or consecutively," Toomin said.

"It will be the judgment and sentence of this court as to the jury's verdict finding the defendant guilty of murder of Anton Schuessler, that Kenneth Hansen be remanded to the custody of the Department of Corrections for a determinate sentence of not less than two hundred nor more than three hundred years.

"As to the verdict of the jury finding the defendant guilty of murder of John Schuessler, the court will also impose a sentence of not less than two hundred or more than three hundred years.

"And, finally, as to the jury's verdict finding the defendant guilty of the murder of Robert Peterson, the court will impose a sentence of not less than two hundred or more than three hundred years."

On her two-by-three-foot drawing pad, a freelance sketch artist captured the impenetrable look on Hansen's face. As Toomin delineated concurrent sentences and Hansen's right to appeal, the artist's right hand moved rapidly across the paper, capturing the closing moments of a arduous, emotional, four-week trial. Members of the media sat on the edge of their seats, scanning the room for the persons they wanted to interview. The mood of the court was somber. A few people who had sat intently throughout the entire proceeding hugged one another as if the weight of the world had just been lifted from their shoulders. Some were smiling, others looked perplexed.

Toomin pounded the gavel on his bench. The court was at last in recess.

Looking back on the trial from an eight-year perspective, Toomin called it "a horrendous case," but "people were watching it. It was a high-profile case, and I wanted to make sure that things were done right, that the *t*s were crossed and *i*s were dotted.

"I've been at this for a long time, and normally, I don't get involved emotionally. There were times when I'd feel things but didn't show it," he said. "I think that definitely at the sentencing, I got caught up in that. The judge has the last say, and I [was] kind of unloading everything that had built up for a year or two since I got the case, and that's when it came out." Judge Toomin said that he would have liked to impose the death penalty upon Kenneth Hansen but couldn't because it did not exist at the time of the murders.

As to why the defense did not object to the state's emotional closing, Jed Stone commented, "There is always a difficult issue raised in objecting to the closing arguments of our opponent." Stone continued, "By not objecting you let it pass and may waive the issue for appeal. Here I did not object but was convinced that homophobia of the prosecution was clearly documented and the issue clearly presented for appeal. In the end I was right. Judge Toomin's critique is armchair lawyering at its best. Was he reversed on appeal? Did Ken win a new trial based on our posttrial motion? Were the issues of errors preserved for appellate review? Yes to all three."

Kenny Hansen sat mute in an eight-by-five cell at Pontiac Correctional Center until October 1995 when Fox News reporter Larry Yellen persuaded him to talk about his life, the murders, and the guilty verdict. The two-hour interview was conducted in Ken's jail cell. "He never budged regarding his guilt," the investigative reporter told one of the authors. "He was very callous. I showed him the pictures of the victims. They meant nothing to him. 'Larry,' Hansen said, 'I'd like to help you, but I don't know anything about them.'

"As I think back on the interview, I was . . ." Yellen paused, searching for the right word. "I learned a few things about his private life. He was active in theater and student government when he was in high school. How does somebody go from being president of the student council to . . . " Once again Yellen hesitated. "The more I learned about his past, the more surprised I was that he committed these crimes." This is not to say that the veteran news reporter was convinced of Hansen's innocence. Yellen said he didn't have an opinion because he didn't attend the first or second trial.

He described Hansen as "friendly and engaging." Then after more thought, he said, "You know what surprised me? If, in fact, he was wrongly convicted, that he wasn't angrier. He didn't express that anger during the interview. He didn't seem to have the anger that somebody who was wrongfully convicted should have."

In a later interview, Hansen answered Yellen's assessment, "You know I've had a conversation with my minister [after the first trial]. I try getting angry. Joe Plemmons," Hansen sighed, "and Herb Hollatz, I didn't know him that well, but I can see how he could get himself involved with these people [prosecutors]—he was kind of a bragger with a big mouth. Uh, if what he said was true, he would have been the first one to tell his father. His father would have been a hero. His father would have ended up the commissioner [of the Chicago Police Department]. Uh, but, anyway, Joe Plemmons, Roger Spry, Bobby Stitt. I raised Bobby Stitt. I took him to school."

Hansen spoke at length about how he disliked and distrusted Red and explained that his heart was filled with forgiveness but no anger. "What can I say? I had nothing to do with those boys. What's supposed to be my response?"

In 2003, the authors telephoned and left messages for Cheryl Hollatz, one of the daughters of the prosecution's star witness, Herb Hollatz, who had admitted he had consensual sex with Kenneth Hansen and that Hansen had told him that he killed the three boys. When Cheryl finally returned the phone calls, her introduction was blunt—"I think my father killed those boys." She said that not long after the trial, she received a call from her dad. Surprised to hear from him after such a long time had passed, Cheryl listened as her father pointedly admitted, "I'll never forget the look in the boys' eyes before they died." The authors promised Cheryl that this stunning admission would not be revealed until after Herb passed away. Herb Hollatz died on September 23, 2003.

19

Requiem

LEAVING THE GRIDLOCKED EXPRESSWAYS of Chicago behind, over-the-road truckers familiar with the monotonous expanse of Illinois prairie land drink their coffee strong and black in order to stay awake. Miles and miles of telephone poles and cornfields, overpasses, and the occasional silo and gas station provide the view along I-55, the main road to Pontiac, Illinois. Pontiac hosts the eighth-oldest correctional facility in the United States, which opened as a boys' reformatory on June 22, 1871.[1]

Separated from the Far Northwest Side of Chicago by a distance of 101 miles, Pontiac is a maximum-security prison housing some of the most criminally violent inmates in the state. Most are former City of Chicago residents assigned to disciplinary segregation. Every thirty minutes, correctional officers check on the segregated prisoners. Within these drab and sterile, white and gray walls, inmates are accorded few privileges and permitted only a handful of items, which are included on the administrator's check list and must be preapproved by the staff.

Kenneth Hansen is Pontiac inmate #H70860. He is a permanent resident at Pontiac, following his transfer from the Cook County Jail. While certainly not the oldest inmate to mark time in the Illinois prison system, he is one of only a handful of prisoners past the age of sixty to be incarcerated at Pontiac. The populations of elderly male prisoners—like child murderer William Heirens, whose appeals for parole are repeatedly and predictably turned down—are, for the most part, lodged in the downstate Dixon correctional facility where conditions are far less austere.

Jack Reed and Sergeant Mark Baldwin, both of the Cook County Sheriff's Police, drove down to pay a visit to Hansen in 1997. They were intent upon unraveling the secrets of the Ralph Probst murder, a cold-case file for over thirty years involving a slain Cook County Sheriff's Police officer. Hansen's name surfaced in connection with the conspiracy to kill the officer in the spring of 1967, and Reed and Baldwin were anxious to learn more.

As they interviewed the balding, diabetic horseman with fierce, deep-set eyes, they took particular note of his buoyant manner. "He was very upbeat," recalls Reed. "A professor from the Northwestern University School of Law promised him that he would assist him in beating the rap [his conviction]. He expected to get out at any time."

Reed and Baldwin were unable to pry loose any useful information from Hansen. They were surprised, however, at the apparent eagerness of well-meaning "bleeding hearts" to embrace the cause of a man that in the estimation of law enforcement was a killer who had corrupted several generations of young boys for his personal sexual gratification. Kenneth Hansen had, indeed, managed to recruit sympathetic allies from among a circle of left-leaning attorneys and idealistic law students sincerely committed to overturning death penalties and sentences of Illinois prison inmates they believed were unjustly convicted.

Pushing the envelope on behalf of the vocal opponents of capital punishment, the Center on Wrongful Convictions at Northwestern University Law School prevailed upon then Governor George Ryan, a moderate-to-liberal Republican immersed in a "driver's license for bribes scandal" that had occurred under his watch as Illinois Secretary of State. The group asked Ryan to issue blanket clemency for all death-row prisoners.[2] Theirs was not a campaign of half measures. In the minds of Director Lawrence Marshall and the campus advocates volunteering time to the center, the Hansen case underscored the dangerous tendency of the Illinois criminal justice system to convict an innocent man for the most spurious reasons.[3]

Jed Stone alerted Marshall to a possible new suspect who came forward the day after the case ended, offering Hansen renewed hope. Marshall called upon criminal defense attorney Leonard Goodman, a member of the center's advisory board, to take up Kenny's cause. Executive Director Rob Warden, however, said, "We do not [currently] represent Kenneth Hansen, though I believe there is a strong likelihood that he is innocent. The case was and is very weak."

With no vagueness of purpose, Goodman set out to prove the verdict wrong on all counts. He would do this with the understanding that no fees would be no collected from the convicted man or his family. "Yes, I do a lot of pro bono work," he said matter-of-factly. "I pick and choose my cases." Characterizing the Hansen prosecution as "an absolute fraud," Goodman said there was "no evidence the kids were even molested. *They* [the prosecution] made it about sex."

Arthur O'Donnell, Hansen's family lawyer of many years, passed away at his California residence on November 7, 2000, at age seventy-six, after losing his battle with leukemia. Before O'Donnell died, he wrote an appeal.

Jed Stone, the showy and at times spellbinding cocounsel during the difficult trial, was not retained.

To pay for his father's legal defense, Mark had taken out a thirty-year mortgage on his farm in Crete, but the outcome of the first trial left a bitter taste in his mouth. He was not entirely pleased with Stone's handling of the case and realized when it was too late to make a difference that Art O'Donnell had passed his prime as a trial lawyer. "He was too old to be effective," Mark said. "He wasn't as sharp as he could have been, and he let a lot of things slide." Without the means to pay for a high-profile criminal-defense attorney to replace Stone in the second trial, Mark accepted the offer of pro bono help from the Center for Wrongful Convictions. Hansen's fading hopes for a successful appeal were left to Goodman, an alumnus of the Northwestern Law School and Jenner and Block, the downtown megafirm.

If Kenneth Hansen has one true friend left in this world apart from his youngest son, it is the serious-minded and reserved Leonard Goodman, who believes his client is a victim of overaggressive prosecution and the wild stories of hired informants. "Ken worked hard all of his life. He's a nice guy, but nobody special," opined the lawyer over drinks at Nick's Fishmarket. "He never put on airs, and his homosexuality caused him to have relationships with some extremely shady people." Goodman would base his appeals on the claim that the "improper admission of evidence" of three of four paid witnesses to the defendant's deviate sexual conduct with children was so prejudicial that the verdict required reversal. For the moment, at least, the linchpin to any hope of Hansen securing freedom seemed to revolve around a long-dead mystery man named Jack Reiling.

Shortly after Kenny's first conviction on September 13, 1995, Margie Mack and Joyce Saxon, the daughter and ex-wife of Jack Reiling, respectively, spun a weird but thought-provoking tale to members of the defense team, offering Hansen's lawyers fresh hope for a reconsideration of the verdict that had shipped Hansen off to Pontiac Correctional Center for three hundred years. Mack and Saxon said Kenneth Hansen was innocent of the terrible crime and that Jack Reiling, the father and husband they thought they knew, had killed those boys. After forty-plus years of self-imposed silence, they were finally prepared to publicly disclose long-buried secrets surrounding the triple homicide.

Jack Reiling—Indiana born but Chicago raised—was a sodden, violent man, whose life was raucous and discordant. He was arrested for numerous petty crimes, including check-kiting, fraud, and armed robbery of a currency exchange, and accused of siring babies with a circle of ex-wives and unhappy girlfriends and putting the children up for sale on the black market in a vile and disgusting money-making scheme.[4] Because Reiling was not a homosexual and unlikely to be cruising for pickups, what possible motivation could he have for soliciting three young boys on a street corner on a Sunday night?

Mack said she believes that her father picked up the boys at Milwaukee and Lawrence and drove them to the home of his sister Peggy Cavaness, a nurse who had lived in an apartment building on Logan Square Boulevard not far from the same elevated train station where Bobby, Anton, and John had transferred earlier that afternoon. "In back of the apartment stood a small greenhouse where Peggy grew vegetables and fruit," Mack said. "He took the boys out to the workroom of the greenhouse to show them hobby models, but at some point, he must have become very upset and killed them all." A greenhouse is a likely place to find the kind of three-pronged garden tool that was used to strike at least one of the boys down.

Joyce Saxon had said nothing about it to her daughter Margie until 1970 when the teenaged girl was planning to travel to California with her fiancé to reunite with a father she had lost contact with years earlier. Only then did Saxon speak up for the first time and tell her daughter about her father.

Saxon said that her husband came home drunk one morning and while sitting at his kitchen table provoked an argument with her. At one point, he said, "I killed those three boys." On the table was a newspaper with the story about the boys' murders, including a crime-scene photo.

Kenny's only hope was that Margie or Joyce would take the stand—which neither did. Kenny said he was disappointed because he was hanging his freedom on their testimonies.

"If Saxon genuinely believed the story in 1955, she would have come forward then," argued Thomas Gainer, assistant state's attorney, in reply to Goodman who based his petition for a new trial on the Saxon testimony in a May 1998 evidentiary hearing.

Saxon, a former nightclub singer, said she had her own personal reasons for keeping this deadly secret for so many years, but in a moment of candor, she also revealed that she had divulged this information to several acquaintances as early as 1963. Were her motives in 1998 true and honorable? That was the question that plagued Judge Toomin and the prosecutors in the first trial.

What better way to knock Jack off the pedestal on which his daughter had placed him than to accuse him of one of the most notorious crimes to happen in the City of Chicago? More troubling than the personal attacks against her credibility leveled by the prosecution team was Saxon's decision to accept an invitation to appear on a 1999 segment of an Oprah Winfrey show with her daughter and Leonard Goodman after first refusing to discuss the case or answer the questions of investigators. Mack admits she is disappointed by the outcome of her mother's television appearance. "The glare of lights bothered mom's eyes. They wouldn't let her wear sunglasses, and she was very uncomfortable all through the taping," she said. To compound matters, Winfrey abruptly cut them off.

Back in Pontiac, however, inmate #H70860 elicited a surprising outpouring of public sympathy resulting from the television publicity. Hansen, looking old, frail, and pathetic, was interviewed before a national television audience from inside the confines of the prison. "God gets me through," Hansen said in deep humility. "I sleep very well at night. I go to chapel twice a week. I put the whole thing in God's hands, and then here comes Margie out of nowhere. It's a miracle!" Kenny is a model prisoner, who turned to God for solace. He said he loved all children and animals. He works in the prison library, completes crossword puzzles as a part of his daily routine, and listens to "old-time country music" on his Walkman to assuage the tedium of prison life.

Margie Mack volunteers much of her time trying to reverse this perceived injustice, but her occasional missteps only serve to cast further doubts. From 1996 on, Mack has kept a research diary of her tireless efforts to unlock the secret history of Jack Reiling. The journal was later given to attorneys on both sides of the aisle to mull over, but she badly misread a set of prison records claiming that her father suffered from "antisocial schizoid personality disorder." It turned out that the records were for another inmate, not Reiling.

Jim Delorto said he believes the tearful daughter is probably sincere in her beliefs in an idealistic way, but her theory does not hold up. "Mrs. Saxon said she *knew* that Jack Reiling was the genuine killer because he just happened to be driving a green Packard in 1955," Delorto said. "Based on a few shaky eyewitness reports, the four Chicago newspapers published inaccurate information that the suspect vehicle was, in fact, a Packard. But there's one problem with that. The rubber floor mats creating the impressions on the [boys'] skin were also found in Chevys for the model year 1955—the same car owned by Kenneth Hansen. That did not come out in the press back in '55." Delorto knew this because he had attended a classic car show with his son Tony and the boy's friends. Mingling among the antique-car buffs, Delorto's interest was piqued by a vintage 1955 Chevy. The owner of the vehicle was inspecting the engine when Jimmy spoke up. "Can I take a look in the trunk?"

The puzzled man looked at Delorto.

"I'm a private investigator, and I was wondering if you have an original mat in the trunk."

The state's evidence, however, tended to refute the story told by Joyce Saxon but did not deter Goodman, who stood implacably before Judge Michael P. Toomin on May 26, 1998, arguing that Saxon's allegations raised enough reasonable doubt about Hansen's guilt to merit a new trial. Toomin sided with the prosecution and rejected the request for a new trial, declaring that whatever information the two women could offer at this late date "would not be likely to change the result of the first trial involving Hansen—in part because Saxon, who couldn't remember key facts, wasn't creditable."

Toomin's unfavorable ruling proved to be a temporary setback for Goodman and his team as they pressed on with fresh appeals. Meanwhile, Hansen bided his time in Pontiac, waiting to learn what God and a new judge might have in store for him in the months ahead. The earnest young litigator went on to ask the Illinois Appellate Court to weigh the improper admission of testimony from witnesses testifying to Hansen's sexual escapades as an unrelated issue that might have unfairly swayed jurors. "There was no evidence that any of the four [Roger Spry, Herb Hollatz, Joseph Plemmons, and Red Wemette] had ever spoken of Hansen's confession prior to speaking with government [ATF] investigators in 1993 or 1994," wrote Goodman in his appellate brief. In a split decision handed down on May 18, 2000, the conviction of Kenneth Hansen was reversed and remanded to the Circuit Court of Cook County by the Illinois Appellate Court.[5] Writing for the majority opinion, Judge Thomas E. Hoffman concluded "that the trial court erred in admitting the above-specified testimony of Spry, Wemette, [Lance] Williamson, Officer [John] Farrell, and Assistant State's Attorney [Barbara] Riley regarding the defendant's practice of picking up young male hitchhikers and sexually assaulting them. We cannot say that the error was harmless. Improper admission of evidence of a defendant's sexual conduct with children is so prejudicial as to normally require reversal."[6] In her dissent, Justice Shelvin Louise Hall argued that the pattern of sex crimes committed against young boys years after the Schuessler-Peterson murders was admissible because it demonstrated a pattern of violence and "renders harmless any error that may have occurred" in admitting the disputed testimony.

Leonard Goodman described his client as "just choked up with emotion, speechless," but even with that high note, Goodman remained cautiously optimistic. "There's a lot of information that has come to light since they tried him the first time," he said. "I think that there's a real question as to who committed these murders."

On November 30, 2000, Director Lawrence Marshall from the Center of Wrongful Convictions bestowed upon Goodman an award for his advocacy on behalf of the wrongly convicted at a festive charity dinner attended by a number of prominent public figures including Governor George Ryan, former Senator Dawn Clark Netsch, and Seymour Simon, former Chicago alderman and Illinois Supreme Court justice. Goodman was honored this night (in part) for "developing compelling evidence that the [Schuessler-Peterson] murders had been committed by a violent criminal named Jack Reiling who died in 1980."[7]

From the podium, Governor Ryan singled out the resolute young barrister for his work on behalf of Hansen and the other alleged innocents languishing in Illinois prisons. "Leonard Goodman is a lawyer who certainly could be doing a lot of other things than working on behalf of the wrongly convicted," gushed the effusive Ryan from the dais. "But he learned from his grandfather Henry Crown and his uncle Lester Crown that it is important to give back to your community, and he has decided to fight on behalf of people who have few champions and little hope. And I want to say thank you."[8] It was a strange and ironic twist that so prominent one of the Crown offspring should want to become so actively engaged in Hansen's defense, given the major role the Colonel's former protégé, the lackluster former Cook County State's Attorney John Gutknecht, once played in the hunt for the killer back in 1955.[9]

At the end of the year 2000, the Illinois Supreme Court granted Kenneth Hansen a new trial with a new judge—Mary Ellen Coghlan, a former assistant Cook County public defender and assistant Illinois attorney general—scheduled to preside.[10] "There is no bail until such time as this court sets a bail because bail was obviously revoked at the time of sentencing," Coghlan declared. Kenny would not be coming home for Christmas after all. Instead, he would undergo quadruple-bypass surgery.[11]

A few months later came better news. Citing a landmark U.S. Supreme Court decision, Coghlan ruled on March 27, 2001, that Goodman had met his burden, and Joyce Saxon's testimony would be admissible in the second trial. Whether Leonard Goodman would exercise his option and summon the mother and daughter back for another go-around was an entirely different matter.

The battle-tested litigants in this forty-seven-year-old drama returned to their respective corners to plot opening moves, knowing that the next time they gathered on Monday, August 12, 2002, inside the justice mill fronting California Avenue, they would be playing for keeps.

Leonard Goodman and Steven Weinberg, the legal team representing Hansen, stepped out from the elevator into a broad corridor carrying two boxes of files. They walked side by side in silence until they reached room 300, a courtroom borrowed by Judge Mary Ellen Coghlan because in her regular courtroom, visitors would have had to sit behind gray-tinted windows and listen to the trial through old speakers that crackled and buzzed.

Lawyers for both sides began by debating obscure points of law as the judge ruled on a series of motions that determined what witnesses and evidence would be allowed at the trial. Judge Coghlan hoped to avoid making the same missteps as had been made in the first trial. "I appreciate the opportunity to consider some of these legal issues in advance because I think it makes it easier," she said. "This will not be a trial by ambush on either side.

"I will not allow any allegations about Mr. Hansen's past sexual behavior—including testimony about a pattern of pedophilia." Coghlan urged the state to refrain from asking their witnesses about "what others said," not even for the words of key witnesses who had died. She did, however, allow a "few important phrases that fall under specific legal exceptions," but the lawyers would have to work around the gaps inherent in such an old case.

As the attorneys hashed out last-minute motions, the defense revealed that some forensic materials that could bolster their claims of innocence were no longer available. Weinberg pointed out some of the missing evidence would discredit the prosecutors' contention of exactly when the boys were killed. The evidence was likely disposed of because it was thought to be no longer of evidentiary value.

At sixty-nine, Hansen appeared worn-out in his dark-brown, well-fitted but old suit. With tie askew, he strolled into the courtroom. Few people, however, recognized him. *Chicago Sun-Times* reporter Robert C. Herguth wrote, "He looked like an absent-minded professor" in his dark-rimmed glasses. Alice Hohl, a young reporter from the *Daily Southtown*, had a similar reaction. She didn't think the defendant looked wanting at all. "Is that Kenneth Hansen? He looks more like an old professor."

Much to the surprise of the bailiffs, the courtroom was only half-filled. The men and women of the jury, although an entirely different group from the first jury, bore the unmistakable "Why am I here? He's got to be guilty" facial expression that was so disconcerting to Jed Stone and Art O'Donnell seven years earlier. Bill Bailey was there, in the second row, hoping to hear a crumb of testimony that would exonerate his brother the con man, Richard Bailey, who had been Helen Brach's boyfriend. Eleanor Schuessler's stepchildren were also present. They made themselves available to the media even before the second trial started and were very outspoken about their feelings towards Kenny Hansen throughout the second trial.

In his opening statements, prosecutor Linas Kelecius recounted the horror of the crime, describing the victims as "three ordinary American boys, dressed in baseball jackets and jeans. Three ordinary young boys hitchhiking down Milwaukee Avenue. They made the biggest mistake of their entire lives. They got in the car of this man." Kelecius approached the witness box and made eye contact with each juror before he continued. "Living witnesses and transcripts from those now dead will show that on nearly twenty occasions, Hansen discussed killing the boys or hinted he was involved in their slayings. Some [of the people Hansen told] were gay sex partners afraid to go public. He threatened [them] with violence.

"He killed these three angels out of fear that they would report his molestation," the veteran prosecutor categorically announced. "Mr. Hansen rationalized the murders by saying, 'It was either the boys or me.' Being gay was unacceptable in 1955."

Weinberg, the youngest of the attorneys, tried to derail the state's case by telling the jurors it was built on seasoned criminals, "con men, a pornographer, an accused arsonist, and paid informants." He cautioned the jury that they were about to enter "the ugly world of the Chicago horse industry" and would not like the characters who were intimately involved. He asked the jury to keep level heads and open minds. "You're not going to like the defendant either. But whether you like him or not is irrelevant."

The witnesses were by now familiar to the public. Hetty Salerno was older, but her testimony was still compelling. "The first scream—a loud, piercing, to me, frightening scream—came from the direction of the stables. The second scream came. It was softer, more subdued." Salerno wasn't sure who exactly said what but remembered that either her husband or a neighbor commented, "Someone is beating the hell out of a kid."

William "Red" Wemette, who had put on about twenty pounds, repeated essentially the same stories told to him years earlier by Hansen. Ralph Helm filled in the details about his walk home from the movies the night of October 16, 1955, when he saw the boys thumbing a ride on the corner of Lawrence and Milwaukee. "It was rainy," he said. "Blowing rain." Before Goodman ended his questioning, the witness expressed with certainty that it was the boys he saw. "No doubt in my mind that it was Anton. I never saw any car pull up. I don't know if they were picked up by anybody. But it was Anton I saw hitchhiking."

The defense team dwelled on the contentious issue of the food content found in two of the boys' stomachs. Former Cook County Medical Examiner Dr. Shaku Teas testified that based on the 1955 postmortems, the pasta in the stomachs of the Schuessler brothers confirmed in her mind that they were killed "hours before" the time the prosecutors asserted. "My opinion is if it is a fact that they ate at 1:30 PM, they couldn't have died at 9:30 PM," she said, pinning the time of death closer to 4:30 PM, which was, of course, impossible.[12] "Even at that time there was a question as to the time of death with regards to the stomach contents."

On cross-examination, Kelecius assailed Teas's testimony on multiple fronts and got her to admit that there was no specific mention of pasta being found in the lining of the boys stomachs in the 1955 postmortems and that other experts say that digestion of food content can take up to six hours. If the boys were slain late in the afternoon, as Teas believed, how would she account for eyewitness accounts placing them in the bowling alleys after 7:00 PM? If the hypothesis was accepted, it would require jurors to reject the iron-clad testimony of witness Ernest Niewadomski, who was the last person to speak with the boys before they disappeared. "According to you, [was he] talking to three ghosts?" Kelecius asked sarcastically. "Doesn't that cast doubt on your opinion?"

"I am looking at scientific evidence that is there," Teas responded. "Eyewitness testimony that night is unreliable."

On the second day, Cook County Medical Examiner Dr. Edmund Donoghue, who had reviewed the autopsy reports of the boys, rebutted the testimony of Teas. Weinberg asked, "Can the gastric contents determine time of death?"

"No," Dr. Donoghue said.

Weinberg drilled the medical examiner for five to ten minutes about the "noodle theory."[13] Donoghue provided a reasonable explanation as to why the macaroni found in the stomachs during the autopsy may *not* have been fully digested. The pasta was in soup and, therefore, not fully chewed. He also suggested that the digestive process might have been slowed because of the boys' "intense excitement" about going downtown. Beyond the issue of whether Hansen worked at the Idle Hour Stable, much of the defense's case rested on old information found in 1955 documents that there was undigested macaroni in the stomachs of the slain Schuessler brothers when the boys' bodies were found near a bridle path near the stable.

Weinberg trolled for explanations as to why the boys were stripped naked. "Could there be other evidence on the clothes? Manure? Hay? Horse hairs?"

"Yes," the doctor said in a hard voice, admitting that an insecticide, the type commonly used at stables, was found in some of the wounds. The defense argued that, in the absence of any physical evidence of sexual molestation, such an opinion was beyond the pathologist's expertise.

Now fifty-three years old, Roger Spry took the witness stand on the second day of deliberation with a defiant attitude—more noticeable now than during the first trial. In a heavy West Virginia accent, Spry said, "Kenny tried to hold him [Peterson] and [in] trying to keep the two younger ones from getting away, he accidentally choked one to death. They were screaming and hollering. He said [Jayne] helped him load the kids into the trunk of the car. He said they dumped them off in the forest preserve."

"Why did you wait so long before you came forward?" Prosecutor Cassidy asked.

Spry responded with emotion, "Because he lied to me! He [Hansen] told me Bev killed herself. But he killed her!"

Goodman reminded jurors that Spry was being held in an Arizona jail on July 23, 1993, on a charge of arson when he was offered a deal. "Instead of facing three to seven years in jail, you were going to get probation, so killing thirty-five horses became a criminal damage to property." Spry's girlfriend, Colleen Quinn, followed; almost verbatim from the first trial, she recalled the disturbing conversation the young couple had as they drove from Chicago to Texas and how Roger said Ken had threatened, "If you ever do that again, you will end up like the Peterson boy!"

The second day of the trial, sixty-five-year-old optometrist Richard Ritt was to identify the film he had shot at the crime scene in Robinson Woods in 1955. "The only person at the crime scene [when I got there] was an employee of the Park District." Ritt wasn't certain who had edited the film but said it did air on all four local TV stations about five hours after the boys' bodies were found. In the years since 1955, Ritt's grainy, 16 mm footage, capturing the images of the murdered boys' lifeless bodies lying in a ditch, had been transferred to VHS-tape format. The prosecutors rolled out two, twenty-five-inch color monitors that were hooked up to a single videotape machine. The press hung around to catch a glimpse of the 1955 film. Then the bailiff took one of the television setups and wheeled it into the judge's chambers. In the quiet of the small room, the litigants and the judge watched the copy of the newsreel play silently on the television set. After the five-minute sequence faded to black, Coghlan closed her eyes tightly and sighed. "I believe that the jurors should see the film. Not all of it, but some of it." For fifteen minutes, the attorneys dickered over what to leave in and what to leave out.

Just back from their midday break, the jurors stared intently at the video. It was the most intense moment of the trial. First came scene-setting shots of a sign announcing Robinson Woods Forest Preserve, and then images of the unclothed, pasty-white bodies of the three boys lying at the bottom of a grassy trench flickered on the Sony monitors. Jurors held their hands to their mouths, many looked away, and still others grimaced and inhaled sharply through clenched teeth. Hansen was impervious—or numb—to the drama played out before him. The film showed several items of clothing, including white jockey shorts and a boy's T-shirt, tossed in amongst the broken twigs and tall grass a short distance away from the place where the bodies lay. Using a tree branch, investigators at the scene picked up the tattered clothing remnants and catalogued them as evidence.

Deliberately edited out of the jury's viewing copy were shots of Harry Glos flipping the naked bodies over, as if they were life-sized rag dolls—evidence that the investigation was compromised from the start. The film was prejudicial beyond repair—at least that is what Weinberg and Goodman believed as they muddled forward questioning the next round of witnesses.

Anne Caldwell-Movalson was another equestrian enthusiast who claimed to have met Kenny in 1950 or 1951. Caldwell-Movalson had boarded her horse at Happy Day Stables, which she claimed was owned by Si Jayne. The young horsewoman showed horses, took people on trail rides, and often volunteered to ride with Hansen "because I was a good rider."

Cassidy handed Caldwell-Movalson a photograph and asked if she recognized who was in the picture.

"It looks like Kenny," she replied. Like so many young girls hanging around Idle Hour in the 1950s, she thought that Kenny was cute. She was almost fourteen years old; Kenny was at least eighteen. "I thought he was employed at the stables."

Goodman prodded Caldwell-Movalson with questions about who actually owned the stables, "Si Jayne or George Jayne?" The defense attorney said that if George had owned the stables, which was likely because at one point in the early 1950s, big brother Si sold Happy Days to George, then the person Caldwell-Movalson had a crush on who may or may not have been Kenny Hansen and would *not* have known Si Jayne. This, according to Goodman, was overlooked in the first trial. Caldwell-Movalson, however, said she was certain Happy Days was owned by Si because "My father said so."

Witness after witness testified to the crux of the state's argument—that Kenneth Hansen not only knew Silas Jayne but actually worked for him at the Idle Hour Stable and was, therefore, entangled in the criminal aspects of Jayne's violent world. The prosecution also maintained that after an argument with Jayne, Hansen moved his part of the livery business to the south suburbs.

The horse business world was indeed a tar pit. Get close to it, and it stuck to you. The testimonies of ATF Agent Jim Grady and hooved-animals advocate Donna Ewing attested to it. Then the prosecution called upon Dave Hamm, who avowed that in 1971, he had a conversation with Hansen. "I was with the Illinois State Police. [Ken and I] talked specifically about his discharge from the military in 1955. He said he knew Silas Jayne prior to going into the military and that he worked for him at the Idle Hour Stables in 1955." After Hamm's testimony, the state rested its case.

Ironically, Judge Coghlan had ruled that Glenn and Bruce Carter could not testify as evidence for the Schuessler and Peterson boys' "state of mind" because of the strict hearsay rules. The jury never learned that the boys were planning a trip to Idle Hour Stable. On the other hand, Joyce Saxon was allowed to testify that her ex-husband, Jack Reiling, who died of a heart attack in 1980, told her he killed the boys, but Saxon did not show up in court. "She's ill," Goodman, who fought so hard to get her testimony admitted, said little about her absence.

The Goodman-Weinberg team likely erred in their decision not to allow Hansen to testify on his own behalf, but Mark Hansen said they did a better job than Art O'Donnell and Jed Stone had done in the first trial, by prudently sidestepping the unbelievable Gacy defense and producing witnesses more favorable to Kenny's interests, including the Jaynes.

Frank M. Jayne Sr. reiterated, "Kenny never worked at Idle Hour in 1955. From 1950 to 1960, my brother Silas owned the Idle Hour Stables, and Hansen didn't work there. I saw [Hansen enough] times at horse shows to recognize him, and he was not [at the Idle Hour]. Heck, he didn't meet Si until '61 . . . '62."

Dorothy Jayne, Si Jayne's widow, stated that she was a former champion rider who had worked at Idle Hour from 1954 until it closed in the mid-1960s. She was composed, articulate, and very clear that she had never seen Hansen at the Idle Hour Stables in 1955 "or any time thereafter. Si Jayne had nothing to do with livery horses." Under cross-examination from Assistant Cook County State's Attorney Jennifer Coleman, the widow admitted that she probably attended a horse show in Kansas City around the time of the murders and that her day-to-day contact with the stable hands was only "minimal." Mrs. Jayne, who in her prime was one of the best women riders in America, indirectly admitted that she spent a lot of time out of town showing horses. Dorothy Jayne's testimony was supplemented by Barbara Beitzel Ashbaugh, who worked at the stables and said there was a night watchman there, and the gates and doors to the barns were locked at night. Trained Dobermans also guarded the property.

Dan Strong testified that he served in the military with the defendant. After Hansen was discharged from the service in 1955, he and his wife visited Strong in Texas. Strong believed it was in October 1955 but could not recall the exact dates. Rendered inadmissible at a previous motion trial was a letter Hansen had written to Strong dated September 16, 1994. The following is a relevant portion: "This is a cry for help from your old friend from Korea, Kenneth Hansen. The years have gone by and we seem to have fallen out of touch. I have never forgotten the wonderful time Beverly and I had with you in October of 1955, the trip to Six Flags, Mexico, Corpus Christi, Padre Island, et cetera, and all the rest. . . . My son Mark is trying to reach you to explain what is happening and hoping you still have some snap shots or mementos of that visit." The defense did introduce a box of photographic slides from the above-mentioned vacation. During an interview after the first trial, Mark Hansen allegedly told a reporter, "My dad said that my mom was mistaken when she dated the slides in question September 1955 and that the trip actually took place in October 1955." The box of slides was included in the trial, but the interview tape was not.

Although law enforcement and prosecutors were well aware of retired horseman Bob Breen, who said he heard no screams during his short stay at the Idle Hour Stables in October 1955, and neither had his daughter who corroborated his story, the defense team did not know about either of them, and, thus, neither was summoned to testify. Had he done so, Breen would have cast serious doubt on the tenuous Ken Hansen–Idle Hour connection.

By the end of the fifth day of the hearings, it was obvious that a defense team, for the second time, had failed to impugn the credibility of the state's four star witnesses—Spry, Plemmons, Wemette, and Hollatz. Plemmons admitted that for years Hansen was his good friend. Plemmons said he kept the "dirty secret" out of loyalty. But all that changed, he said curtly, when he "learned the truth" about how Hansen's wife, Beverly, lost her life, suggesting Hansen might have played a role in her death. "We were on the same side, and then he lied." The jury never heard that Ken's wife died allegedly by hanging in 1989 and that the death was ruled a suicide. After his testimony concluded, the defense attorneys asked for a mistrial, telling the judge the jury had been prejudiced by the testimony.

Cassidy recited his closing argument, which sounded undeniably like the emotional speech he made in 1995: "Your time has come, Johnny, Tony, and Bobby." In his closing arguments, he told a story about the three young murdered boys in heaven consoling each new child crime victim and telling them, "Be patient, your time will come; justice will be served." He talked about the three little angels whose innocent lives were taken by a monster.

"Sleazy witnesses are sleazy witnesses, but can they tell the truth on their best day?" pondered one juror. The answer, of course, was yes.

In their first vote, the jury of eight men and four women voted eleven to one to convict. A second poll was unanimous after a careful review of the witness statements. "That's how we came to our conclusion," said juror Mae Martin. "We went through everything with a fine-toothed comb."

The jury deliberated for less than two hours. Hansen was found guilty on all six counts.

Ken's inability to produce a suitable alibi for his whereabouts the night of October 16, 1955, was convincing. "If I am going to defend someone, I am going to tell you where my guy is," commented another juror who asked to remain anonymous. "We don't even know where Mr. Hansen was at on that day. And they never bothered to give us any explanation."

A barrage of reporters surrounded Cassidy, who said, "It is not so much about punishing Hansen, as it is about giving hope to [the families of] victims in other so-called cold cases."

Calling the state's case "Swiss cheese" because of its many holes, Leonard Goodman said it was "inconceivable" to him that the prosecution witnesses would have kept silent on their own volition all these years. "A crime does not go unsolved for forty years if the killer is a blabbermouth," Goodman said. He accused Spry and company of trying "to work their own deals," but the insinuation fell on deaf ears, as it had seven years earlier.

Weinberg gathered up his papers, and as he walked out of the courtroom, he was encircled by reporters. "Mr. Hansen was convicted twice by two different juries. What can I say," he said. "I believe in the judicial system."[14]

Family members of the victims said that two separate juries believed Hansen killed the three boys, and even though he would be eligible for parole in eleven and a half years, they believed that he'd never again see the light of day. "I think his time has run out," Nancy Kujawa Rauscher, Eleanor Schuessler's stepdaughter, articulated. "Twenty-four people have said he is guilty now, not just twelve," reminded Karen Kujawa, the wife of Eleanor's stepson Gary. Rauscher unclenched her hand from the tight grip she had on a religious medal given to her by Eleanor years earlier. She held it up so the press could see it and said softly, "She said it would bring luck, and it did. I held tight and didn't let go of it."

"Kenneth Hansen changed a city which has lived in fear since the day that three naked bodies of these young boys were found discarded like trash," Assistant State's Attorney Thomas Biesty said after the verdict was read. "Today, Tony, Bobby, and John are gone, but their killer sits right here awaiting justice. After forty-seven years, these three angels are finally getting some justice."

A group of defense attorneys who watched the trial intently whispered loudly in earshot of the press. "This wasn't justice," one man concluded. "The trial was based on emotion—if a child is dead, then somebody must be held accountable. Hansen was doomed from the get-go. How do you try a forty-seven-year-old case?"

Leonard Goodman, who was behind his colleagues, spoke slowly and clearly, "I plan to appeal the conviction. Cook County prosecutors failed to provide any evidence and relied solely on accounts given by informants."

Rauscher said she doesn't know if the family could go through it all again. "I'm glad it's over. Hopefully totally, because we can't do this any more."

Cassidy said if the conviction is overturned again, there will be another trial because the state will not give up the prosecution.

Jimmy Delorto and his partner, John Mazzola, sat in the unfinished basement office of their newly formed private-investigation firm. The phone rang, disturbing their focus. "Another slam dunk," Grady said, leaving nothing about the verdict to Delorto's imagination.

There wasn't much for the federal agents to say to one another, and nobody felt like celebrating. Delorto summarized, "I know that all three of us believe that Kenneth Hansen killed the Schuessler and Peterson boys. We checked everybody out, even Herb Hollatz. The stool. The trunk pad. These items left impressions in the muscle of John Schuessler's thigh. Hansen did it. There was probably somebody else involved, but Hansen's as guilty as shit."

"No words can describe the horror, the disbelief, and the shock that overcame my family," said Nancy Kujawa Rauscher at the sentencing hearing, reading from a handwritten letter by Eleanor Schuessler's sister, Beatrice Blane, who was ailing and unable to participate in the second trial. "How could a human being do something so heinous, so terrible to three young boys? This was not a human being who did this. It was some animal, some monster, someone not fit to walk this earth. But walk he did."

As Rauscher finished describing the devastation to her family, Hansen sat up slightly and leaned forward in his chair. "I didn't do it," he said in a loud, nervous voice.

The judge quickly asked him to be quiet.

Kenneth Hansen has maintained his innocence throughout. In the closing moments of the sentencing hearing on October 1, 2002, he stood before Judge Coghlan to make his one and only public statement before being shipped back to Pontiac.

"As God is my witness, I would not, I could not, I did not kill those children. Talk to my friend. I was in Texas or Mexico with my wife when the murders took place," Hansen said. Wearing tan jail garb, he stood between his two attorneys. "These stories that have come forth horrify me. If I were all of you and I heard all those stories, I would hate myself, too."

(In prison, Hansen refused to waver from the belief he was railroaded. In a handwritten note to Bobby Stitt given to Gloria Sykes, he said, "I know in my heart you were forced to do what you did and I certainly bear no ill-will. I think of all the good times with Bev and you and I relive those beautiful memories of all of us together while I am in my cell." He said at the end of the prison interview, "I had little hope of an innocent verdict, especially after the film of the boys was shown to the jury." He said the jury "had to convict someone, and it was me." Hansen still regrets that he didn't take the stand, but his lawyers felt that it wouldn't help or hurt him, so there was no reason to put him through intense scrutiny.)

Inside her tiny courtroom, the judge addressed the defendant. Coghlan called the slayings "vicious, brutal, and senseless." She said that the crime "forever changed our city and will never be forgotten, that such tremendous evil could exist and exists. . . . Words are truly inadequate to convey the horror of these young children. Kenneth Hansen will never ever have the ability to inflict harm on another human being."

"On a personal note," Delorto said, "in my lifetime, this was the most significant crime that was ever committed in Chicago. Perhaps in the United States. There was never another situation where three innocent children had their lives taken away from them at the same time. I can't remember another case where a pedophile, for whatever selfish reason, killed three kids. Just for his obsession, he squeezed the life out of these three kids. Gacy took one life at a time. These boys were younger than Gacy's victims. Hansen's a homosexual, but he's also a pedophile, and it should go as a warning for everyone just how dangerous pedophiles are. The laws are good. We should know who these pedophiles are. The reason we have these laws is because a man like Ken Hansen is incurable. Pedophiles are incurable. He admitted he abused over one thousand kids. He doesn't think anything of it. He doesn't think this is a bad thing. As far as I'm concerned, they should have killed the bastard, and if I ever have the opportunity, I will pull the switch."

Delorto glanced over at a photograph on his desk of his children—Michael, 18, Tony, 16, Melissa, 29, and Amanda, 27—and smiled.

Epilogue

> This hideous crime remains, however, the blackest stain ever inflicted upon Chicago as a place where innocent children could live in safety and their parents in peace of mind. Any citizen may be the one to turn up the revealing link. The hunt must go on, harder than ever. This crime *must* be solved.
>
> *Chicago Daily News*, October 25, 1955

MUCH HAS BEEN WRITTEN about the baby-boomer generation's "end of innocence," the closing psalm of America's last so-called golden age when our nation enjoyed a privileged position in the world. In the collective consciousness, the belief persisted that the attainment of middle- or upper-class status, and with it our contentedness to live out our days for the sake of the kids and the little acre of property we called home, made us somehow exempt from the violence of the streets that had taken root in the poorer, crime-ridden areas of our cities.

Whether or not we still buy into nostalgic notions that life in the 1950s was less complicated and more virtuous than today, no one would argue the point that the world we once knew has become quite a different place. Today, we lock our front and back doors and secure the basement windows with thick glass blocks. We install motion-sensor lighting on the roof of the garage to ward off prowlers. Kids attend martial-arts classes to learn defense techniques so they can protect themselves against the criminally inclined. Patrol boys and girls have all but vanished from the street corners they once protected, because most every child in America these days either rides a bus to school or is chauffeured to the playground by mom or dad. We know there are "bad people" out there. This is the nature of world we live in, and it is useless to ponder the whys and the wherefores of the matter, other than to say something went terribly askew in our culture somewhere between the era of *Your Hit Parade* and MTV.

Though, statistically, the number of child-abduction cases committed by strangers is not significantly higher today that it was in 1955, the media does a far better job of drawing attention to the problem of sexual predators. In turn, parents and national advocacy groups have rallied behind tough, new legislation aimed at isolating child molesters from society and have maintained pressure on legislators to do more. In response, Congress had passed tough, new laws requiring the states to implement registries of sex offenders and crimes against children. Is it enough to say that it is the nature of the times in which we live and simply let it go at that?

But we also know—or think we do—that it wasn't always like this. There was a time not so long ago when people living in the big cities didn't always bother to lock their doors, and only the members of the mental-health community understood the true meaning of the clinical term *sociopath*. When did trust surrender to the onrushing new realities? When did the world we thought we had made safe for kids by virtue of winning World War II and freeing the enslaved nations from the yokes of dictators suddenly reveal itself as a place of hidden perils?

One key date was October 18, 1955, the day the naked bodies of three young boys were found lying in a ditch near the Robinson Woods bridle path. The crime was made more grisly by the controversial decision of fanatical TV and newspaper executives to publish the stark and horrifying images of the unclad victims over the airwaves and on the back of the morning papers. Apart from the obligatory crime-scene photos of dead gangsters and hold-up men routinely appearing in the scandal sheets and tabloids of the day, the Schuessler-Peterson case marked the first time in memory that a graphic depiction of underage murder victims was shown in the national press and by the networks. Today, crime-scene photos involving children (and adults as well) are no longer published in newspapers. Addresses of victims and perpetrators are withheld from publication in order to keep the cranks and curiosity seekers away. The names of young victims are not released until their next of kin have been notified.

Echoes of 1955 and the crime that shook the nation deeply resonate on the Far Northwest Side of Chicago even today, where a graying population still shares the common values of family, parish, thrift, and self-reliance. Indeed, this is a very different side of the Windy City, separate and apart from the congested streets and flourishing urban life along the lakefront east of Ashland Avenue. Most residents of the trendier neighborhoods brushing up against Lake Shore Drive know very little about the bedroom communities of Jefferson Park, Norwood Park, Portage, Gladstone, or South Edgebrook.

As housing values continue to appreciate, the marked deterioration of the Jefferson Park and Portage Park commercial districts in recent years is a growing concern. Empty storefronts and vacant lots portend an economic decline and, perhaps, the final blow for the remaining ma-

and-pa shoe stores, bakeries, and ladies' apparel shops that welcomed families of the area in the 1950s. Today's residents prefer to do much of their socializing and shopping in the sprawling suburban malls.

The old Gateway Theater, where Bobby Peterson and his friends wiled away the hours on lazy Saturday afternoons in the "last really good decade" of our memory, is no longer a neighborhood popcorn palace showing second-run double features with a newsreel. Today it is a Polish-American cultural center. The former S. Rosenau Jewelers, an Art Deco building at the intersection of Milwaukee and Lawrence where many people believe that Ken Hansen rendezvoused with the three boys, was demolished in 2002. A chain drug store occupies the site. The streets that Bobby, Tony, and John knew so well in their short time on this Earth more closely resemble those of a ghost town than a hub of local commerce.

For many years, the Schuessler-Peterson murders tugged at the collective conscience of the community until an acceptable interval had passed, and the shared sorrows began to recede—but the boys were never completely forgotten. That is because the triple homicide is singularly unique in the pantheon of American crime. To the best recollections of investigators, it was the first time three children were abducted and slain by a complete stranger and for reasons that baffled the sharpest minds of law enforcement.

There was no evidence any of the three boys had been sexually molested, no ransom demand was ever phoned in, and the killer never once attempted communication with the families, as had happened in the middle of the Grimes investigation when an anonymous caller taunted Loretta Grimes with details about the girls only the mother could have known. Thus, the Schuessler-Peterson case has became an enduring subject of mystery and speculation, adding to a growing list of famous, brutal Chicago crimes constantly discussed, debated, and dissected.

Pondering the identity of that individual becomes a guiltless Sherlockian exercise in which everyone can freely partake. The Chicago child murders of the 1950s, however, represent a more complex cloth to unravel than merely postulating a killer's true identity. It suggests a bleaker, more modern reality—one that is more and more the subject of around-the-clock news coverage: sensational crimes in which children are targeted.

The fear-evoking crimes of the 1950s exposed terrible weaknesses in a culture deemed morally superior by conservative, church-going America settling into the slower pace of a post-war world. In the intervening decades, these crimes have come to symbolize the painful erosion of innocence that began in an era that we have idealized. The crimes and their terrible aftershocks were a metaphor of a changing America—a more violent America on the brink of reaping a great social whirlwind. In 1955, however, the gathering storm was but a gust of wind, a harbinger of the coming unrest.

A decade after the second reopening of the Schuessler-Peterson investigations, skeptics and nonbelievers still refuse to weigh the evidence and adjudge Kenneth Hansen guilty or admit there is even a remote possibility he was a participant in this savage act of murder. If the doubters were willing to concede the point, they would have to admit that Ken Hansen is a disappointingly benign stand-in for the imaginary kind of fiend crafted by the makers of our popular culture and literature. Lacking a mysterious and cunning archcriminal to embrace, we are left to ponder the harsh verdict leveled against this dull and unassuming murder suspect and, indeed, against all of the other pathetic wretches who commit stupid, senseless crimes, clog our prison system, and plead for redress. The first newswire photos circulated of the inconspicuous-looking horseman shortly after his arrest in 1994 reveal a face in the crowd of history: an average man—a working man.

Perhaps it is easier in the long run to believe in the existence of a ghostly, faceless bogeyman than to acknowledge that a real human scourge lived among us all along, managing all this time to outwit the sharpest thinkers in law enforcement. This is truly a frightening enough scenario, but perhaps it makes much more sense for doubters to reject the evidence out of hand and press on with the hunt for a more sinister force loosened upon the land than to admit their own vulnerabilities.

Skeptics will likely want to know why Kenneth Hansen never killed again after 1955, if, in fact, he killed at all. Did Hansen ever use the word *we* when he confessed his involvement in the murders to Spry, Wemette, and company, instead of the singular *I*? Hansen refuses to talk about it. He is unwavering in his declarations of innocence. The belief that an innocent man was denied due process and railroaded into prison is firmly planted in Attorney Leonard Goodman's mind. "The heavy-handed way in which the prosecution . . . " Shaking his head and staring down at the table, he does not complete the thought. How can anybody prosecute or defend a forty-year-old crime when evidence has been lost or destroyed, and the witnesses (if any) are either dead or unable to remember? Perhaps, in the final analysis, there is truth in the axiom, justice delayed is justice denied.

The authors respect the fine investigative work of ATF agents Jimmy Delorto, John Rotunno, and James Grady, but not all the critical information was presented to jurors by either the prosecution or defense counsel. In all criminal trials, it is incumbent upon lawyers to gather and distill all cogent facts so jurors can gain a complete understanding of the many complex strands of a murder case. In the Schuessler-Peterson deliberations, additional suspects were overlooked, and key witnesses like the Carter boys and Bob Breen (who might have aided the defense team) were not heard from.

Given the amount of evidence, the question we must now consider is if not Hansen, then who? Kenneth Hansen has insisted all along that he was honeymooning in Texas at the time of the murders, but the devil is in the details, and thus far, the horseman has failed to substantiate his alibi with dates, times, and/or places. Even a photo would suffice, but Ken could not produce a single dated image capturing the celebration of his and Bev's honeymoon, and isn't that rather peculiar? Does it not generally follow that a young couple would want to preserve the joyous and treasured moments of their early married life with an album of snapshots? "He *has* the photos," counters Goodman, "but they are dated a month earlier" and therefore useless to the defense.

Hansen maintains that upon his return to Chicago, he and Beverly relocated in 1955 to the southern suburbs to open the Bro-Ken H Stables at 8214 Kean Ave. in the village of Willow Springs. No listing for the stables can be found in the commercial Yellow Pages until 1960. Unless he was leasing this property from the Illinois State Toll Highway Commission (the then-owners of the one acre of land where the Bro-Ken H was situated), the historical record does not jibe with Hansen's account.

Ruling out the ludicrous notion that thirteen-year-old John Wayne Gacy lured the boys to his garage and murdered them before Daddy Gacy came home to read him the riot act, a handful of other potential suspects are left to ponder over—a small-time hustler named Charles Dahlquist, the former stable hand and star prosecution witness Herb Hollatz, the politically connected Northwest Side steel-factory owner accused of complicity by Detective James Lanners but never interrogated or charged with a crime, and the notorious stable owner Silas Jayne.

Within days of the boys' slayings, Detective Lanners and his partner, Robert Ekenborg, had other suspects, but politics and greed played heavy roles in hampering investigations.

"I grabbed two guys over at Si Jayne's stables sleeping in an old, blue

Ford," Lanners said. "I go over there on Higgins Road, and these two guys are in the back seat." According to Lanners, one of the guys was "a homosexual." "I was concerned," the detective said. "Homosexuals around all these kids."

One of the men was Larry Mallek, 23, of 4863 Northwest Highway, who was questioned and cleared of any connection with the triple slayings. He sued Lanners, Ekenborg, Lieutenant Deeley, and Sergeant John McNellis for $2 million in damages. Mallek, a cable splicer for Illinois Bell, claimed that he had been "beaten, kicked, and punched" by police and held incommunicado for more than sixty hours after his arrest, newspaper articles reported.

But Lanners said, "None of this happened. We were good to them. The vehicle the boys [Mallek and friend] were sleeping in looked similar to the car coming out of the parking lot where the bodies were found. This one guy was an admitted homosexual. The other guy, Mallek, wasn't; I didn't worry about him because he answered questions accordingly."

The law suit against the Chicago police officers was quickly dropped because, Lanners said, "Mallek was involved in ransacking the abandoned homes soon to be torn down to build the Kennedy Expressway. Mallek told me that his lawyer told him to sue us."

The art and science of link analysis are provocative and increasingly popular techniques of criminal investigation used to establish and prove the existence of relationships between seemingly disparate people that otherwise might slip under the radar of law enforcement. In recent years, sophisticated software programs like *Analyst's Notebook* have been developed to aid police and private investigators as they uncover conspiracies and hunt down killers.

Charles Dahlquist is a provocative and interesting candidate for an *Analyst's Notebook* research assessment of possible motives and complicity. The former golf caddy living only a few blocks away from the Schuessler family at the time of the murders kept surfacing in the preliminary stages of the investigation. Two eyewitnesses placed Dahlquist near River Road and Belmont Avenue in the company of a boy who resembled Anton Schuessler Jr. just three months before the boy's disappearance and murder. The odd coincidence? Or is it possible that Dahlquist, who was known to hang out at the local riding stables, spent time at the Idle Hour Stable during one of Bobby Peterson's occasional Saturday afternoon visits with Glenn and Bruce Carter in 1954 and 1955? After a flurry of renewed interest in Dahlquist in 1957, his trail grew cold when he served out a minor sentence in Chicago. A search of the Social Security Death Index reveals that Charles Dahlquist expired in San Mateo, California, in 1991. His name never once came up during the courtroom deliberations in 1995 or in the second trial seven years later. Attorneys on both sides of the aisle were never made aware of this man or his possible role as a conduit to Kenneth Hansen or to Herb Hollatz, the court witness who made the startling confession to his daughter of his complicity in the crime before he passed away.

Infiltrating the hidden world of Silas Jayne, a hostile and devious horseman guilty of fratricide and much more, may have cleared up some of the unsolved mysteries, but unfortunately it is no longer possible. Si Jayne died in 1987, taking to the grave a lifetime of secrets, including, perhaps, a final chapter to the Schuessler-Peterson murders.

The Idle Hour Stable remained open for business and a Silas Jayne holding. In 1962, there was another mysterious devastating barn fire. New generations of girls and boys, including one of the authors, continued to enjoy hayrack rides and Saturday-morning equestrian lessons in the company of rootless stable hands who would drift in and out on a whim (given the transient nature of the business). The day came when the nearby operations of competitors investigated and hastily cleared by police in October 1955 were shuttered and the grounds cleared for other purposes. In November 1965, Silas Jayne sold off forty horses and riding equipment at a public sale and closed the operation. The property was subdivided and redeveloped. Townhomes, a Dominick's grocery store, and an office complex fill in other areas of the property once owned by Jayne.

A few decades of land development quickly reshaped this lonely outpost of hay barns, horses, truck farms, and prairie land to undistinguished O'Hare sprawl. Heavy traffic whisks by the former location of the Idle Hour on Higgins Avenue. The defining characteristics of a stable vanished long ago, although two old wooden buildings predating modern development are tucked away in a remote corner at the back end of the property.

We can only surmise that the boys were hustled to some remote location on the open prairie where they were accosted and murdered and that the horrific crime did not take place inside the tack room of the Idle Hour Stable. Until someone else steps forward, the location of the crime scene remains a vexing mystery.

For the surviving family members, there has been a restoration of peace but little spiritual renewal following the close of a murder trial that established legal precedents likely to be studied for years to come. The Peterson family only wanted to forget the blackness of those days, nothing more. Through both trials, Eleanor Schuessler's stepdaughter Nancy Kujawa Rauscher clutched the St. Francis medal given to Eleanor by a priest at St. Tarcissus on the morning of the funeral. "She [Mrs. Schuessler] said it would bring me good luck, and it did," Rauscher happily told reporters moments after Hansen was convicted for the second time on August 19, 2002.

Lunatics and crackpots telephoned Eleanor and her second husband, Valentine "Bud" Kujawa, at all hours to threaten, cajole, and otherwise vocalize stern opposition to their betrothal so soon after the boys' funerals. The couple packed up the Hudson and escaped to Florida after the elder Mayor Daley gently suggested that it might be the best and only way for them to escape the hounding of the press and the meddling of the neighbors. "All I can say is dye your hair and move out of state," Daley advised. Eleanor listened and became a strawberry blonde. The couple took Daley's words to heart and drove nonstop to Florida. There they would remain for five full years, before returning north and beginning anew. Eventually, they made their way to Wisconsin in search of an elusive peace. Eleanor went to her grave in 1986 unable to reconcile or fully comprehend how so simple a thing as a harmless Sunday outing into the city with a school chum could take away her two sons and her husband.[1] *Because some men are wicked, the innocent must suffer.*

We cannot say that Ken Hansen is innocent of this crime—the circumstantial evidence that never made its way into court is most compelling. Nor do we believe that this one man subdued and murdered the boys on his own. By the same token, with the lack of physical evidence and the high probability that Roger Spry and other prosecution witnesses harbored deeply rooted hatred toward Hansen, there is room for reasonable doubt with respect to the guilt or innocence of the convicted man. Therefore, we would not be terribly surprised or shocked to see the 2002 conviction voided, and a third trial ordered.

The final question and perhaps the most important one of all is this— can we adequately protect our children from deviant pedophiles and other predators? Given the evidence before us and pedophiles in the churches and our public schools, the answer seems to be an unqualified no. Does it then follow that no matter how many times a parent warns a child to flee from strangers, the man (and the occasional woman) who solicits a kid for sex seems to know every trick in the book to lure an unsuspecting juvenile into his or her car for illicit purpose?

Parents must remain vigilant to potential danger and react to sudden changes or mood swings in a child's behavior. Sadly, the experts agree that there is no special "look" to a person who sexually feeds off kids, nor is it likely that there is a cure for such fixations. They come from all walks of life—they are business leaders, educators, contractors, Little League coaches, clergy, neighbors, trusted relatives . . . and even stable owners who attend to the care and feeding of animals. If anything, there have been a crisis of confidence and a loss of faith. And that may be the most terrible tragedy of all.

Lost in the dramatic windup of the Schuessler-Peterson case was the discovery of the ultimate fate befalling Helen Brach, catalyst for the original investigation of the child murders. But in the hush of an empty office late one afternoon, words spoken in confidence by a valued government informant opened a Pandora's box of old and deadly secrets. Solving the Schuessler-Peterson case as a result of Red Wemette's confessional was a private victory for Jim Delorto, a guy from the neighborhood who turned a defining moment from childhood into something far more personal. Bringing closure to the Helen Brach disappearance was less personal but positive validation of the skills and talents of Delorto—pure cop and cold-case specialist.

Agent Delorto revealed his private theory behind a stunning development in the Brach case occurring on October 1, 1978. A young Indiana couple, out for a walk in a dismal patch of woods near 159th Street and Wentworth Avenue in Thornton Township, found a partially clad skeleton not far away from the Calumet City sin strip.

Suspicions immediately arose that these were the worldly remains of an elderly woman, likely to be Mrs. Brach after it was ascertained that Helen wore dentures, and this particular skeleton had no teeth. The size of the clothing matched what Brach might have worn on her last day on Earth. Wisps of graying reddish hair found at the death scene seemed to confirm suspicions that this was the lost candy heiress, but Dr. Robert Stein, Cook County's first duly appointed medical examiner following the abolition of the coroner's office in 1976, said that the skeleton was a much younger woman and that Mrs. Brach did have all of her teeth.[2]

"Everything about the body was consistent with Helen Brach," fired back Dave Hamm. "How many other women do you know who wear pink and purple? The underwear, the clothing, the hair, the height, and weight—the two posts anchoring the bridge in the skull were identical to Mrs. Brach's dental records." Nevertheless, Dr. Stein remained adamant in his opinion that the skeleton of the Jane Doe was shorter than Mrs. Brach, who in her younger years stood five-feet, seven inches tall. A measurement of the remains clearly showed that in life this person was only five-feet, four and a half inches tall. The explanation for the inconsistency is simple, "Mrs. Brach suffered from osteoporosis. In her declining years, *she had actually shrunk* and was only five feet, four and a half inches tall at the time of her disappearance," said Hamm, who was closer to this investigation than anyone and has no doubt.

The deceased met a violent death. A moon-shaped indentation on the side of the skull identically matched the bottom of an empty Coke bottle lying only a few feet away from the body. The murder weapon was cast into the weeds and left for investigators to find, suggesting that the killer was arrogantly taunting law enforcement, in effect saying, "Come and get me!"

An astonishing thing happened. The skull of the Jane Doe, aka Helen Brach, turned up missing—disarticulated from the body. "Stop and think about that a moment. Who would have the authority to walk into the Cook County Medical Examiner's office to remove a skull prior to a forensic examination without anyone noticing?" Dave Hamm answered his own question, "Let's say a police officer is throwing a bachelor party or a birthday party for a friend, and he wants to a pull a gag on his houseguests. He drives down to the morgue and, in his official capacity, gains access to the Rose Room (where forensic remains were stored) and walks out with a skull, and no one is the wiser. That's one possible explanation. Or else . . . "

Or else, the theft was perpetrated by an individual acting in his official capacity for the gang of high-class con men known as the Horse Mafia. "Si Jayne didn't give a rip about who killed Helen," Hamm continued. "All he wanted was to collect the $250,000." The presumption in law-enforcement circles is that Jayne coveted the reward offered by the Brach estate and the Brach Foundation, one of the richest charitable trusts in the state. As proof of Silas Jayne's involvement in the conspiracy–murder-reward scheme, Hamm cites a secretly taped phone conversation between Jayne and Maurice Ferguson, a former Illinois Department of Corrections inmate, who was promised a job by Si once Si was released from prison. An exchange of phone calls followed. In one of them, the top dog of the

Horse Mafia was caught on tape bellowing to Ferguson, "Give them the head!" The plot to remove the skull of Helen Brach from the Rose Room allegedly revolved around a former Skokie, Illinois, police sergeant now living in the interior of Mexico. The sergeant had some prior dealings with the Jayne gang. Hamm believes this man in his "official capacity" must be considered the prime suspect in the theft of the skull.

As for Ferguson, he was summoned to Chicago to meet with Richard Bailey and the Jaynes to discuss the elimination of Jack Matlick, the Brach houseman who called Helen's dentist the day *after* she was reported missing. Matlick said that Helen Brach required dental cement, and could he please come down and pick some up for her? When the dentist suggested that this was a procedure only a dentist could do, and Helen should come over right away, Matlick ended the call.

Glenview Police questioned Matlick about eleven checks that cleared Brach's bank account after she had disappeared. Even more disturbing was his failure to notify police of her disappearance. He waited two weeks to place the phone call. In the years following Frank Brach's death, Matlick had became Helen's Rasputin—a controlling, manipulative figure who took charge of nearly every aspect of her pathetic, withered life. "I had the strange feeling that Matlick had taken over her entire personality," an investigator told *Time* magazine in 1978. "He even used her glasses to read."

The forty-seven-year-old former deliveryman failed two lie-detector tests and for many years thereafter was considered suspect #1 in Helen's disappearance, but a battery of police and private investigators failed to pin anything on him. "Jack Matlick was a party to the scheme from the very first moment," Hamm states unequivocally. "Cathy Jayne, daughter of Frank Jayne, walked in on a conversation and overheard them talking about killing Mrs. Brach." Cathy Jayne was not considered a reliable witness, and her testimony in *le affaire Brach* was discounted.

In 1979, the skeletal remains of the Jane Doe were interred in a potter's field, and there they would languish until 1990 when federal agents, the U.S. attorney's office, and detectives from the Illinois State Police launched an investigation into the thirteen-year-old unsolved murder. A series of forensic tests were planned. Looking to crack the mystery using the resources of modern science and technology, Delorto and Hamm ordered the skeleton exhumed. "I was hopeful that we could do some DNA testing. We got the order to have the grave opened," Hamm recalls. "However, we were later told that nothing could be determined by DNA with so much time having already passed. The FBI sent us a guy who was a *dentist*. A dentist! It was a cover-up for Stein, the whole damned thing."

The skull had once been lost or stolen while in the custody of the medical examiner, and then it had disappeared. "Yeah, that happens once in a while," Dr. Stein told Jim Delorto, who had to wonder how many other missing Cook County people would never be identified because of this kind of ineptitude.

Silas Jayne was in prison when Helen Brach disappeared, but few people doubt that he had a hand in it, from abduction to murder to cover-up. Time being money, Jayne wanted it done quickly and cleanly. Recalled Hamm, "Joe LaPlaca told us that Frank Jayne visited Si in prison two weeks prior to the day that Helen disappeared. The purpose of his visit was to solicit his permission to make Mrs. Brach disappear."

Another strange twist to the story was reported in April 2005 when Kenny's former protégé Joe Plemmons emerged from his self-imposed exile in a sleepy southeastern Pennsylvania town to bare his soul to ATF agent John Rotunno. The fifty-seven-year-old horseman said he shot Helen Brach in 1977 on orders from Curtis Hansen, who delivered the battered and unconscious candy heiress wrapped in a blanket to Kenny's Tinley Park stable. Plemmons and Ken Hansen unloaded the body from the trunk of the Cadillac, while Curtis ominously cradled a shotgun. "Put holes in the blanket, or there will be two of you in the trunk!" barked Ken's hoodlum brother. Plemmons hesitated then pulled the trigger—twice. He is convinced that Brach was "already dead" by the time the remains were lifted from the trunk and that he would "never have done such a thing" if Curtis hadn't been standing there. The woman under the blanket was beaten badly, that much he could see. Joe Plemmons pointed an accusing finger at the former suburban police officer identified by Delorto and Hamm.

According to Plemmons, Brach's lifeless remains were driven to a Gary, Indiana, steel mill off of Interstate 65 and incinerated in a blast furnace. Plemmons said he never forgot the awful smell. The memory of the rancid stench, a guilty conscience, and failing health compelled him to seek absolution for these old crimes. "I was tired of feeling the way I felt. There were at least some things I could get straight . . . for me, I am not a killer. I am not a terrible person."

The startling confession headlined Chicago newspapers in April 2005. Apart from offering the glib but imprisoned con man Richard Bailey a ray of hope that he might yet be granted a new trial, Plemmons's claim is unproven, and many law-enforcement professionals, including Delorto, are unconvinced. Joe Plemmons's history and his personal motives were called into question as the Brach case once again went cold.

Attorney John Cadwalader Menk, a former president of the Chicago Bar Association and named Helen's guardian ad litem in the posthumous administration of her estate, was convinced that the swindler Bailey and his cohorts were responsible for the disappearance of the Candy Lady. He had stared deep into the heart of the Equestrian Mafia and saw only blackness. "The horse crowd," he said with a heavy sigh, "can be ruthless and cruel."

Delorto and Mazzola's firm assists various municipalities with issues of discovery when they are threatened by outside litigation. The work is fast-paced and interesting, and from time to time Jimmy is called out of town. To the chagrin of his patient and long-suffering wife, Debbie, who frets over his health every minute of the day, high-calorie restaurant food remains a staple of his diet.

Jimmy's mother, who had been living with his family since 1995, passed away on March 11, 1998. She was eighty-one years old. Just as devastating was the death of his kid brother Frankie in 2000. His family had just finished a wonderful Thanksgiving dinner with laughter, love, and gaiety. Frankie stretched out on the couch to watch a football game. He fell asleep and never woke up. At the age of fifty-four, he died of a heart attack. Mindful of his own vulnerabilities, Delorto has quit smoking, one cigarette at a time.

On April 4, 2006, in a *Chicago Sun-Times* article headlined "Did someone else help kill the boys in '55?", Thomas Frisbie, staff reporter, wrote, "The authors of a new book say they've found evidence that the full story of the infamous fifty-one-year-old Peterson-Schuessler murders—in which three Northwest Side boys were killed—has yet to be told, including the possibility that someone never charged in the killings might have been involved."

After reading the article, Cheryl Hollatz, a daughter of the prosecution's star witness Herb Hollatz, e-mailed the authors of this book. Cheryl opened the brief conversation with Sykes by saying, "Did my sister call you?" The question was really meaning to ask if Cheryl's sister had told the authors that Herb Hollatz killed the boys. According to Cheryl, her sister had turned on the family. Sykes reminded Cheryl about their conversation in 2002, in which Cheryl said, "I think my father killed those boys" because he had said to her, "I'll never forget the look in the boys' eyes before they died."

Cheryl said in reply, "I don't think my dad did it."

Although asked to call back with a statement for the epilogue of this book, Cheryl never called.

The statement "I'll never forget the look in the boys' eyes before they died" is very strong and conclusive. Whether Herb Hollatz was really present when the boys were killed has gone with him to the grave. But what is known is that Bobby, John, and Tony saw the person or persons who murdered them.

NOTES / BIBLIOGRAPHY / INDEX

1. The Telephone Call

1. Judge Joseph Force Crater is a famous missing man in America. On August 6, 1930, after telling friends he was going to a Broadway play, Crater disappeared, never to be heard from again. Crater, "the most missingest man in New York," has become a pop-culture synonym for mysterious disappearances.

2. A juice loan is an organized-crime, street term in the big cities for making loans at exorbitant amounts of interest to deadbeats who cannot otherwise secure credit legitimately. The loans are typically carried out by Mafia "soldiers" and street collectors. Failure to pay back the loans often results in a terrible beating—or death. This practice is also known on the street as *Shylocking*, after the character in Shakespeare's *Merchant of Venice*.

3. The two gangland victims were Paul Gonsky and Patrick "Patsy" Ricciardi. Both were involved in the distribution of pornographic materials and the management of adult theaters.

4. Dr. Denton's are sleepers (or pajamas), usually flannel, with built-in feet and a drop seat.

2. No Indian Summer This Year

1. The sharp decline in the birthrate during the Great Depression and the national unity and sense of purpose in the following war years were contributing factors to low levels of criminal violence in America in the 1930s and 1940s. The uptick in youth crime in the mid-1950s was gradual, but it slowly escalated through the decade and as the first of the baby-boom generation approached adolescence. Statistical studies have demonstrated that the population group between the ages of fourteen and twenty-four commits the most crimes.

2. "Rock Around the Clock," a song made famous in 1955 by Bill Haley and the Comets, became the national anthem of rock-'n'-roll and rebellion. The song topped Chicago deejay Howard Miller's WIND top-ten evening play list in the late summer months of 1955.

3. Restrictive covenants were often inserted into property deeds to prohibit the selling of a home to persons of color.

4. In the fall of 1955, the Chicago City Council finally got around to repealing a 1942 wartime ordinance prohibiting women from drinking at a bar unless properly escorted by their husbands or other "suitable" male companions.

5. The local scene in the mid-1950s was re-created in the musical *Grease*, which originally opened as a play on February 5, 1971, in Chicago. *Grease* was written in part by Jim Jacobs, a neighborhood man and a self-avowed greaser who graduated from Taft High School in Norwood Park.

6. The Chicago forest preserves are swaths of greenery and original forest land preserved and maintained by the Chicago Park District as a historic reminder of the flora, fauna, and tall trees of the region before the arrival of the white settlers.

7. The *Schühplatteler* is a traditional Upper Bavarian folk dance preserved and maintained by the ethnic German fraternal and choral societies for many decades and practiced by first- and second-generation immigrant families and their offspring. The man slaps his heels and kneecaps while his partner dances around him. The literal translation is "shoe-slap."

8. Crown Point, Indiana, had achieved national notoriety a little over two years before when bank robber John Dillinger escaped from the local jail and the custody of Sheriff Lillian Holley.

9. By the 1990s, the factories and machine shops lining Touhy Avenue had largely disappeared and had been supplanted by retail strip malls.

10. In former years, this particular patch of Milwaukee Avenue real estate had been a disreputable "roadhouse" district, where Al Capone and his Northwest-suburban gangster rival Roger Touhy had battled for control of the bootleg rackets during Prohibition. In the 1950s, the Guys and Dolls Tavern and the adjoining Riviera Lounge were syndicate buckets-of-blood (that is, disreputable, tough bars) sponsored by Rocco "the Parrot" Potenza, a powerful vassal of organized crime.

3. The Last Bus Ride

1. A cultural icon in his day, Broadway columnist and television variety-show host Ed Sullivan graced the cover of *Time* magazine the week of October 17, 1955.

2. In 1956, Mike Spiotto was promoted to head D-3, a newly formed division within the reshuffled detective bureau of the Chicago Police Department.

3. Although Helm testified that the boy was facing south, which would indicate the three were looking to go north on Milwaukee Avenue, other testimony and evidence confirm that the boys were hitchhiking east on Lawrence Avenue.

4. A Time to Grieve

1. O'Hare International Airport and a strip of land connecting the terminals and runways to the existing city boundary line were annexed to Chicago on April 9, 1956, largely through the political influence wielded by Mayor Richard J. Daley. The strip extended from Chicago to O'Hare and included East River Road from the city limits at Lawrence Avenue north to Higgins.

2. The formal dedication of O'Hare Field and the inauguration of airline service from what would become a major hub began on October 29, 1955—less than two weeks after the boys disappeared.

---

3. Chief Ranger Daniel Conway bitterly complained to the press later that week that he had only two men assigned to cover the forest preserves from the south end of Cook County north to Touhy Avenue. That crime had moved beyond the decaying core of the inner city and was spreading into the outlying areas was a concept the hidebound politicians on the county board failed to grasp in their debate over law-enforcement staffing and appropriations.

Cook County Sheriff Joseph D. Lohman was indignant towards Don Gudeman and made his feelings plainly known even before the bodies were identified and removed. The crime had occurred outside the city limits and technically fell within the jurisdiction of the sheriff's police.

4. Child murders were on the rise. Earlier that summer, an eight-year-old South Side girl named Mary Manzo was abducted from the streets near her home while running to the neighborhood grocery store for her mother and was bludgeoned to death. An adolescent boy, described as a "mental defective," was quickly arrested and charged with the crime. Mary was the third child slain in Chicago in 1955, but the little girl's tragic death was only a prelude to the larger horror that was to come with the Schuessler-Peterson murders.

Sociologists blamed the rising tide of crimes involving juvenile perpetrators on the ills of the modern era—changing social and sexual mores and the shifting role of parents in an industrial society. "There was a time when boys lived virtually twenty-four hours a day with their parents or were apprenticed to adults," said Lloyd E. Ohlin, director of the University of Chicago Center of Education and Research in Corrections, to a women's study group that fall. "Now in large urban areas their elders are at jobs quite remote from the boys."

"In Chicago in the 1950s, there were no complex societal explanations of bad behavior," Alan Ehrenhalt notes in *The Lost City*, his fine narrative study of urban social forces at work in the insular neighborhoods of that time. There were "no histories of child abuse or substance abuse or low self-esteem, no failure on the part of insensitive parents or authorities. The explanation was that these were bad people—sinners. If you were smart, you kept your distance."

5. The coroner decided that rigor mortis had already come and gone, thus allowing the bodies to be "rearranged" by investigators. Livingston and the rangers he immediately summoned found Robert Peterson lying stomach-down with his head pressed up against the east side of the ditch. John Schuessler was lying facing north with one leg under the Peterson boy. Anton Schuessler Jr. was facing south and lying on his back. His hands were neatly folded across the lower part of his chest suggesting that the killer deliberately arranged them that way as a sign of remorse before fleeing the scene.

6. Cinema Processors, owned by Ike Bartimocca and Morrie Bleckman, was the only Chicago laboratory used by the major news media.

7. Walter McCarron was reelected to a second term the following year

8. In 1955, Forest Glen was an alternate name for South Edgebrook. Now the area is just called Forest Glen.

9. Statistically, the number of child abductions in the U.S. hasn't changed all that significantly since the mid-1950s, but a *New York Times* poll shows that in

1980, only 12% (or less) of parents drove their children to and from school. By 2000, the same survey revealed that 42% of parents who were questioned said they routinely provided school transportation for their kids, suggesting that adults pay far closer attention to the media saturation of a handful of high-profile child abductions than to the empirical data suggesting that children are relatively safe walking to school by themselves or with friends.

5. The Mysterious Marks

1. The *Chicago American* was one of the flagship papers of the Hearst chain and renowned for its tough, uncompromising investigative reporting.

2. PUBLISHER'S NOTE: Detective Lanners gave the authors the full name of his prime suspect, but the suspect was never charged with the crimes.

3. Statistics, of course, can be conjured up in various ways. For example, departmental critics and civic "do-gooders" often accused the cops of chronically underreporting crime. But, overall, the crime picture reflected a stunning 69% increase in the number of arrests made in Chicago between 1950 and 1954. (Buried in the favorable statistics were more ominous indicators. The citywide murder rate had remained static, and crimes against juveniles were on the rise.)

4. The boundaries of the district have been redrawn since 1955, but at the time, the Jefferson Park Police Station (aka the Irving Park District or simply Gale Street) covered the Far Northwest Side of Chicago.

5. In law-enforcement terminology, a *heater case* is a high-profile, front-page investigation demanding swift resolution.

6. Leroy F. "Buddy" McHugh, like many of his colleagues who covered the crime beat for the Chicago dailies, was himself the son of a police officer. He was one of the first reporters to show up in Robinson Woods shortly after the discovery of the bodies on October 18, 1955.

7. Early in his career, Patrick J. Deeley was taken under the wing of Detective Chief William "Shoes" Schoemaker, a legendary rackets-buster who investigated scores of Mob killings during the Prohibition Era. Schoemaker was the first appointed commander of the "Scotland Yard" investigative unit. With a powerful sponsor like Schoemaker in back of him, Deeley's rapid advancement in the police cadre was virtually assured.

8. Lieutenant Deeley was promoted to chief of detectives on January 3, 1956, replacing the ailing John O'Malley. Deeley named as his SIU successor Mike Spiotto, a twelve-year veteran of police work who lived in nearby Edison Park and knew the lay of the land. Spiotto was advanced to the rank of sergeant in August 1955 and lieutenant a year later.

9. Deeley was the unlucky number-two man in the futile search to find State Representative Clem Graver, a shady West Side politician in league with the Mob. Graver was abducted outside his Pilsen home on June 11, 1953, in the front of his wife, who was standing on the porch when the kidnappers' car sped away. Graver vanished into thin air, but Deeley and his men relentlessly grilled two thousand witnesses and even searched the sewers for Graver's re-

mains before the whole thing was called off. Clem Graver was officially MIA and may lie buried beneath the Grant Park parking garage, according to old and persistent rumors.

10. Before 1960, when Superintendent Orlando W. Wilson abolished the practice, police were often comped by restaurant owners and presented with cash gifts and other emoluments at Christmastime. While many business owners considered it a token of good will and were happy to reward the cop on the beat, some disgruntled shopkeepers objected to what they considered a shakedown but paid up anyway because they feared they would not receive adequate police protection in the coming year if they didn't.

11. Fifteen-year-old Judith Mae Andersen was a sophomore at Austin High School on Chicago's West Side. On the night of August 16, 1957, Judy went to visit Elena Abbatocola, a school chum. Around 11:00 PM, Judith telephoned her mother requesting permission to spend the night with Elena, but Mrs. Andersen told her to please come home right away. Judith said she would be home in twenty minutes, but she never showed up. Four days later, a typed ransom note arrived at the Andersens': "If you want your daughter, leave $10,000 at 3419 Janssen Ave." Police believed the note was the work of a crank until two days later when a fifty-five-gallon oil drum containing the headless torso of a young female was pulled out of Montrose Harbor. On August 24, a five-gallon drum with the girl's severed head inside was found in the water at the same location. Both drums bore the marking "EN-ARCO," a designation of the National Refining Company, but police were unable to trace the drums back to their owner. Fingerprints and dental records established that the victim was the missing girl. Commissioner O'Connor vowed complete interdepartmental cooperation and promised that his finest detectives would solve the case. Finally, in February 1958, the cops picked up Barry Zander Cook, a husky North Side construction worker who confessed to the July 22, 1956, murder of Margaret Gallagher, a fifty-one-year-old beauty operator, who had been sunbathing on the Foster Avenue beach. From his cell in the Joliet penitentiary, Cook admitted he was the Spyglass Murderer. (A high-rise resident viewing the lakefront from his apartment at 4980 N. Marine Dr. with binoculars accidentally witnessed the murder in progress, hence the press nickname.) Detective Sergeant Charlie Fitzgerald believed that Cook was responsible for the Judith Mae Andersen murder and quite possibly the murders of the Schuessler-Peterson boys as well, though lie-detector tests eventually cleared Cook of complicity in the triple homicide. Cook had met Judy in the offices of a Loop modeling agency where she was a part-time telephone solicitor and where his mother was employed as a consultant. The police later found out that Cook had been working construction jobs in the Austin neighborhood where Judy resided. On the night in question, Cook drove his mother to Midway Airport where she was to catch a flight to Dallas. Detective Fitzgerald surmised that Cook spotted Judy on his way home and lured her into the car where he shot her several times. The young man was relentlessly grilled by Fitzgerald, who was in the habit of sleeping inside the prison in order to be close to the suspect. Police had already built a

solid case against Cook for the Spyglass Murder, and an indictment quickly followed. Incredibly, a jury acquitted Cook in 1959, despite what appeared to be overwhelming evidence of guilt. The acquittal sparked public outrage. Cook served out the remainder of his earlier sentence at the Stateville Penitentiary and was quietly paroled in June 1967. Cook, with his supportive parents in tow, moved to Houston. In many respects, the officially unsolved Andersen case is remarkably similar to the Schuessler-Peterson murders and the 1957 abduction-slayings of the Grimes sisters (discussed in chapter 6):

1. All six youths were missing for some time before they were found.

2. All were found in or near water—the Schuessler-Peterson boys near the Des Plaines River, the Grimes girls adjacent to Devil's Creek, and Judy Andersen in Lake Michigan.

3. The six victims were stripped of their clothing and the bodies disposed of in such a way that they would easily be found by passers-by.

4. The Grimes sisters and Judy Andersen disappeared on a Friday. The Schuessler-Peterson boys were abducted on the sixteenth of October, the Andersen girl the sixteenth of August. Because the victims were slain in widely separated areas of Chicago, policing agencies discounted the theory that all three sets of murders were linked though the parallels are striking.

12. Appointed to the detective bureau in 1951, Jim McGuire rose to the rank of lieutenant in Chicago, deputy chief of the Cook County Sheriff's Police during the administration of Richard B. Ogilvie (1962–1966); and head of the Illinois State Police a year after Ogilvie was elected governor in 1968.

13. In the 1950s, *fruit* was a common designation applied by police to homosexual men.

6. Deadly Screams

1. In a backwoods grocery store, Emmett Louis Till allegedly made a sexual overture to an older white woman who was working behind the counter. A few days later, her husband, Roy Bryant, and his friend J. W. Milam forced their way into the shack where the boy was staying. They dragged him to the river and demanded a swift apology. When Till refused, he was beaten, shot, and tossed into the river. The south's peculiar form of justice prevailed, and Milam and Bryant were acquitted in a sham trial. The murder of Emmett Louis Till shamed the nation, and after nearly fifty years, there is renewed interest in identifying additional participants who allegedly formed an automobile "caravan" to assist Bryant in what amounted to a southern lynching. The documentary film *The Untold Story of Emmett Till*, produced by Keith Beauchamp, was released in 2002. Till's mother, Mamie Till Mobley, passed away on January 6, 2003, at the Jackson Park Hospital on Chicago's South Side. A seven-mile stretch of Seventy-First Street was renamed "Emmett Till Road" as a lasting legacy to the boy and the Civil Rights movement.

2. Edward C. Johnson, Michigan State Police chief of detectives, said, "There was enough evidence surrounding the two sets of murders to warrant checking the facts." In April 1956, Lieutenant Mike Spiotto and the SIU were on the lookout for Charles Ficher, a forty-two-year-old nurse from Muskegon who was in Chicago around the time Bobby, Anton, and John were abducted. The man had been accused of "making improper advances" to a twelve-year-old boy. "Charles Ficher" turned out to be an alias used by Herman Barmore, a career criminal and child molester who spent twenty-one of his forty-four years locked up in various New York state prisons. Barmore was arrested in May 1957 while in Arizona and was returned to Michigan where he was prosecuted on a charge of manslaughter, rather than first- or second-degree murder, in connection with the death of Gorham. The judge ruled that the state failed to show elements of premeditation. No link could be found to the Schuessler-Peterson case.

3. During World War II, the original Scotland Yard detectives brutally interrogated suspected German spies. In the tense post-war years, communist sympathizers, syndicate hoodlums, and other malefactors were routinely taken down to the "blue room," where, it was rumored, unspeakable tortures were inflicted to pry loose confessions. The unit was dissolved in June 1956 by an indignant Mayor Richard J. Daley after wiretaps placed by Chicago PD's "Scotland Yard" were discovered inside Democratic headquarters at the Morrison Hotel.

4. Within hours of the discovery of the bodies, detectives found a tattered shirt lying 150 feet from the bodies in Robinson Woods. It was the first compelling piece of physical evidence to turn up in the investigation. "Strips torn from the shirt may have been used to bind the boys' arms and legs, we believe," said Sergeant Thomas Mulvey. Detectives James Kennedy and James Mullaney easily solved the mystery of the ragged shirt. With the help of the laundry-mark unit, they traced ownership back to one John Bannach Sr., who had passed away in 1953. The dead man's garments had been given over to charity and wound up in the possession of a youth incarcerated at the Illinois Industrial Home for Boys in Sheridan, Illinois. The boy was ruled out as a suspect.

5. The *Chicago American* reported on October 27, 1955, "A police squad searched the Idle Hour and Timber Ridge stables along Higgins Road but found no clues."

6. Arnold Spenser Leese (1878–1956) was the founder of the Imperial Fascist League, a virulent anti-Semitic sect founded in England in November 1928. According to an anonymous piece appearing on a neo-Nazi Web site *Unity: Truth about Judaism and Zionism* (http://www.thirdworldplanet.com/jubel/jrm. htm), Leese was sent eight copies of the *Daily News* article in question by Van Hyning and was prepared to "investigate" the Schuessler-Peterson murders in order to establish "proof" that the boys were slain by Jewish cultists when he died suddenly in 1956, and all of the documents pertaining to the case mysteriously disappeared. On his Web site, Steven R. Centner (son of Robert Centner, former Palatine, Illinois, police chief and now deceased) had mentioned this conspiracy nonsense in his otherwise informative accounts of the case:

The coroner turned all the documents over to the DA's office and recommended individuals be prosecuted of perjury and murder. The coroner also made bitter remarks to the newspapers about the case. He received an official order from the DA's office to make no more public comment on the case. Several nights later a small bomb blew the front door off the coroner's house.

The Unity Web site writer states that "Dr. Leon Steinfeld" of the Forest Sanitarium flew to Switzerland for a "rest cure" but committed suicide in his hotel room. Centner then says that "the authorities" (and not Eleanor Schuessler) committed Anton to the home immediately after he took his lie-detector test, buying into notions that a sinister intrigue was afoot. The Unity writer calls it "house arrest." Centner qualifies his theory by telling readers that he is not sure if the father's death occurred immediately after the murders or six weeks later. In truth, Anton Schuessler was admitted to the sanitarium on November 9, 1955—a fact easily verified by a cursory examination of the Chicago newspapers. The Unity Web site further misidentifies Dr. Julius Steinfeld as Dr. Leon Steinfeld. Centner refers to the Cook County State's Attorney as the "DA." The District Attorney designation has never been used in Cook County. Nor does Centner correctly refer to Walter McCarron as the "coroner" (in fact, the Unity Web site incorrectly refers to him as "Dr. Thomas McCarron"), raising even more doubts about the dubious assertion that McCarron's home was bombed because he had publicly defied John Gutknecht's gag order. Was such a gag order even issued? There are no published reports of a bomb exploding outside of McCarron's residence or the director's alleged suicide in Switzerland.

7. Eleanor's parents, Mr. and Mrs. John Holz, lived at 3704 N. Southport Ave. in Lakeview, or what was then the city's "German Town." Charley Weber was a colorful personage; one of the last of the old-fashioned Chicago "saloon politicians." He represented the Lakeview community as state representative and alderman for nearly thirty years, up until the moment of his death in August 1960. Weber and wife perished under suspicious circumstances. Carbon monoxide fumes seeped into their upstairs bedroom late one night from the attached garage. Either by accident or design, Weber's Cadillac was left running all night.

7. A Case Grown Cold

1. F. Lee Bailey represented Silas Jayne in the trial of the defendants accused of murdering Si's brother George Jayne. Si was sentenced to six to twenty years in prison.

2. The Marjorie Hipperson murder was one of three puzzling slayings of young women in Los Angeles at that time. Marjorie's parents resided in Chicago.

3. There is a strong likelihood that Charles Dahlquist also worked at a local stable. A Chicago newspaper reported it, though it is not readily apparent that the stable was the Idle Hour. That Ed Kline, Charles Driscoll, and quite possibly Dahlquist were connected to the stable at one time or another, and all

were viewed as suspects suggests that it was at this crucial juncture when the investigation was blown.

4. Some reporters privately speculated that one or more of the boys were fruit hustlers. That theory was withheld out of respect for the grieving parents.

5. *DA* is short for *duck's ass*, a popular hairstyle for men and boys in the 1950s.

6. Wilson may have been confusing Charles Dahlquist with Barry Zander Cook in the Judith Mae Andersen case.

7. PUBLISHER'S NOTE: Because the spelling of the name is not known and there is no corroboration of the name, it is not printed here.

8. The murders of the Grimes sisters also brought to mind the Roberta Rinearson slaying nine years earlier. Rinearson was a ten-year-old west suburban girl whose lifeless form was pulled out of a ditch on County Line Road, dividing Cook and Du Page counties, December 18, 1948. The parallels between these two sets of homicides are uncanny. The Rinearson girl and the Grimes sisters were products of broken homes. A movie theatre figured prominently in both cases. On the day of her disappearance, Roberta left home at 5:30 PM to see a film at the Park Theater in LaGrange—just a short distance from her Brookfield home. Roberta was abducted, sexually assaulted, and strangled to death. Nineteen months later, the Lyons Police Department charged George Lettrich, a thirty-six-year-old alcoholic and thief, with the crime. Suburban police held Lettrich incommunicado for sixty hours while they tortured a confession out of him. Prosecuted for murder in 1951, Lettrich was spared a rendezvous with the electric chair, and his conviction was reversed on appeal to the Illinois Supreme Court. His sentence was eventually reduced to one to ten years in Stateville prison for sexual assault. Whether or not he was the actual killer or the hapless victim of the brutal police tactics common in that era remains a mystery. If he really was a "wronged man," a strong possibility exists that the Rinearson killer also murdered the Grimes sisters based on the striking similarities between the two cases.

9. It is interesting to note that Roberta Rinearson, the Schuessler-Peterson boys, and the Grimes girls attended a movie before their abductions. Is it possible that their killer or killers attended the movies?

10. Long-time residents of Willow Springs recall the rough character of "Liberty Grove," a remote no-man's land located east of Wolf Road and north of Columbia Woods where the nightly debauch between prostitutes and their johns inside portable trailers was indulged by local authorities. South Sider Larry Raeder believes that Liberty Grove, only a mile-and-a-half from the German Church Road crime scene, might be linked to the mystery of the Grimes sisters. Is it possible that the girls were taken to this disreputable trailer park and raped? Armed guards cradling shotguns patrolled the main road leading into Liberty Grove. The area has since been partially paved over.

11. Bedwell received ten thousand letters of sympathy from people all over the country who expressed belief in his innocence. Freed by Adamowski, the most famous "skid-row dishwasher" in America was extradited to DeLand, Florida,

in May 1957 to stand trial for moral turpitude against a thirteen-year-old girl he met while working as a carnival roustabout three years earlier. Bedwell was eventually acquitted on a charge of statutory rape. He hurried back to Chicago in August to live with his mother and hunt down a job in the construction industry. Several female admirers had provided him with enough money to pay for his Florida-to-Chicago bus fare. Bedwell is believed to have died in Tennessee.

12. Sixteen years passed and the investigation into the Grimes case remained open. Homicide detectives in the Brighton Park area reported in December 1972 that they "continue to interview up to seventy persons a year who claim to have some knowledge of the case." Most were dismissed as nuisance calls but nothing could be taken for granted. As hard as they tried, investigators were never able to link the two sets of child murders. No one was ever prosecuted for the Grimes murders, and the Schuessler-Peterson case would remain an even larger enigma for many years to come. "We didn't have DNA back then. Maybe if we did, those two sets of crimes would have been solved years ago," Mike Spiotto said, looking back on those days with a sense of frustration. "It was not unusual for all kinds of mentally disturbed people to come forward and confess to killing these kids. If a fellow went to a district and said 'I did it,' I'd have to go down there and try to prove it, and about ten times out of ten, they were repeating what they had read in the newspaper."

13. According to a letter dated October 14, 1970, from an assistant state's attorney in Gutknecht's office, Adamowski "not only continued this practice but he added more to each cash stipend because he felt the staff was grossly underpaid, etc."

14. For most residents and line officers counting down the days to retirement, Jefferson Park was a dream assignment—safe surroundings in a cooperative, nearly crime-free environment. Year in and year out, incidents of serious crime remained the lowest in the city. In 1967, a dozen years after the Schuessler-Peterson murders, it was the only police district in Chicago without a homicide to report.

8. Suspects in the Shadows

1. The assailants had driven their terrified captive to Joliet where one of them sexually abused her at knifepoint. The rapist and his cohort were never found, and the crime was destined to go unpunished.

2. A name amazingly close to but not to be confused with that of John Gacy who appears later in this chapter.

3. Kayo, a chocolate-flavored beverage, was popular in the 1950s.

4. The questions and answers from this interview appeared in the *Chicago American* on June 5, 1957.

5. Gacy, whose father was a first-generation Pole, abducted and murdered thirty-three teenaged boys and young men in the 1970s, burying most of them in the crawlspace of his Norwood Park Township ranch house, not far from O'Hare Airport. By the time the crawl space underneath house was dug up in December 1978 and the gruesome remains of the missing boys and young men

exhumed, the search for Frankenstein and Mr. Potato Head, which might have helped unlock the secrets of the Schuessler-Peterson case, was long abandoned, buried in the past.

9. Wild Horsemen

1. *Spin and Marty,* one of the most popular segments on the *Mickey Mouse Club,* premiered on November 4, 1955. It was the story of a snooty, rich boy, Marty, who shows up a boys' dude ranch, the Triple R, with his butler, Perkins. Marty hates the outdoors and horses but is gradually brought around by Spin, a cool kid who befriends Marty.

2. Investors and equestrians serious about owning horses purchase hunters and jumpers for competition purposes. The hunter variety is judged strictly on style. The rider trots his or her hunter show horse before a panel of judges rating the animal for artistry and graceful presentation. Jumpers compete for cash prizes in two-round competitions requiring the rider to leap over hurdles in the first round and essentially repeat the procedure in round two, with an emphasis on speed and time.

3. Hansen later claimed that he and Beverly were enjoying a belated honeymoon in Allen, Texas, and Mexico at the time of the Schuessler-Peterson murders. He cited as proof the birth of their first son, Danny, in June 1956. Beverly allegedly referred to her first-born as a "Texan by conception." Danny Hansen is three years older than his brother Mark.

4. The Bro-Ken H at 8214 Kean Ave. is gone; the original buildings were razed long ago. Local residents with long memories believe Hansen's stable suffered the same fate as two riding stables at 9400 Kean Ave. and a stable adjacent to the Bro-Ken H; that is, they were destroyed by an arsonist for the insurance money.

5. Judith Anderson, who engaged Hansen in conversation at Idle Hour in August 1955, should not be confused with Judith Mae Andersen, the West Side girl who was abducted and murdered in 1957.

6. Tragedy marred the Jayne family as far back as 1938, when De Forest Jayne, a younger brother of Si, committed suicide. The twenty-eight-year-old champion rodeo rider ended his life five days after Mae Sweeney, his former riding student and wife, downed arsenic in a fit of depression. Decked out in his favorite Western attire that Mae dearly loved, De Forest drove to Calvary Cemetery in Evanston, where she had been buried only the day before, and discharged a twelve-gauge shotgun round into his head.

7. Ace crime reporter John O'Brien relates a Silas Jayne story that never fails to shock or amuse the listener, depending, of course, on the person's point of view, concerning the humane and ethical treatment of animals. It seems that when Silas Jayne was a young roughneck chasing the girls and importing wild horses from the Western rangelands, a cantankerous goose bit him. Si extracted vengeance not only against the hapless fowl but by killing the entire flock as well. Whether the tale is apocryphal or has a kernel of truth to it is a matter for discussion. Other sordid aspects of Silas Jayne's checkered life are more easily verified and would later become of utmost importance to investigators.

8. From Edward Baumann and John O'Brien's "Vengeance and Violence," *Chicago Tribune Magazine*, January 3, 1988, p. 6.

9. Richard Bailey owned a stable at 9453 Harms Rd., in the forest preserves of Morton Grove. This was the staging ground for the sale of two worthless horses to the doomed candy heiress Helen Marie Vorhees Brach and other equally worthless horses to elderly women he seduced through lonely-hearts ads placed in suburban newspapers. Shy and rather quiet by nature, Helen Brach did not warm up to strangers and was ill at ease in most social situations. She much preferred the solitude of her sprawling Glenview mansion on seven wooded acres. But Richard Bailey was different than most superficial fortune hunters and tinhorns. Between 1973 and 1976, he coaxed the candy heiress into parting with $300,000 of her money on racehorses worth only a fraction of what she ultimately paid. Richard's brother Paul "P. J." Bailey became Mrs. Brach's personal horse trainer. He purchased three broken-down horses that were eventually sold to Brach for $17,500.

10. "Si always had fires," said Bob Breen, who started out as a groom and fox-and-hounds bugler at the tony Onwentsia Country Club in Lake Forest back in the 1920s. "Personally, he was a nice enough guy. He never got into killing horses but he might burn a barn down from time to time." Breen chuckled as he remembers one of the arson fires that turned bad. "It was a brick building . . . it wouldn't burn down! It seemed there was nothing he could do, so he decided to blow the place up. There was another incident when a man wanted a refund on a bad horse that Si had sold him. He never got his money back, and his house was blown up."

11. The feuding Jaynes shared the same mother but had different fathers. Si's father, Arthur Jayne, was a truck driver who had ties to Prohibition-era bootleggers plying their trade in the Northwest suburbs in the 1920s. George was the son of Si's mother and Waukegan attorney George William Spunner. George was born out of wedlock and adopted by the Jaynes. The antagonism between the two brothers can be traced back to an ugly incident in 1924 that had nothing to do with George, who was in diapers at the time. One night Silas took his sweetie Elsie Schultz out for ride in his roadster. In a dark, deserted location, he became amorous with the girl, but she refused to submit to his advances. Elsie was a girl of good moral character. She resisted, but the muscular boy she thought she knew had his way. She reported the rape to her outraged father, and charges were hastily filed. George Spunner declined to ask for leniency for the rambunctious young man in the mistaken belief that hard prison time might bring the boy down a peg. Justice was meted out. Silas cooled his heels in the state reformatory at Pontiac, Illinois. Si never forgot the shambles that his mother's lover had made out of his arrest and prosecution for what he considered a minor infraction against morality. At a deeper, subconscious level, Jayne transferred his loathing of Spunner to young George. The difference in age between Silas and George undoubtedly enflamed existing sibling rivalries, though Si's apologists assert that the problem rested solely with George, whom

they accused of stealing customers and doping horses to make the animals appear docile in the presence of prospective buyers.

12. Silas Jayne was married twice. After he was divorced by his first wife, Martha, "a tough old girl who opened a stable on the West Side," according to Bob Breen, Jayne married Dorothy McCloud, a champion rider, who remained his life companion until 1987 when he passed away.

13. Bob Breen pinpoints the origin of the feud to the moment Si convinced George to assume ownership of the Happy Day Stable at Montrose and Cumberland.

> George had a place in the woods at Dempster and Waukegan when Si asked him to come in. Well, Si had a customer—a money guy named Bill McGinley who wanted to buy a horse from him for $20,000. Si sent him over to George for just this one transaction, but then George kept McGinley as a customer on a permanent basis and made a fortune from him. That's when it started. George didn't belong in that family, and that's the truth.

14. The Jayne brothers made a gentleman's agreement not to interfere with one another and promised to refrain from entering into direct competition in the same horse-show circuits. The arrangement called for George to register his stable for shows in the far western reaches of the United States. Silas claimed the entire eastern seaboard and the Ohio Valley for his own, demanding territorial exclusivity. George broke the agreement and went head to head with Si on his own turf ten to fifteen times a year on average. Most men placed in a tight position by a recalcitrant business rival who violated the terms of a noncompete agreement would submit the matter to the arbitration of the courts but not Si Jayne. Si was a man who liked to get even. George and Marion Jayne were vacationing in Hot Springs, Arkansas, on January 28, 1952, when they received word that their seven-room home off Waukegan Road in Morton Grove had burned to the ground. On the same grounds as the house, the younger Jayne brother, a rising star in show circles, operated a stable with forty-three horses. A night watchman slept inside the barn, but he saw nothing. Silas was strongly suspected, but there was no explanation as to why the furniture was conveniently removed from the house a week earlier and why the water and other utilities had been shut off.

15. The blood feud claimed its first victim on June 14, 1965. Twenty-two-year-old horsewoman Cherie Lynn Rude was blown to bits by three sticks of dynamite planted inside the engine compartment of George's 1965 gold-colored Cadillac. Cherie was a fearless and determined championship rider from the affluent western suburb of Hinsdale. She had been trained by George Jayne from the time she was eleven years old and only a week earlier had captured a second-place trophy at the Lake Forest Horse Show at the swank Onwentsia Country Club. Now she was dead—her right leg was severed, and flying debris sliced her jugular vein. "It should have been me!" sobbed George to her grieving

parents. Moments before the mishap occurred, George tossed Cherie the keys to his car while he repaired to the washroom. Cherie and her boss were scheduled to drive out to Hinsdale that afternoon to pick up a horse. The pretty, dark-haired equestrian rider had worked as an instructor the three years leading up to the murder. Aware of the volatility of the feud and fearing for her personal safety, Cherie Rude began carrying a loaded pistol with her at all times—in the glove compartment of her car and in her riding clothes. She fully understood the serious threats leveled against her employer but was loyal to him right up to the bitter end. The murder of Cherie Lynn Rude would go unsolved for the next thirty-four years.

A jury convicted James Blottiaux of the Cherie Rude murder on July 15, 1999, two years after Cook County State's Attorney Dick Devine indicted him for the murder-for-hire scheme linked to Silas Jayne. The court imposed a hundred-to-three-hundred-year prison sentence, bringing an end to a mystery that had plagued law enforcement for decades. A truck driver and garage owner at the time of his arrest, Blottiaux had worked at the Idle Hour Stables in the 1960s. He was allegedly offered $10,000 by Silas Jayne to kill George. It was determined that Blottiaux and various accomplices took part in eleven bombings between June 1962 and October 1966, gaining proficiency by detonating blasting caps on the bank of the Cal-Sag Canal near Lemont, Illinois. With practice and refinement of technique, Blottiaux was able to rig a bomb to a car in eight seconds. With better central coordination among agencies at the time the crime was committed, Cherie's killer might have been apprehended immediately. In 1963, Blottiaux and an accomplice named Thomas Hanna were arrested after a pipe bomb was found in their automobile during a routine traffic stop. Efforts to indict Blottiaux during the George Jayne murder investigation fell short after Ruth Engel, a key witness for the prosecution who was present at Tri-Color Stable on June 14, 1965, did not appear one hundred percent credible to ASA Nick Motherway. "Just how sure are you, Miss Engel?" asked Motherway. Engel beamed, "I'll be as sure as you want me to be!" Moments later, she was discharged. In 1995, police again picked up Blottiaux, this time on a weapons violation. The state originally zeroed in on Hanna as a suspect, but the case was blown. It took many years, but in 1999, Blottiaux was finally convicted as a result of the tireless investigation led by a task force of agents from the Bureau of Alcohol, Tobacco, and Firearms, the Cook County Sheriff's Police, and Chicago homicide detectives. They cultivated Hanna as the key informant who would be willing to go on record after thirty-two years and finger Blottiaux. According to James Delorto, Hanna provided Blottiaux with a vehicle used in connection with the Rude bombing. The explosive device was rigged together by a third man, Haldane Clemmensen, a friend of Blottiaux from Port Townsend, Washington, whose name surfaced in the trial. When Jim Grady and John Rotunno, the ATF agents who investigated the case, turned up at Clemmensen's place of residence in Omaha, Nebraska, the surprised bomber asked Rotunno, "So what took you so long?" Only one surviving relative of Cherie Rude, her sister Marla, was on hand to see justice served. She made the journey in from Oklahoma.

16. On the twenty-year anniversary of the Probst slaying, CCSPD officer Robert Borowski took out newspaper ads soliciting information from the public that might shed light on the murder of his friend and partner.

17. By 1970, Hansen had merged Sky Hi and High Hopes into one location—Sky Hi Hopes at the Central Avenue location in Tinley Park. He advertised "hunters & jumpers" and riding instructions.

18. In 1988, Lieutenant Reed cracked a six-year-old murder mystery exposing a seamy web of police corruption in his own department and in the south suburban municipalities. Dianne Turner Masters disappeared in December 1982. Her remains were pulled from the trunk of a submerged Cadillac dumped in the Chicago Sanitary and Ship Canal in Willow Springs. Reed pinned the murder on Dianne's estranged husband, Alan Masters, a corrupt suburban attorney, and Willow Springs Police Chief Michael Corbitt, a former Kenny Hansen stable hand. Both were convicted on murder-conspiracy charges. The case inspired two books and a 1992 TV movie titled *Deadly Matrimony*, starring Brian Dennehy as Detective Sergeant Jack Reed. The actor reprised the role in several other TV movies including *A Search for Justice* and *Badge of Honor*. Reed is no longer in law enforcement. His confidence in the integrity of the sheriff's office shaken by the politicized nature of the department, the inertia he encountered during the Probst investigation, and unpunished corruption, he retired in 1998. He is presently employed in the private-security industry.

19. "Mad" Sam DeStefano, a forty-year veteran of Chicago organized crime, was shotgunned to death inside the garage of his house on April 14, 1973. He was awaiting trial for the murder of Leo Foreman, president of a small insurance agency.

20. Marion Jayne's accomplishments in the world of sport were considerable. Married to George Jayne in 1944 at the tender age of seventeen, Marion was already a skilled athlete destined for greatness. At age thirteen, she participated in the Olympic diving trials. Under George's tutelage, she evolved into a world-class equestrian and was among the first to jump a horse over a seven-foot fence. In the 1950s and 1960s, she cofounded several stables with her husband that likely placed her in harm's way with respect to Silas. She is best remembered today as a top aviatrix, beginning as a Powder Puff tournament competitor before going on to win twenty-six first-place victories in cross-country speed-racing. Featured on CNN, CBS, ABC, and other television outlets, she is the only U.S. pilot to have raced her plane twice around the world. Mrs. Jayne founded the Grand Prix Air Race and cofounded the Air Race Classic. A third competition event was re-named the Marion Jayne U.S. Air Race following her death in Denton, Texas, on December 14, 1996, at age seventy.

21. Formal and dignified in appearance and manner, Robert Lee Brown was a party to the horse swindles engineered against elderly women by the gigolo and con man Richard Bailey. According to Gretchen Reynolds, Brown acted as a "sympathetic intermediary" between Bailey and Carol Karstenson, the wealthy widow of a Sears executive who was cheated out of $193,000 while hospitalized in Evanston. When she threatened Bailey and his confederates with exposure,

her family barn was burned down. She was also thrown from a horse when a mysterious car suddenly veered in front of her, and death threats were received at her home. Reynolds quotes an unnamed source: "These were very sophisticated con games. Bailey, Brown, the others—they all had their particular established role to play." Brown is one of the threads linking Silas Jayne and Richard Bailey to Kenneth Hansen. In 1995, Brown was convicted of one count each of racketeering, mail, and wire fraud. He was sentenced to fourteen months in prison, a $2,000 fine, and three hundred hours of community service.

22. Curtis Hansen is believed to have participated in a raft of unsolved contract murders. In his peak-earning years, Curtis was aligned to a bevy of powerful hoodlums including the late Vince Solano, Mike Glitta, and James "Monk" Allegretti, who ran prostitution and gambling on the North Side, and Jimmy "the Bomber" Catuara and Albert "Caesar" Tocco, overseers of the chop-shop racket in the southern suburbs. Curt owned the Valley View Young Adults Club (YAK, pronounced *yak*), an after-hours social club for area teens until a mysterious fire destroyed the building. Curt blamed it on a faulty electrical system, but given the history of arson fires linked to the Jaynes and Ken Hansen, the story sounds dubious. Suffering the ravages of cancer and diabetes, Curtis passed away in 1993 at a veteran's hospital. Wemette lived at Ken Hansen's Sky Hi Stables in Tinley Park for several years "between 1968 and 1973" and assisted Hansen in the procurement of young boys by his own account. Wemette was an FBI mole from August 1971 until 1989.

23. Hansen later changed the name to the Camelot Stables and operated the business until 1987, when the property was sold.

24. For clarification, Frank Jayne Sr. was Si's brother. Frank Jayne Jr. is Si's nephew. Frank Jayne Jr. was charged with hiring a man to set fire to Junior's Northwestern Stables in Morton Grove, Illinois, in 1984 for the $88,000 in insurance money. On June 26, 2003, the trial ended with a hung jury, and the judge declared a mistrial.

10. *Till Death Do We Part*

1. Mark Hansen disputes this. He says he is unaware of any purchase of furniture made by his mother. James Delorto related this version of events.

2. For a chilling but clinical description of common personality traits manifested by psychopaths, see *Psychopathy: Theory, Research, and Implications for Society* by David J. Cooke, Adelle E. Forth, and Robert D. Hare. Hare is a member of the Department of Psychology at the University of British Columbia in Vancouver, Canada, and is regarded by many to be the preeminent scholar in the field today.

3. See Cooke, Forth, and Hare, *Psychopathy: Theory, Research and Implications for Society*, 129.

12. *"Oh, by the Way . . ."*

1. The term *ghetto* is law enforcement slang for inner-city-gang crimes investigations.

2. Claremont Avenue is located on the Northwest Side of Chicago.

3. Danny Hansen is three years older than his brother, Mark. Danny operates the White Birch Farm in the northern suburbs of Chicago.

4. Beverly is referring to Roger Spry, the "throwaway boy" the Hansens had "adopted."

13. Born into Misery

1. Hansen's attorneys denied such an arrangement had ever occurred. Kenny's son Mark testified that Roger slept contentedly in his own bedroom upstairs and not with the dogs. However, Mark would have been too young to remember Spry's arrival.

2. The Hansen residence at the Bro-Ken H burned down forcing the family to move to a cottage at the back of the property. For a brief spell, the family lived in Bridgeview and then finally at the Sky Hi Hopes (later renamed Camelot).

3. Spry corroborated Red Wemette's statements regarding Farmer, Ryder, and Brown.

4. Forest View Farms remains in business. Opened in the 1950s, the stable provides hayrides, trail rides, and Western-style riding.

5. This information is from an interview with Roger Spry at Glenview, Illinois, by James Delorto and David Hamm on November 14, 1991.

6. Country singer Johnny Cash recorded one of his most famous albums at Folsom Prison. It is currently home to Charles Manson and Erik Menendez.

7. Wemette testified that Hansen has said that the two older boys were on a horse or a pony, and he had taken the youngest boy (Anton) into a separate room and performed fellation on him. He then sent the younger boy out and had John come in. Anton told Bobby what had happened and that they needed to get his brother out and should call their parents and the police.

8. Presumably it was Robert Peterson who put up the greatest resistance and was the first to die.

9. At the time of the first investigation, the SIU was reasonably certain that the bodies were not placed in Robinson Woods until late Tuesday morning, based on the account of Edward and Herman Rohlfes and other passersby.

10. Kenneth Hansen's lawyers contended that the amount of money paid to Spry was closer to $8,000. In exchange for his testimony in court against Ken Hansen, felony arson charges filed against Spry for the August 14, 1970, Forest View Stable fire were reduced to a misdemeanor charge of criminal damage to property without jail time.

11. This quote is from the testimony of Colleen Quinn on pages H53 and H54, transcript of record, appeal to Appellate Court of Illinois, First District, Circuit Court 94 CR 21926.

12. Three exceptions to the rule are recognized: (1) where local law-enforcement authorities are unlikely to prosecute a crime the federal government has interest in, (2) if the case has significant organized crime involvement (this was a contentious issue throughout the Brach case and the spin-off prosecutions),

or (3) the prosecution of a public figure or politician that may present problems for local prosecutors.

13. Jack O'Malley succeeded Cecil Partee as Cook County State's Attorney following the ascension of Richard M. Daley (Mayor Richard J. Daley's son) to the mayoralty in 1989. O'Malley won a four-year term in 1992 but went down to defeat four years later amid partisan criticism that his prosecutorial record was sub-par, and his operating budget overinflated.

14. Citing the case of *Payton v. New York*, §445 U.S. 573, Arthur J. O'Donnell, attorney for Ken Hansen, argued unsuccessfully that minus a search warrant, the officers had entered the home illegally and without consent, thereby constituting a Fourth Amendment violation. On August 10, 1995, O'Donnell told the court, "And I think on the basis of that, any testimony of any person who was . . . whose identity was revealed to them by virtue of this prior illegality of the entry into the house without consent and the seizure of those documents violates the Fourth Amendment." Assistant State's Attorney Pat Quinn replied that no witnesses were found "as a result of using . . . looking at the materials recovered from the Hansen home on August 11th." Judge Michael Toomin concluded that on the basis of a reasonable suspicion that Hansen might take flight, Schak's entry into the home and the seizure of Hansen's personal items were valid. O'Donnell's motion to suppress was denied.

15. Judge John A. Wasilewski of the Markham Branch of the Cook County Circuit Court signed the search warrant authorizing the removal of the photos, address books, proof of residence, "and any other documents indicating a location of ownership of property where Kenneth Hansen may be located" at 3:15 PM, August 11, 1994.

16. Farrell noted the presence of empty suitcases in the back of Kenny's truck but determined he wasn't trying to flee.

17. Hansen's contention that he was never read his Miranda rights and was denied right to counsel is outlined by defense attorneys Arthur J. O'Donnell and Kenneth N. Flaxman in their Brief and Appendix of Defendant-Appellant to the Illinois Appellate Division, First District, Sixth Division (case no. 94 CR 21926).

18. Barbara Ann Riley served as an assistant state's attorney at Twenty-Sixth and California, Chicago's main Criminal Courts Building, from 1985 until 1996. She was elected to the bench in 1996 and presently serves as a judge in the Domestic Relations Division of the Cook County Circuit Court.

19. In 1956, following the exhumation of the boys' graves, SIU detectives embarked on a search of greenhouses and industrial plants—automobile repair shops and dealerships were generally overlooked.

14. A Man Without a Horse

1. *Black Beauty: The Autobiography of a Horse* was written by Anna Sewell and first published in 1877. It was the first major work to draw attention to the cruel mistreatment of horses.

2. First known as Pennyville (1853) and changed to Brickton in 1855, the name was changed a third time to Park Ridge. Park Ridge borders Chicago on the Far Northwest Side.

3. The actual name of the horse is not known.

4. This incident is related on page H60, Transcript of Record of Appeal to the Appellate Court of Illinois First District, Circuit Court, No. 9 CR 21926.

5. This quote is from pages H64 through H68, Transcript of Record of Appeal to the Appellate Court of Illinois First District, Circuit Court, No. 9 CR 21926.

6. While maintaining that he kept his past homosexual encounters to himself, family members admitted that Hollatz led "an openly gay lifestyle" for at least twenty years.

15. Showdown at Twenty-Sixth and Cal

1. *Venire facias* is the entire jury panel from which a trial jury is selected.

2. In 1994, prosecutors told Judge Cawley that they had a witness who would testify that Hansen admitted to bothering over two thousand boys beginning in 1955.

3. Art O'Donnell proved to be something of a prophet when he predicted in 1994 that Cawley's ruling would result in a "long-term reversal" if Hansen was convicted.

4. Arguments regarding the use of Silas Jayne's name during court proceedings are quoted from trial transcripts, pages F57 through F62.

5. A Toomin quote from the September 5, 1995, transcripts, pages F7 and F8, reads, "The presumption of innocence means that since there is no burden for the accused to prove himself innocent, he need not testify in the case, unless he elects to do so. He need not present any evidence in the case unless he elects to do so. He may do nothing but sit here and rely upon what he and his counsel perceive to be the inability of the People to prove him guilty beyond a reasonable doubt."

6. *In limine* means "at the outset."

7. *Voir dire* is the oral examination of prospective jurors by the opposing attorneys or by the judge and attorneys. The goal of the process is to eliminate jurors who might be biased against one side of the case.

16. Memories and Nightmares

1. *Probative* means "serving to test, try, or prove; furnishing evidence or proof."

2. There was a boys' reformatory in St. Charles, Illinois.

3. Actress Loretta Swit played "Hot Lips" Houlihan in the long-running, 1970s' television comedy series *MASH*.

4. Swit's quote is taken from an HAHS Web site.

5. Donna Ewing, president of Hooved Animal Humane Society, lives in Woodstock, Illinois. A horsewoman for more than thirty years, Ewing said

that she has witnessed many agonizing, inhumane horse deaths. She said that people need to be educated about their responsibility for providing a quality life and a humane death to their companion horses. She feels very strongly about the inhumane transport of horses.

6. Edmund Donoghue, PhD, is a graduate of the University of Notre Dame (1966) and the Marquette School of Medicine in Milwaukee (1970). He did his internship at the Mayo Clinic in Rochester, Minnesota. He joined the Cook County Medical Examiner's office on July 1, 1977, after a stint in the U.S. Navy.

7. Stone was only partially correct. Kearns originally reported that the deaths occurred between 9:00 PM and midnight.

8. Diatomaceous earth is soil consisting of diatoms, a class of minute planktonic, unicellular, or colonial algae.

17. Dog Days of Testimony

1. A stipulation is an agreement between the parties, in this case the prosecution and defense attorneys, with respect to the conduct of legal proceedings.

18. Judgment Day

1. Mark Hansen disputes the contention that Kenny was an abuser. "My father bought underfed horses from a killer buyer," Mark said. "Horses were expensive back then, and this was a good way for him to build up his livery business. He actually saved the lives of many horses on their way to slaughter." Mark repeated his side of the story to reporters throughout the trial, but he never got any ink. "If I was a juror and heard all of this stuff about my dad, I'd think he was a sick SOB and needed to sit in jail, too!"

2. Accused bomber James Blottiaux was convicted of the Rude murder by a Cook County jury on July 15, 1999, and was sentenced to one hundred to three hundred years in prison.

3. *Gregg v. Georgia* was a pivotal U.S. Supreme Court ruling handed down July 2, 1976, marking the beginning of the modern period of capital punishment. By a seven-to-two decision, the Gregg case legitimized the imposition of the death-penalty verdict, thus reversing a 1972 decision that had declared a moratorium on the death penalty when it ruled in *Furman v. Georgia* that all existing death-penalty statutes were unconstitutional.

4. This is an incorrect statement. Capital punishment was in effect in Illinois in 1955. Cop killer Richard Carpenter was put to death in the electric chair on December 19, 1958. Before capital punishment was temporarily abolished in 1972, two more men were executed in "The Land of Lincoln"—Vincent Ciucci and James Dukes, both in 1962.

19. Requiem

1. In 1933, the Pontiac reformatory school became a part of the Illinois State Penitentiary System (reorganized as the Illinois Department of Corrections in 1970).

2. A moratorium on executions was declared in January 2000. Governor

George Ryan appointed a fourteen-member, bipartisan commission to study the Illinois capital punishment system. In April 2002, they returned a damning report, declaring the criminal justice system "broken" and in need of a complete overhaul. His administration in shambles because key employees of the secretary of state's office had engaged in a long-standing pattern of awarding driver's licenses to unqualified applicants in consideration of bribes that were funneled back into Ryan's political coffers, the governor deemed it prudent not to seek reelection in 2002, was criminally indicted three years later, and convicted April 17, 2006 of, among other things, bribe-taking in exchange for state contracts. Before his last day in office on January 13, 2003, Ryan commuted the death sentences of the remaining 160 inmates condemned to death.

3. In 1990, a volunteer legal team led by Lawrence Marshall agreed to represent death-row inmate Rolando Cruz during his appeals. Cruz was convicted of the 1983 rape-murder of seven-year-old Jeanine Nicarico, when there was clear and compelling evidence that a criminal named Brian Dugan was the actual killer. An investigation headed by Rob Warden, who was then attached to the staff of *Chicago Lawyer,* succeeded in reopening the case. The Illinois Supreme Court reversed Cruz's conviction in 1994. Governor Ryan formally pardoned him in 2003.

4. Baby-selling rackets drew the attention of the U.S. Congress in 1955. In November, Senator Carey Estes Kefauver, a Democrat from Tennessee, convened Senate subcommittee hearings to investigate the link between the sale of unwanted infants and patterns of juvenile delinquency in America. The practice was found to be widespread and involved many so-called "distinguished" civic leaders across the country. Judge Harry Woodward of the Richmond County (Georgia) Juvenile Court admitted that he had sent "hundreds of babies" from Augusta into homes from coast to coast in consideration of fees ranging from $100 to $300 per child. The excuse given was that unwed and desperate young mothers were being forced to surrender their babies after being turned away by social-welfare agencies. From the 1930s through the 1950s, a once-respected, patrician judge of the Memphis, Tennessee, Juvenile Court named Camille Kelly ran an infamous but thriving baby-selling operation. The highly publicized Congressional hearings may have given Jack Reiling ideas, if, indeed, there is truth to Mack's accusation.

5. The three-judge panel voted two to one to overturn the verdict. Justice Leslie Elaine South voted with Justice Thomas E. Hoffman against Justice Shelvin Louise Hall.

6. As precedent, Hoffman cited a 1996 ruling *People v. Bobo,* 278 Ill. App. 3d 130, 133, 662 N.E. 2d 1203, and *People v. Novak,* 242 Ill. App. 3d 836, 858, 611 N.E. 2d 1203, a case tried in 1993. "In addition," Hoffman said, "the only evidence linking the defendant to the victims' murders was the testimony of Spry, Wemette, Plemmons, and Hollatz. The credibility of most of these witnesses had been significantly impeached. Therefore, we cannot say that the evidence that the defendant sexually assaulted innumerable young boys over a period of twenty years did not influence the outcome of his trial."

7. Information about this event, was on Centner's Web site page, http://www. lawnorthwestern.edu/depts/communicate/newspages/Fa1100/charitydinner. htm, but the page has been taken down.

8. Goodman's father is Irving Crown, brother of Henry Crown who was nicknamed "Colonel." He founded the powerful Material Services Corporation (MSC), supplying ready-mixed cement to the city and campaign contributions to Democratic politicians.

9. John Gutknecht, whose brother-in-law was Henry Crown, passed away in 1972.

10. In March 1995, Coghlan was appointed a judge in the Circuit Court of Cook County. She was elected to a six-year term in November 1996. Coghlan served in the criminal division as the supervising judge of the evening division until 1998, when she was transferred to the day division.

11. Hansen made medical history as the first prison inmate to undergo this procedure.

12. Anton and John had eaten a home-cooked noodle soup with their parents prior to going over to the Petersons.

13. Steve Weinberg believed that Tony and John went home before going to the bowling alley and ate some of their mom's home-cooked soup, the same meal they had for lunch. If his theory is correct, the time of death would have to be pushed back to the wee hours of the morning, and the screams, heard by the Park Ridge neighbors, could not have belonged to the Schuessler-Peterson boys.

14. Weinberg would not be part of Hansen's appeal.

Epilogue

1. Gary Kujawa and his sister Nancy Kujawa Rauscher recalled "how afraid" their parents were of letting the kids out of their sight. As the Kujawa children entered their teens, stepmother Eleanor would always caution them that "there were bad people out there, and you don't know who they are or where they are." Many other Northwest Side children growing up in the 1950s and 1960s heard that same frightening refrain.

2. Robert Stein served as Cook County Medical Examiner from 1976 until his retirement in 1993. The Cook County Institute of Forensic Medicine was renamed the Robert J. Stein Institute of Forensic Medicine in 1994. On average, the Medical Examiner performs 4,500 autopsies a year. Among the 12,000 deaths reported each year, only about half are actually accepted for investigation.

B I B L I O G R A P H Y

Books

Bailey, F. Lee, with John Greenya. *For the Defense*. New York: Atheneum, 1975.

Baumann, Ed, and John O'Brien. *Getting Away with Murder: Fifty-Seven Unsolved Murders with Reward Information*. Chicago: Bonus, 1991.

Bloun, Nancy, ed. *Park Ridge, Illinois: A Photo History*. Skokie, IL: Great Lakes Graphics, 1993.

Borchers, Stanley. *History of Park Lake: Park Ridge, Illinois*. Self-published, 1993.

Cahill, Tim, and Russ Ewing. *Buried Dreams: Inside the Mind of a Serial Killer*. New York: Bantam, 1986.

Colander, Pat. *Thin Air: The Life and Mysterious Disappearance of Helen Brach*. Chicago: Contemporary, 1982.

Cooke, David J., Adelle E. Forth, and Robert D. Hare, eds. *Psychopathy: Theory, Research and Implications for Society*. Dordrecht, The Netherlands: Kluwer Academic, 1995.

Corbitt, Michael, with Sam Giancana. *Double Deal: The Inside Story of Murder, Unbridled Corruption, and the Cop Who Was a Mobster*. New York: Morrow, 2003.

Crowe, Richard T., with Carol Mercado. *Chicago's Street Guide to the Supernatural*. Oak Park, IL: Carolando, 2001.

Demaris, Ovid. *Captive City: Chicago in Chains*. New York: Stuart, 1969.

Ehrenhalt, Alan. *The Lost City: Discovering the Forgotten Virtues of Community in the Chicago of the 1950s*. New York: Basic, 1995.

Englade, Ken. *Hot Blood: The Money, the Brach Heiress, the Horse Murders*. New York: St. Martin's, 1996.

Erzinclioglu, Zakaria. *Every Contact Leaves a Trace: The Greatest Scientific Detective Cases of the Twentieth Century*. New York: Carlton, 2001.

Freeman, Lucy. *"Before I Kill More . . ."* New York: Crown, 1955.

Garland, Norman M., and Gilbert B. Stuckey. *Criminal Evidence for the Law Enforcement Officer*. 4th ed. New York: McGraw, 1998.

Geberth, Vernon J. *Practical Homicide Investigation: Tactics, Procedures, and Forensic Techniques*. 3rd ed. Boston: CRC, 1996.

Halberstam, David. *The Fifties*. New York: Random, 1993.

Kellerman, Jonathan. *Savage Spawn: Reflections on Violent Children*. New York: Ballantine, 1999.

Lindberg, Richard C. *To Serve and Collect: Chicago Politics and Police Corruption from the Lager Beer Riot to the Summerdale Scandal, 1855–1960*. 1990. Carbondale: Southern Illinois UP, 1998.

Moss, Jason, with Jeffrey Kottler. *The Last Victim*. New York: Warner, 1999.

Possley, Maurice, and Rick Kogan. *Everybody Pays: Two Men, One Murder, and the Price of Truth*. New York: Putnam, 2001.

Rakoff, Jed S., and Howard W. Goldstein. *RICO: Civil and Criminal Law and Strategy*. New York: Law Journal, 1994.

Silberman, Charles E. *Criminal Violence, Criminal Justice*. New York: Random, 1978.

Stopp, Margaret T. *Evidence Law in the Trial Process*. 1st ed. Albany, NY: Delmar, 1998.

Wilson, Colin. *Written in Blood: The Criminal Mind and Method*. New York: Warner, 1989.

Zonderman, Jon. *Beyond the Crime Lab: The New Science of Investigation*. New York: Wiley, 1998.

Newspapers

Chicago American
Chicago Daily News
Chicago's Northwest Side Press (Nadig)
Chicago Sun-Times
Chicago Today
Chicago Tribune
Daily Southtown
Milwaukee Journal
Norwood-Edison Times (Pioneer Press)
St. Louis Post-Dispatch

Periodicals and On-Line Resources

"AHSA Hearing Committee Notices of Penalty." *Equestrian Times*. June 1997. <http://www.horsenews.com/break/mayjune97/indict.htm>.

"Alleged Horse Killers Charged with Murder." *Animal People News*. September 1994. <http://www.animalpeoplenews.org/94/7/horsekillers.html>.

Baumann, Eddie, and John O'Brien. "Vengeance and Violence." *Chicago Tribune Magazine*, 3 Jan. 1988: 6–15.

Blum, Howard. "The Horse Murders." *Vanity Fair* Jan. 1995: 92–101.

"Case of the Missing Widow." *Time* 6 Mar. 1978: 24.

Centner, Steven. "The Men Who Killed George Jayne." Aug. 1, 1999. <http://www.angelfire.com/sc/Centner/JayneG.html>.

———. "Village Confidential: Palatine Police." Aug. 1, 1999. <http://www.angelfire.com/sc/Centner/PalatinePPD.html>.

Clendenen, Richard, and Herbert W. Beaser. "The Post Reports on Juvenile Delinquency: The Shame of America, Part 2." *Saturday Evening Post* 15 Jan. 1955: 32–33, 70–73.

Damman, Marilyn, with Jimmy Breslin. "Who's Got My Baby?" *Saturday Evening Post* 9 June 1956: 23–25, 126–31.

"Death Awaited Three." *Newsweek* 31 Oct. 1955.

Grogan, David, Barbara Sandler, and Alysia Tate. "Rakish Romeo." *People* 15 Aug. 1994: 55–57.

Halem, Dan, and Jennifer Pruitt. "The Ghost of Jack Reiling." *Chicago Magazine* June 1999: 52–65.

Harty, Erin. "Chicago Jury Believes Burns, Convicts Lindemann of Fraud." *Chronicle of the Horse.* 29 Sept. 1995. <http://www.erinharty.com/clips/lindemann.html>.

Jaynes, Gregory, with Mark Shuman. "All the Pretty Horses." *Time* 8 Aug. 1994: 30.

Johnson, Flora. "If I Should Die." *Chicago Magazine* July 1976: 114–15.

Joravsky, Ben, with Richard Lindberg. "Backstabbbers." *Reader* 13 Apr. 2001: 1, 16–19, 22–31.

Kiger, Patrick J. "The Horse Lady Vanishes." *GQ* May 1995: 187–94.

O'Donnell, Paul, with Karen Springen and Matt Bai. "Like Candy from an Heiress." *Time* 8 Aug. 1994: 60.

Reynolds, Gretchen. "Horses, Money, Murder." *Chicago Magazine* Dec. 1994: 68–73, 96, 98, 100, 102.

Rodkin, Dennis. "Love with the Improper Stranger." *Chicago Magazine* Sept. 2001: 145–47, 190.

Shaffer, Tamara. "Death and the Maidens." *The Reader* 21 Mar. 1997: 10–18.

Vachula, Richard. "The Gacy Connection." *Chicago Magazine* July 1989: 112–14.

Weiner, Lori. "Did Homophobia Play a Role in Conviction of Gay Man in the 1955 Killing of Three Boys?" Outlines. 24–30 Sept. 1997. <http://www.suba.com/~outlines/current/outlines/archives/092497/bias.html>.

"Who Saw These Boys?" *Life*, 31 Oct. 1955.

Special Reports and Court Transcripts

Chicago Police Department Annual Reports. 1955–1958; 1960–1964.

Lohman, Joseph D., sheriff. *Cook County Sheriff's Office, Four Years of Progress: 1954–1958.* Chicago: Cook County Sheriff, 1958.

People of the State of Illinois v. Kenneth Hansen. No. 94 CR 21925. Circuit Ct. of Cook County, Criminal Division. Michael P. Toomin, trial judge.

———. No. 94 CR 21926. Ill. Appellate Ct., 1st Dist., 6th Div. Appeal from the Circuit Ct. of Cook County. Brief and Appendix of Defendant-Appellant. Michael P. Toomin, trial judge.

Peterson, Virgil. *A Report on Chicago Crime for 1955*. Chicago: Chicago Crime Commission, 29 Feb. 1956.

———. *A Report on Chicago Crime for 1966*. Chicago: Chicago Crime Commission, 11 Aug. 1967.

United States of America v. Richard Bailey. No. 94 CR 481. US Ct. of Appeals for the 7th Circuit. Appeal from the US Dist. Ct. for the N. Dist. of Ill., E. Div. Milton I. Shadur, trial judge.

Sweeney, Rev. Kenny, 88
Sweitzer, Leon (Chicago PD, detective), 101–2
Swit, Loretta, 258, 363n3 (chap. 16)
Sybers, Peter (Rusk County, Wisc., sheriff), 89

Teas, Dr. Shaku, 320
Thomas, Edwin P. "Junior," Jr., 196, 283–84, 286–87, 289, 300–301
Thorne, Marion, 64
Thorne, Montgomery Ward, 64
Thorsen, Wesley B., 60–61
Till, Emmett Louis, 85, 350n1
Tisinai, Mrs. Stephen, 101
Tocco, Albert "Caesar," 360n22
Toman, Dr. Andrew J., 127
Toomin, Michael P. (judge, Cook County Circuit Court), 224–29, 231–34, 239–40, 245–46, 285, 297–99, 305–6, 308–9, 315, 362n14, 363n5 (chap. 15)
Touhy, Roger, 346n10
Town, Harry, 79
Tremore, Ancil Earl, 157–58
Trivers, Linda Hoffman, 146, 264, 266
Tucker, Ernest E., 89, 121–22
Tynan, James, 205–6

University of Chicago Center of Education and Research in Corrections, 347n4
Untold Story of Emmett Till, The (film), 350n1

Vachula, Richard, 137
Valanis, Adolph, 133–34, 136
Valley View Young Adult Club (YAC), 12, 181–82, 360n22
Van Hyning, Mrs. Lyle Clark, 106
Varley, Judy, 135
Vazquez, Gloria, 88, 97
Verkle, Donald (Chicago PD, detective), 89
Vince, Joe, 2, 187
Voderberg, Kurt, 277–78

Wall, Noel, 261
Walloch, Anthony F., 100–101
Walloch, Sylvester, 100
Walsh, Carol, 46
Warden, Rob, 312
Wasilewski, John A. (judge), 362n15
Webber, Alfred, 76
Webber, Catherine, 76
Weber, Charles (Chicago alderman), 107–8, 352n7
Weinberg, Steven, 318–21, 323, 366n13
Werner, Cathy, 121
Weisgerber, Elsie, 41, 82
Wemette, Robert R., Sr., 274
Wemette, William "Red," 9–17, 156, 168, 176–87, 196, 201, 206, 238, 249, 270–75, 277, 284, 296, 300, 304, 316, 320, 325, 332, 337, 360n22, 365n6
Werner, Cathy, 121
White, Minnie, 145
White, Robert Denton, 145
Wilk, Herbert (detective), 80
Williamson, Lance, 270, 316
Willis, Benjamin C., 86
Wilson, Orlando W., 130, 349n9
Wilson, Sloan, 18
Wilson, Tony, 119
Winfrey, Oprah, 315
Wisilinski, Dolores, 100
Wisilinski, Edward, 100
Woods, Orville (Ladysmith, Wisc., police chief), 89
Woodward, Harry (Richmond County, Ga., juvenile court judge), 365n4
Wright, Linda, 155
Wright, Mickey, 155

Yellen, Larry, 309–10
Young, Ray (Chicago PD, sergeant, mobile crime laboratory), 51
Your Sheriff Reports (television series), 74

Zielke, Arlene, 216, 221–22, 252

Richard C. Lindberg, a lifelong Chicagoan, is a journalist and research historian, who has authored eleven books dealing with aspects of the city's history, politics, criminal justice, sports, and ethnicity. Among his publications is *To Serve and Collect: Chicago Politics and Police Corruption from the Lager Beer Riot to the Summerdale Scandal, 1855–1960*. Lindberg is a past president of the Society of Midland Authors and the Illinois Academy of Criminology and a 2001 recipient of the Frederic Milton Thrasher Award for excellence in research and reportage of Chicago organized crime and street gangs.

Born and raised on Chicago's Northwest Side, **Gloria Jean Sykes** has been a national documentary film and news magazine producer, writer, and director and an investigative producer for three decades. Sykes, winner of two Angel Awards, has received eight Emmy Award nominations for her work, which includes the television specials *Homelessness: A Prayer, Campaign 90: The Propositions,* and *Children of Alcoholic Parents* and an HBO Original Feature movie *Cheaters* spotlighting the 1995 Steinmetz High School academic decathlon scandal and starring Jeff Daniels. She also served as the producer of the prime-time NBC series *What Happened?*